Don C

Project Risk Management

Project Risk Management

Processes, Techniques and Insights

Chris Chapman and Stephen Ward

School of Management
University of Southampton

JOHN WILEY & SONS

Chichester • New York • Brisbane • Toronto • Singapore

Copyright © 1997 by John Wiley & Sons Ltd,
Baffins Lane, Chichester,
West Sussex PO19 1UD, England

National   (01243) 779777
International (+44) 1243 779777
e-mail (for orders and customer service enquiries): cs-books@wiley.co.uk
Visit our Home Page on http://www.wiley.co.uk
or http://www.wiley.com

Reprinted August 1997, May 1998

Other Wiley Editorial Offices

John Wiley & Sons, Inc., 605 Third Avenue,
New York, NY 10158-0012, USA

Jacaranda Wiley Ltd, 33 Park Road, Milton,
Queensland 4064, Australia

John Wiley & Sons (Canada) Ltd, 22 Worcester Road,
Rexdale, Ontario M9W 1L1, Canada

John Wiley & Sons (Asia) Pte Ltd, 2 Clementi Loop #02-01,
Jin Xing Distripark, Singapore 129809

Library of Congress Cataloging-in-Publication Data

Chapman, C. B.
    Project risk management : processes, techniques, and insights / Chris Chapman and Stephen Ward.
        p.   cm.
    Includes bibliographical references and index.
    ISBN 0-471-95804-2 (cloth)
    1. Industrial project management.   2. Risk management.   I. Ward, Stephen (Stephen C.)
    II. Title.
    T56.8.C52   1997
    658.4′04—dc20   96–30345
                                                                          CIP

British Library Cataloguing in Publication Data

A catalogue record for this book is available from the British Library

ISBN 0-471-95804-2

Typeset in 10/12pt Palatino from the author's disks by Laser Words, Madras, India
Printed and bound in Great Britain by Bookcraft (Bath) Ltd, Midsomer Norton, Somerset
This book is printed on acid-free paper responsibly manufactured from sustainable forestation, for which at least two trees are planted for each one used for paper production.

IT WAS AT THAT MOMENT THAT MAURICE KNEW HE WAS DIFFERENT FROM OTHER LEMMINGS.

Contents

Foreword

All projects involve risk—the zero risk project is not worth pursuing. This is not purely intuitive but also a recognition that acceptance of some risk is likely to yield a more desirable and appropriate level of benefit in return for the resources committed to the venture. Risk involves both threat and opportunity. Organisations which better understand the nature of the risks and can manage them more effectively can not only avoid unforeseen disasters but can work with tighter margins and less contingency, freeing resources for other endeavours, and seizing opportunities for advantageous investment which might otherwise be rejected as 'too risky'.

Risk is present in every aspect of our lives; thus risk management is universal but in most circumstances an unstructured activity, based on common sense, relevant knowledge, experience and instinct. Project management has evolved over recent years into a fully-fledged professional discipline characterised by a formalised body of knowledge and the definition of systematic processes for the execution of a project. Yet project risk management has, until recently, generally been considered as an 'add-on' instead of being integral to the effective practice of project management.

This book provides a framework for integrating risk management into the management of projects. It explains how to do this through the definition of generic risk management processes and shows how these processes can be mapped onto the stages of the project life cycle. As the disciplines of formal project management are being applied ever more widely (for example, to the management of change within organisations) so the generic project risk management processes set out here will readily find use in diverse areas of application.

The main emphasis is on processes rather than analytical techniques which are already well documented. The danger in formalised processes is that they can become orthodox, bureaucratic, burdened with procedures, so that the practitioner loses sight of the real aims. This book provides the reader with a fundamental understanding of project risk management processes but avoids being over-prescriptive in the description of the execution of these processes. Instead, there is positive encouragement to use these generic processes as a starting point for elaboration and adaptation to suit the circumstances of a particular application, to innovate and experiment, to simplify and streamline the practical implementation of the generic processes to achieve cost effective and efficient risk management.

The notion of risk efficiency is central to the theme. All risk management processes consume valuable resources and can themselves constitute a risk to the project which must be effectively managed. The level of investment in risk management within projects must be challenged and justified on the level of expected benefit to the overall project. Chris Chapman and Steve Ward document numerous examples drawn from real project experience to substantiate the benefits of a formal process-oriented approach. Ultimately, project risk management is about people making decisions to try to optimise the outcome, being proactive in evaluating risk and the possible responses, using this information to best effect, demonstrating the need for changes in project plans, taking the necessary action and monitoring the effects. Balancing risk and expectation is one of the most challenging aspects of project management. It can also be exciting and offer great satisfaction, provided the project manager is able to operate in a climate of understanding and openness about project risk. The cultural change required in organisations to achieve this can be difficult and lengthy but there is no doubt that it will be easier to accomplish if risk management processes are better understood and integrated into the practice of project management.

This book is a welcome and timely addition to the literature on risk management and will be of interest to all involved in project management as well as offering new insights to the project risk analyst.

Peter Wakeling
Director of Procurement Policy (Project Management)
Ministry of Defence (Procurement Executive)

Preface

The projects which motivated initial development of many of the ideas in this book were primarily large engineering projects in the energy sector: large-scale arctic pipelines in the far north of North America in the mid 1970s, BP's North Sea projects from the mid 1970s to the early 1980s, and a range of Canadian and US energy projects in the early 1980s. In this period the initial focus was 'the project' in engineering and technical terms, although the questions addressed ranged from effective planning and unbiased cost estimation to effective contractual and insurance arrangements and appropriate technical choices in relation to the management of environmental issues and related approval processes. An earlier book and underlying papers discuss some of the ideas which developed during this period (Cooper and Chapman, 1987).

The projects which motivated evolution of these ideas from the mid 1980s to the present involved considerable diversification: defence projects (naval platforms, weapon systems, and information systems), civil information systems, nuclear power station decommissioning, nuclear waste disposal, deep mining, water supply system security, commodity trading (coffee and chocolate), property management, research and development management, civil engineering construction management systems, electric utility long-term and medium-term corporate planning, electric utility generation unit construction and installation or enhancement, commercial aircraft construction, the construction of Channel Tunnel rolling stock, and the risk and benefit management of a major branch banking information systems project, to mention a few used directly or indirectly as examples in this book. In this period the focus was on what aspects of project risk management are portable, in the sense that they apply to garden sheds and nuclear power stations, and in what way do ideas have to be tailored to the circumstances, in the sense that garden sheds and nuclear power stations require some clear differences in approach.

The reader may be concerned with projects with features well beyond our experience, but we believe that most of what we have to say is still directly relevant, provided the projects of concern involve enough risk to make formal consideration of that risk worthwhile. Even if this condition is not satisfied, informal or intuitive project risk management will benefit indirectly from some of the insights offered.

WHAT THIS BOOK IS ABOUT

This book makes no attempt to cover all aspects of project management. However, it addresses project risk management as a process which is an 'add-in' to the project management process as a whole, rather than an 'add-on'. The need to integrate these processes is central to the argument and to the basic position adopted by this book.

The need to start to understand project risk management by understanding processes is also central to our case. The details of models or techniques or computer software are important, but they are not of direct concern here.

Senior managers who want to make intelligent use of risk management processes without depending on their risk analysts need to understand most of this book (the exceptions are signposted). Those who wish to participate effectively in risk management processes also need to understand most of this book (the exceptions are similar). Those who wish to lead risk management processes need to understand this book in depth, and a wide range of additional literature on technique, model and method design, and computer software.

We introduce the acronym RMP (for 'risk management process') at the outset because it is required so often, with the promise that the conventional PLC (for 'project life cycle') is the only other acronym of this kind to be employed, and both will be redefined when first used in each chapter.

A very important message emphasised here is that project risk management in the context of any particular project can be viewed as a project in its own right, as part of a multi-project environment concerned with all other aspects of project management, such as planning resources, building teams, quality management, and so on. An immediate implication of this view is a need to 'plan the risk management process' as part of a process of 'planning the project planning process', a second-order level of planning associated with planning the project itself. In the absence of another source of quality audit for project management, this also implies using risk management process to make sure all other desirable aspects of project management are in place. A more subtle and far-reaching implication is that everything we know about project management in general, and multi-project management in particular, applies to the project risk management process itself.

There is an inevitable circularity in the ideal structure for such a book, largely because of the iterative nature of risk management processes. The authors have restructured it several times to avoid approaches which overtly failed. We believe the present structure works, but the reader will have to be the judge. A range of different approaches to this book might be suggested, from 'work your way through each chapter in detail before going on to the next', to 'skim the whole book and then go back to the bits of most interest'. We leave the readers to judge what best suits their inclinations, with a few hints we hope are useful.

THE LAYOUT OF THIS BOOK

The book is in three parts. Part One sets the scene and introduces a generic risk management process. Part Two examines each phase of this process in detail. Part Three considers modifications to the generic process.

Part One Setting the Scene (Chapters 1-4)

Chapter 1 considers the roots of uncertainty in projects, the nature of project risk, and the role of risk management.

Chapter 2 considers the implications of the project life cycle (PLC), for two linked but separate reasons. First, a significant source of project risk is process related, and its nature is dependent upon the issues the process addresses, which are in turn heavily dependent upon the stage in the PLC of primary concern. Second, appropriate risk management processes, even in broad generic terms, must be grounded in the context of a particular stage in the PLC to be described with any clarity. Most of this book assumes that the particular stage is the 'Plan' stage of the PLC described in Chapter 2.

Chapter 3 considers the motives for formal risk management processes. Some of these motives are sophisticated, 'soft', and not well understood. The benefits of risk management processes are most effectively viewed as potential objectives. Risk management processes need to be selected or designed to achieve the benefits or objectives required. Appropriate risk management processes, even in broad generic terms, must be grounded in appropriate objectives to be described with any clarity. Most of the book assumes the comprehensive set of objectives outlined in Chapter 3, and a correspondingly comprehensive approach to the risk management process.

Chapter 4 provides an outline of project risk management as a generic process. In addition to assuming that a comprehensive formal risk management process is required at the Plan stage of the PLC, this chapter assumes 'a client' perspective, and that 'the client' is one organisation with one project. The nine-phase structure outlined in Chapter 4 provides the pattern for Part Two.

Part Two   Elaborating the Generic Process (Chapters 5–13)

Part Two elaborates the nine-phase generic process of Chapter 4, one chapter per phase. The elaborations are a distillation of processes we have found effective and efficient in practice. This is 'theory grounded in practice', in the sense that it is an attempt to provide a systematic and ordered description of what has to be done in what order to achieve the deliverables each phase should produce. It is a model of an idealised process, intended to provide an understanding of the nature of risk management processes. This model needs to be adapted to the specific terrain of specific studies to be useful. Examples are provided to help link the idealised process back to the practice they are based on, to facilitate their application in practice.

Much of what most experienced professional risk analysts do is craft, based on craft skills learned the hard way by experience. Part Two is an attempt to explain systematically as much as we can in a particular generic process context, indicating along the way areas where craft skills are particularly important. Some specific technique is also provided, but technique in terms of the 'nuts and bolts' or mechanics of processes is not the focus of this book.

Part Three   Modifying the Generic Process (Chapters 14–17)

Chapter 14 starts the process of relaxing the three assumptions used to provide the focus essential to clarify the risk management process description in Part Two, addressing the 'implications of different project life cycle positions', and the merits of using the Plan stage position selected for Part Two as a basis for initial introduction of risk management processes into an organisation.

Chapter 15 addresses 'alternative points of view', in particular 'a contractor perspective'. The 'client perspective' used in Part Two is a general one, in that it has to include consideration of contractors, and a contractor can view 'his or her project' defined as a subset of 'the client's project' as a client would in many respects. However, a number of issues not addressed earlier are considered in Chapter 15.

Chapter 16 addresses 'selecting short cuts'. It can be very valuable for organisations to select initial risk management processes in a context which allows a comprehensive approach and a broad view of the benefits and objectives, as part of a rich, deep and balanced training process. However, taking short cuts is a necessity most of the time. The issues this raises are discussed in Chapter 16.

Chapter 17 completes the process of 'modifying the generic process' by discussing the introduction of risk management process into an organisation, which can be viewed as a high risk project in its own right. 'Physician heal thyself' is an apt quote in this context, which we explore in a preliminary manner in Chapter 17.

As its title suggests, this book is about primarily processes, in terms of the insight necessary to use risk management processes effectively and develop efficiency in doing so. It uses examples to focus on very specific lessons provided by practice. These examples may be viewed as the basis for, or evidence of, 'theory grounded in practice', or they may be viewed as 'war stories with a moral', depending upon the reader's preferences.

Acknowledgements

Part of the motivation for this book was our awareness of a growing interest in project risk management guidelines for specific industries, and in more general standards, in the UK and elsewhere (e.g. PMI, 1992). Chapman considerably developed his thinking interacting with other specialists in project risk management while working on the CCTA (The Government Centre for Information Systems) publication *Management of Project Risk* (CCTA, 1995), and while working with AEA Technology on their project risk management guidelines. Both authors developed their thinking while working with the Association of Project Managers (APM) Specific Interest Group (SIG) on Project Risk Management, to the extent that the chapter structure of this book was changed more than half way through writing it to reflect the SIG's agreed process description in the *Project Risk Analysis and Management (PRAM) Guide* (APM, forthcoming).

The PRAM Guide complements this book. Both books have a very similar generic process chapter (Chapter 4 in this book, Chapter 3 in the PRAM Guide, both drafted by Chapman), describing the generic process in terms of nine phases, a characterisation which we believe is likely to become a standard. The support of that characterisation by the organisations represented by more than a hundred people active in the APM SIG on Project Risk Management is the basis of this belief, but the nine-phase structure has worked well when developing this book. If readers prefer other structures, the nine phases used here will map onto all those the authors are aware of, with two specific examples of such mapping provided in Chapter 4.

Members of the APM SIG on Project Risk Management who were involved in the working party which contributed to the generic process definition described in Chapter 4 (and their organisations) are: Paul Best (Frazer-Nash), Adrian Cowderoy (City University, Business Computing), Valerie Evans (MoD-PE), Ron Gerdes (BMT Reliability Consultants Ltd), Keith Gray (British Aerospace (Dynamics)), Steve Grey (ICL), Heather Groom (British Aerospace (Dynamics)), Ross Hayes (University of Birmingham, Civil Engineering), David Hillson (HVR Consulting Services Ltd), Paul Jobling (Mouchel Management Ltd), Mark Latham (BAeSEMA),

Martin Mays (CORDA, BAeSEMA), Ken Newland (Quintec Associates Ltd), Catriona Norris (TBV Schal), Grahame Owen (IBM (UK) Ltd), Philip Rawlings (Eurolog), Francis Scarff (CCTA), Peter Simon (PMP), Martin Thomas (4D Management Consultancy), and David Vose (PVRA). We would particularly like to thank Peter Simon (chair of the working party and editor of the PRAM Guide) and David Hillson (secretary to the working party).

Most of Chapter 2 is reprinted from the *International Journal of Project Management*, Volume 13, S. C. Ward and C. B. Chapman, 'A risk management perspective on the project life cycle', pages 145–149, Copyright (1995), with kind permission from Elsevier Science Ltd, The Boulevard, Langford Lane, Kidlington OX5 1GB, UK.

Chapter 15 uses material reprinted from the *International Journal of Project Management*, Volume 12, S. C. Ward and C. B. Chapman 'Choosing contractor payment terms', pages 216–221, Copyright (1994); Volume 9, S. C. Ward, C. B. Chapman and B. Curtis 'On the allocation of risk in construction projects', pages 140–147, Copyright (1991); and Volume 9, S. C. Ward and C. B. Chapman, 'Extending the use of risk analysis in project management', pages 117–123, Copyright (1991); with kind permission from Elsevier Science Ltd, The Boulevard, Langford Lane, Kidlington OX5 1GB, UK.

Figures 8.2, 11.5 and 11.6 are reproduced from C. B. Chapman, D. F. Cooper and M. J. Page, *Management for Engineers*, John Wiley & Sons. Figures 8.3 and 14.1 are reproduced by permission of the Operational Research Society, Seymour House, 12 Edward Street, Birmingham B1 2RX, UK.

The authors would like to acknowledge the contributions of a large number of colleagues we have worked for and with over a number of years. It would be inappropriate to list them and their contributions, but we would like to express our gratitude. Only the errors and omissions are entirely our own.

Part One

Setting the Scene

Chapter 1

Uncertainty, Risk, and Their Management

I keep six honest serving men, They taught me all I knew; Their names are what and why and when and how and where and who.

Rudyard Kipling

1.1 THE ROOTS OF UNCERTAINTY IN PROJECTS

The need to manage uncertainty is inherent in most projects which require formal project management. Consider the following illustrative definition of such a project:

> an endeavour in which human, material and financial resources are organised in a novel way, to undertake a unique scope of work of given specification, within constraints of cost and time, so as to achieve unitary, beneficial change, through the delivery of quantified and qualitative objectives. (Turner, 1992)

This definition highlights the one-off, change-inducing nature of projects, the need to organise a variety of resources under significant constraints, and the central role of objectives in project definition. It also suggests inherent uncertainty which requires attention as part of effective project management processes.

The roots of this uncertainty are worth clarification. In the authors' experience careful attention to formal risk management processes (RMPs) is usually motivated by the large-scale use of new and untried technology while executing major projects, and other obvious sources of significant risk.

However, the key issues such processes help to resolve are often unrelated to the motivating difficulties, and they are usually central to virtually all projects. For example, a common issue is 'do we know what we are trying to achieve in clearly defined terms which link objectives to planned activities?' It is important to understand why this situation arises, and to respond effectively, in the context of *all* projects.

A convenient starting point is consideration of the project definition process portrayed in Figure 1.1. The roots of project uncertainty are associated with six basic questions which need to be addressed:

1. *who*   who are the parties ultimately involved?   (parties),
2. *why*   what do the parties want to achieve?   (motives),
3. *what*   what is it the parties are interested in?   (design),
4. *whichway*   how is it to be done?   (activities),
5. *wherewithal* what resources are required?   (resources),
6. *when*   when does it have to be done?   (timetable).

For convenience we refer to these question areas as 'the six Ws', using the designations in brackets as well as the W labels for clarity when appropriate. We cannot discuss 'the six Ws' in a seminar with a straight face, particularly when talking about the *'whichway'* and *'wherewithal'*, but it is a useful device to remind us of the need to consider all six areas. (We are grateful to an anonymous referee for suggesting the use of *'whichway'*, to complete the set.)

The flow lines in Figure. 1.1 show influences on project definition which are the roots of uncertainty. In the context of roots of uncertainty, these arrows can be interpreted as indicating the knock-on effects of uncertainty in each entity. As Figure. 1.1 shows, the roots of uncertainty may extend back to the level of resources available, the basic purpose of the project, and even the identity of the relevant parties. Any uncertainty associated with entities earlier in the cycles portrayed by the diagram are of fundamental importance later. In the earliest stage of a project, during conception, uncertainty is at its greatest. The purpose for which the project is required and the parties who will be involved may not be clear. In principle, much of this uncertainty is removed during design and planning by attempting to specify what is to be done, how, when, by whom, at what cost. In practice, a great deal of uncertainty may remain.

As indicated in Figure 1.1, 'project initiators' are a subset of the *who*, the 'project parties ultimately involved'. Project initiators kick the whole process off.

One or more project initiators first identify the basic purpose of the project, or intended benefit from it, the *why* or motives for the project. These motives will usually include profit, involving revenue and cost, along with 'other motives'. Initially the nature of these motives will be

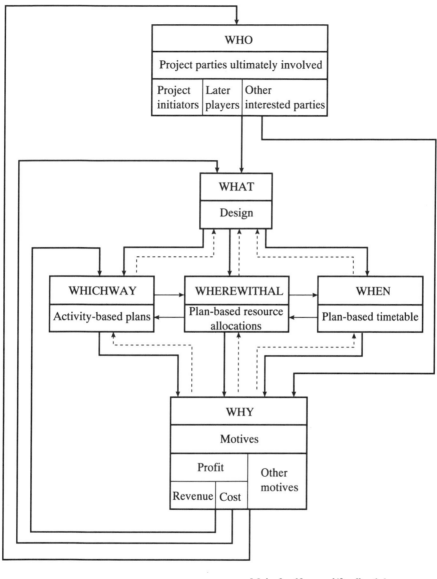

Figure 1.1 The project definition process.

defined, but they will not be quantified as objectives. That is, in terms of the mission–goals–objectives hierarchy often used to move from an overall mission statement to quantified objectives, the initial focus of the *why* may be on mission and broadly defined goals. The solid influence line from *who* to *why* in Figure 1.1 indicates this initial influence sustains itself as a main feed forward relationship.

Why, in terms of the initial conception of purpose, may influence the initially assumed *whichway* (activity-based plans, the activities, or the how), as indicated by the dotted influence line between *why* and *whichway* in Figure 1.1. In a similar way, *why*, in terms of the initial concept or purpose, may influence the *wherewithal* (plan-based resource allocations, the resources), and the *when* (plan-based timetable, the timetable) in a broad strategic sense. On occasion these influences may be negligible, but this is just a special case.

The *what* of the project, the design, be it a building, other physical product, service or process, is the direct responsibility of the *who*, as indicated by a feed forward solid line on Figure 1.1. Initially, the *what* may be constrained by the assumed activity-based plans and associated resources and timetable, the initial *whichway*, *wherewithal* and *when*, which are in turn driven by the initial *why*. All these links are dotted influence lines. Further, the *what* is driven directly by the *why*, as indicated by a solid main feedback loop on Figure 1.1. The initial *what* then confirms or revises the *whichway*, the activities required to execute the design, as indicated by a feedforward solid line on Figure 1.1.

The *what* and *whichway* then confirm or adjust the *wherewithal* and the *when*, with significant feedforward and feedback along the *whichway–wherewithal–when* dimensions. The *whichway–wherewithal–when* entities then feed forward into quantification of cost, possibly revenue and other motives, *why* in terms of a more developed measured definition. These considerations may relate to capital cost only, or more complex through-life approaches.

Why in this more developed sense may now lead to one of three major feedback loops:

1. to *whichway*, with linked feedback loop changes to the planned activities, resources or timetable without affecting the basic design (*what*) or the *who*;
2. to *what*, with more fundamental changes to the design itself;
3. to *who*, with changes of a still more fundamental nature involving the project initiators, 'later players' and 'other interested parties'.

In each case these feedback loops result in subsequent feedforward through the solid influence lines.

As the project evolves it may be appropriate to bring in further later players, enlarging the *who*, for resource reasons, for example. It may also become appropriate to consider other interested parties who are not direct players (regulators, for example).

This brief description of the project definition process in terms of the six *W*s involved is an over-simplification for many projects, but it is sufficiently complex to highlight the nature of important roots of uncertainty in projects. In particular, if we recognise that the *what*, *whichway* and *wherewithal* together describe the quality of a project, and ignore revenue and other motives, then the bottom half of Figure 1.1 corresponds to the well-known cost–time–quality triad. The limited perspective inherent in the simple cost–time–quality triad is then apparent from the expansion of this triad by Figure 1.1.

A particularly pervasive source of uncertainty may arise from the involvement in a project of a multiplicity of people or organisations. In any organisational setting, even small projects invariably involve two or more parties working together, where each party may be an individual, some unit of the same organisation, or representatives of entirely separate organisations. The relationships between the various parties may be complex, often involving a hierarchy of contractual arrangements. Such relationships bring fundamental complications which have a profound influence on project uncertainty and project risk. The other interested parties in Figure 1.1 reflect the potentially important roles of regulators and others who are not direct players, but may require careful attention, because they are important sources of uncertainty. It is important to ensure a *broad* view of the *who*, to include all relevant interested parties, and a *rich* view, to distinguish individual players or groups within single organisations who may have significantly different agendas.

1.2   THE NATURE OF PROJECT RISK

A broad definition of project risk is 'the implications of the existence of significant uncertainty about the level of project performance achievable'. A source of risk is any factor that can affect project performance, and risk arises when this effect is both uncertain and significant in its impact on project performance. It follows that the definition of project objectives and performance criteria has a fundamental influence on the level of project risk. Setting tight cost or time targets makes a project more cost or time risky by definition, since achievement of targets is more uncertain if targets are 'tight'. Conversely, setting slack time or quality requirements implies low time or quality risk. However, inappropriate targets are themselves a source of risk, and a failure to acknowledge the need for a minimum level of performance against certain criteria automatically generates risk on those dimensions. Morris and Hough (1987) argue for the importance of setting clear objectives and performance criteria which reflect the requirements of various parties, including stakeholders who are not always recognised as players (regulatory authorities, for example). The different project objectives held by interested parties and any interdependencies between different objectives need to be appreciated. Strategies for managing risk cannot be divorced from strategies for managing project objectives.

Whatever the underlying performance objectives, the focus on project success and uncertainty about achieving it leads to risk being defined in terms of a 'threat to success'. Suppose success for a project is measured solely in terms of realised cost relative to some target or commitment. Then risk might be defined in terms of the threat to success posed by a given plan in terms of the size of possible cost overruns and their likelihood. This might be termed 'threat intensity'.

From this perspective it is a natural step to regard risk management as essentially about removing or reducing the possibility of underperformance. This is unfortunate, since it results in a very limited appreciation of project risk. Often it can be just as important to appreciate the positive side of uncertainty which may present opportunities rather than threats. Two examples may help to illustrate this point.

Example 1.1

North Sea offshore pipelaying involves significant uncertainty associated with weather. Relative to expected (average) performance, long periods of bad weather can have significant sustained impact. It is important to recognise and deal with this 'threat'. It is also very important to recognise that the weather may be exceptionally kind, providing a counterbalancing opportunity. Making sure supplies of pipe can cope with very rapid pipelaying is essential, for obvious reasons. Also important is the need to shift following activities forward, if possible, if the whole pipeline is finished early. If the implications of good luck are not seized, and only bad luck is captured, the accumulated effect is obvious. This is a characteristic of risk which demands management, and a fundamental part of what has to be understood and responded to.

Example 1.2

The team responsible for a UK combined cycle gas turbine (CCGT) electricity project were concerned about the threat to their project's completion time associated with various approvals processes which involved important novel issues. Gas was to be provided on a take-or-pay contract in which gas supply would be guaranteed from an agreed date, but gas not required from that date would have to be paid for anyway. This made any delay relative to the commitment operating date very expensive, the cost of such unused gas being in effect a project cost. The response to this threat was to seize the opportunities offered by the only response identified—moving the whole project forward three months in time (starting three months earlier, and finishing three months earlier), and arranging for standard British Gas supplies for testing purposes if the project actually finished three months early. Using British Gas supplies for testing was a non-trivial change, because its gas composition was different, requiring different testing procedures and gas turbine contract differences. This response would deal with planning delays, the motivation for first suggesting it, and it would also deal with any other reasons for delay, including those not identified. Further, it provided a very high degree of confidence that the CCGT plant would be operational very shortly after the main gas supply initiation date. This in turn made it practical to maintain the strategy of using British Gas supplies for testing, but move the whole project back in time (starting and finishing later) in order to time the take-or-pay contract date to coincide directly with the beginning of the peak winter demand period, improving the corporate cash flow position. The opportunity to improve the cash flow position in this way while maintaining confidence with respect to the take-or-pay contract for gas was deemed to be a key impact of the risk management process.

These two examples illustrate the importance of opportunities as well as threats, the first in cost terms at an activity level, the second in cost and revenue terms at a project level. On occasion opportunities may also be very important from a morale point of view. High morale is as central to good risk management as it is to the management of teams in general. If a project team becomes immersed in nothing but threats, the ensuing doom and gloom can destroy the project. Systematic searches for opportunities, and a management willing to respond to opportunities identified by those working for them at all levels (which may have implications well beyond the remit of the discoverer), can provide the basis for systematic building of morale.

More generally, it is important to appreciate that project risk is by nature a very complex beast with important behavioural implications. Simplistic definitions, such as 'risk is the probability of a downside risk event multiplied by its impact', may have their value in special circumstances, but it is important to face the complexity of what project risk management is really about if real achievement is to be attained when attempting to manage that risk.

1.3   THE ROLE OF RISK MANAGEMENT

The essential purpose of risk management is to improve project performance via systematic identification, appraisal and management of project-related risk. A focus on reducing threats or adverse outcomes, what we might call 'downside' risk, misses a key part of the overall picture. An aim of improving performance implies a wide perspective which seeks to exploit opportunities or favourable possibilities, what we might call 'upside' risk.

To realise in practical terms the advantages of this wide perspective, it is essential to see project risk management as an important extension of conventional project planning, with the potential to influence project design and base plans on a routine basis, occasionally influencing very basic issues like the nature of the *who* and the *why*.

A 'base plan' is a target scenario, a portrayal of how we would like a project to go. This plan provides a basis for project preparation and execution, and control of the project. Underlying the base plan is a design, which may be worth identifying as a 'base design', if possible changes are anticipated.

Control involves responding to threats and opportunities, and revising performance targets where appropriate. 'Contingency plans' are a second level of plan, a portrayal of how we would like to respond to threats or opportunities associated with a base plan. Risk management is usually associated with the evaluation and development of contingency plans supporting the base plan, but effective risk management will also be instrumental in the development of project base plans. Really effective risk management will influence design as well, and it may influence motives and parties. Planning and risk management in this sense is proactive, rather than reactive. Where uncertainty presents potential future threats or opportunities, proactive planning and risk management seeks to modify the future incidence and quality of threats or opportunities and their possible impact on project performance. This does not mean that reactive planning will not be necessary, or that all possible out-turns will have been predicted. It means that proactive planning will have been carried out to an extent which allows reactive planning to cope without nasty surprises most of the time. Reactive risk management, responding to the control function, will be reasonably panic free, without a need for crisis management most of the time. A degree of crisis management may be essential even in the context of a very effective and comprehensive risk management approach, but relatively few crises should come totally 'out of the blue'. Proactive planning, in the sense of developing base plans and contingency plans as appropriate, is fundamental to risk management. Significant reactive planning will still be required, and sometimes crisis management will be necessary, as a subset of the reactive planning process. However, effective risk management will reduce crisis management to an acceptable level.

To illustrate these points, consider another example, building on Example 1.1.

Example 1.3

Off-shore oil or gas pipelaying in the North Sea in the 1970s involved a number of serious risks. If no proactive planning had been undertaken, the potential for overwhelming crisis management was obvious.

The pipes laid in the North Sea at this time were constructed from sections of rigid steel pipe coated with concrete, welded to the pipeline on the lay barge, then eased over the stern of the barge by taking up the tension on sets of bow anchors, maintaining a smooth S shape of pipe between the barge and the ocean floor. As bow anchors approached the lay barge, they were picked up by tugs, carried ahead, and reset. Improperly controlled lowering of new pipeline sections could result in a pipe buckle, a key pipelaying risk. Excessive waves greatly increased this risk. Barges were classified or designated to indicate maximum safe wave heights for working, 3 metre or 1.6 metre, for example. In the face of excessive wave heights the operators would put a 'cap' on the open end of the pipe and lower it to the ocean floor, retrieving it when the waves reduced. These lowering and lifting operations could themselves lead to buckles.

The base plan for laying pipe assumed no significant risks (opportunities or threats) would be realised, only the minor day-to-day variations in performance which could be expected to average out.

The potential opportunity provided by unusually good weather, and the potential threat posed by unusually bad weather, was assessed by direct reference to historical weather records. Control was exercised by monitoring progress relative to the base plan, aggregating all reasons for being early or late, until a significant departure from the base plan was identified. A control response could be triggered by an accumulation of minor difficulties, or the realisation of a significant, obvious threat like a pipe buckle. Once the need for a control response had been identified and an appropriate response selected reflecting the nature of the realised threats or opportunities, the associated response became part of the revised base plan.

Effective comprehensive contingency planning ensured that the most crucial prior actions necessary to implement the preferred revisions to the base plan would be in place if it was cost effective to put them in place. The implications of not putting them in place were understood when making a decision not to do so.

Should a pipe buckle occur, there would be a potential need for additional pipe. This had to be ordered well in advance of starting the pipelaying if a delay associated with awaiting delivery were to be avoided. Effective contingency planning needed to ensure that enough pipe was available most of the time. However, it would not have been cost effective to ensure buckles never led to a shortage of pipe. Nor would it have been cost effective to undertake detailed planning to deal with all the knock-on effects of a pipe buckle.

Proactive and reactive planning are not alternatives, they are complementary aspects of planning as a whole, with proactive contingency planning supporting reactive contingency planning when this is cost effective. Similarly, crisis management is not an alternative to risk management, it is a consequence of its failure, but even the most effective risk management must fail on occasions if it is to remain cost effective on the average. Only if risk management fails completely, or is simply not addressed, will crisis management become the dominant management mode.

Much good project management practice could be thought of as risk management. For example, good practice in planning, coordination, setting milestones, change control procedures and so on, involves general responses to pervasive sources of risk such as human error, omissions, communication failures and so on. However, most texts on project management do not consider the way risk management should be integrated with project management more generally, in terms of a wide view of what a coordinated approach to proactive and reactive risk management can achieve. This is the role of risk management addressed here. It is important to appreciate the breadth and complexity of this risk management role if the opportunities effective risk management offers are to be realised.

Many experienced project managers perceive a gap between good practice as advocated in project management textbooks (project management 'theory') and good practice as they have experienced it. This gap may reflect the collective failure of the project management profession to define comprehensive approaches to project risk management fully integrated with project management. The concern here is providing a step on the road to filling this gap.

Chapter 2

Implications of the Project Life Cycle

The Moving Finger writes; and, having writ, Moves on: nor all thy Piety nor Wit shall lure it back to cancel half a line, Nor all thy Tears wash out a Word of it.

Edward Fitzgerald

2.1 INTRODUCTION

The six Ws framework of Figure 1.1 identified broad categories of uncertainty associated with any project, a generic structure related to six entities, and the cycle of attention as it moves from one entity to another. Within this framework the precise nature of many project risks will be situation specific. However, many important sources of risk are common to all projects because they are associated with the fundamental management processes that define the project life cycle. It follows that comprehensive project risk management is not just an extension of project management; it should also encompass risk management of the project management process itself. In order to fully appreciate the potential scope for risk management that this implies, it is necessary to examine the structure of the project life cycle (PLC) in some detail. As we shall see, the six Ws introduced in Chapter 1 are closely related to the different stages of the PLC, and the focus of any risk analysis needs to vary with these stages.

For most of this chapter we consider a single, generic project in isolation, so as to focus on the PLC. However, projects usually exist in an organisational context which includes other related projects and programmes.

Accordingly, this chapter ends with a short discussion of this multi-project framework and considers the implications for managing risk in a single project.

2.2 EIGHT STAGES

The PLC is a convenient way of conceptualising the generic structure of projects over time. It is often described in terms of four *phases*, using terms like: conceptualisation, planning, execution and termination (Adams and Barndt, 1988). Alternative phraseology may be used, such as formation, buildup, main programme, and phaseout (Thamhain and Wileman, 1975), but the underlying phases identified are essentially the same.

The PLC can be described in terms of the extent to which each phase differs in terms of the level of resources employed (Adams and Barndt, 1988), the degree of definition, the level of conflict (Thamhain and Wileman, 1975), the rate of expenditure and so on. This can help to show how management attention to the factor plotted needs to vary over the life of the project. By way of example, Figure 2.1 shows how costs typically accumulate in projects, with the majority of expenditure taking place in the execution phase, although the precise shape of the cost curve may vary greatly from one project to another. For example, in the context of military equipment and other projects with very high ongoing operating costs, full life cycle costing approaches address the implications of quite different cost curve shapes.

For risk management purposes, life cycle diagrams like Figure 2.1 point to the desirability of addressing project risk earlier rather than later

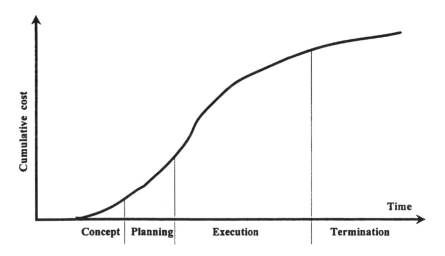

Figure 2.1 Cost in the project life cycle.

in the PLC, before major resource commitments are made. However, a deeper appreciation of the scope for risk management of PLC processes requires consideration of the individual phases, and of the processes within each phase.

Table 2.1 breaks down the typical four *phase* characterisation of the PLC into eight *stages*. We use stage rather than phase to emphasise the difference, and to reserve the word phase for the decomposition of the risk management process (RMP).

This breakdown into eight stages goes some way towards highlighting sources of process risk. However, a still more detailed description of the PLC is useful to underline where particular risks arise in the PLC and where risk management might be most effective. Specifically, it is useful to break the eight stages into a larger number of *steps*, as listed in Table 2.1. In the early stages, these steps imply a process of gradually increasing detail and focus on the provision of a product or service deliverable.

The Conceive Stage

It is useful to think of the Conceive stage as part of an innovation process, and draw on ideas from Lemaitre and Stenier's description of the innovation process (Lemaitre and Stenier, 1988), although the scope of our Conceive stage is somewhat different. The Conceive stage involves identifying a deliverable to be produced and the benefits expected from the deliverable. It begins with a 'trigger event' (Lyles, 1981), when a member of an initiating organisation perceives an opportunity or need. At this point the project deliverable may be only a vague idea, and some initial development may be associated with the 'concept capture' step. 'Clarification of purpose' involving the identification of relevant performance objectives and their relative importance is another key step in the Conceive stage. This step may be problematic to the extent that different views about the appropriate objectives are held by influential stakeholders who try to negotiate mutually acceptable objectives. Objectives at this stage are likely to be ill-defined or developed as aspirational constraints (for example, latest completion, minimum levels of functionality, maximum cost and so on). Before the concept can be developed further, in a 'concept elaboration' step, sufficient political support for the idea must be obtained and resources allocated to allow the idea to be refined and made more explicit. Other individuals, organisations or potential stakeholders may become involved. Support at this stage may be passive, merely allowing conceptualisation to proceed, rather than an expression of positive approval of the project. The focus of this stage is the early cycles of the six Ws of Figure 1.1.

Eventually an evaluation of the project concept and objectives as defined to date becomes necessary, the 'concept evaluation' step in Table 2.1. Evaluation here (and later) is not simply a *go/no-go* decision, but a

Table 2.1 Phases, stages and steps in the project life cycle.

Phases	Stages	Steps
Conceptualisation	Conceive	Trigger event Concept capture Clarification of purpose Concept elaboration Concept evaluation
Planning	Design	Basic design Development of performance criteria Design development Design evaluation
	Plan	Base plan Development of targets and milestones Plan development Plan evaluation
	Allocate	Base design and plan detail Development of allocation criteria Allocation development Allocation evaluation
Execution	Execute	Coordinate and control Monitor progress Modification of targets and milestones Allocation modification Control evaluation
Termination	Deliver	Basic deliverable verification Deliverable modification Modification of performance criteria Deliver evaluation
	Review	Basic review Review development Review evaluation
	Support	Basic maintenance and liability perception Development of support criteria Support perception development Support evaluation

go/no-go/maybe decision. A *go* decision takes the process into the Design stage. A *no-go* decision causes it to stop. A *maybe* decision involves iteration through one or more previous steps. The basic process risk in this stage is moving on to design before the project concept and objectives have crystallised, and before effective concept evaluation.

The Design Stage

A *go* decision in the Conceive stage initiates a 'basic design' step in the Design stage, giving form to the deliverable of the project. The focus of this stage is giving substance to the *what* entity, although loops through the other five Ws will be involved. This usually requires a step increase in the effort or resources involved. 'Development of performance criteria' builds on the base design and project objectives. For many projects this involves refining project objectives, but it may involve the identification of additional objectives and further negotiation where pluralistic views persist. This step influences 'design development' which leads to 'design evaluation' using the developed performance criteria to assess the current design in *go/no-go/maybe* terms. As in the concept stage, *no-go* will end the process. A *maybe* evaluation is most likely to lead to iteration through one or more development steps, but if fundamental difficulties not anticipated in the concept stage are encountered, the loop may go back to the concept stage. *Go* takes the process on to the Plan stage. The basic process risk at this stage is moving on to the Plan stage before effective design evaluation. The decomposition of the Table 2.1 'planning phase' into Design, Plan and Allocate stages serves to emphasise this risk.

The Plan Stage

A *go* decision in the Design stage initiates development of a base plan, indicating how the design will be executed (*whichway*), what resources are required in broad terms (*wherewithal*), and how long it will take (*when*). The focus of this stage is these three Ws, but loops through the other three will be involved. Yet more individuals and organisations may become involved. 'Development of targets and milestones' involves determining specific targets for producing the project deliverable, typically in terms of cost and time, but sometimes in terms of resource usage or other considerations as well. 'Plan development' follows and leads to 'plan evaluation' in *go/no-go/maybe* terms. A *maybe* decision may require further development of targets and milestones within the Plan stage, but more fundamental difficulties may take the process back to design development or even concept elaboration. The basic process risk at this stage is moving on to the Allocate stage before effective programme evaluation.

The Allocate Stage

A *go* decision in the Plan stage takes the process on to the Allocate stage, and a detailed allocation of internal resources and contracts to achieve the plan. The detail of the *what* (design) drives the detail of the *whichway* (activities) which drives the detail of the *wherewithal* (resources) which drives the detail of the *when* (timing), with iterative, interactive loops. The Allocate stage is a significant task involving decisions about project organisation, identification of appropriate participants and allocation of tasks between them. The *who* may be substantially redefined. Either implicitly or explicitly the allocation process involves allocation of execution risks between participants. This activity is an important source of process risk in that this allocation can significantly influence the behaviour of participants and hence impact on project performance. In particular, allocation of execution and termination phase risks influences the extent and manner in which such risks are managed. This warrants careful consideration of the basis for allocating tasks and risks in the 'development of allocation criteria' step.

'Allocation development' necessarily involves detailed design and planning in order to allocate tasks unless this whole stage is contracted out along with the balance of the project. Contracts and subcontractual structures may require development. Again the nature of the issues changes with the change of stage, and the level of effort may escalate. As in the earlier project stages, development during this stage is followed by 'allocation evaluation'. A *maybe* decision which goes back to the Plan, Design or even Conceive stage is extremely unwelcome, and a *no-go* decision will be seen as a serious disaster in many cases.

The Rationale for Separate Design, Plan, and Allocate Stages

A possible argument against decomposition of the Table 2.1 'planning phase' into Design, Plan and Allocate stages is their interdependent nature, and the need to iterate within this phase. We believe that the importance of this dependence and the process risks it generates is highlighted by their separation. Quite different tasks are involved, with different end products, and different process risks. The decisions to move from Design to Plan to Allocate are very important. This makes it important to treat them as separable, recognising their important interdependencies.

There is a related question about the focus on *whichway*, *wherewithal* and *when* in the Plan stage, and the subsequent detailed treatment of these same three Ws plus design in the Allocate stage. Why not separate them to yield still more stages? In this case we view the interdependence as too strong to make separability useful for present purposes. However, Figure 1.1 clearly suggests it will be important to distinguish these Ws in each of these two stages for some purposes.

More generally, we view the decomposition of the Table 2.1 'planning phase' into three stages as useful because it captures useful separability, but in our view further formal decomposition is not useful at the level of generality of concern here.

Figure 2.2 emphasises the inter-stage feedback loop structure of the Conceive–Design–Plan–Allocate stages, and following stages. 'Primary feedback loops' are 'primary' in the inter-stage sense, ignoring the more

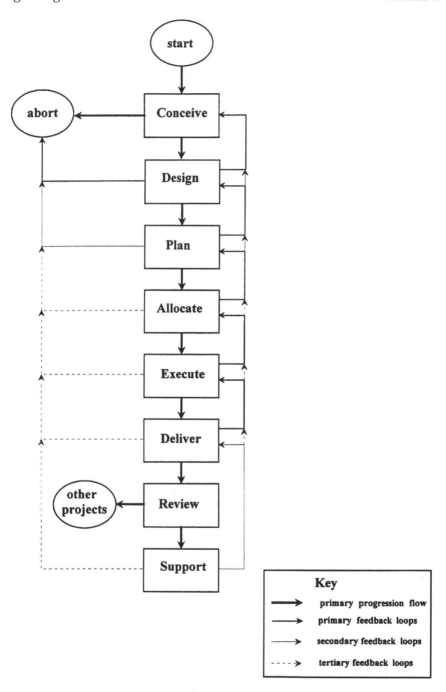

Figure 2.2 Inter-stage progression and feedback structure.

fundamental feedback loops within each stage. 'Secondary' and 'tertiary' feedback loops indicate more costly feedback to be avoided if possible.

Figures 1.1 and 2.2 are both pictures of the same process, from different perspectives and in different dimensions. Figure 1.1 takes the six Ws as its basis, while Figure 2.2 takes the eight stages of the PLC as its basis. Iterative loops following the feedback structure between the six Ws of Figure 1.1 can take place within each of the Figure 2.2 stages.

The Execute Stage

A *go* decision in the Allocate stage initiates the main body of the project, the Execute stage. The start of this stage signals the start of order-of-magnitude increases in effort and expenditure. The planning is over, the action begins. During execution, the essential process risk is that coordination and control procedures prove inadequate. A common perceived source of risk in the Execute stage is the introduction of design changes. but these may be earlier risks coming home to roost. Consequent adjustments to production plans, costs and payments to affected contractors ought to be based on an assessment of how project risks are affected by the changes and the extent to which revised risk management plans are needed.

For most projects repeated iteration will be necessary through the steps in the Execute stage. Exceptionally, loops back to earlier stages may be necessary. Very nasty surprises could take some aspects of the project right back to the concept stage, or lead to a *no-go* decision, including project abortion. Nasty surprises are realised risks from earlier stages which were not identified, indicating a failure of the risk management process in earlier stages.

The Rationale for Separate Deliver, Review and Support Stages

The project 'termination phase' of Table 2.1 involves three distinct aspects, captured in the Deliver, Review and Support stages, each encompassing different risk management concerns. The rationale for their separation, and no further separation, has the same form as the argument for separation of the Design, Plan and Allocate stages. However, arguably the case for separation is even stronger in terms of the very different nature of these stages.

The Deliver Stage

The Deliver stage involves commissioning and handover. Again the issues are different from previous stages. The 'basic deliverable verification' step involves verifying what the product of the project will do in practice, its actual performance as distinct from its designed performance. An important risk is that the deliverable fails to meet expected performance criteria. Modification of product performance may be achievable, but modification of performance criteria or influencing stakeholder expectations and perceptions may be necessary. However, unless they were explicitly anticipated these are not process risks in this stage, they are a realisation of earlier unmanaged risks. 'Delivery evaluation' focuses on the need for quality assessment and modification loops, including compensating for unanticipated weaknesses by developing unanticipated strengths. Loops back to the concept stage or a *no-go* abort decision are still possible.

The Review Stage

The Review stage involves a documented audit after delivery of the product. Some lessons will be obvious, the 'basic review' starting point. But allocating resources to systematic study to draw out lessons which were not obvious, 'review development', is important. Missing important lessons means mistakes will be made again, the key process risk in this stage. Not having such a stage explicitly identified almost guarantees the realisation of this risk. Hindsight may suggest some actions were successful or not, for unanticipated reasons. Such occurrences ought to be noted for future reference. An important aspect of the review should be documentation of the manner in which performance and other criteria relevant to each project stage developed, in particular the rationale for any changes. 'Review evaluation' involves evaluating the likely relevance and usefulness of review data for informing future project management practice. Review evaluation does not lead to abort or loops back to earlier stages. Unlike evaluation steps in previous stages, the Review stage as conceived here is not concerned with the possibility of abort or loops back to earlier stages. As indicated in Figure 2.2, the purpose of review evaluation is to inform practice on other projects. A positive approach to the Review stage is important, with the emphasis on capturing good practice and rewarding the deserving, not highlighting bad practice and punishing the guilty.

The Support Stage

The Support stage involves living with the ongoing legacy of apparent project 'completion', possibly in a passive 'endure' mode, until the product of the project is discarded, decommissioned, or otherwise disposed of. 'Basic maintenance and liability perception' is the starting point when the project is complete in the handover sense, noting that handover may be an internal matter in organisational terms. 'Development of support criteria' and associated 'support perception development' leads to 'support evaluation' which may be repeated periodically. The focus of this evaluation may be a within-stage loop back to development of perceptions, or a limited loop back to the Deliver stage. Exceptionally, the outcome could be a *no-go* decision involving product withdrawal or other explicit withdrawal of support for the project's product. Again, surprises are not risks inherent in this stage, but process risks in earlier stages realised in this stage.

2.3 ELABORATIONS TO THE EIGHT-STAGE FRAMEWORK

Despite the number of steps in Table 2.1, the possibility of iteration at each evaluation step, and the iterative six W process loops of Figure 1.1 within each stage, our description of the PLC is still a simple one by comparison with the complexities of real projects. Nevertheless, to the extent that we are concerned with highlighting sources of process risk, it is a useful basic framework. In any event, this framework is easily elaborated to describe a variety of common project situations. Some examples follow.

Project Dimensions

In practice, projects are planned and executed in several dimensions: physical scope, functionality, technology, location, timing, economics, financing, environmental, and so on. Thus each step in Table 2.1 could be viewed as multi-dimensional, with each step considering each dimension in parallel or in an iterative sequence. In this latter case, the PLC might be visualised as a spiral of activities moving forward through time, where each completed circle of the spiral represents one step in Table 2.1 completed, and each spiral represents sequential consideration of the various project dimensions.

Parallel Components

Many projects, especially large ones, may be managed as a set of component projects running in parallel. The steps in Table 2.1 can still be used to describe the progress of each component project, although there is no necessity for the component life cycles to remain in phase at all times. 'Fast tracking' is a simple example of this, where completion of the parent project can be expedited by overlapping project Design, Plan, Allocate and Execute stages. Thus, some components of the parent project can be designed and planned, and allocation and execution commenced for these components, before designing and planning is complete for other components. As is widely recognised, such staggered execution is only low risk to the extent that the design of components first executed is not dependent on the design of subsequent components. Plans which involve an element of 'fast tracking' should be supported by an appropriate risk analysis, with a focus on feedback from more advanced components into the life cycle steps of following components.

Objectives not Easily Defined

For many projects objectives and related performance criteria can be refined progressively through the Conceive, Design, Plan and Allocate stages of the PLC. However, in some projects, for example information systems or software development projects, it may not be practicable to ensure that all project objectives are well defined or crystallised prior to the Execute stage. This becomes apparent in previous stages, where *go* decisions acknowledge the situation. In this scenario 'control evaluation', undertaken each time a milestone is achieved, ought to include a 'configuration review' (Turner and Cochrane, 1993; Turner, 1992) of objectives currently achievable with the project. If these are unsatisfactory, further stages of Design and Plan may be necessary.

Contracting

When allocation of tasks in the Allocate stage involves the employment of contractors, the tendering and subsequent production work of the contractor can be regarded as a project, or component project, in its own right. For the contractor, all the steps in Table 2.1 are passed through on becoming involved in the parent project. What the client regards as the Allocate stage is regarded by the contractor as the Conceive, Design, Plan and Allocate stages. In the case where the contractor has a major responsibility for design (as in turnkey or design and build contracts), the client will move quickly through the Conceive, Design and Plan stages, perhaps considering these stages only in general outline terms. Then the contractor carries out more detailed work corresponding to these stages. For the contractor's project, the 'trigger' involves both a need and an opportunity to tender for work, usually managed at a high level in the contracting organisation. The Conceive stage corresponds to a preliminary assessment of the bidding opportunity and a decision to tender or not (Ward and Chapman, 1988). This is followed by costing design specifications and plans provided in more or less detail by the client, perhaps some additional design and plan development, evaluation of the tendering opportunity, price setting and submission of a bid. For the contractor's project, the Allocate stage involves further allocation of tasks, perhaps via subcontracting, detailed design work and production scheduling as indicated above.

Incomplete Definition of Methods

In some projects, such as product development projects, it may not be practicable to define completely the nature or sequence of activities required prior to commencing the execution phase (Turner and Cochrane, 1993). In such cases management expects Design, Plan, Allocate and Execute stages to take place alternately on a rolling basis, with achievement of one milestone triggering detailed Design, Plan, Allocate and Execute stages of the next part of the project deliverable. In this scenario, previous *go* decisions in the Design, Plan and Allocate stages are made on the understanding that subsequent control evaluation steps will send the process through further Design, Plan and Allocate stages as necessary when the appropriate milestone has been achieved. In effect, the Design, Plan, Allocate and Execute stages are managed as a sequence of mini-projects.

Prototyping is a special case of this scenario, and a natural approach where the intention is to mass produce a product, but the product involves novel designs or new technology. For the production project, the PLC Conceive and Design stages are managed as a prototype project (with its own PLC). On completion of the prototype, the production PLC proceeds from the Plan through to the Support stages in Table 2.1.

2.4   IMPLIED OPPORTUNITIES FOR RISK MANAGEMENT

The value of breaking down the PLC into such a large number of stages and steps might be questioned on three grounds:

1. these steps and stages will be difficult to distinguish cleanly in practice;
2. in practice some of these steps may not be necessary;
3. this level of detail adds complexity, when what is required to be useful in practice is simplification.

For example, it might be argued that some of the later evaluation steps may be regarded as non-existent in practice because the decision to proceed is not usually an issue beyond a certain point. However, we would argue that it is worthwhile identifying such steps beforehand, given their potential significance in managing process risks.

Many of the really serious risks projects are late realisations of unmanaged risks from earlier project stages. The detailed stage and step structure of Table 2.1 and the associated Figure 2.2 help to make this clear. In many projects there is a failure to give sufficient attention to *go/no-go/maybe* decisions. Such decisions should involve careful evaluation of risk, both to appreciate the risks inherent in a *go* decision and the rewards forgone in a *no-go* decision. Equally important is the need to recognise when a *go/no-go* or *maybe* choice should be on the agenda. Many projects appear to involve just one *go/no-go* decision—at the end of the Conceive stage. Yet the large number of projects that run into major problems of cost escalation, time overruns and quality compromises suggests that explicit *go/no-go/maybe* decision points in later stages would often have been worthwhile.

A further reason for the detailed step structure is to highlight the process of objectives formation and its significance for project risk management. As noted in Chapter 1, risk is measured in terms of uncertainty about the attainment of project objectives. In the PLC, objectives and performance criteria are often initially vague for good reasons, but they must be progressively clarified and refined during the Conceive, Design, Plan and Allocate stages. This process needs to be recognised and the implications understood. A situation where the objectives of a project change imprecisely during the project without proper recognition of the new situation implied is particularly risky. From a risk management viewpoint, any changes in objectives and performance criteria at any stage of the PLC need to be carefully evaluated for risk implications.

Much of 'good project management practice' could be thought of as management of pervasive and fundamental process risks such as human error, omissions, communication failures and so on, which are not necessarily explicitly identified or confined to particular stages of the PLC. The framework presented here focuses on more specific process risks with different PLC stages involving rather different risk management considerations. There is obvious value in being clear about which risks are specific to particular stages in the PLC and which are not.

Specifying the PLC as a number of stages and steps highlights the potential opportunities for risk management in projects. Table 2.2 gives examples of the ways in which risk management could contribute to each stage of the PLC, and suggests that risk management could usefully be applied on a piecemeal basis in one or more stages of a PLC without the necessity for risk management in any previous or subsequent stages. For example, risk analysis could form part of the 'evaluation' step in any stage of the PLC, and be instrumental in producing an iteration back through earlier steps. Alternatively, risk analysis might be used to guide the first step of each stage. In these circumstances, the focus of risk analysis is likely to reflect immediate project management concerns in the associated project stage. Thus risk analysis might be undertaken as part of the Plan stage primarily to consider the feasibility and development of the work schedule for project execution, for example. There might be no expectation that such risk analysis would or should influence the design, although it might be perceived as a potential influence on the subsequent Allocate stage decisions. In practice, many risk analyses are intentionally limited in scope, as in individual studies to determine the reliability of available equipment, the likely outcome of a particular course of action, or to evaluate alternative decision options within a particular PLC stage.

To view risk analysis as an add-on to individual stages or steps of a PLC is to take a restricted view of project risk that is likely to limit the effectiveness of the risk management effort. As we have seen, it is only by considering the complete PLC as an integrated whole that the significance of risks and the interdependencies of risks between stages can be fully appreciated and managed. Wherever it is carried out in a PLC, risk analysis

Table 2.2 Applications of risk management in the project life cycle.

Stages of the PLC	Roles for risk analysis
Conceive	Identifying stakeholders and their expectations Identifying appropriate performance objectives
Design	Testing the reliability of design Testing the feasibility of design Setting performance criteria Assessing the likely cost of a design Assessing the likely benefits from a design Assessing the effect of changes to a design
Plan	Identifying and allowing for regulatory constraints Assessing the feasibility of a plan Assessing the likely duration of a plan Assessing the likely cost of a plan Determining appropriate milestones Estimating resources required Assessing the effect of changes to the plan Determining appropriate levels of contingency funds and resources
Allocate	Evaluating alternative procurement strategies Defining contractual terms and conditions Determining appropriate risk sharing arrangements Assessing the implications of contract conditions Assessing and comparing competitive tenders Determining appropriate target costs and bid prices for contracts Estimating likely profit following project termination
Execute	Identifying remaining execution risks Assessing implications of changes to design or plan Revising estimates of cost on completion Revising estimates of completion time of execution stage
Deliver	Identifying risks to delivery Assessing feasibility of delivery schedule Assessing feasibility of meeting performance criteria Assessing reliability of testing equipment Assessing requirement for resources to modify project deliverable Assessing availability of commissioning facilities
Review	Assessing effectiveness of risk management strategies Identifying of realised risks and effective responses
Support	Identifying extent of future liabilities Assessing appropriate level of resources required Assessing profitability of the project

needs to be regarded as a contribution to risk management of the whole project. The opportunities for risk management include looking forwards and backwards at any stage in the PLC, addressing all the issues indicated by Table 2.2 as appropriate.

2.5 A WIDER PERSPECTIVE

As well as recognising the detailed internal structure of individual project life cycles, it is also important to recognise the role of a project as part of a larger, corporate picture. Projects are invariably embedded in a wider context which involves other projects. Three basic contexts are: the Chain Configuration; the Parallel Configuration; and the Project Hierarchy. Figure 2.3 illustrates these configurations.

In the Chain Configuration a sequence of component projects follow one another over time to complete an overarching, primary project. In the Parallel Configuration a number of component projects run in parallel, perhaps with interdependencies, to complete an overarching, primary project. In either case the 'primary project' may be thought of by senior management in terms which go beyond that associated with projects, as a strategy or long-term programme. The discipline and techniques of project management may be considered of limited use in managing strategy or programmes in this sense, leading to a separation of strategy ('primary project') management and project management of the component projects. This separation may be formalised by organisational structures, and may increase the chances of risk management of component projects being treated separately from consideration of strategic risk.

An obvious example is a contracting organisation where the ongoing business involves tendering for individual contracts. Each contract won is treated as a project, and these contracts form a mixture of the Chain and Parallel Configurations. Interdependencies exist between contracts to the extent that they utilise common corporate knowledge, skills and other resources. An important task for senior management is to manage the (often implicit) 'primary project', the organisation's short- and long-term strategy. Unless this is managed explicitly at 'the top', strategy is likely to emerge *ad hoc* from the 'bottom-up' in an unintended rather than deliberate manner (Mintzberg, 1978).

In a Project Hierarchy the 'primary project' is broken down by management into a hierarchy of component projects. The Project Hierarchy shown in Figure 2.2 is a simple example with embedded Parallel and Chain Configurations. Much more complex configurations involving a combination of these three configuration types exist in most organisations.

Large engineering or construction projects are invariably managed as Project Hierarchies. As noted earlier, large projects may be managed as a set of component projects running in parallel, with each parallel component comprising a hierarchy of component projects. Management of the 'primary project' can be tackled as a complex version of project management and is typically managed at a more senior level than management of the component projects. As a practical matter, managers of primary projects may

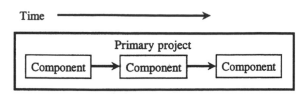

(a) Chain Configuration: primary project as a chain of component projects.
Stages in a primary project may be managed as a chain of component projects

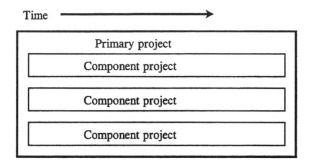

(b) Parallel Configuration: primary project as a set of parallel component projects.
Aspects of a project may be managed as a set of parallel projects

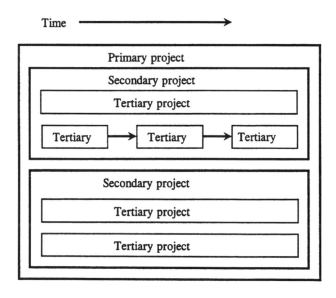

(c) Project Hierarchy: primary project as a three-level hierarchy of component projects

Figure 2.3 Configuration of project systems.

not be interested in the 'nuts and bolts' of individual component projects, but they will have to understand them well enough to make sure the component projects fit together as a whole. To achieve this they need to pay special attention to how the six Ws of each of the various component projects fit together, with obvious implications for managing risk.

More generally, a Project Hierarchy can be thought of as a hierarchy of an organisation's long-, medium- and short-term planning activity. In a top-down approach, long-term strategy leads to the development and implementation of medium-term projects. These may be achieved by a programme of short-term projects, or may otherwise constrain short-term operations. Scope for managing risks exists at each level reflecting the corresponding key issues at each level. However, management at each level also needs to be aware of potential impacts from adjacent levels. In particular, managers of medium-term projects need to take into account potential impacts on their projects from both short-term and long-term issues.

Example 2.1

An electric utility, providing electricity to a set of private and corporate consumers, might start with a corporate level assessment of annual profit, P_t, equal to annual revenue, R_t, less annual costs, C_t, for $t = 1, 2, \ldots n$, up to the chosen long-term planning horizon.

Revenue might be a key source of risk, worthy of major risk management effort. Forecast demand might be important here, but existing competing utilities, possible new competitors, market regulators, and other political players may be important parties to consider.

Cost might also be important. At the corporate level, cost may be driven by long-term strategic planning decisions: what mix of sources of power should be aimed for 25 years hence, what proportion of nuclear, gas-fired, coal-fired units should be planned for, and so on. Through-life costs will be important, including fuel costs, the effects of environmental legislation or technology development, and liability for pollution or accidents.

At an operational level, management is concerned with the day-to-day utilisation of existing units. At an intermediate level, an important management concern is the timing of decisions to start building new power generating units. Such decisions may be coupled to both short-term, operational issues and longer-term strategic issues. Sudden failure of an existing unit may trigger a need to bring plans forward. Political events may alter the need for a planned unit significantly, perhaps even eliminate the need for the unit, possibly doing so when construction of the unit is already underway.

The project manager for the construction of such a unit clearly needs to manage the project in a way that deals effectively with the risks he or she is responsible for and the risks other members of the organisation are responsible for.

Motivation to undertake risk analysis in a top-down strategic manner needs to come from the organisation's board level managers. This involves issues beyond the scope of this book, but discussed elsewhere (Chapman, 1992a). However, even if a project manager's organisation chooses to ignore such issues completely, a competent project risk manager cannot do so. At the very least, it is important to identify the complete set of corporate risks which impact on the project manager's project and which may require responses from the project manager or other parties.

2.6 CONCLUSION

To be fully effective, risk management needs to address the whole PLC rather than selected stages. Assuming a whole project approach to risk management, we would expect risk analysis to guide and inform each and every stage of the PLC. Moreover, we would expect the scope and depth of analysis to increase as the project progresses towards the Execute stage. Prior to each stage a preliminary risk analysis could guide the first step, but as more details and options are considered in subsequent steps, further risk analysis could be performed with increasing detail and precision to continuously guide and inform the project management process. Thus risk management should be an integral part of each stage of the PLC.

In all multi-project configurations, any designated project is but a particular reference point in a larger system, affected by the wider system and with potential to affect the wider system in turn. A key management issue, and risk management issue, is the degree of interdependency between (component) projects. The greater this interdependency, the greater the desirability of risk analysis which addresses the overall system.

Chapter 3

Motives for Formal Risk Management Processes

The Light of Lights looks always on the motive, not the deed, The Shadow of Shadows on the deed alone.

William Butler Yeats

3.1 INTRODUCTION

Formal risk management processes (RMPs) offer a number of important benefits which need to be appreciated if the best use is to be made of RMP. Many people who are not familiar with formal RMPs see them as processes whose sole concern is risk measurement, and see risk measurement as a response to the question 'is this too risky?' in terms of selected performance criteria. Bankers or management boards requiring comfort before releasing funds may seem to be instrumental in causing RMPs to be viewed in this way. There is clearly nothing wrong with banks or boards using risk management to serve this end, but if this is the sole rationale, RMP will be largely wasted, and may prove ineffective in relation to even this limited goal. That is, effective risk measurement may not be feasible unless a richer set of organisational performance criteria is considered.

The range of ends which can be served depends upon the characteristics of the RMP employed, and associated dependencies are complex. The easiest way to explain these relationships is to begin by addressing RMP in its most comprehensive form, looking at all the possible motives and ends served by such a process, and then consider what is lost as a consequence of an efficient set of short cuts, simplifying the process. This is the line of attack taken in this book. At this stage in the line of argument it is important to develop a broad understanding of what is possible, and the general concepts associated with the key motives for a formal RMP.

This chapter begins with the central role of RMPs, the pursuit of risk efficiency. Arguably the most difficult motive to understand, it is certainly the most important. It is the central reason why risk management should not be seen as an 'add-on', an overhead, with a focus on questions like 'is it worth it?' It is the central reason why risk management should be seen as an integrated 'add-in', an improvement to the basic project planning process, always worthwhile, a key issue being 'how much formal risk management in what style is best on this occasion?' Organisations like the UK Ministry of Defence now clearly and explicitly accept this argument, requiring *appropriate* formal RMPs for *all* procurement, without being too prescriptive about what is appropriate (MoD(PE)-DPP(PM), 1991, or PERAG, 1991). A central issue this book considers at length is 'what do we mean by appropriate?', and in particular, how the style or form of analysis should change with the circumstances, including the motives for formal risk management processes.

3.2 RISK EFFICIENCY

Assume for the moment that achieved performance can be measured solely in terms of cost out-turn, and that achieved success can be measured solely in terms of realised cost relative to some approved cost commitment. In this context, risk can be defined in terms of the threat to success posed by a given plan in terms of the size of possible cost overruns and their likelihood, what we will call 'threat intensity'. More formally, when assessing a particular project plan in relation to alternatives, we can consider the expected cost of the project as a basic measure of expected performance (what should happen on average), and we can consider associated risk or threat intensity in terms of possibilities of exceeding some approved cost commitment and related probabilities.

In this context some ways of planning a project will involve less expected cost and less risk than others—they will be better in both respects, and relatively more efficient. The most efficient plan for any given level of expected cost will involve the minimum feasible level of risk. The most efficient plan for any given level of risk will involve the minimum feasible level of expected cost. 'Risk efficiency' in this sense defines a set of what economists call Pareto optima: given a risk efficient plan, expected cost can only be reduced by increasing the risk; risk can only be reduced by increasing the expected cost. This concept is most easily pictured using a graph like Figure 3.1.

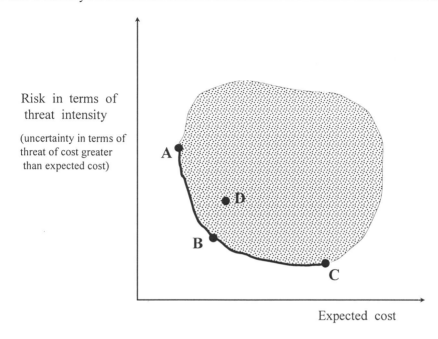

Risk in terms of
threat intensity

(uncertainty in terms of
threat of cost greater
than expected cost)

Expected cost

Figure 3.1   Risk efficient options.

Consider a set of feasible project plans, and a set of non-feasible plans, portrayed in relation to expected cost and threat intensity as indicated in Figure 3.1. The feasible set has an upper and lower bound for both threat intensity and expected cost because there are limits to how good or bad plans can be in both these dimensions. The boundary between the feasible and non-feasible sets need not be a smooth, continuous curve as shown in Figure 3.1, but it is convenient to assume this for illustrative purposes.

The 'risk efficient boundary' is portrayed by the curve A–B–C, that set of feasible project plans which provides a minimum level of risk in terms of threat intensity for any given level of expected cost, the minimum level of expected cost for any given level of risk in threat intensity terms.

Any point off the boundary, like D, represents an inefficient plan, which can be improved upon with respect to both threat intensity and expected cost, moving to B, for example.

If a base plan and associated contingency plans are risk efficient, any change to these plans which reduces the associated risk will increase the expected cost, and any change which reduces the expected cost will increase the risk. Resources are allocated to base and contingency plan activities to put the project plans on the risk efficient boundary.

A key characteristic of risk is that some ways of planning a project have a higher expected cost and they are riskier than others. Searching for risk efficiency is the key to understanding and dealing with risk. A focus on threats associated with one particular plan misses the point. Understanding how to move from a risky plan to a less risky plan and reduce the expected cost at the same time is a central issue.

We can never be sure our plans are risk efficient. However, we need to search systematically for improvements in risk efficiency, otherwise we will never find them. This implies that the form of risk analysis selected must be geared to a search for opportunities to improve risk efficiency, to do things better in the risk efficiency sense. Usually what is involved is identifying where extra money or other resources expended up-front will reduce later risk and overall expected cost. Diagnosis of potential changes to base or contingency plans to improve risk efficiency is the central purpose of effective project risk management. Consideration of risk efficient choices in the following example motivated an oil major to adopt formal risk management on a worldwide basis for all significant or sensitive projects.

Example 3.1

A major North Sea offshore oil project was about to seek board approval and release of funds to begin construction. Risk analysis was undertaken to give the board confidence in the plan and its associated cost. One activity involved a hookup, connecting a pipeline to a platform. It had a target date in August. A 1.6 metre barge was specified, equipment which could work in waves up to a nominal 1.6 metre height. Risk analysis demonstrated that August was an appropriate target date, and a 1.6 metre barge was appropriate in August. However, risk analysis also demonstrated that, because this hookup was late in the overall project sequence, and there was considerable scope for delays to earlier activities, there was a significant chance that this hookup would have to be attempted in November or December. Using a 1.6 metre barge at this time of year would be time consuming and might mean delays until the following spring, with severe opportunity cost implications. A revised analysis was undertaken assuming a 3 metre wave height capability barge, costing more than twice as much per day. This more capable barge avoided the risk of going into the next season, significantly reducing risk in terms of the threat of a significant cost overrun. It also significantly reduced the expected cost. This significant improvement with respect to both expected cost and risk in terms of the threat of a major overrun provided a significant improvement in risk efficiency. The base plan was changed, and it was recognised at board level that this one change paid for the risk analysis study many times over.

In the event, hookup was actually completed in October in good weather conditions.

This example illustrates three separate roles for risk analysis in relation to risk efficiency:

1. diagnose desirable changes in plans;
2. demonstrate the need for such changes;
3. facilitate, demonstrate and encourage 'enlightened caution'.

Diagnose Desirable Changes in Plans

Sometimes risk analysis can diagnose difficulties and identify a need for changes in project base plans or contingency plans which were previously obscure and not recognised. Risk analysts should be motivated to search for such changes, and they should enlist the support of the project team as a whole to join the search. In this context risk analysis can be usefully portrayed as a treasure hunt—the 'treasure' is increases in risk efficiency through changes in plans. Put another way, risk analysis is a search for opportunities, not for reasons to kill a project. This positive perspective is extremely important for staff motivation and morale, as well as for the direct pay-off in terms of more efficient plans and designs, and a more effective approach to achieving efficiency.

Demonstrate the Need for Such Changes

Sometimes risk analysis is not necessary to identify a need for changes in plans in the sense that exploring the intuitions of project team members will reveal an understanding of the need for such changes. However, whether or not recognition by specific project team members is the result of risk analysis, risk analysis can allow the demonstration of the need for that change to others, like the board in Example 3.1. Demonstration of this need is a separate and very important aspect of making the changes. For a variety of reasons, if it is not possible to demonstrate clearly the need for changes, such changes may not be made, even if most of those involved acknowledge the need to make the changes. One basic reason is determined resistance to changes by those with vested interests. Another is inertia. Yet another is a business culture which discourages the 'enlightenment' essential to achieve risk efficiency, about to be introduced in terms of 'enlightened caution'.

Facilitate, Demonstrate and Encourage Enlightened Caution

'Enlightened caution' is defined as willingness to commit resources which may not be needed, because in expected value terms (on average) it will be cost effective to commit them.

Had problems in the earlier part of the project of Example 3.1 caused the hookup to take place in November or December, with seasonably bad weather, the change to a 3 metre barge would have been clearly justified. The enlightened caution associated with the changes would have been verified empirically. The hookup taking place in October in good weather demonstrated enlightened caution which was not verified empirically. This was a very important demonstration, because if enlightened caution is part of a corporate culture, money will be spent which 20:20 hindsight will suggest would have been saved whenever we are lucky, and it is important to appreciate that this money was not wasted.

If no formal risk analysis process had been followed in relation to the Example 3.1 decision to use a 3 metre barge, the decision being made on intuitive grounds by the project manager, his career might have looked much less promising when it became clear he could have got away with a 1.6 metre barge. That is, the risk analysis made it clear that the project manager had done well to achieve hookup by October, and he had been lucky with the weather. Without a formal risk analysis, his good luck might have been confused with bad management regarding this decision, overlooking completely his good management of the project (getting to the hookup by October), and blighting his career. A worldly wise project manager would explicitly recognise this possibility, and might opt for the 1.6 metre barge in the absence of formal risk analysis, deliberately making a bad management decision because good luck would subsequently be confused with good management, and bad luck would subsequently just be interpreted as plain bad luck. If an organisation cannot distinguish between good luck and good management, bad luck and bad management, individuals will manage risk accordingly. Without risk analysis to demonstrate support for their decisions, astute managers who are naturally and reasonably cautious with respect to their own careers will see risk efficient decisions comparable to choosing the 3 metre barge in Example 3.1 as unwise, potentially dangerous to their careers, seeming to demonstrate a whimpish uncalled-for caution whenever they actually manage the preceding work effectively. Very astute managers will avoid even looking for opportunities to increase risk efficiency in this way, to avoid the moral hazard of the obvious conflict of interests. More generally, if good luck and good management cannot be distinguished, such opportunities will not be looked for, and for the most part they will be passed over if they are stumbled upon.

Risk analysis can facilitate and demonstrate enlightened caution in partic-ular instances, and by doing so encourage a more general culture change associated with circumstances which are not worth formal analysis as used in relation to Example 3.1.

If everyone involved understands the lesson of examples like Example 3.1, the culture can change as a consequence of everyone looking for and making changes which increase risk efficiency through enlightened caution. This means that sometimes most people will spend money on 'insurance' that is not needed. However, any organisation which never spends unnecessary money on 'insurance' which is not needed is habitually 'under-insured'. Enlightened caution needs to be facilitated and demonstrated to overcome this widespread cultural phenomenon, the demonstration of instances when enlightened caution was not empirically verified being of particular importance.

Quantification of Risk

With respect to all three of these aspects of risk efficiency, quantification of risk is clearly useful. With respect to demonstration, quantification is virtually essential. The spread of enlightened caution as a culture change depends on demonstration. This implies that any approach to risk management which does not lend itself to comparative quantification of risk to assist with the process of ensuring risk efficiency is likely to prove defective.

3.3 TRADE-OFFS BETWEEN RISK AND EXPECTED PERFORMANCE

Closely linked with the concept of risk efficiency is the possibility of making trade-offs between alternative risk efficient project plans.

Continue for the moment with the assumption that expected cost and associated risk as measured by threat intensity are adequate measures of performance. The level of risk associated with most risk efficient plans can be reduced given an increase in expected cost, and the level of risk can be decreased given an increase in expected cost. In relation to Figure 3.1, point A represents the minimum expected cost project plan, with a high level of risk despite its risk efficiency. Point C represents the minimum risk project plan, with a high level of expected cost despite its risk efficiency. If an organisation can afford to take the risk, A is the preferred solution. If the risk associated with A is too great, it must be reduced by moving towards C. In general, successive movements will prove less and less cost effective, larger increases in expected cost being required to achieve the same reduction in absolute or relative risk. In practice, an intermediate point like B usually needs to be sought, providing a cost effective balance between risk and expected cost, the exact point depending upon the organisation's ability to take risk.

The scale of the project relative to the organisation in question is a key issue in terms of the relevance of plans A, B or C. If the project is one of hundreds, none of which could threaten the organisation, plan A may be a sensible choice. If the organisation is a one-project organisation, failure of the project probably leading to failure of the organisation, a more prudent stance may be appropriate, closer to C than A.

If an organisation can afford to minimise expected cost and not worry about risk in terms of threat intensity, this has the very great merit of simplicity. This in turn implies it is very worthwhile defining a level of potential threat below which the organisation can ignore threat intensity, above which threat intensity needs to be considered and managed.

Risk analysis can serve three separate roles in relation to trade-offs between risk and expected performance, two almost (but not quite) directly analogous to those associated with risk efficiency, the third somewhat different (but complementary):

1. diagnose possibly desirable changes in plans;
2. demonstrate the implications of such changes in plans;
3. facilitate, demonstrate and encourage 'enlightened gambles'.

Diagnose Possibly Desirable Changes in Plans

The treasure hunt for difficulties associated with current plans and associated changes in plans or opportunities to improve risk efficiency may identify desirable moves around the risk efficient boundary. Consider a fabricated alternative to Example 3.1 to illustrate this issue.

Example 3.2

Assume that Example 3.1 involved different perceived uncertainty. Assume risk analysis suggested that the 3 metre barge would effectively avoid the risk of major delays (a lost season) costing £100 to £200 million, but increased expected cost by £15 million.

Assume that after due consideration the board decided to specify the 1.6 metre barge, taking an enlightened gamble.

Assume that in the event, the hookup activity was reached in October, but the weather proved unseasonably bad, and hookup was delayed until the following spring.

The out-turn of Example 3.2 might make some boards wish they had not been told about the gamble. However, we argue that whatever the decision and whatever the outcome, boards should be pleased such decisions are brought to their attention. Further, we argue that decisions involving trade-offs at lower levels also benefit from formal diagnosis in a similar manner. The rationale may become clearer as we consider the two further roles of risk analysis in relation to trade-offs between risk and expected performance.

Demonstrate the Implications of Changes in Plans

It might be obvious to all involved that a change in approach, like using a 3 metre barge instead of a 1.6 metre barge as in Example 3.2, would increase expected cost but reduce risk. Identification of the trade-off situation involved might not be an issue.

Demonstration of the implications as just discussed is still extremely valuable, and a separate and very important part of the process of ensuring appropriate trade-offs between risk and expected performance are made. Indeed, arguably the importance of demonstration increases when a trade-off is involved, relative to a case like the basic Example 3.1, because the judgement is a much finer one.

Facilitate, Demonstrate and Encourage Enlightened Gambles

The quantification of uncertainty in Example 3.2 might lead many people to the conclusion that a 3 metre barge was clearly worthwhile. Had risk analysis not been carried out, but figures of this order of magnitude been generally anticipated, caution might seem even more obviously desirable. However, while promoting enlightened caution, formal risk analysis can and should also encourage 'enlightened gambles', defined as risk efficient gambles involving significant risk which is considered bearable.

For oil majors involved in £1000 million projects in the 1970s and 1980s, potential losses much greater than £100–200 million were part of the territory. To enable them to live with these risks, joint ventures were common. Over ten such projects, taking the risk just described equates to an expected cost saving of £15 million times ten, or £150 million. Oil companies could not afford to pass up expected cost savings on this level in order to reduce risks which did not need to be reduced. Enlightened gambles were a key part of the culture. Organisations which do not take enlightened gambles reduce their average profitability, and may guarantee eventually going out of business. The authors have experience of programmes specifically designed to demonstrate the need for such enlightened gambles in organisations which spend too much on avoiding gambles, the equivalent of persistent over-insurance. Formal risk management can facilitate, demonstrate and encourage enlightened gambles as a basis for engineering-associated organisation culture changes.

In the context of Example 3.2, if the gamble had paid off, the virtue of the enlightened gamble would have been verified empirically. However, the occasional visible high level failure of such gambles is extremely important, because it demonstrates that good managers who take risk efficient gambles are sometimes unlucky. If no quantified risk analysis had been undertaken to demonstrate the expected cost saving associated with the Example 3.2 enlightened gamble, this message would have been lost, whatever the outcome. In the absence of a demonstrated expected cost benefit and an organisational culture which promotes enlightened gambles, astute managers do not take such gambles, and very astute managers don't even look for them.

Risk analysis can facilitate a search for opportunities to take enlightened gambles, demonstrate that such gambles are worth taking, and encourage a culture change where this mode of thinking and behaviour becomes the norm even when formal risk analysis is not involved. Enlightened caution means that sometimes money will be spent on proactive risk management which in the event proves unnecessary. Enlightened gambles mean that sometimes money will not be spent on proactive risk management which in the event proves unlucky. The general cultural issue is concerned with distinguishing between good luck and good management, bad luck and bad management, in order to persuade people to take the right risks and avoid the wrong ones, in risk efficiency and risk/expected performance trade-off terms.

Particularly at middle and lower levels of management, involving decisions risk analysis may not reach directly, changing the culture to provide enlightened gambles can have a significant impact on organisational performance. 'Unenlightened gambles' (gambles which are not risk efficient, or risk efficient but inappropriate) are an obvious concern of risk analysis, to be rooted out and avoided. 'Unenlightened caution' (risk reduction measures which are not risk efficient, or risk efficient but not necessary) is arguably an even more important target for risk analysis and associated culture change. Risk management as opportunity management is particularly concerned with enlightened gambles, and the need to distinguish between bad management and bad luck.

Quantification of Risk

With respect to all three aspects of risk/expected performance trade-offs, quantification is clearly even more useful than it is with respect to risk efficiency. The judgements required are finer, and more difficult, making quantification even more valuable.

3.4 RISKS AS A 'GOOD THING', AND RISK MANAGEMENT AS 'FUN'

The culture changes associated with facilitation, demonstration and encouragement of enlightened caution and enlightened gambles as just discussed are extremely important in their own right. They are also extremely important drivers of second-order effects, which flow from the increased confidence in the face of risk associated with looking for opportunities posed by uncertainty.

If risk is seen as a 'bad thing', a source of fear to be avoided, people develop blinkers, as a natural defence mechanism. If risk is seen as a 'good thing', an opportunity and source of satisfaction to be seized, people take off their blinkers. They start to look for opportunities. This can go well beyond enlightened caution and enlightened gambles, to include entirely new ways of seeing an organisation's purpose.

If culture change is on the agenda when introducing formal risk management, it is extremely important to address these second-order effects. Second-order effects associated with risk as a 'good thing' are concerned with a conscious, systematic search for all potentially useful new opportunities, whether or not formal risk management is relevant, but following examples provided by formal risk management which are suitable visible demonstrations of the possibilities.

When people take their blinkers off and start searching for opportunities they generally enjoy themselves. Lateral thinking becomes the order of the day, and people start to think of risk management as 'fun'. It is fun because it is tackled in advance, in a calm and creative way, while there is time to work around the obvious and important problems. Reactive crisis management is not eliminated, but it is reduced to a tolerable level. For years we have suggested to seminar audiences that *good* formal risk analysis processes are not inhibiting, and they are not about 'doom and gloom' they are about creative thinking, seizing opportunities, and having fun—the acid test of a good risk management process is 'do the people involved have a smile on their face?'

While it may not seem so at first sight, this is a *very* serious point. If a manager wants to attract and keep the best people, and get the most out of them, morale is a key issue. Good morale cannot be bought, it has to be developed. Good risk management processes can help to build good morale in a number of ways. Encouraging creative and lateral thinking is one way. Other ways include the order-of-magnitude increases in communication between all project staff which tend to flow from the process, breaking down 'them-and-us', enlarging cooperation across group and company boundaries, and so on. These benefits should not simply be allowed to happen. They should be encouraged by designing them into the process.

3.5 BIG PICTURES AND CONSTRUCTIVE INSUBORDINATION

A common experience for risk analysts is being asked to answer what they soon perceive to be 'the wrong question'. It is important for analysts, and for those who ask them questions, to understand that this does not necessarily imply an error of judgement on the questioner's part—it may be the natural consequences of a need for focus prior to the insights provided by analysis. It may be useful for analysts to assume that this is the case, and indulge in 'constructive insubordination', attempting to answer 'the right question', after some time spent attempting to formulate 'the right question'.

An experience which is common to those who ask questions of analysts is a provisional answer to what is perceived as 'the wrong question'. This too may be the natural consequence of a need for focus, or part of the process of negotiating 'the right question', which may be usefully understood as 'constructive insubordination', not an error of judgement on the analyst's part.

Encouraging a dialogue, an interactive process, which both facilitates and promotes constructive insubordination, can be an important part of the overall culture change process. It is vital to teams working across different management levels. The following example illustrates what may be involved.

Example 3.3

An offshore project on the east coast of Canada being planned in the early 1980s involved two possible technologies.

One technology involved a gravity platform, a larger-scale version of an approach used by the Norwegians for North Sea projects. A large concrete doughnut is cast in a deep-water harbour, sunk, and another section cast on top. This process is repeated until a large concrete 'pipe' about 100 metres across and 200 metres long is formed. This 'pipe' is then floated and towed to the site. After sinking it at the desired location, it is half filled with iron ore to make it heavy enough to withstand the impact of icebergs. The other half is used to store oil when production begins.

The other technology involved a submarine well-head connection via a flexible hose to 'ship-shapes', effectively tankers, which produce the oil, moving off station if icebergs become a threat.

Political pressures were an important part of the decision process. Gravity platforms would have to be constructed in an east coast Canadian harbour, an area of high unemployment. Ship-shapes could come from anywhere. A number of other factors also favoured the gravity platform approach.

Initially it was assumed that the gravity structure was the preferred approach, and the focus of a risk assessment Chapman was asked to undertake was on the cost of a gravity platform. However, the initial analysis concentrated on the technology choice question, in terms of uncertainty associated with recoverable oil in the reservoir, the price of oil when it is produced, and the capital costs and operating costs for both technologies. A key issue was the high capital cost and low operating cost structure of the gravity platform approach versus the low capital cost and high operating cost structure of the ship-shape approach. This analysis demonstrated that as things then stood, a gravity platform approach involved unacceptable risk. A low oil volume/low oil price/high platform capital cost scenario involved betting the company and losing. A ship-shape approach did not pose this threat, because of its low capital cost.

The company's management were not pleased by this result, addressing a question they had not asked, but they accepted its validity, and managed the risks it identified.

Subsequent to this analysis, further exploratory wells confirmed the anticipated volume of oil, and the risk associated with the gravity approach was managed in other ways, to make this technology (design) choice effective and efficient.

An important motive for RMPs can be the much more effective team working which should result from working relationships which encourage big picture perspectives, discourage tunnel vision, and encourage productive questioning of sacred cows. This does not imply an absence of discipline, or a tolerance of unconstructive insubordination. The goal is a process which is creative and supportive, built on mutual confidence and trust, give and take. It deliberately avoids the assumption that more senior management 'know better' than their juniors, and seeks to liberate the creativity of all levels of management responsibility. Even hard-nosed military commanders in the heat of real battle understand the value of constructive insubordination, the origin of the term, and the obvious illustration of a context in which unconstructive insubordination would not be tolerated.

3.6 DISTINGUISHING BETWEEN TARGETS, EXPECTATIONS AND COMMITMENTS

An important reason for quantifying uncertainty is that it forces management to appreciate the significance of differences between 'targets', 'expected values' and 'commitments', with respect to costs, durations and other performance measures. This in turn forces management to clarify the distinction between 'provisions' and 'contingency allowances'. This clarification was a central concern when BP International introduced RMPs in the mid 1970s, and it should be a central concern for most organisations.

In cost terms, expected values are our best estimate of what costs should be realised on average. Setting aside a contingency fund, to meet costs that may arise in excess of the expected cost, defines a 'level of commitment' (probability of being able to meet the commitment). The contingency allowance provides an uplift from the expected value which is not required on average if it is properly determined. Determining this level of commitment ought to involve an assessment of perceived threats and the extent to which these may be covered by a contingency fund, together with an assessment of the implications of both over- and under-achievement in relation to the commitment. High penalties associated with being over cost relative to the penalties associated with being under cost can justify a higher probability of meeting commitments than the 50–60% chance an expected value might provide. An 80% or 90% chance of meeting commitments is common.

Targets, set at a level below expected cost, with provisions accounting for the difference, need to reflect the opportunity aspect of risk. Targets need to be realistic to be credible, but they also need to be lean, to stretch people. If optimistic targets are not aimed for, expected costs will not be achieved on average, and contingency funds will be used more often than anticipated. If expected costs together with contingency funds are treated as targets, following a version of Parkinson's law, work will expand to fill the time available for its completion, leaving insufficient margin when anything goes wrong. Targets are usually associated with 1–20% chances of being achieved. Sometimes differences between targets, expectations and commitments are kept confidential, or left implicit. We argue that they need to be explicit, and a clear rationale for the difference needs to be understood by all, leading to an effective process of managing the evolution from targets to realised values.

Organisations which do not quantify risks have no real basis for distinguishing these three very different kinds of estimates. As a consequence, single values attempt to serve all three purposes, usually with obviously disastrous results, not to mention costly and unnecessary dysfunctional organisational behaviour. 'The cost estimate' or 'the completion date' become less and less plausible, there is a crisis of confidence when they are moved, and then the process starts all over again. Senior project managers involved when RMPs were introduced by BP in the mid 1970s stated that the avoidance of this cycle was the key benefit of RMPs for them. The ability to manage the gaps between targets, expected values and contingency levels, and setting those values appropriately in the first place, is a central concern of risk management. The recommended basis for managing the relationship between targets, expected values and commitments is developed briefly at various points in later chapters.

3.7 DOCUMENTATION

Documentation of RMP can include information in a wide variety of forms, describing activities, risks, responses, decisions taken, identified trigger points, and so on. Such documentation might be regarded as a byproduct of project risk management, rather than a central concern. However, this documentation serves a number of useful purposes which may be worth pursuing in their own right.

1. Documentation can provide focus for the initial thinking process. If people have to explain their thinking to others in writing, ambiguities get ironed out that might otherwise remain.
2. Documentation can provide an unambiguous vehicle for communication at any given point in time. If people explain what they mean in terms of designs and activities, risks and responses, in writing in detail, the scope for misunderstanding is significantly reduced. This can be particularly important in communications between different organisational units or in client–contractor situations. In such settings a number of questions concerning the risk management effort need to be addressed. For example: who is responsible for which activities?, who bears which risks?, and who will respond to realisation of shared risks? Clear documentation can also be an essential part of making all risks and all key assumptions clearly visible to all interested parties. A key role for any formal analysis process is the collective use of team input to a joint decision, drawing on a range of expertise as appropriate. Communication is a vital aspect of this process.

3. Documentation can provide a record to assist new project team members to 'get up to speed' quickly. Staff turnover on a project can be a significant source of risk, which documentation helps to mitigate. Risk management documentation is a very valuable training tool specific to the project to which new staff are attached.

4. Documentation can provide a record which explains the rationale for key decisions. In some industries (and for some careers), this may become a very important document if a decision goes badly wrong due to bad luck, as illustrated by Example 3.1.

5. Documentation can provide a record which captures corporate knowledge in a manner useful for subsequent similar project teams. If the kernel of the thinking behind one project is available, in a readily accessible form, for those doing the next, the value of this information can be very great. For contracting organisations this information may even amount to a competitive advantage over rival firms. Such information can also be the basis of ongoing training as well as an individual learning tool, and a basis for fundamental research.

6. When organisations first introduce a formal RMP, appropriate data is usually difficult to come by. However, the use of a formal RMP clarifies the nature of appropriate data, and generally leads to the systematic collection and appreciation of such data, as part of the documentation process. The importance of this development is difficult to understand for organisations which have not been through the process of introducing a formal RMP, but it is recognised as a major benefit by those who have introduced such processes. It is important to ask whether this issue is relevant up-front, because it means a current lack of data which could be collected in the future does not distort the development of an approach which best serves long-term needs.

If only the first of these six purposes is of interest, limited documentation may be appropriate. The others deserve careful prior attention, even if the design of the documentation has a fairly free format. Important factors which should influence the design of documentation include:

1. the nature of existing documentation on similar prior projects;
2. the likelihood of similar projects in the future;
3. for contractor organisations, the potential competitive value of documentation;
4. for client organisations, the potential value of documentation for assisting with choice of contractors and terms of contract, and for communicating effectively with contractors during negotiations and subsequently during project execution;

5. the need for 'visibility', involving non-technical readers who require a carefully crafted summary, for example non-executive directors or various stakeholder groups.

In addition, the format and level of documentation will be influenced by project specific features. As a general rule, a single rigid policy on risk management documentation for all projects is not usually appropriate.

At a very simple, practical level, if documentation requirements for risk management purposes (and all other project management purposes) are not thought about in advance, enormous inefficiencies will arise when the risk management process addresses the shortcomings of the basic project planning documentation. If these shortcomings are not addressed because RMPs are not introduced, ineffective management of the project is an inevitable result.

3.8   CONCLUSION

This chapter has considered the main generic motives for undertaking risk analysis rather than an exhaustive analysis of all likely motives. For example, it has not addressed the value of quantitative analysis as a means of assessing what is important, to direct further analysis and data acquisition efforts. Further, it has not considered issues such as when qualitative analysis alone may be appropriate, or when well-developed contingency plans may be irrelevant. These and other issues like them will be addressed later, and summarised in Chapter 17.

Successful RMPs are not driven by a simple wish to measure risk, although the measurement of risk may be a byproduct of the process. They are driven by a search for opportunities to change base plans and contingency plans in ways which display enlightened caution and enlightened gambles. That said, risk measurement can be a vital tool in this process, especially if the full potential value of cultural changes is to be realised, and dysfunctional organisational behaviour associated with confusing targets, expectations and commitments, provisions and contingency sources is to be avoided.

An important observation is that the approach taken to risk management ought to reflect the motives driving it. The very useful documentation associated with risk analysis should also be shaped directly by the motivations for the analysis.

Chapter 4

An Outline Generic Process

Some people regard discipline as a chore. For me, it is a kind of order that sets me free to fly.

Julie Andrews

4.1 INTRODUCTION

This chapter outlines a formal risk management process (RMP) for projects in generic terms. It provides some of the detail essential to understanding the nature of practical risk management processes for particular applications, but maintains a general view applicable to all types of projects. The discipline provided by the formality of the process outlined in this chapter is not a source of restriction, it is a source of liberation. This is a key message of this book as a whole. This chapter provides an overview which Part Two builds on.

As indicated in the Acknowledgements, the basis of this chapter was drafted by Chapman for the Association of Project Managers (APM) *Project Risk Analysis and Management (PRAM) Guide*. The process is a distillation of the experience of a large number of organisations which have used RMPs successfully for a number of years, as understood by a working party of more than twenty people drawn from an APM Specific Interest Group (SIG) of more than a hundred who reviewed working party drafts representing a very broad spectrum of organisations in the UK. We believe the structure of the process it provides will become a standard because of this wide authorship and support, we know it works well in practice, and we believe it works well as a framework for discussion.

Formal risk management processes (RMPs) should be applied at all stages in the project life cycle, by clients (project owners) and contractors (other parties associated with a project). It is most easily explained, and applied for the first time, when implemented in a comprehensive manner on behalf of a client at a sanction point towards the end of the Plan stage. This chapter assumes that this is the perspective and stage of interest initially, revisiting these assumptions later. Further, it assumes that the 'client' is one organisation with one project for the time being.

Most specific RMPs are described in terms of phases (stages) which are decomposed in a variety of ways, some related to tasks (activities), some related to deliverables (outputs/products). The nine-phase structure used here is more detailed than most specific processes (methods). A

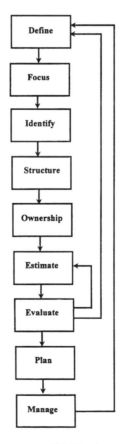

Figure 4.1 Risk management process (RMP) phase structure flow chart.

consequence of the additional detail provided by nine phases is clarification of the relative importance and role of aspects of the process which other specific RMP descriptions emphasise in varying degrees. This includes making explicit several very important aspects which none of the earlier descriptions addresses directly. The methodology described here is comprehensive, encompassing all important aspects of all methods familiar to all the APM SIG authors. Short cuts are possible, and some of the more important ways to simplify the process are developed later. More sophisticated processes are also possible within the framework provided. These are also addressed later.

The nine phases are discussed in a start-to-start precedence sequence. Once started all phases proceed in parallel, with intermittent bursts of activity defined by an iterative process interlinking the phases. Each phase is associated with broadly defined deliverables. Each deliverable is discussed in terms of its purpose and the tasks required to produce it. Significant changes in purpose underlie the boundaries between phases.

Figure 4.1 summarises the phase structure in flow chart format, indicating only the key or primary feedbacks. Figure 4.2 indicates in linked bar chart form the way effort expended in each phase might be focused over the life cycle of a typical RMP. Table 4.1 summarises the phase/deliverable structure.

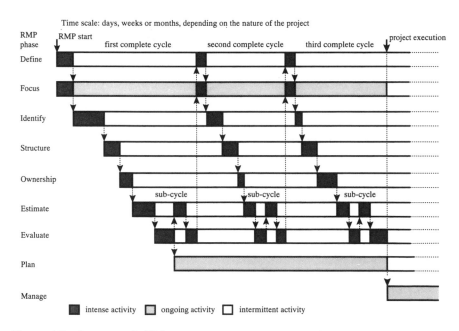

Figure 4.2 An example Risk management process over time.

Table 4.1 A generic risk management process structure (client perspective/plan stage initiation).

Phases	Purposes	Deliverables (may be targets not achieved initially)
Define	Consolidate relevant existing information about the project. Fill in any gaps uncovered in the consolidation process.	A clear, unambiguous, shared understanding of all relevant key aspects of the project, documented, verified and reported.
Focus	Scope and provide a strategic plan for RMP. Plan RMP at an operational level.	A clear, unambiguous, shared understanding of all relevant key aspects of RMP, documented, verified and reported.
Identify	Identify where risk might arise. Identify what we might do about this risk, in proactive and reactive responses terms. Identify what might go wrong with our responses.	All key risks and responses identified, both threats and opportunities, classified, characterised, documented, verified and reported.
Structure	Testing simplifying assumptions. Providing more complex structure when appropriate.	A clear understanding of the implications of any important simplifying assumptions about relationships between risks, responses and base plan activities.
Ownership	Client/contractor allocation of ownership and management of risks and responses. Allocations of client risks to named individuals. Approval of contractor allocations.	Clear ownership and management allocations, effectively and efficiently defined, legally enforceable in practice where appropriate.
Estimate	Identify areas of clear significant uncertainty. Identify areas of possible significant uncertainty.	A basis for understanding which risks and responses are important. Estimates of likelihood and impact in scenario or numeric terms, the latter including identification of assumptions or conditions, sometimes with a focus on 'show-stoppers'.

(*continued overleaf*)

Table 4.1 (*continued*)

Phases	Purposes	Deliverables (may be targets not achieved initially)
Evaluate	Synthesis and evaluation of the results of the estimate phase.	Diagnosis of all important difficulties and comparative analysis of the implications of responses to these difficulties, with specific deliverables such as a prioritised list of risks, or a comparison of base plan and contingency plans with possible difficulties and revised plans.
Plan	Project plan ready for implementation and associated risk management plan.	1. Base plans in activity terms at the detailed level required for implementation, with timing, precedence, ownership and associated resource usage/contractual terms where appropriate clearly specified, including milestones initiating payments, other events or processes defining expenditure, and an associated base plan expenditure profile. 2. Risk assessment in terms of threats and opportunities, prioritised, assessed in terms of impact given no response is feasible and potentially desirable, along with assessment of alternative potential reactive and proactive responses. 3. Recommended proactive and reactive contingency plans in activity terms, with timing, precedence, ownership and associated resource usage/contractual terms where appropriate clearly specified, including trigger points initiating reactive contingency responses and impact assessment.
Manage	Monitoring. Control. Developing plans for immediate implementation.	Diagnosis of a need to revisit earlier plans, and initiation of replanning as appropriate, including on a regular basis specific deliverables like the monitoring of achieved performance in relation to planned progress, and prioritised lists of risk/response issues. Exception (change) reporting after significant events, and associated replanning.

Other specific RMP descriptions can be mapped onto the nine-phase description provided here. For example, the four-phase SCERT description used earlier by Chapman (Chapman, 1979), and the slightly different four-phase structure plus an Initiation phase used by the UK Ministry of Defence (MoD(PE)-DPP(PM), 1991) align as indicated in Table 4.2. Part of the purpose of the APM PRAM Guide project was the provision of a standard process description and terminology to avoid the unnecessary confusion generated by slightly different descriptions of common concepts.

Table 4.2 Risk management process (RMP) phase structure comparisons.

APM (used here)	UK MoD (1991)	SCERT (Chapman, 1979)
Define	Initiation	Scope
Focus		
Identify	Identification	
Structure	Analysis	Structure
Ownership		
Estimate		Parameter
Evaluate		Manipulation and interpretation
Plan	Planning	
Manage	Management	

4.2   DEFINE THE PROJECT FOR RISK MANAGEMENT PURPOSES: THE DEFINE PHASE

All specific RMPs have a Define phase, but much of it is usually implicit. Its purpose is to define project effort to date in a form appropriate for RMP to:

1. consolidate in a suitable form relevant existing information about the project which RMP addresses—for example, project objectives should be clearly stated, project scope (including breadth and time frame) and strategy need to be defined, activity plans need to be defined at an appropriate simple overview level, associated timing and resource usage implications specified, underlying issues like design described, and stakeholders' interests defined;

2. undertake project management activities to fill in any gaps uncovered in the consolidation process—in principle such gaps should not exist,

but in practice this is a crucial aspect of RMP, a form of risk assessment of the project management process to date, and response to any concerns.

Achieving both purposes of the Define phase is essential, a basic foundation for what follows.

The deliverables provided by the Define phase may be a single document or parts of several documents. Whatever their form, a comprehensive and complete Define phase should clarify all relevant key aspects of the project which RMP addresses, in a manner accessible to all relevant client staff. The target deliverable is this clear, unambiguous, shared understanding of the project.

Tasks required to provide this deliverable include:

1. *consolidate*: gather and summarise in a suitable form relevant existing information;
2. *elaborate*: fill in the gaps, creating new information;
3. *document*: record in text with diagrams as appropriate;
4. *verify*: ensure all providers of information agree as far as possible, important differences in opinion are highlighted if they cannot be resolved, and all relevant providers are referred to;
5. *assess*: value the analysis to date in context, to ensure it is 'fit for purpose' given the current status of the risk management process;
6. *report*: release verified documents, presenting if appropriate.

The first two of these tasks are specific to the Define phase. The last four are common to all phases.

Because aspects of the project may not be clearly defined when RMP begins, and may take some time to be clearly defined, important and central aspects of the Define phase may be ongoing. However, the initial concern of RMP should be making as much progress as possible with the Define phase before moving on to later phases. The greater the level of unfinished business from the Define phase, the lower the efficiency and effectiveness of the following phases. Figure 4.2 indicates the way effort expended on the Define phase might be timed in a typical RMP, with the bulk of the effort at the outset, but further bursts of effort at the start of subsequent cycles through the process, three complete cycles being illustrated in Figure 4.2 by way of an example. Ongoing Define-phase activity throughout the process is another way Figure 4.2 might portray this phase.

4.3   FOCUS THE RISK MANAGEMENT PROCESS: THE FOCUS PHASE

All specific RMPs have a Focus phase, although it may be given other titles. Its purpose is to define RMP scope and strategy as distinct from the strategy of the project RMP addresses, and to plan RMP in operational terms as a project in its own right. For example, if RMP is being applied to test the viability of a new project, a purely qualitative approach may be appropriate, but if RMP is being used to assess budgets or bid prices, a fully quantitative (probabilistic) approach may be required, these differences having important specific method and resource requirement implications.

Achieving both purposes of this phase is essential, as basic to what follows as the Define phase. Some specific RMPs make more of this phase than others. For example, the MoD Risk Strategy Plan (MoD(PE)-DPP(PM), 1991) requires more formalisation of both aspects of this phase than most. The deliverables provided by the Focus phase may be a single document or parts of several documents. Whatever their form, a comprehensive and complete Focus phase should clarify all relevant key aspects of RMP as a project in its own right in a manner accessible to all relevant client staff. The target deliverable is this clear, unambiguous, shared understanding of RMP.

Tasks required to provide this deliverable include:

1. *scope the process*—this task addresses issues such as who is doing the analysis for whom?, why is the formal project risk management process being undertaken (what benefits must be achieved)?, and what is the scope of the relevant risk?
2. *plan the process*—this task addresses issues such as using what resources over what time-frame, using what models and methods (techniques), what software and so on, and culminates in a 'tactical' plan for the risk management process, to make the process operational.

The repetitive common tasks (*document, verify, assess* and *report*) are also involved, with some specific *assess* tasks.

The Focus phase may be largely concurrent with the Define phase, but updating RMP plans will necessarily be ongoing. Figure 4.2 indicates the way effort expended on the Focus phase might be timed in a typical RMP, assuming bursts of activity linked to the Define phase, and some additional ongoing activity.

The Define phase and the Focus phase may be thought of jointly as a higher level 'initiation phase' as indicated for the UK MoD process in Table 4.2. The Define and Focus phases are part of the even larger 'scope phase' in the SCERT process, as indicated in Table 4.2. They are separated here because they are concerned with very different deliverables, both of which are essential to what follows.

4.4 IDENTIFY THE RISKS AND RESPONSES: THE IDENTIFY PHASE

All specific RMPs have an explicit Identify phase, some, for example PERAG (1991), using this designation (omitting to worry about the identify/identification distinction). We cannot manage risk if we do not understand:

1. where it is coming from, in terms of what detrimental effects might be experienced, and the mechanisms underlying these effects;
2. what we might do about it, in proactive and reactive response terms;
3. what might go wrong with our responses—that is, secondary risks.

All RMP methods emphasise a need to identify sources of risk at the outset of the process. Some specific RMPs concentrate initially on impact or effects of these risk sources, leaving root causes or root sources until later. Some specific RMPs which defer the issue of root causes until later also defer the related issue of responses (to effects and root causes), and then only consider alternatives in relation to major risks. However, at least one response, even if it is 'do nothing and accept the risk' (which may not be feasible) must be identified and assumed in order to understand the impact of a risk later in the first pass (iteration) through the process. RMPs are iterative, with frequent loops back, so specific RMPs which in theory do things in different orders can prove much the same in practice.

Identifying risks and responses involves two specific tasks:

1. *search*: for sources of risk and responses, employing a range of techniques such as pondering, interviewing, brainstorming and checklists;
2. *classify*: to provide a suitable structure for defining risks and responses, aggregating/disaggregating variables as appropriate;

plus the four common tasks (*document*, *verify*, *assess* and *report*).

The deliverables provided by the identification phase should include a risk list or log or register, indicating at least one assumed response, a generic 'do nothing' being one option. The immediate deliverables may include a preliminary assessment of response options associated with these risks, but more detailed lists of response options may be deferred. The key deliverable is a clear common understanding of threats and opportunities facing the project. Opportunities (upside risks and more effective ways of proceeding in general) and associated responses need to be identified and managed with the same resolve as threats. Often RMPs are particularly successful because the process of generating and reviewing responses leads to the identification of important opportunities with implications well beyond the risks which led to their identification.

Figure 4.2 indicates the way Identify-phase effort might be focused in a typical RMP, assuming significant preliminary assessment of responses at the outset of this phase, and renewed response option identification effort later in areas where risks remain a concern.

4.5   DEVELOP THE ANALYSIS STRUCTURE: THE STRUCTURE PHASE

It is useful to decompose the UK MoD 'analysis phase' into four phases (Structure, Ownership, Estimate and Evaluate), because they each have different deliverables serving different purposes.

All RMPs have a Structure phase, usually part of another phase, like the MoD 'identification phase'. Some aspects are necessarily integrated with earlier phases, like the structure implied by the lists of activity risks and responses. Other aspects are necessarily left until now, or later. In some specific RMPs structure is implicit, assuming a simple standard structure by default. In general, we want the structure used for RMP to be as simple as possible, but not misleadingly so. The purpose of the Structure phase is to test simplifying assumptions, and provide a more complex structure when necessary. Failure to structure can also lead to lost opportunities. For example, some responses (general responses) to particular risks can in practice deal with sets of risks, possibly all risks up to that point in a project. It is important to recognise the opportunities provided by such general responses.

Structuring involves three specific tasks:

1. *refine classifications*—this involves the review and development (where appropriate) of existing classifications, in the sense that a 'new' response may be defined because the understanding associated with an 'old' one may be refined, and in the sense that a new classification structure may be introduced, distinguishing between specific and general responses, for example;
2. *explore interactions*—this involves reviewing and exploring possible interdependencies or links between project activities, risks and responses, and seeking to understand the reasons for these interdependencies;
3. *develop orderings*—this involves possible revisions to the precedence relationships for project activities assumed in the Define phase. An ordering

for risks is also needed for several purposes, including priorities for project and process planning, and for expository (presentation) purposes. In addition, this step involves developing a priority ordering of responses which takes impacts into account, including secondary risks.

In terms of documentation, the Structure phase involves completing the generation of a set of pictures or graphs, and defining associated mathematical models where appropriate, which capture all the key relationships in terms which are as simple as possible.

The key deliverable of the Structure phase is a clear understanding, on the part of the analysts and all users of the analysis, of the implications of any important simplifying assumptions about the relationships between risks, responses, base plan activities and all the other Ws.

4.6 CLARIFY OWNERSHIP ISSUES: THE OWNERSHIP PHASE

All RMPs have an Ownership phase, with three purposes:

1. to distinguish the risks and associated responses that the client is prepared to own and manage from those the client wants other organisations (such as contractors) to own or manage;
2. to allocate responsibility for managing risks and responses owned by the client to named individuals;
3. to approve, if appropriate, ownership/management allocations controlled by contractor(s) and third parties.

The first of these three purposes should be achieved before moving on to the following phase of RMP. Some organisations will consider this first purpose as a part of project strategy, which the Define phase will identify. Deferring achievement of the other purposes until later is usually appropriate, as indicated by Figure 4.2. This suggests modest effort initially, increasing in subsequent cycles as the first purpose is replaced by the second and third.

The deliverables provided by the Ownership phase are clear ownership and allocations of management responsibility, efficiently and effectively defined, and legally enforceable as far as practicable. The tasks required to provide this deliverable may be very simple or extremely complex, depending upon contract strategy. For expository purposes we assume no fixed corporate contracting policy. In these circumstances the Ownership phase involves two specific tasks:

1. *scope the policy*—this task addresses issues such as what are the objectives of the ownership strategy (the *why*)?, which parties are being considered

(the *who*)?, and what kinds of risk require allocation (the *what*)? This task culminates in a policy for risk allocation issues;
2. *plan the contracts*—this task considers the details of the approach (the *whichway*), the instruments (the *wherewithal*), and the timing (the *when*). This task transforms risk ownership policy into operational contracts.

4.7   ESTIMATE IN TERMS OF SCENARIOS AND NUMBERS: THE ESTIMATE PHASE

All RMPs have an Estimate phase, concerned with cost, time and other appropriate performance measures, although it may be given an alternative designation like the 'parameter phase' of the SCERT process as indicated in Table 4.2, or embedded in a broader phase, like the MoD 'analysis phase' of Table 4.2. It should have two purposes, which are related but important to distinguish:

1. to identify areas of the project 'reference plan' which *may* involve significant uncertainty and *may* need more attention in terms of data acquisition and analysis;

2. to identify areas of the project reference plan which *clearly* involve significant uncertainty and *clearly* require careful decisions and judgements by the client team.

A single pass to achieve the second purpose is not usually a cost-effective approach to analysis. We want to minimise the time spent on relatively minor risks and risks with simple response options, to use the time on major problems involving complex response options. To do this a first pass with a focus on the first purpose can be used, looping back until the second purpose can be achieved with confidence. Initial loops back can involve just the estimate and evaluate phases, illustrated in Figure 4.1 by the Evaluate–Estimate loop back, and in Figure 4.2 by one such loop (sub-cycle) within each of the two complete loops back to the Define phase from the Evaluate phase. Later, more complete loops will be effective, providing more attention to detail and some revisions in relation to all the previous phase outputs in those areas where unresolved risk issues suggest it is worth applying more effort. Attempting to achieve all the required outputs via a single pass process is not effective, because it will involve attention to detail which proves unnecessary in some areas, as well as skimped effort in areas where more effort would be very productive. Part of the process of managing RMP as a project in its own right is concerned with responding to those areas where risk (in threat or opportunity terms) is identified and better solutions are required. RMP has a clearly defined formal structure, but it cannot be applied in a mechanical manner. Most experienced risk analysts understand this, but many formal statements of RMP methodology do not make this very important point clearly enough.

The deliverables provided by the Estimate phase are estimates of likelihood and impact in terms of cost, duration, or other project criteria for risks identified earlier. Some specific RMP methods suggest numeric probability distributions from the outset. Some suggest likelihood and criteria ranges associated with labels like High (H), Medium (M) and Low (L) initially, and numeric measures later if appropriate. Most methods recognise that assessment of some risks may be best handled by identifying them as conditions, associated with assumptions, deliberately avoiding estimation in the usual sense. Most methods recognise that estimation in the usual numeric (or H/M/L label) terms may be a waste of time, and at best eliminated: for example, if on a first pass the concern is identifying and then managing any 'show-stoppers', 'estimation' reduces to looking for show-stoppers. The key deliverable is a basis for understanding which risks and responses are important.

The key deliverable of the Estimate phase is the provision of a basis for understanding which risks and responses are important. Three specific tasks are required to provide this deliverable:

1. *select an appropriate risk*—as the basis of a process of successive estimation of a set of risks, select an appropriate place to start and each successive risk in terms of initial estimates and refinement of those estimates;
2. *scope the uncertainty*—provide a simple numeric subjective probability estimate, based on the current perceptions of the individual or group with the most appropriate knowledge, to 'size' the risk;
3. *refine earlier estimates*—if the impact of the risk being estimated given chosen responses warrants, or the sensitivity of associated response decisions warrants, refine the initial scoping estimate. This may be undertaken in conjunction with refining the response-related decision analysis.

4.8   EVALUATE THE NUMBERS AND SCENARIOS: THE EVALUATE PHASE

All RMPs have an Evaluate phase, although it may be coupled with the Estimate phase and embedded in a broader analysis phase, like the MoD 'analysis phase', or it may be coupled with planning and management, as in the SCERT process description. Its purpose is synthesis and evaluation of the results of the Estimate phase, with a view to client assessment of decisions and judgements.

The deliverables will depend upon the depth of the preceding phases achieved to this point, looping back to earlier phases before proceeding further being a key and frequent decision at this stage. For example, an important early deliverable will be a prioritised list of risks, while a later deliverable might be a diagnosed potential problem associated with a specific aspect of the base plan or contingency plans, and suggested revisions to these plans to resolve the problem. The key deliverable is diagnosis of any and all important difficulties, and comparative analysis of the implications of responses to these difficulties.

Specific loops back to all earlier phases are not indicated on Figure 4.1 to keep the figure simple, but they could be shown to all phases.

Generic tasks other than the three common tasks cannot be usefully defined at the level of generality used here, but specific tasks are discussed and illustrated later in Chapter 11.

The Evaluate phase should be used to drive the distinction between the two purposes of the Estimate phase indicated earlier. That is, a first pass can be used to portray overall uncertainty and the relative size of all contributing factors, and further passes can be used to explore and confirm the importance of the key risks, obtaining additional data and undertaking further analysis of risks where appropriate, before moving on to consideration of project decisions and judgements. However, to make these judgements as part of the Evaluate phase, careful consideration has to be given to such judgements in the Estimate phase, to capture both uncertainty 'in nature' (inherent in the project) and uncertainty related to our understanding of this inherent uncertainty.

Most experienced risk analysts argue in favour of reaching the Evaluate phase for the first time early in RMP, much of RMP time then being spent in iterative loops concerned with the development of project plans. Figure 4.2 assumes this is the case, the illustrative three complete cycles being used to revise and reassess developing plans as well as refining analysis of risks and responses where this seems worthwhile. In practice, early achievement of the first pass may not be achievable, but the benefits of RMP will be reduced as a direct consequence. Separate identification of the loop back from the Evaluate phase to the Define phase on Figure 4.1 emphasises the special importance of this feedback process (as for the Evaluate–Estimate feedback loop).

4.9 PLAN THE PROJECT AND THE MANAGEMENT OF ITS RISK: THE PLAN PHASE

All RMPs have a Plan phase. It may be called that, as indicated for the MoD process in Table 4.2, or coupled with ongoing risk management, as for the SCERT process description. The Plan phase uses all preceding RMP effort to produce a project base plan ready for implementation and associated risk management plans (actions) for the project management process. Ensuring these plans are complete and appropriate is the purpose of this phase. The plans are the deliverables. The specific tasks are reasonably obvious in relation to the specific deliverables, as for the Evaluate phase. Some of the key specific deliverables any RMP Plan phase should provide are:

1. base plans in activity terms, at the detailed level required for implementation, with timing, precedence, ownership and associated resource usage/contractual terms where appropriate clearly specified, including milestones initiating payments, other events or processes defining expenditure, and an associated base plan expenditure profile;
2. risk assessment in terms of threats and opportunities, prioritised, assessed in terms of impact given no response if feasible and potentially desirable, along with an assessment of alternative potential proactive and reactive responses;
3. recommended proactive and reactive contingency plans in activity terms, with timing, precedence, ownership and associated resource usage/contractual terms where appropriate clearly specified, including trigger points (decision rules) initiating reactive contingency responses, and impact assessment.

Proactive responses will be built into the base plans, and reactive responses will be built into the associated contingency plans, when they become part of the overall project plans. All phases of RMP should be closely coupled with project planning in general, but the need for this coupling is perhaps particularly obvious in this phase.

Figure 4.1 shows no loop back from the Plan phase to the Define phase (or other phases), this aspect of 'planning' being built into the Evaluate phase as far as possible.

Some specific methods suggest a formal separation between base plans (which are owned by the project planning function) and the risk management plans (which are owned by the risk management function). This can be required by organisational constraints, but it is not desirable. It highlights the practical need to separate project management and risk management in some organisations, but the general desirability of seeing risk management as an integral part of project management.

4.10 MANAGE THE PROJECT AND ITS RISK: THE MANAGE PHASE

All RMPs have a Manage phase, ongoing once the project is implemented, concerned with monitoring actual progress with the project and the associated risk management plans, responding to any departures from these plans, and developing more detailed plans for the immediate future. One key deliverable is diagnosis of a need to revisit earlier plans, the basis of control, and initiation of replanning as necessary. Another is rolling development of plans ready for implementation. The specific tasks relate to the specific deliverables as in the Evaluate and Plan phases. Some of the key deliverables any RMP Manage phase should provide on a regular cycle (monthly, for example) include measures of achieved performance in relation to planned progress, a short prioritised list of risk/response issues requiring ongoing management attention, with recent changes in priority emphasised and trends assessed, plus related lower-level, more detailed reports drawing appropriate management attention to all issues requiring action. In addition to reports on a regular cycle, significant events should initiate appropriate replanning and exception/change reporting.

4.11   A RISK MANAGEMENT PROCESS EARLIER OR LATER IN THE PROJECT LIFE CYCLE

Guidelines for the use of RMP earlier or later in the project life cycle than the plan stage are discussed in Part Three, Chapter 14, but some comments are offered here.

Implementing RMP earlier in the project life cycle than the plan stage is in general more difficult, because the project is more fluid, and less well defined. A more fluid project means more degrees of freedom, more alternatives to consider, including alternatives which may be eliminated as the project matures for reasons unrelated to RMP. A less well-defined project means appropriate documentation is harder to come by, and alternative interpretations of what is involved may not be resolvable. At a very early stage in a project's life cycle, just after conception, RMP can be like attempting to nail jelly to the wall.

That said, implementing RMP earlier in the project life cycle is in general much more useful if it is done effectively. There is scope for much more fundamental improvements in the project plans, perhaps including a risk-driven redesign or initial design of the product of the project. The opportunity aspects of RMP can be particularly important for early RMP implementation. It can be particularly important to be very clear about project objectives, in the limit decomposing project objectives and formally mapping their relationships with project activities, because preemptive responses to risks need to facilitate lateral thinking which addresses entirely new ways of achieving objectives.

Some broad, general features of RMP earlier in the project life cycle include characteristics such as it is usually less quantitative, less formal, less tactical, more strategic, more creative, and more concerned with the identification and capture of opportunities.

Implementing RMP later in a project life cycle gives rise to somewhat different difficulties, without any compensating benefits. Contracts are in place, equipment has been purchased, commitments are in place, reputations are on the line, and managing change is comparatively difficult and unrewarding. RMP can and should encompass routine reappraisal of a project's viability. In this context early warnings are preferable to late recognition that targets are incompatible or unachievable. That said, better late than never.

As a general rule, the earlier the better, but organisations that want to introduce RMP and have some choice about when in the context of a range of possible projects to use as test cases would do well to start with a project which has been well managed to the project approval stage. Being thrown into the deep end may prove an effective way to learn to swim, but there are preferable alternatives.

4.12   ALTERNATIVE PERSPECTIVES

Guidance associated with alternative perspectives and associated approaches to contracting insofar as we can provide them are addressed in Part Three, Chapter 15. However, it is useful to understand the following points at this stage:

1. if risk ownership is not clearly defined, a client's risks can be a contractor's opportunities;
2. clients and contractors necessarily have different objectives, but a contract which leads to confrontation is perhaps the biggest single risk most projects encounter, a contract which seeks congruence in objectives being absolutely critical;
3. clients and contractors both need to undertake separate RMPs, but they need to establish a constructive dialogue involving input to each other's RMPs, and 'fixed' price contracts mitigating against this;
4. the trend towards 'partnering' and other forms of contracting which facilitate cooperative working is a trend to follow, but not blindly, when developing a comprehensive procurement strategy;
5. a carefully and thoughtfully executed RMP should address all the really difficult and sometimes obscure questions, like how should contracts be structured and defined, as well as the comparatively obvious ones like how much will the project cost, if for no other reason than the fact that the answers to the simple questions usually depend upon the assumptions about the difficult ones.

4.13   SELECTING SHORT CUTS

The comprehensive RMP outlined here and developed in detail in Part Two should be understood as a cohesive, internally consistent, integrated process in full before attempting the short cuts and modifications which are essential in most practical applications. Practical projects require short cuts, but explaining how short cuts should be selected is not a simple matter. This issue is addressed in Part Three, Chapter 16.

4.14   CONCLUSION

This chapter is comprehensive in the sense that it is designed to include all specific methods in current use the authors and SIG reviewers of the APM Guide were familiar with, discussed in terms of a comprehensive RMP, to give the reader an overview. Chapters which follow will give this overview more operational content, and clarify its nature with examples.

Several key issues should be clear from this chapter:

1. RMPs are highly structured, but they do not imply a rigid 'paint by numbers' approach. Creativity, lateral thinking and imagination are stimulated by the process, not discouraged.
2. RMPs are in many important respects largely a formalisation of the common sense project managers have applied for centuries. RMP described here is not a new way of thinking, or the engine of an intellectual revolution, which requires a significant change in mindset to be appreciated.
3. The formalisation involved in RMPs is central to capturing the benefit of RMPs, as part of the communication processes involved. The level and kind of communication RMP can generate can lead to significant culture changes within organisations. These changes can be quite fundamental, and they can be very complex.
4. Because RMPs can be concerned with very complex issues, it is very important to see 'keep it simple' as a guiding principle, adding complication only when benefit from doing so is perceived.
5. The iterative nature of RMP is central to 'keeping it simple', using early passes of the process to identify the areas that need more detailed assessment in later passes.

Part Two

Elaborating the Generic Process

Chapter 5

Define the Project for Risk Management Purposes: The Define Phase

If you are sure you understand everything that is going on, you are hopelessly confused.

Walter F. Mondale

5.1 INTRODUCTION

Part Two (Chapters 5–13) elaborates the phases of the risk management process (RMP) outlined in Chapter 4. For clarity, each of the nine phases is discussed in a separate chapter, although the depth of the treatment and the length of each chapter is not uniform.

In Part Two it is convenient to repeat three key assumptions used in Chapter 4:

1. the RMP is concerned with 'the client perspective', and 'the client' is one organisation with one project;
2. the RMP is initiated in the Plan stage of the project life cycle (PLC);
3. a comprehensive RMP is required.

Given these assumptions, the phases in the RMP become much easier to explain, and the explanation provides a convenient direct guide for some first-time users. In Part Three (Chapters 14–16) we consider the implications of relaxing each of these assumptions in turn.

As indicated in Chapter 4, the Define phase, concerned with clarifying the project definition for risk management purposes, is the first phase of the project risk management process. In principle, the Define phase should not be necessary, but in our experience it is always vital. It provides a basic foundation for everything that follows. This chapter explores in more detail what is involved.

The purpose of the Define phase is to consolidate and elaborate the nature of the project effort to date in order to define the project in a form suitable for the rest of the project risk management process. Two somewhat different but closely linked specific tasks are involved:

1. *consolidate* relevant existing information about the project and its management processes in a suitable form;
2. *elaborate* project management activities to fill in any gaps uncovered in the consolidation process, by stimulating the project team to develop their plans and processes.

Four common tasks are also involved:

1. *document*: record data and analyses, in text and tables with diagrams as appropriate;
2. *verify*: ensure that all relevant providers of information are referred to, that all providers of information agree as far as possible, and that important differences in opinion are highlighted if they cannot be resolved;
3. *assess*: value the analysis to date in context, to ensure that it is 'fit for purpose' given the current status of the risk management process;
4. *report*: release verified documents and formally presenting findings if appropriate.

Typically these common tasks need to be carried out sequentially in each phase, and for each distinct step that may be identified in each phase. A final phase specific *assess* task with a positive result ends the current iterations within each phase.

The target deliverable is a clear, unambiguous, shared understanding of the project and its management processes suitable for the risk management process which follows.

In expanding on the outline of the Define phase provided in Chapter 4, this chapter adopts a structure based on the six Ws of Chapter 1, beginning with the *who*, the project parties. It is convenient to portray by addressing each of the six Ws as six steps within the Define phase, as shown in Figure 5.1.

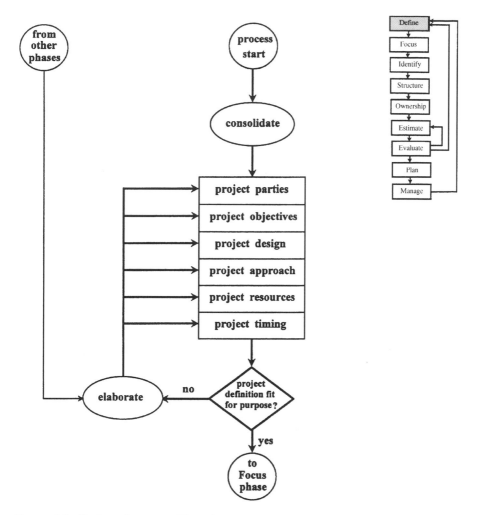

Figure 5.1 Define phase specific tasks.

Figure 5.1 portrays starting the Define phase in a *consolidate* mode. Each of the six Ws is addressed in turn. The overall results are assessed. Loops back to individual Ws are initiated by a specific *assess* task as appropriate, to fill the gaps in an *elaborate* mode, until the specific *assess* task gives a positive result, allowing the process to move on to the next phase. Recurring common tasks (*document, verify, assess,* and *report*) are not shown to keep the diagram simple enough to clarify key issues.

In practice it may be more effective to aim for separate *consolidate/elaborate* loops for each of the six steps, as well as the overarching loop structure of

Figure 5.1. This figure is an idealisation which helps to capture and illustrate the spirit of the process in tractable, simple terms. Our intent is to make Figure 5.1 complex enough to say something interesting and useful, but simple enough to say it clearly and concisely. Figure 5.1 is not a restrictive definition of the ideal process, it is a caricature.

When attempting to implement this process, the distinction between the steps may seem artificial, with fuzzy overlaps being a routine fact of life. However, the purpose of a detailed specification of the Define phase with separate steps is to provide focus and keep the implementation in practice as simple as possible. Trying to keep too many balls in the air at one time makes it much more likely one will be dropped. Even at this level of detail the method described here is not a 'cookbook' recipe, to be followed blindly. It is more a description of culinary techniques, to be used to create specific recipes.

Figure 4.2 portrays the way the effort associated with the Define phase might be timed in a typical risk management process, as discussed in Chapter 4.

5.2 PROJECT PARTIES, THE *WHO*

The identity, nature and relationships between the key players in a project, the *who*, is clearly a general project management issue. However, it is inseparable from risk management. For example, in marketing terms distinguishing between purchaser and ultimate user of a product can be very important. A memorable illustration concerns the launch (some time ago) of a new carbon paper for copy typing which did not make black smudges on secretaries' fingers and clothes. Initial marketing effort was targeted at corporate supply departments. It failed. A revised approach aimed at secretaries was an overwhelming success.

It may suffice to draw up a simple list of the parties, supplemented by a paragraph or two about their nature, and a paragraph or two about each key relationship. This information may be readily available. However, usually fundamental information is not available in a concise documented form because it is presumed to be too basic to bother to record.

Two sets of parties are worth distinguishing: agents of the client, and 'other stakeholders'. The latter set includes parent organisations, partners, regulatory bodies, competitors and customers. The client may have little choice about their involvement in the project and limited ability to control their objectives and actions, yet their ability to influence the project and its performance may be substantial. Agents of the client are, in theory, more controllable by the client, but this set of parties may also include subcontractors not directly under the control of the client. Their potential for liquidation is an obvious concern. Their ownership may be an issue, as illustrated by the following example.

Example 5.1

Government managers of a weapon system contract believed that no risk was involved because they had a very tight specification with onerous performance penalties. When the prime contractor reported a major shortfall on performance, it was assumed that the contractual provisions could be used. It was discovered too late that the prime contractor could pass the liability to a subcontractor, and the subcontractor was owned by the government.

The value of documenting the identity, nature and affiliations of all parties to a project is further illustrated with the next example.

Example 5.2

A government established organisation was partly owned by its major customers. The project '*who*' was a particularly useful starting point because the risk arising from the built-in conflict of interest inherent in the ownership/customer structure was identified formally for the organisation's board of directors by a third party. Steps were taken to resolve the position, and the subsequent risk management process clearly allocated significant particular risks to specific customers/shareholders.

It is important to understand that 'the home team' is worthy of careful inspection as well as 'the opposition'. For example, two nations which are partners in a new weapon system development project may seem to want the same thing, but one may be desperate for completion by the agreed date, and the other may prefer significant delay. Those party to the negotiation of the agreements between the two countries may understand this very clearly, but those implementing the contract may not, with obvious implications. A few pages of background to the agreement making such issues clear to everyone involved can be very valuable. Complex relationships may benefit from formal exploration using the identification methodologies discussed in Chapter 7.

   An essential deliverable of the Define phase is a comprehensive list of all the players who may prove central to the project. The purpose is to provide sufficient detail for following steps, and sufficient summary information to trigger later recognition of risks which can be generated by all parties to the project.

5.3 PROJECT OBJECTIVES, THE *WHY*

A key aspect of project risk analysis is appraising the implications of project objectives and related performance criteria, the project *why*, whether these are well defined or not. Any changes in objectives and performance criteria at any stage of the PLC need to be carefully evaluated for risk implications.

A clear idea of prevailing project objectives is also important in planning for risk analysis because the structure and form of project objectives ought to drive the structure and form of the risk analysis. This assessment needs to consider the nature of the objectives, their relative importance, how they might be measured, and the extent to which trade-offs can be made between them. For example, project managers must generally consider the relative priorities to be placed on cost, time and quality, recognising that trade-offs are possible between these basic performance criteria. If this is not done, different parts of the project team will make internally inconsistent decisions, and the project organisation as a whole will show confusion and lack of focus.

It is important to be clear about the full range of relevant performance criteria which may relate to a corporate perspective as much as a particular project's perspective. Thus corporate concerns about strengthened market position, a more favourable position with regulating authorities, or a 'greener' public image, may be important. In the context of an oil major, for example, strengthened market position is a subset of the issues ultimately driving profit, a more favourable position with regulatory authorities is a subset of the considerations driving market position, and a 'greener' public image is a subset of the considerations driving position with regulatory authorities. Each successive member of this quartet (profit–market position–regulatory position–perceived 'greenness') is more difficult to describe in formal terms. Other performance criteria may not have a simple hierarchical structure like this, and relatively difficult criteria to describe and manage like perceived 'greenness' may be extremely important. More than one major engineering project has failed as a direct result of a failure to manage these issues, which can be a much more important driver of profit (through revenue, project capital cost and operating costs) than the direct technical choices which tend to receive the attention of technically driven project teams.

It may be appropriate to consider the relative importance of criteria in the context of the project as a whole, although different parts of a project may involve different priorities. In both cases it may be useful to consider these priorities and consequent risks in an analytical structure which records different objectives and related activities explicitly. For example, in projects with a high science content, clarification, detailing and hierarchical structuring of project objectives to correspond with activity structures can be extremely useful. The basis of the rationale is that planned activities are only one way of achieving objectives, what may currently seem the best way of executing the project, but serious threats to completion of those activities may be best responded to by doing something quite different, or simply abandoning the associated objective. If the relationship between activities and objectives is made explicit at the outset, the subsequent risk management process becomes much more efficient and effective.

In a risk management context, if quantification of risk is involved, the need to be clear about priorities is intensified, because the risk management process must exploit these priorities and the structure of the risks involved. Quantification can serve to force organisations to clarify priorities. An important motive for quantification can be forcing this clarification.

Often it is feasible and sufficient to select one primary criterion, and convert other criteria into primary criterion equivalents. Other criteria may also be treated as constraints, and the effect of varying these constraints on performance in terms of the primary criterion are investigated. Consider an example.

Example 5.3

The structure of the initial risk analysis of a civil engineering construction project assumed that the primary criterion was cost. Delay was treated as a secondary criterion, converted into cost equivalents by assessing (in probability distribution terms) a cost per unit time for delay during construction. Quality (performance in relation to the design specification) was treated as a constraint. When the analysis was complete in terms of a representation which users were satisfied broadly reflected the reality of the situation, trade-offs began. In particular, the project as planned at that stage was deemed too expensive, re-engineering being applied to reduce the cost. It was not just a question of reducing quality or increasing time. The project objectives were revisited, and a significant change in approach adopted.

Initial risk analysis often adopts time (delay) as the primary criterion in the first instance. Cost is defined later as a function of time and the variability of other costs which are not time dependent. This is particularly true of North Sea projects, and is implicit in associated risk management methods (see, for example, Chapman, 1979).

Other ways of relating cost and time, or other possibilities for treating quality, may be preferable in other cases. For example, safety critical software for a weapon platform or a nuclear power station may require a very different approach. Performance may be the primary criterion, followed by cost, with time dependent upon performance and cost risk choices.

These issues are not relevant just because project risk management is a concern. They are central to project management in general.

A further consideration is how objectives should be measured. If time risk is the key concern, choosing a suitable metric is relatively straightforward, but some important issues need considering. For example, time to milestone payments may be the key concern for a contractor; time until a system achieves a satisfactory level of performance may be the key concern for a client. Earlier sensitising to the *who* is important if this kind of distinction is going to get recognised. Delay may have very different cost implications for different parties, so which party is considered is crucial. Defining payments in terms of milestones to ensure contractor performance may be the client's ultimate concern, to ensure a compatible sense of urgency applies to all parties.

For cost risk these issues become more complex. For example, is life cycle cost the issue, or just capital cost? Both can involve a common starting point, but the overall approaches are very different.

For performance (or quality) risk these issues become still more complex. For example, the trade-off between complete and partial degradation of a system may raise very complex issues which affect basic system design. If risk analysis is insensitive to key issues it may prove a costly waste of time, so these issues need up-front treatment.

In some cases it may be useful to define a metric for criteria measurement which links time, cost and performance in a more direct manner. For example, computer software projects have a long-standing love–hate relationship with 'the mythical man-month' (Brooks, 1975). 'Standard-months' can be used as a basis for estimating work content, cost and time, with associated performance risk analysis and efficiency risk analysis working on a standard-month basis.

5.4   PROJECT DESIGN, THE *WHAT*

Review of project design, the *what*, is an important part of the consolidation and elaboration process which is often ignored, at considerable cost.

A highly valued feature of successful project risk management reports is often a carefully crafted summary of project design issues, the project *what*. Usually the material is selected from design reports prepared by the project team as part of the normal project planning process. In such cases the added value of the risk analysis reports is simply pulling it together in an integrated form accessible to all project staff. Sometimes this integration process reveals missing detail, occasionally it reveals major flaws. In effect, it is an independent review, by a risk analyst who is by vocation someone prepared to ask lots of dumb questions, in order to write his or her simplified view of what the design is all about, with a strong drive for internal consistency and clear definitions of relationships. Sometimes the apparently dumb questions have no effective answers, revealing cracks which need serious attention.

Linking design issues or components to objectives or benefits of the project in a more formal and structured way would seem to be a key area for method development. Science-based projects, like research or research and development projects, lend themselves to formalisation of these links. Another good example is the development of 'benefit management' processes for information technology projects. The benefit structure used to justify the projects is formally mapped onto the system design and the tasks required to achieve the projects, and the risks associated with the tasks and design linked back to the benefits. Whether or not this is done, an early review of the project *what* is vital, and the positioning suggested in this section has worked well in practice in many successful studies.

5.5 PROJECT ACTIVITY PLANS, THE *WHICHWAY* (OR HOW)

The need for a simple high level activity structure for risk management purposes is now widely understood, although not universally practised. The advice 'target about 20 activities, with an upper limit of about 50' (Chapman, 1979) has proven appropriate for a wide range of project types and values.

Example 5.4

Offshore North Sea projects in the late 1970s could involve total expenditures of the order of £1000 million. Even in the context of projects of this size aiming for 20 activities was deemed appropriate, with 50 activities perceived as the upper limit for effective risk analysis. Example activities were: design the platform, fabricate the platform, design the modules (which sit on the platform), fabricate the modules, install the platform, install the modules, design the pipeline, procure the pipe, coat the pipe, lay the pipe, hookup (connect the pipe to the platform), and so on.

Each of these activities is clearly a project in its own right. Separating components of a project into activities at this level allows for the separation of sources of risk which are largely different and unrelated, the responsibility of different people, amenable to different types of responses or solutions, and other rules of thumb of this nature. There is no point attempting detailed risk management within these activities until risk associated with the relationships between these activities is managed. If the detailed questions are addressed at the outset, we tend to 'lose sight of the wood for the trees'.

It is vital not to assume that risks associated with different activities are independent or unconnected. Rules of thumb which are useful when defining an initial activity structure, and revising it to meet changes in perceived needs as the project or the analysis progresses, are worth some attention here.

For risk management purposes, the basic rule of thumb is keep things as simple as possible. Only break down an activity into more detailed activities if it seems it will be useful to do so. For example, offshore oil pipeline projects might treat purchase of the pipe, delivery of the pipe, coating the pipe, and laying the pipe as separate activities, but might not consider how pipe laying operations vary in different seasons of the year.

Another rule of thumb is 'don't separate activities which involve complex interactions'. For example, fabrication of the modules to be installed on an offshore platform (providing power, accommodation, and so on) might be treated as one activity, and their installation might be treated as another activity, without attempting to deal with the complex interrelations within these activities for overall risk management purposes, although for some planning purposes (implementation, for example) the exact nature of inter-connections is clearly critical.

The discipline required to 'keep it simple' is not always easy, and the issues associated with where to decide to draw the line dividing (defining) activities are complex. Associated expertise is a craft rather than a science to a significant extent, requiring practice involving mistakes.

5.6 PROJECT RESOURCES, THE *WHEREWITHAL*

A review of resource requirements implied by the activity plans must be part of the *consolidate* and *elaborate* tasks because an obvious source of risk is key resources not being available when needed. If a risk management process has not been in place from the outset of the project, the identification of resource requirements is usually part of a process to provide base cost estimates. This process can be somewhat separate from the design and activity planning processes, which may proceed in parallel to some extent.

In large engineering or construction projects, usually the group doing the base cost estimation is not the same as the group doing the activity planning, and the designers are a third group. Often they have very different backgrounds. Sometimes these functional and cultural differences are exacerbated by departmental or contractual structures. Risk analysts often feel like they have been parachuted into the middle of a 'three-ring circus', with quite separate uncoordinated acts in the three rings. They may be viewed by the three acts as a new clown, but they have to operate to some extent as a ringmaster, without offending the ringmaster.

The relationships between professions needs to be tackled directly, to avoid associated risks being realised, otherwise they may have to be addressed on a contingency response basis which may prove extremely costly. This point raises the issue of the order for the *whichway* and *wherewithal* steps. For convenience it is usually safe to assume the order used here, but the design process may suggest considering *wherewithal* first, then *whichway*.

5.7 PROJECT TIMING, THE *WHEN*

In the authors' experience, it is very important to construct a simple activity-on-node precedence diagram to portray clearly the assumed precedence relationships between the activities selected for the *whichway* portrayal of the project. It is also important to construct a separate but directly related Gantt chart to portray the implied timing. Modern linked bar-chart software makes it tempting to combine these two traditional graphs in a single graph, but clarity and generality is lost if this is done.

It might seem that good project management practice ought to make review of the *when* largely redundant if formal risk analysis is introduced at the end of the 'allocation' stage of the PLC. Given the more detailed networks and Gantt charts normally used for project planning, it might be reasonable to expect that obtaining information about activities and schedules in a form suitable for risk analysis would be relatively straightforward. However, we have yet to find this the case.

At a very detailed planning level, it may seem that precedence relationships are always strict and simple, and defined by the task nature of the activities. The water must be boiled before we make the tea, for example. At the strategic planning level, the level most appropriate for initial risk management, precedence relationships tend to be fuzzy and complex, and defined by design and resource issues as well as the task nature of activities.

The strategic level views of activity precedences and timing used for project risk management should capture very important alternative approaches to the project which detailed portrayals obscure, and alternatives need to be identified to clarify the options available. Consider two examples.

Example 5.5

Planning the fabrication of modules for offshore platforms (for accommodation, control functions, etc.) in a conventional critical path network manner, focusing on the project *whichway*, naturally assumes modules are completed before taking them out to install on the platform. In practice it is much more expensive to complete fabrication offshore, but it may be cheaper to do so than missing a weather window. Hence, the planning process ought to reflect the trade-off between the cost of onshore/offshore fabrication and the risk of missing a weather window.

Example 5.6

Two sequential activities associated with preparing to sink a deep-mining shaft project were assumed to be on a sub-critical path. When it became apparent that they might be critical, the possibility that they might take place in parallel was raised. It transpired they had been put in series because it was assumed that the same resources would be used. This was cost effective if this path was sub-critical, but not if it was critical.

Being aware of the trade-offs described in these two examples was essential for good project management, whether or not formal project risk management was an issue. These examples also illustrate an interdependency between the project *whichway*, *wherewithal* and *when* which needs explicit attention. The questions of *whichway*, *wherewithal* and *when* are not really separable in many situations. However, it is useful to distinguish them for consolidation purposes, because they are often treated separately in project planning.

5.8   THE ONGOING NATURE OF THE DEFINE PHASE

The Define phase deliverable is a clear, unambiguous, shared understanding of all relevant key aspects of the project, appropriately documented, verified, assessed as 'fit for purpose' and reported. The written form of this deliverable may be a single document, or parts of several documents. Whatever their form, a comprehensive and complete Define phase should clarify all relevant key parts of the project which the risk management process addresses, in a manner accessible to all relevant client staff. A single document achieving these ends is often held to be a key benefit of a formal risk management process, especially by senior managers.

Part of the documentation should be a 'reference plan' for the project which may be modified and augmented as a result of the subsequent risk analysis. Usually ensuring an appropriate reference plan is available is not just a question of capturing in simplified form an existing common perception of the six Ws. In practice, this step is a risk analysis of the project planning process which requires responses to errors of omission and commission in the project management process. Responses may involve project management as distinct from project risk management, involving people and organisations not necessarily part of the risk management process.

Even if project risk management is first implemented when the project is well developed, the Define phase as just outlined may reveal gaps in the reference plan which need to be filled. In principle, such gaps should not exist, but in practice some are inevitable. Because some aspects of the project may not be clearly defined when the Define phase begins, and they may take some time to be defined, important and central aspects of the Define phase may be ongoing. However, the initial concern of the risk management process should be making as much progress as possible with the Define phase before moving on to the other phases. In general, the greater the level of unfinished business from the Define phase, the lower the efficiency and effectiveness of the following phases.

Treating project management and project risk management as closely coupled processes is central to the approach outlined here. Some separation may be essential because different people and organisations may be involved, and other differences are important. However, the separability should be limited, to avoid imposing constraints which can prove very expensive. Risk management is an 'add-in' to project management, not an 'add-on'.

Chapter 6

Focus the Risk Management Process: The Focus Phase

All men are equal—all men, that is to say, who possess umbrellas.

E. M. Forster

6.1 INTRODUCTION

The opportunities for risk management in projects are considerable and pervasive. Any systematic efforts at project risk management must be carefully managed if cost-effective use of risk management resources is to be achieved. A well-designed RMP is not proof against risk any more than a well-designed umbrella is proof against rain, but it is a distinct advantage. This suggests considering the risk management aspect of a parent project as a project in its own right, with a specific planning phase prior to execution of risk analysis, and periodic, ongoing development of this plan for the risk management process.

Viewing the risk management process as a project in its own right suggests that systematic consideration of the six Ws as they apply to risk management effort would be appropriate. Thus the Focus phase in the risk management process ought to address the following questions:

1. *who* wants risk analysis to support a formal risk analysis process, and *who* is to undertake the analysis?
2. *why* is the analysis being undertaken?
3. *what* form should the analysis take?
4. *whichway* should the analysis be carried out?

5. what resources (*wherewithal*) are required?
6. *when* should the analysis be undertaken?

As with the Define phase in Chapter 5, it is useful to address these six questions in terms of a six-step structure.

For expository convenience, consider a situation where risk analysis is to be undertaken on a 'green field site', in the sense that an approach has not been prespecified. In these circumstances the Focus phase involves two specific tasks:

1. *scope the process*—this task addresses issues such as who is doing the analysis for whom?, why is the formal project risk management process being undertaken (what benefits must be achieved)?, and what is the scope of the relevant risk? It culminates in a 'strategic' plan for the risk management process. A strategic plan is useful for two reasons. First, it ensures that management is aware of its limitations (if any) in addressing other parts of the project life cycle (PLC), which may warrant further risk analysis. Second, it helps determine the appropriate structure and level of detail in the risk analysis;
2. *plan the process*—this task addresses issues such as using what resources over what time-frame, using what models and methods (techniques), what software and so on, and culminates in a 'tactical' plan for the risk management process, to make the process operational.

The repetitive common tasks (*document, verify, assess* and *report*) are also involved, with some specific *assess* tasks.

The deliverables provided by the Focus phase may be a single document or parts of several documents. Whatever their form, a comprehensive and complete Focus phase should clarify all relevant key aspects of the risk management process as a project in its own right in a manner accessible to all relevant client staff. The target deliverable is this clear, unambiguous shared understanding of the process.

Figure 6.1 outlines an elaboration of the structure of the Focus phase. It portrays starting the Focus phase in *scope the process* mode. Each of the first three Ws is addressed in turn. The process then loops back to the first three individual Ws as appropriate to fill in the gaps in the *scope the process* mode, until the specific *assess* task, *assess process scope*, gives a positive result, this being a strategic plan 'fit for purpose' at present. The process then moves on in *plan the process* mode, working within the strategic plan on each of the last three Ws, until the specific *assess* task, *assess process plan*, gives a positive result. Both specific *assess* tasks can fail to reach an acceptable position, stopping the project or the process.

As in Figure 5.1, the recurring common tasks, *document, verify, assess* and *report*, are not shown, to keep the diagram simple.

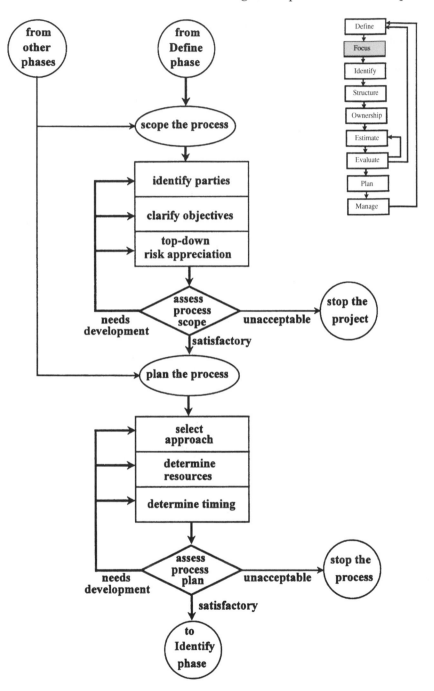

Figure 6.1 Focus phase specific tasks.

In practice it may be more effective to aim for separate assess/elaborate loops for each of the six steps, with parallel converging strategic and tactical planning processes once the basic shape of the strategic plan is in place.

Figure 6.1 is not a restrictive definition of the ideal process. As with Figure 5.1, it is an idealisation to capture and illustrate the spirit of the process.

6.2   IDENTIFY PROCESS PARTIES, THE *WHO*

The first step in the Focus phase deals with the process *who*: who is undertaking risk analysis for whom. The key players should be:

1. senior managers, to empower the process, to ensure the risk analysis effort reflects the needs and concerns of senior managers, and to ensure it contains the relevant judgements and expertise of senior managers;
2. all other relevant managers, to make it part of the total management process and ensure that it services the whole project management process;
3. all relevant technical experts, to ensure it captures all relevant expertise for communication to all relevant users of that expertise in an appropriate manner;
4. a risk analyst or risk analysis team, to provide facilitation/elicitation skills, modelling and method design skills, computation skills, teaching skills which get the relevant messages to all other members of the organisation, and allow the risk analysis function to develop and evolve in a way which suits the organisation.

In the context of each project, the relationship between the risk analysis team and other players needs early and clear definition. In a client–contractor situation when the risk analysis team is part of the client organisation this issue may seem straightforward, but very important issues still need to be addressed in an explicit manner. For example, does the team report to the project manager and act as a support function for the project manager, or does the team report to the board and act as an auditor of the project team on behalf of the board? In the authors' view the risk analysis team must be seen by the project team as a support function providing feedback of immediate practical value to the project team. If this is not the case, the cooperation necessary to do the job will not be forthcoming and the risk management process will flounder. However, it is equally important that the risk analysis team be seen by the board as unbiased, with a demonstrable record for 'telling it as it is', as providers of an 'honest broker' external review as part of the process. If this is not the case, the risk management process will sink without trace.

In relation to all key players the process must be seen as immediately useful and valuable, in the sense that it more than justifies the demands made upon them. Furthermore, if it threatens any of the players, there must be a balance of power in favour of meeting that threat rather than avoiding it. If the quality of the project management process or staff is a serious issue, this can be the biggest source of risk to the risk management process as a project, as well as to the project itself. If this is the case, it deserves careful management, for obvious reasons.

More generally, risk management processes can themselves be very high-risk projects, and some of the key risks require careful attention to the process *who* question in the Focus phase.

A common question at risk management seminars is 'can I as a client ask my prime contractor to do a risk analysis for me?' The answer is yes, but while such an analysis may be a useful starting point for the client, it is only that. The problem here is that to the extent that the client and contractor have different objectives and information, their perception of project risks will be different. In particular, what the client sees as risks the contractor may see as opportunities. The contractor may be unwilling to reveal such opportunities to the client if doing so is likely to lead to a reduction in those opportunities. This issue is considered in more detail in Chapter 15.

More generally it is extremely important to be very clear and explicit about who is undertaking risk analysis for whom, and how the reporting process will be managed.

To clarify the importance of the reporting process, consider a simple practical issue. If the project risk analyst reports to the project manager, using information obtained from a set of groups within the project team, it is very important to keep the whole team on-side. This means each group must be aware of the implications of their assessments before they go beyond the group, and they must have time to change their minds, perhaps several times, until they are confident about exposing their assessments to the rest of the project team. Some project teams may be fairly uninhibited about this, but others may be extremely sensitive, with consequential major impacts on risk management plans. A project team made up of contractors who have scope for competition as well as collaboration can be a source of this problem, and a risk of sufficient importance to warrant a project team design which avoids it. Designing the project team reporting processes as whole is itself a part of the project definition process which needs to be risk managed.

Major doubts about who is undertaking risk analysis for whom may invalidate all following steps, so this a good reason for putting this step first in the Focus phase.

While the process *who* question arises because of concerns associated with the risk analysis process, this step raises issues which are inherent or implicit in good project management as a whole. That is, this *who* step can be used as a catalyst for clarifying who is working for whom in the project management process as a whole, or the process *who* can be defined in this broad sense. If the risk analyst or the project manager, or some other member of the project team, does not take it upon themselves to clarify process party issues in this broad sense, they will be mismanaged or unmanaged.

Some organisations refer to risk analysts in the above sense as risk *managers*. There may be good reasons for doing so, but this can imply a confusion of roles. Risk is a pervasive aspect of a project which can be delegated in terms of analysis but not in terms of management. In the authors' view proper integration of project risk management and project management more generally requires that the project manager takes personal responsibility for all risk not explicitly delegated to managers of components of the project.

6.3   CLARIFY PROCESS OBJECTIVES, THE *WHY*

Explicit consideration of why risk analysis is being carried out, the process *why* question, helps to clarify further the scope of the risk management process. In particular, an awareness of the purpose and scope of the risk analysis can help determine the desirability or necessity for quantification. Consider two contrasting examples.

Example 6.1

An engineering construction project was approaching the point of a board level 'go/no-go' decision. It was the first project the organisation had subjected to a formal risk analysis process. If a 'go' decision was taken, the project could be executed within a few years, with no major anticipated changes in management. The project management team wanted board approval for a budget they could live with and control within the organisation in an effective manner, but they recognised that if they asked for funds they did not need, they would increase substantially the risk of a 'no-go' decision. This was a very unwelcome possibility. These concerns made a quantitative risk analysis essential, in order to distinguish clearly between targets, expectations, and commitments.

Example 6.2

A commercial aircraft manufacturer managed production as a 'programme' of projects, each aircraft as a project. Each aircraft was costed on a materials and labour basis, using 'standard hours' for all tasks. Production was planned using standard CPA (Critical Path Analysis) deterministic planning tools. The basics of most aircraft conformed to a standard production model, but each aircraft involved significant variations according to the instrumentation and finishing requirements of the airline or other customers ordering the aircraft. Two sources of uncertainty plagued the manager of each aircraft's production: materials might not arrive when they were required; and staff might not be available when they were required, because another aircraft manager 'stole' them by pleading higher priority, or because of illness and staff turnover.

If materials did not arrive on time they were 'chased', and work rescheduled to use materials and staff that were available.

Airlines wanted to know how long it would take to deliver an aircraft when ordering it. Keeping delivery promises was an important marketing strategic weapon. Forecasting delivery date to the day over the last 30 days was also a contractual matter, with a cost of about £10 000 per day early or late, because of the airline's need to put new aircraft into their service schedules.

Consistent failure to deliver on time with substantial variations in performance suggested the need for a formal risk management system.

Discussions with those involved in managing the system suggested that replacing the CPA-based planning system with one capturing the uncertainty involved would hinder rather than help the shop-floor managers. No changes to the existing system were recommended at this level.

To deal with the forecasting problem, a system was suggested that went back to the basic standard hours calculations used for costing, measuring the efficiency associated with converting standard hours into completed work as a function of aircraft percentage completion, and using this model plus forecast staff availability to forecast completion.

The efficiency associated with converting standard hours into work achieved could be shown to fall off in a predictable way as aircraft neared completion, because work was increasingly difficult to do out of order due to missing components, and less flexibility was available when rescheduling to cope with shortages of components or key labour.

This modelling also provided a 'what-if' capability for addressing higher level programme management questions, such as: would it be better to let one aircraft which is in trouble carry on as planned, rather than borrow staff from two others which are currently ahead of schedule, but could be induced to fail if we 'steal from Peter to pay Paul'?; or would it be a good idea to recruit 10% more staff than we think we need over the next six months?; or how much is it costing us to have materials arrive late, and what is the most cost-effective way to reduce these costs?

These examples illustrate the value of being clear about the purpose of any risk analysis before it is attempted. A corollary is that there is no best way to pursue all risk analyses—much of the need to vary the approach taken hinges on why it is being undertaken.

A basic axiom of those who build successful models for decision-taking purposes is 'there is no one best model for all purposes'. The same can be said for the processes built around such models. Effectiveness and efficiency demand we design or select our models and processes according to our purposes. If more than one purpose is being pursued, we may need more than one model and process, running in a separate but linked manner.

At a more complex but equally practical level, if the concept of risk efficiency is not clearly understood and rigorously searched for, it will not be found. The resulting increase in cost, with no compensating reduction in risk, will be a function of the riskiness of the project. In a low risk project it might be of the order of a few percent of total project cost. In a high risk project the resulting increase in cost could be considerably more and might well be a major element of project cost.

Such issues are of central and critical importance in most projects. The sums involved warrant considerable attention in the context of large, high risk projects, and generally those involved in such projects recognise this is the case. What is not so widely appreciated is the extent to which risk management objectives need to be considered and pursued formally in small projects, especially if novelty is involved.

6.4 TOP-DOWN RISK APPRECIATION AS A BASIS FOR PROCESS DESIGN, THE *WHAT*

A competent project risk analyst must undertake a limited top-down strategic view of corporate risks affecting his or her project, even if the organisation chooses to ignore such issues completely. Given the essential nature and pivotal role of such 'corporate' risks, this is the logical place to start consideration of risks. From a risk management perspective, it really is a waste of everybody's time to do otherwise. If this involves 'constructive insubordination' which is likely to be so unwelcome that it may cut short the project risk analyst's career in this organisation, he or she may wish to keep this part of the analysis to themselves!

An important reason for undertaking a top-down risk appreciation of the project context is to determine where the limits of the project manager's responsibilities for managing project-related risk lie.

Example 6.3

When Chapman started work on one organisation's risk management processes his remit did not include an assessment of strategic risks, but an early priority was to persuade the directors that such an analysis would be a good idea. Several preliminary analyses were undertaken to indicate what would be involved. The highly political nature of the project made the issues identified extremely sensitive. A full analysis was not undertaken by Chapman, but he was encouraged to provide the directors with a suitable framework and to clarify key corporate risks as he saw them. This process helped to shape corporate policy on major strategic issues, was used as the basis for a report to the board, and added substantial value to the overall risk management process.

Apart from its direct value as a strategic analysis for the directors, the strategic overview set the project risk management in context. For example, it was recognised in a formal corporate sense that a range of major design changes might take place for political reasons, or for reasons related to customer plans. However, those responsible for the design underlying the project were explicitly relieved of responsibility for worrying about such changes, responsibility being formally placed with the board.

The rest of Part Two assumes a simple division of 'external' and 'internal' risks between board level and project management for most illustrative purposes, but a more complex, hierarchical division of risks can be helpful, for reasons considered in Chapter 9.

Once it is clear, in broad terms, which risks are external and which are internal to the project, it is useful to take a top-down view of internal project uncertainty, quantifying this in terms of cost, revenue, and/or delay as appropriate. What is important here is an appreciation of the kind of overall picture a top-down analysis can provide by portraying the views of senior staff in a carefully structured but relatively simple framework which can be implemented in a matter of weeks (days or even hours if necessary given appropriate experience). A top-down approach begins with a broad categorisation of risks which can then be progressively decomposed into a hierarchy of component risks. This helps to identify areas of dependence between risks and may identify further risks which ought to be regarded as external to the project for project management purposes. Consider an extension of Example 6.3.

Example 6.4

When risk management was introduced, the board had approved fairly detailed 'high' and 'low' cost estimates for the project involving around a thousand identified cost components. Early top-down interpretation of these estimates in probabilistic terms was desirable, in a manner compatible with bottom-up risk analysis processes being put in place.

The 'low' cost estimate was an optimistic base estimate. All cost items the cost estimators were aware of had been costed on a 'no significant problems' basis, and added up to provide an overall 'low' cost estimate.

The 'high' cost estimate was a pessimistic base estimate in terms of 'problems the estimators could see' which were clearly risks owned by the project, such as variations in the volume of concrete required for a foundation. The estimators excluded risks clearly owned by the board, such as major design changes. They excluded the impact of delays, due to construction difficulties or planning processes. They excluded a range of minor design changes and other issues related to unclear ownership. They also excluded 'risks the estimators could not see', by definition.

The top-down project risk analysis started by providing the overall total 'high' and 'low' cost estimates with a probabilistic interpretation in terms of those risks they included. It then identified all the risks the project was responsible for, in broad terms, which were not included. The impact of these risks was then assessed, one at a time on a conditional basis, within a structure which facilitated consideration of dependence. About a dozen sources of risk were separately identified and combined in relation to overall cost, to provide the board with a senior management judgement of what the previously approved 'high' and 'low' figures meant. Even the 'high' figure had a significant chance of being exceeded, but the important messages were why this was the case, and what had to be addressed via the bottom-up analysis in order to reduce the cost.

6.5   ASSESS PROCESS SCOPE

Document, verify, assess and *report* common tasks associated with the first three steps of the Focus phase provide a 'strategic' framework which serves to guide detailed planning of the risk management process, completing the *scope the process* specific task. *Assess the scope* of the risk management process is the next *specific* task, providing a convenient place to pause and consider the project risk perceived to date.

Stopping the project may be a possibility if assessing the project, and the associated risk management process plan, raises serious questions. However, answering these questions then becomes central to the objectives of the risk management process, requiring further development of the process strategic and operational plans. At its simplest, the assessment may identify a single potential 'show-stopper', the *scope* and *plan the process* tasks may address how best to assess the extent to which this show-stopper can be revised, removed, resolved or dissolved. This *assess* task may reduce to deciding whether it is worth planning a risk management process, or whether it is better to bring the whole project to a stop without further work.

When a project is in doubt, a different kind of risk management process is required to one based on the assumption the project will proceed. What is particularly critical is an understanding, on the part of the whole project team, that the whole purpose of project planning changes if the viability of a project is seriously called into question. If a project that was assumed to be 'a goer' suddenly looks like 'a maybe', project planning and project risk management need to address the question 'is the project worth doing?', considering how to do the project only insofar as it is necessary to do so to address this question, to avoid excessive planning process delays. The details of how to do it are a complete waste of time should the project be stopped, and resources should be allocated to how to do the project details with this potential nugatory expenditure effect clearly in mind.

In principle, this issue should be addressed via appropriate risk management processes earlier in the project life cycle, as discussed in Chapter 14. In practice, it often requires attention in the face of a mindset which does not easily accommodate the idea of planning a project to obtain an unbiased view of costs and revenues with no immediate direct interest in implementing the project, especially if the project team are threatened by the possibility of the project stopping and this threatens their livelihood.

6.6   SELECT A PROCESS APPROACH, THE *WHICHWAY*

As shown in Figure 6.1, the *plan the process* specific task involves considering how the risk analysis effort is to be carried out, first addressing the process approach or *whichway* question, then expanding on the closely related process design or *what* question, finally considering the *when* question.

It is very important to understand that there is no one best method or process for all project risk management purposes. We would not expect to use the same approach for the construction of all buildings or the development of all weapon systems or the implementation of all information systems. Even within these industry sectors, we must expect to arrange the planning effort in a manner tailored to the needs of the specific project. The same applies to planning the project risk management effort.

Planning for the risk management process begins with selecting an appropriate model or set of models. A 'model' in this context is the deliberate simplification of reality we use to carry out analysis. Most models of interest have a mathematical form, but of particular concern is their associated graphical form, which forms the basis of our conceptual understanding of their implications.

A key point here is that there is no one best model for all project risk management purposes. Even in an organisation with well-established risk management processes in place, decisions need to be made, consciously and regularly, about which models to use. If these decisions are not made consciously, then decisions are being made by default which may prove very costly. On some occasions the models used may be too simple, obscuring important issues which should be addressed. On other occasions the models may be too complex, involving effort which is not cost effective. Using an inappropriate model to analyse risk is a risk management planning error directly comparable to undertaking a construction project with an inappropriate plan.

Failing to consider this issue is rather like operating a car hire firm that always offers a Rolls Royce, or a Mini, regardless of the potential customer's wallet or needs. It is difficult to overemphasise this point because the systematic nature of risk management processes can easily seduce those who ought to know better into the adoption of a single modelling approach for all activities in all projects. 'If the only tool in your toolbox is a hammer, every problem looks like a nail', is a situation to be avoided.

It is also worth noting that the selection of suitable models for risk management purposes can influence other project planning models in important ways, and these issues need joint consideration.

The simplest project activity planning models which explicitly consider risk are PERT (Programme Evaluation and Review Technique) models, which portray project activity structure via an activity-on-arrow or activity-on-node diagram representing precedence constraints, and uncertainty associated with the duration of each activity directly via a probability distribution, which may be pictured as a cumulative probability curve. First introduced in the late 1950s (Moder and Philips, 1970), these models are still the basis of much current project risk management.

A key shortcoming of basic PERT models is the assumption that activity probability distributions are independent, both causally and statistically. This shortcoming was recognised and addressed in part in the early 1960s via Generalised PERT (Moder and Philips, 1970), which addresses causal dependence by embedding decision trees in a PERT network. For example, if activity B, following activity A, can be accelerated if activity A is late, a decision tree is used to recognise and model this possibility.

A second key shortcoming of basic PERT models is the need for direct estimates of how long an activity will take. Direct estimating ignores the possibility of more accurate assessment by asking the question 'at what rate can we proceed', and using the answer to work out how long an activity might take. This alternative to direct estimating can be particularly important when repetitive processes are involved. This shortcoming was recognised and partially resolved in the mid 1960s as part of the GERT (Graphical Evaluation and Review Technique) approach by employing a Markov or semi-Markov process model, which can be embedded in a generalised PERT model. In a Markovian process one probability distribution defines the 'state' the system is in (how much of the activity has been completed) and another defines the 'transitions' between time periods (activity rates of progress) which are used to update the 'state'.

A further key shortcoming is the need to understand the nature of the risk realised before considering effective responses. For example, delay to a pipelaying activity because the contractor proves incompetent requires a different response to delay caused by bad weather. This shortcoming was recognised and resolved in the mid 1970s as part of the SCERT (Synergistic Contingency Evaluation and Review Technique) approach (Chapman, 1979). The SCERT approach involves a fault tree or event tree model embedded in a GERT model.

Choosing the appropriate level of model sophistication can be left to later in the risk management process if a nested set of compatible models of the SCERT variety is the basis. However, specific simplifications at this stage in the process which preclude more sophisticated models later can have serious ongoing consequences.

For present purposes we assume a comprehensive model of the SCERT variety may be required. The question of possible simplifications or short cuts will be addressed in Chapter 16.

6.7 DETERMINE PROCESS RESOURCES, THE *WHEREWITHAL*

Just as resources for the project require explicit consideration, so too do resources for effective risk analysis, the process *wherewithal* question. In the short term there may be specific constraints on cost and time, perhaps imposed by the parent project. Resource questions are likely to revolve around the availability and quality of human resources, including the availability of key project personnel, and the availability of information processing facilities.

Computing power is no longer a significant constraint for most project planning, with or without consideration of risk. Even very small projects can afford access to powerful personal computers. However, software can be a significant constraint, even for very large projects. It is important to select software which is efficient and effective for an appropriate model and method. It is also important to prevent preselected software from unduly shaping the form of the analysis.

Our current preference is a flexible unstructured software system to get started, '@Risk' being a typical industry standard example. It is effective in expert hands because it is flexible, but it is not very efficient because it is flexible and requires expert users. When the type of models used and the associated methods or processes have become reasonably well defined, more specific and more efficient software may deserve attention, at the very least 'macros' or sub-routines constructed from a basic software system.

For similar reasons we believe the personnel used to introduce project risk analysis into an organisation should be a team put together with a focus on effectiveness, not efficiency, in the first instance. Once the nature of the processes involved are understood and accepted throughout the organisation, efficiency can be addressed. However, too early a focus on efficiency may prove very ineffective.

In the early stages of the risk management process the risk analysis team may be seen as the project planning player doing most of the risk management running. However, it is vital that all the other players (as listed earlier in Section 6.1) see themselves as part of the team, and push the development of the risk management process as a vehicle serving their needs. This implies commitment and a willingness to spend time providing input to the risk analysis and exploring the implications of its output.

Consultants can have a very important role in the implementation of such processes and the execution of specific studies. Most organisations cannot effectively self-start in this area. However, project managers and project teams more generally cannot simply buy a risk analysis from a consultant, nor should they attempt to do so.

6.8   DETERMINE PROCESS TIMING, THE *WHEN*

'Physician heal thyself' is a well-known, relevant quote. If a client of the authors' asks 'how long will it take to assess my project's risk?', the quite truthful response 'how long is a piece of string?' will not do. A more useful response is 'how long have we got?' (the process *when*), in conjunction with 'how much effort can be made available?' (the process *wherewithal*), 'who wants it?' (the process *who*), and 'what do you want it for?' (the process *why*). The answer to this latter question often drives the process *what* and the *whichway*.

It is important to understand the interdependence of these considerations. Six months or more may be an appropriate duration for some initial, detailed project risk analyses of a major project, but six hours can be put to very effective use if the question of the time available is addressed effectively in relation to the other process Ws. Even a few minutes may prove useful for small projects. Fitting a risk management process to available time and other resources is central to the issue of short cuts, addressed in Chapter 16. For present purposes, we assume any necessary time is available.

6.9   ASSESS THE PROCESS PLAN

Assessing the process plan is the final specific task within the Focus phase. This provides a convenient place to pause and consider the risks associated with the execution of the risk analysis. The results of the common tasks *document, verify, assess* and *report* with respect to each previous step need to be consolidated at this point.

A key reason for identifying this specific task is to provide a *go/no-go/maybe* decision point in the planning of the risk management process. One possibility is to move directly on to the Identify phase of the risk management process. Another possibility is the need to carry out another pass through the Focus phase, taking in selected steps as appropriate. Stopping the risk management process is a third possibility. There are inappropriate reasons for stopping the risk management process at this stage, such as more risk revealed than the client wishes to see. There are also good reasons, such as nothing can be done about the key risks for the time being, because they are beyond the control of the organisation, and putting the whole process on hold is a sensible strategy. Note that 'stop' need not imply 'abandon'.

Undertaking risk management is a high risk project in itself, especially if embedding effective risk management in the organisation as well as in the project in question is the objective. Often the project planning team provide a high risk environment for risk analysis because, for example, project management is ineffective, or project team members:

1. are not familiar with effective project risk management processes;
2. are familiar with inappropriate risk management processes;
3. come from very difficult cultures;
4. come from competing organisations or departments.

It is one thing to do a consultant's 'hit-and-run', quite another to try herding an assortment of tabby cats and tigers to a mutually agreed destination!

6.10   THE ONGOING NATURE OF THE FOCUS PHASE

The Focus phase may be largely concurrent with the Define phase, but updating risk management plans is necessarily ongoing. Figure 4.2 indicates the way the effort expended in the Focus phase might be timed, as discussed in Chapter 4.

As a risk management process becomes fairly stable, in terms of routine updates for example, the *scope the process* task becomes less relevant, and more detail is required with respect to *plan the process*.

Chapter 7

Identify the Risks and Responses: The Identify Phase

Zaphod ... put on the sunglasses ... They were a double pair of Joo Janta 200 Super Chromatic Peril Sensitive Sunglasses, which had been specially designed to help people develop a relaxed attitude to danger. At the first hint of trouble they turn totally black and thus prevent you from seeing anything that might harm you.

D. Adams, *The Restaurant at the End of the Universe*

7.1 INTRODUCTION

All project risk management process descriptions emphasise a need to identify sources of risk early in the process. Some process descriptions concentrate initially on assessing impacts or effects of these risk sources, leaving consideration of root causes and related responses until later, and then only consider alternatives in relation to major risks. Nevertheless, at least one response, even if it is 'do nothing and accept the risk' (which may not be feasible), must be identified and assumed in order to understand the impact of a risk later in the first pass through the risk management process (RMP). Moreover, while the iterative nature of RMP can allow identification of risks and responses to be revisited, extensive early consideration of both risks and responses is the key to effective risk and opportunity management. In particular, early response identification acts as a catalyst to the widespread search for options, as well as a way of dealing with specific problems. The essence of the matter is:

1. we do not want to waste time considering alternative responses if the first one thought of is both effective and efficient;
2. we do not want to overlook key responses;
3. we do not want to overlook the apparently minor problem which has no effective fix once it occurs;
4. we want to identify opportunities which may have implications beyond the risks which triggered their consideration;
5. we want to explore deeper levels of risks where this is particularly important.

As a whole, the risk management process is about insight, understanding, and asking the right questions. If we identify the right questions and understand what they mean, getting the right answers is a comparative doddle.

Identifying risks and responses involves two specific tasks:

1. *search*: for sources of risk and responses, employing a range of techniques such as pondering, interviewing, brainstorming and checklists;
2. *classify*: to provide a suitable structure for defining risks and responses, aggregating/disaggregating as appropriate.

In terms of documentation the Identify phase involves compiling a risk list, log, or register, indicating at least one assumed response for each identified risk, a generic 'do nothing' response being one option. The documentation may include a preliminary or comprehensive assessment of response options associated with these risks. Detailed lists of response options may be deferred, but early identification of response options can form the basis of a concerted opportunity identification process which goes beyond simple threat management.

The key deliverable is a clear, common understanding of threats and opportunities facing the project. Opportunities (upside risks requiring responses and more effective ways of proceeding in general) need to be identified and managed with the same resolve as threats as part of the same process. Sometimes opportunities and risks are closely coupled, but this need not be the case. Often a project risk management process is particularly successful because the process of generating and reviewing responses leads to the identification of important opportunities, with implications well beyond the risks which led to their identification.

The Identify phase can be treated as an eight-step process, as shown in Figure 7.1.

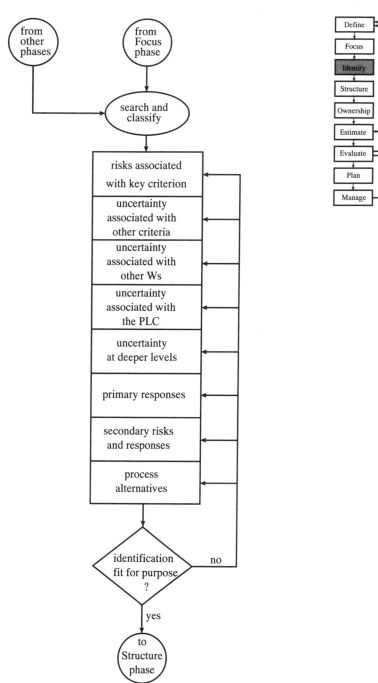

Figure 7.1 Identify phase specific tasks.

The search and classify tasks are not separable to an extent that suggests separate tasks in Figure 7.1, a search and classify mode being required throughout. The first step involves a simple first cut at the identification of risks directly related to a key performance criterion. Steps 2–5 explicitly expand this focus in four important dimensions. Steps 6 and 7 consider associated responses and secondary risks. Step 8 elaborates on the very basic search process used to kick off the first seven steps. A final specific *assess* task initiates loops back to the earlier steps.

As with Figures 5.1 and 6.1, this portrayal is deliberately simplified, to illustrate the spirit of what is involved. In practice, things may not seem to happen according to this model, but the model is a useful target which can help to maintain focus and order.

7.2   RISKS ASSOCIATED WITH A KEY CRITERION

The simplest way to begin the identification phase is to adopt a simple ponder approach to the identification of what might be termed *Key criterion*, *Level one*, *Primary risks*, more conveniently referred to as KLP risks.

Key criterion risks are risks which impact directly on the most important or central project performance criterion.

Level one risks are sources of risk or risk drivers which can be linked directly to an uncertain effect on a performance criterion of interest, without reference to an uncertainty structure involving multiple levels of disaggregated or contributory risk drivers.

Primary risks are risks associated with base plans or designs or other base assumption aspects of the project, as distinct from secondary risks associated with responses to primary risks.

Pondering is a simple approach involving the use of a single person with a 'blank piece of paper and a pencil' (or the computer-based equivalent) to identify risks or responses. This is the most basic approach possible. It may serve as a default option if other approaches are not feasible or suitable. Alternative approaches will be considered in Section 7.9, but pondering should not be dismissed or usurped too readily as a starting point. Most experienced risk analysts start with it intuitively. We rely upon it explicitly as part of the ongoing Focus phase, and the subsequent Structure phase. Its explicit use before involving other people or undertaking a systematic review of available documentation can be very effective for a number of reasons. For example, it can help to kick off an interview process by providing examples of the level of risk aggregation/disaggregation of interest, and stimulating other thoughts.

Pondering can involve formalised processes. For example, an analyst can consider in turn each of the detailed activities making up each of the consolidated activities for risk management purposes, and ask the question 'what might go wrong with this component detailed activity?'

The following example clarifies what is meant by KLP risks.

Example 7.1

Offshore oil and gas projects in the early 1970s experienced widespread planning and costing failure, in that many projects came in late and over cost.

The key criterion was time. Most cost risk was driven by time risk (delay), and trade-offs between time or cost and performance was not a significant issue.

Part of the reason for the planning and costing failure was the absence of a formal process for considering sources of risk, but most of the people involved could provide a list of risk sources at level one without much hesitation. When a formal process was introduced, identification of risks in terms of obtaining a list of risks in level one terms was reasonably straightforward.

Laying offshore pipelines in the North Sea in the mid 1970s was deemed a particularly high risk activity, so examining sources of risk received considerable attention. About 40 risks were identified, including the lay barge arriving late, the lay barge not operating as quickly as planned given good weather, encountering bad weather, pipe 'buckles', and so on.

The large number of risks involved made it particularly obvious that rules of thumb needed to be developed to help decide how many separate risks should be identified, and how risks might be grouped under a common heading or label. This issue is usefully illustrated in relation to pipe 'buckles' which could take two basic forms, a 'dry buckle' or a 'wet buckle'.

A 'dry buckle' involves a kink in the pipe and/or the loss of some of the concrete coating. If a 'dry buckle' occurs, the pipeline can be pulled back on board the lay barge, the buckled section cut off, and pipelaying can then continue. Very little pipe or time are lost.

A 'wet buckle' involves a fracture in the pipe which allows water to rush in. The pipe quickly becomes too heavy for the barge to hold, ripping itself off the barge unless it is released quickly. It then sinks to the ocean floor, and continues to fill with water and debris.

It was very important to distinguish between wet and dry buckles. 'Dry buckles' were a minor problem, conveniently put together with all other 'productivity variations' to cover a range of problems not worth separate analysis, although identification in terms of a comprehensive list of examples was useful. 'Wet buckles' were a major problem, worth designating as a separate risk (called 'buckles' without the need to use the word 'wet' every time they were referred to).

This example also illustrates the two specific tasks of searching and classifying involved in all the Identify phase steps. The *search* task was concerned with the identification of pipe 'buckles' as a source of risk. The *classify* task was concerned with understanding that by 'buckles' we mean 'wet buckles', 'dry buckles' being part of 'productivity variations'. Associated documentation would indicate that the term 'buckles' was to be employed for 'wet buckles', with an appropriate level of description of what is involved, and would record 'dry buckles' as one example (among many) of what was meant by 'productivity variations'.

7.3 UNCERTAINTY ASSOCIATED WITH OTHER CRITERIA

As noted in Chapter 1, there are a number of problems associated with defining risk in relation to performance, which can be viewed as opportunities. One problem (or opportunity) is the multi-dimensional nature of project performance. In some circumstances a case can be made for keeping the measurement of performance and success very simple, but such conditions are comparatively rare. More commonly, project objectives might be viewed in terms of cost, time or quality. Cost might be addressed in terms of capital cost or 'whole life' cost, quality might be divided into technical specification, functionality and appearance, each of which may be 'at risk' to different degrees. Often performance is perceived primarily in terms of dimensions that can be measured, such as time and cost, or particular aspects of quality. The implication is that variations are possible and measurable, and hence risk exists in respect of these performance criteria. Other criteria which are not readily quantified may be treated as inviolate constraints for project management purposes. This may lead to neglect of risk in these dimensions, even though they represent important performance criteria. These problems (opportunities) need to be addressed in this step.

Even if one criterion clearly dominates, such as time in a North Sea offshore project context, other criteria will be important. Uncertainty which will not be identified in the frameworks used for the key criteria will need explicit attention. Consider an example, building on Example 7.1.

Example 7.2

When North Sea offshore project teams were satisfied that time risk had been properly assessed, aspects of cost risk not addressed as part of the process of responding to time risk were assessed. For example, the uncertain duration of a pipelaying activity was multiplied by the uncertain cost of a lay barge per unit time, to compute lay barge cost.

In this case it is relatively simple to build cost risk on a time risk framework. When a clear structure-linking criteria exists, it is worth exploiting. When it does not, more complex approaches may be required, but this complexity requires great care. For example, many complex weapon system and information system risk management processes identify risks in terms of time, cost and/or performance impacts simultaneously, using a matrix format. This may seem simple enough, and sensible enough, for the Identify phase. However, it poses two somewhat different potential problems. First, it does not facilitate a clear, sequential focus on performance criteria which helps to avoid omissions. Second, it leaves structural issues to be addressed later, as they must be for quantification, and this can mitigate against appropriate quantification. By impeding quantification, it impairs the iterative process which is central to a complete risk management process.

Much more detailed analysis of objectives, including their decomposition in a structure directly related to project activities or design components, may be useful in some cases. For example, in a high technology product development project, if a set of components is assessed as very high risk, it may be possible to design out those risks by changing the basic nature of the design, perhaps as part of a formal Value Management process (Green, 1994). This will require a clear understanding of the functional role of the components in the overall design. It involves an interaction between the project *why* and *what*. The groundwork for identification of the risk issues here should have been provided back in the Define phase.

It is important to address these difficulties explicitly as part of the Focus phase or the closely linked Structure phase. Guidance on how to manage such difficulties is beyond the scope of this book, but a starting point for those interested in or compelled to address this issue is provided by Chapman *et al.* (1985) and Klein (1993).

Another problem arising from defining risk in terms of performance uncertainty is that different parties involved in a project are likely to have different performance objectives, or at least different priorities and perceptions of performance objectives. A multiplicity of parties increases the importance of this issue, and this is a major reason for identifying the project *who* in the Define phase.

Even if only one party is of concern, it is very important to define objectives, in writing, and their relative priorities. Often different parts of the same organisation have different objectives. If the differences are very important, treating the different parts of the organisation as separate partners may be appropriate. At the very least agreed priorities in terms of time, cost and performance are essential.

7.4 UNCERTAINTY ASSOCIATED WITH OTHER Ws

In principle, this step could precede the previous two steps in order to assist in the identification of KLP risks and uncertainties associated with performance criteria. However, for present purposes we assume the previous two steps have been taken, and that time is the key criterion, with cost driven by time, as in Examples 7.1 and 7.2.

Project risk management which is largely focused on time (delay) risk is naturally addressed in terms of project activities (the project *whichway*), but the other project Ws are usually important, and associated uncertainty will usually need explicit attention. As a consequence, this step is concerned with considering four Ws: *who, what, when* and *wherewithal*, using as a basis the documentation of all six Ws in the Define phase.

Considering the four Ws other than *whichway* and *why* can reveal some key risks, associated responses, and in some cases secondary risks, with important interactions which require management. Below we consider each of these four Ws in turn, not to generate an exhaustive, generic list of possible risks, which would be impracticable and inappropriate, but to illustrate the range of risk areas that could be considered.

Risks Associated with Other Parties, the *Who*

Chapter 5 indicated the importance of documenting clear descriptions of all the interested parties during the Define phase in a manner which would help to make the identification of associated risks effective in the Identify phase. The issue here is an effective risk identification process using this earlier identification of the relevant parties.

Examples 5.1 and 5.2 illustrate some of the issues, but consider another example.

Example 7.3

Joint venture partners are important to address explicitly, in terms of the interests and roles of all the partners. Many offshore oil projects involve a lead partner who takes operational responsibility and other partners who help to fund the project and share the product. A significant change in plans will require approval by all the partners. If they are not all kept informed of the possible need to make such changes, managing the decision to change the plan can be a question of crisis management rather than risk management, adding to the cost of the incidents necessitating the change, or eliminating the possibility of responding to an opportunity.

Multi-nation military joint ventures, such as the development of new weapon systems or their platforms (aircraft, ships, etc.), make the *who* dimension very rich indeed, due, for example, to different technical requirements, different needs in terms of timing, and different contracting systems between the partners and their contractors.

Regulators, planning authorities and others providing approvals may also prove to be key players. For example, CCTG power stations involve warm water discharges into rivers and vapour plumes which are regulated, in addition to the planning permission issues associated with such plant. Nuclear power stations involve obviously increased levels of regulation, including safety standards which may be changing during construction, necessitating redesigns with delays which yield still more regulation-induced design changes in a vicious circle which can prove extremely expensive. Channel tunnel rolling stock development and production encountered this kind of difficulty. To manage this kind of risk it is important to understand what is driving changes in the regulatory environment and endeavouring to meet the regulations which will be relevant at the appropriate time in the future, not those currently in force. This raises issues picked up in Section 7.6.

Competitors for limited resources (*wherewithal*) can also prove a profitable area of study. For example, oil majors have attempted to avoid bidding up the price for key scarce resources by timing their projects (moving the *when*) to avoid excessive competition. If only a half a dozen players are involved, individual study and perhaps direct collaboration may be feasible. More generally, it may be appropriate to look at the markets for specific resources as a whole. Successful commercial property developers are aware of the need to time new building construction, hopefully while the market for resources and cash are depressed, just before the market for office space takes off. Many failed developers are also well aware of the importance of these considerations too late. This too raises issues picked up in Section 7.6.

Much of the uncertainty inherent in project management arises from agents appointed by the client such as contractors and subcontractors. The client may not be able to rely on an agent performing as the client wishes for reasons related to the nature of the work and the agent's motivation, ability, and understanding of the work (see also Table 7.2). In theory, it should be possible for the client to maximise the chances of satisfactory performance from the agent by careful selection of a suitable agent, careful monitoring of the agent's activities, and ensuring that the agent is appropriately motivated. Unfortunately, lack of knowledge on the part of the client and the presence of uncertainty can make these things difficult to achieve.

The so-called 'principal–agent' relationship, whether between parties in the same organisation, or between a client and contractor, is prone to three fundamental problems: *adverse selection*; *moral hazard*; and *risk allocation* (Eisenhardt, 1989).

Adverse selection refers to misrepresentation of ability by the agent and the principal's difficulty in selecting an agent with appropriate skills. The agent may claim to have certain skills or abilities when hired, but the principal cannot completely verify these skills or abilities either at the time of hiring or while the agent is working. A 'selection' problem can also arise where a contractor misrepresents the work that will be done or the likely final price. Once a contractor has been hired, it may be difficult for the client to ensure that costs are contained and work promised is what is actually delivered.

Moral hazard refers to an agent's failure to put forth the contracted effort. This can be of greatest concern to the principal when it is particularly difficult or expensive for the principal to verify that an agent is behaving appropriately, as when task specifications are inadequate or the principal lacks knowledge of the delegated tasks.

Risk allocation concerns the manner in which project-related risk is allocated between principal and agent. Risk allocation is a very important issue because it can strongly influence the motivation of principal and agent, and the extent to which risk is assessed and managed. Insofar as principal and agent perceive risks differently, and have different abilities and motivations to manage risk, then their approach to risk management will be different. In particular, either party is likely to try to manage risk primarily for their own benefit, perhaps to the disadvantage of the other party. This issue is explored in more detail in Chapter 15.

The uncertainties arising from problems of adverse selection, moral hazard and risk allocation are more likely to arise where principal and agent are separate organisations, as in most client–contractor relationships. Where principal and agent belong to the same organisation it might be expected that such problems would be less likely to arise, to the extent that the parties can share information, responsibilities and objectives more readily. Unfortunately, this is not always the case.

Risks Associated with Project Design, the *What*

Many of the important risks associated with a project relate to the specific physical nature of the project and its design, to the *what* of the project. The relationship may be direct and obvious or indirect and easily overlooked. For example, many risk management methods for high technology products (such as advanced weapon systems) suggest an explicit focus on technical risk issues arising from design because using a design based on the latest technology may involve risks associated with technical failures or reliability problems. Using a design based on established technology may avoid certain technical risks but involve other risks associated with more aggressive competitors who are willing and able to manage the risks of new technology and threaten the market for the product of the project. That is, avoiding a technical risk may involve generating a competitor risk, but where the choice of technology is implicit, competitor risk may be seen as an apparently unrelated, primary risk.

Design changes are often a major threat. However, freezing the design is often not a viable option. Hospitals, military equipment, computer software and comparatively simple consumer products may require design updates during development and production to remain viable. Anticipating these changes in needs may be the key to successful design, as well as the key to a successful project more generally. Attention to procedures for 'change control' (design changes) should be recognised as central to any project involving design which is neither simple nor stable.

Effective anticipation of design changes is part of the risk management process. Links to other Ws may be quite simple but very important, requiring an understanding of the *what*, with the *whichway* and *why* assumed to have been covered earlier, and the *wherewithal* and *when* yet to be considered. For example, property developers will be sensitive to issues like how many car-parking places a planning department may require for a new building now, and whether or not this is likely to increase by next year. A design which fails to reflect this sort of change can put the whole project at risk. At the very least it requires a clear understanding of the technologies involved, and the interface between technological choices and related issues. For example, the development of computer-controlled fly-by-wire technology revolutionised aircraft design because inherently unstable designs which previously would not have been able to fly became feasible, but a whole new set of risks were generated which were not all anticipated at the outset.

It is important to appreciate that *what* is the recipient of impacts from other Ws as well as a source of primary risks, and these impacts can generate substantial second order effects. For example, if some combination of problems from a variety of sources threatens the viability of the target project completion time or date, or its cost, the response may be a change in design. This may have the desired effect, or it may make the situation worse. This impact is well understood in theory in terms of the standard time–cost–quality triangle (Barnes, 1988), but often is overlooked in practice. Part of the role of documenting the six Ws in the Define phase, and review of this documentation with a view to risk identification in the Identify phase, is explicit identification of these issues.

Risks Associated with Project Resources, the *Wherewithal*

The importance of risk management involving resources, the *wherewithal* of the project, is obvious. Lack of the right resources in the right place at the right time is not simply a source of risk. Making sure this does not happen is central to project management. Example 5.6 is a relatively low-key illustration of resource-related risks. In the following example, the availability of one resource was a major risk.

Example 7.4

A very early study by Chapman was totally driven by the impact of a scarce resource: welders needed for the fabrication of a proposed large diameter gas pipeline to bring Arctic gas to US markets. The availability of welders was central to the project because political pressures were forcing a short project duration (a *when* issue) which required a significant proportion (of the order of 10%) of the suitably skilled welders available in Canada. Other factors influencing the availability of welders also needed to be understood, such as immigration rules which would make importing labour difficult or impossible, and a recognition that Arctic construction of this kind often leads to a pattern of employment which involves long hours (and weeks) for an extended period when cash is accumulated by the workforce, followed by a spell on a sunny island until the cash runs out, the duration of both periods depending upon the welders' circumstances and whims.

Potential shortage of various resources is not the only source of risk. For example, in the context of computer software projects, there is a widely held view that adding more staff to a software project which is running very late could be compared in terms of effectiveness to attempting to drown a fire by pouring on petrol.

Usually economic usage of resources suggests self-imposed constraints even if there are no externally imposed constraints. For example, employing 300 people one week, 100 the next, and 200 the next is generally very uneconomic compared with 200 throughout.

If all the resources required are readily available in the required quantities at the required times with no difficulties associated with quality or performance, and no costs associated with highly variable resource usage patterns, the *wherewithal* issue is not worth pursuing. At the very least it is worth confirming that this is the case, in writing if appropriate.

It may be convenient to identify and describe resource requirements (*wherewithal*) within the activity (*whichway*) structure, but common resources mitigate against this, making separate *wherewithal* documentation useful. If a project is subject to political pressure to employ local labour or other resources it makes obvious sense to identify this type of consideration in relation to those resources which are relevant, which has implications for how the resource units are defined. As in the case of activities, the basic rule of thumb is disaggregate resource types only when it looks useful to do so.

Risks Associated with Project Timing, the *When*

Like design (*what*), timing (*when*) can be an important primary source of risk, and a recipient of impacts from other Ws, which can generate important second-order effects. Formal documentation of the Ws is concerned with making sure these issues do not fall down cracks and get lost from sight until they generate a crisis. Example 5.7 illustrates a timing/resource link, in terms of overstated time risk if resource risks could be avoided, because two activities were put in series and allow common resource usage.

Even if no first- or second-order risk impact issues are involved, project duration is an economic choice which needs explicit attention. For example, the study concerned with welders described in Example 7.4 addressed the question of an optimal target project duration explicitly, in response to the political pressure for a shorter duration. But even if no one outside the project team asks questions about project duration, the issue of trade-offs between time (indirect cost) and direct cost is important. At this stage in the process the question needs to be raised in broad terms. For example, if the proposed project duration is 5 years, the question is why not 4, or 6? If the answer is not clear, further attention to the issue will be required, and the need to give it attention should be flagged. From the outset it is important to be clear what level of overhead costs per unit time will be incurred in relation to any project extensions.

A first cut at risk identification might bypass the first two steps, as indicated earlier. It might involve a simple list of all the factors associated with each W and brief notes on relevant issues in relation to each factor. Use of a simple label (or 'handle') for each factor can be very helpful for discussion purposes, while backup descriptions carefully document the associated issues. If all six Ws have not been properly understood, and that understanding documented and shared by the project team, risk identification cannot be effective. For example, failure to consider market and political risks associated with *why* or *what* can render detailed planning and risk analysis of *whichway* and *when* somewhat superfluous, and market and political risks may be driven by technical choices.

The complementary second-cut (or alternative first-cut) approach is to look for risk associated with the elements of a hierarchical framework based on one or more of the six Ws, starting with the obvious framework for the key criteria. Thus a starting point might be a work breakdown structure (WBS) based on a decomposition of the *whichway*, a product breakdown structure based on a decomposition of the *what*, or an objectives breakdown structure based on a decomposition of the *why*. Section 7.2 assumed a *whichway* WBS. Whichever hierarchical basis is chosen, the other five Ws provide a prompt list for identifying risk drivers at each level in the adopted hierarchy.

7.5   UNCERTAINTY ASSOCIATED WITH THE PLC

A project risk management focus on time risk associated with *whichway* risk is almost a basic instinct. Steps 2 and 3 of the Identify phase addressed in Sections 7.3 and 7.4 were concerned with ensuring that other criteria and other Ws did not get ignored. An obvious further elaboration is a review of risks associated with the project life cycle (PLC). Recall that the current analysis assumes we are at the Plan stage of the PLC. Chapter 14 will address the process implications of being at other stages. But a useful step at this point in the risk management process is making sure risks which may not materialise until later in the PLC have been addressed now.

As noted in Chapter 2, many important risk drivers are associated with the fundamental management processes that make up the PLC. A fair number of risk drivers are implicitly acknowledged in lists of project management 'key success factors'. Potential problem areas typically identified in this way are listed in Table 7.1 against the appropriate PLC stages identified in Chapter 2.

The identification of these problem areas in the project management literature is based on substantial project management experience, but it

Table 7.1 Typical process problems in each stage of the PLC.

Stages of the PLC	Process problems
Conceive	Level of definition Definition of appropriate performance objectives Managing stakeholder expectations
Design	Novelty of design and technology Determining 'fixed' points in the design Control of changes
Plan	Identifying and allowing for regulatory constraints Concurrency of activities required Errors and omissions
Allocate	Adequate accuracy of resource estimates Estimating resources required Defining responsibilities (number and scope of contracts) Defining contractual terms and conditions Selection of capable participants (tendering procedures and bid selection)
Execute	Exercising adequate coordination and control Determining the level and scope of control systems Ensuring effective communication between participants Provision of appropriate organisational arrangements Ensuring effective leadership Ensuring continuity in personnel and responsibilities Responding to risks which are realised (implementation difficulties, failure to meet performance milestones)
Deliver	Adequate testing Adequate training Managing stakeholder expectations Obtaining licences to operate
Review	Capturing corporate knowledge Learning key lessons Understanding what success means
Support	Provision of appropriate organisation arrangements Identifying extent of liabilities Managing stakeholder expectations

is somewhat haphazard. Different writers identify different success factors or problem areas, describe them in more or less detail, or identify as single problem areas what may in practice be a whole series of separate problem areas. Another difficulty is that problems are identified as adverse effects rather than in terms of their underlying causes or sources of risk. For example, potential problems in the Execute stage of a project can often be related to weaknesses in particular earlier stages of the project: 'failure of prototype to pass performance trials' may be a consequence of faulty workmanship, unreasonable performance requirements or a choice of new technology or novel design features.

Designing and Planning

A common major driver of project risk is a failure to carry out steps in the Design and Plan stages thoroughly enough. Thus a project proceeds through to execution with insufficiently well-defined specifications for production. During execution this gives rise to difficulties necessitating additional design development and production planning and consequently adverse effects on the performance criteria of cost, time and quality. A related risk, of 'premature definition', is also difficult to avoid entirely except on very routine, repeated projects and is most acute in novel, one-off projects involving new technology. The basis of both problems is that it is extremely difficult to specify in advance how every part of the execution and termination phase will take place; neither is it cost effective to seek to do so. In any case some uncertainty about operating conditions and related factors outside the control of project management will always remain. Inevitably judgements have to be made about the degree of detail and accuracy practicable in the conceptualisation and planning phases, but we would argue that these judgements should be supported and informed by appropriate risk analysis.

Allocation

The Allocate stage is a significant task involving decisions about project organisation, identification of appropriate agents and allocation of tasks between them. As noted in Section 7.4, the introduction of an agent is prone to the three problems of adverse selection, moral hazard, and risk allocation. In particular, this stage of a project can introduce several significant risk drivers:

1. participants have different priorities and risk perceptions;
2. unclear specification of responsibilities (including those relating to the management of risk);
3. communications between different departments or organisations;
4. coordination and control tasks.

Even if client and agents all work for the same organisation, the problems presented by these uncertainties can be substantial. When agents are different organisations, these problems can be particularly challenging.

In a client–contractor situation, the client exerts influence over the contractor primarily via conditions laid down in a contract between the two parties. The contract sets out what is to be produced, what the client will pay, how the client can assess and monitor what the contractor has done, and how things should proceed in the case of various contingent events. In theory, the contract seeks to reduce uncertainty about each party's responsibilities. In practice substantial uncertainties can remain associated with items such as the following:

1. inadequate or ambiguous definition of terms (specifications; responsibilities of parties to cooperate, advise, coordinate, supervise);
2. inappropriate definition of terms (performance specifications; variations; extensions);
3. variations (powers to order; express and implied terms; pricing and payment mechanisms);
4. payment and claims arrangements (timing and conditions for payment);
5. defects liability (who has to be satisfied; who could be responsible; extent of liability).

Execution

During the Execute stage, the essential process risk is that coordination and control procedures prove inadequate. Thus coordination and control ought to include risk management practices as 'good project management practices' which amount to:

1. milestone management;
2. adequate monitoring of activities likely to go wrong;
3. ensuring realistic, honest reporting of progress;
4. reporting problems and revised assessments of future risks.

A common risk driver in the execution phase is the introduction of design changes. These can lead to disruption of schedules and resourcing, and affect cost, time and quality measures of performance directly. A potentially serious concern is that changes are introduced without a full appreciation of the knock-on consequences. Apart from direct consequences, indirect consequences can occur. For example, changes may induce an extension of schedules, allowing contractors to escape the adverse consequences of delays in works unaffected by the change. Changes may have wider technical implications than first thought, leading to subsequent disputes between client and contractor about liability for costs and consequential delays (Williams *et al.*, 1995a, 1995b; Cooper, 1980). Standard project management practice should establish product change control procedures which set up criteria for allowable changes and provide for adequate coordination, communication and documentation of changes. However, adjustments to production plans, costs, and payments to affected contractors ought to be based on an assessment of how project risks are affected by the changes and the extent to which revised risk management plans are needed.

In a repetitive, operational context human failings can be a significant driver of risk. Studies of accidents and disasters often identify 'human error'

Table 7.2 Possible causes of inadequate or incorrect performance by individuals.

Task perception	Following instructions which are incorrect Failure to realise responsibility Personal interpretation of a task required Mistaken priorities, such as taking short cuts through safety rules to save time
Capability and experience	Lack of appropriate training or skills to perform a task Failure to follow instructions Lack of appreciation of consequences of actions Inappropriate choice of procedure to achieve desired outcome Jumping to conclusions about the nature of a situation
Work environment	Information overload makes it difficult to identify important pieces of information and easier to ignore or delay scrutiny Task overload impairs ability to monitor developments and formulate reactive or proactive responses Difficult working environment Inadequate work environment, equipment, or procedures increase the chance of mistakes
Mistake	Random slips Failure to detect very unusual situations or rare events Incorrect assessment of a situation
Motivation	Lack of incentive for high level of performance Lack of concentration on a task Personal objectives
Actions of others	Failure to communicate information Frustration of actions Incorrect or faulty components supplied Insufficient quality of contribution

and 'management error' as major contributory causes (Engineering Council, 1993, Appendix 3; Kletz, 1985). Such risks may be evident in a project setting. Although the novelty of a project can discourage complacency and carelessness to some degree, the project context is often characterised by sufficient novelty, complexity, work pressure and uncertainty as to increase greatly the likely significance of human failure or error.

In any organisational context, a number of factors influence the performance of an individual participant, as shown in Figure 7.2. Failure in individual performance, whether amounting to inadequate or incorrect performance, may be related to one or more of these factors in a wide variety of ways, as listed in Table 7.2.

In a project context, where Figure 7.2 is equally applicable, risk drivers of the kind listed in Table 7.2 could feature in any stage of the PLC. However, seeking to identify risk drivers associated with individuals at every PLC stage may represent an excessive level of analysis. More usefully

Figure 7.2 Factors influencing individual behaviour.

the framework of Figure 7.2 might be applied at an aggregated level to particular groups of individuals or to individual participating organisations. In the latter case it is easy to see how the risk drivers of Table 7.2 might be associated with individual departments or whole organisations acting, for example, in the capacity of contractors or subcontractors.

7.6 UNCERTAINTY AT DEEPER LEVELS

The latter parts of Section 7.5 were motivated by a wish to take a PLC perspective on risk identification, but they were exploring deeper levels of uncertainty than the KLP risk (key criterion, level one, primary risks) examples of Section 7.2. Issues flagged in Sections 7.3 and 7.4 also touched on deeper levels of uncertainty. A further obvious step in the Identify phase is to ensure that deeper levels are explored whenever appropriate. There are a number of ways this can be done. The key issue is to understand the nature of the risks identified well enough to consider responses in an effective manner.

Consider an example, described in more detail elsewhere (Chapman, 1988), which illustrates one way of considering risks at different levels.

Example 7.5

A Beaufort Sea oil project involved oil production on artificial islands. The oil would be sent through pipes to the shore in a sea area known for very deep ice-scours in the ocean bed. These deep scours would put a pipeline at risk even if it were buried 3 or 4 metres beneath the sea bed, many times deeper than conventional pipe burying. The KLP risk Chapman was asked to address (by the project manager) was 'ice-scour damage' to the pipeline. He addressed this question in terms of a second level of uncertainty involving two components to the question 'what was the chance of ice-scour damage?':

1. what was the chance ice would strike the pipeline?
2. what was the chance that an ice strike would seriously damage the pipeline?

Chapman was also asked to take the second of these questions to a third level by the company ice-scour experts, addressing the questions:

1. what was the uncertainty in their data, with a view to assessing what type of additional data would be most useful (more seasons or a wider area within a season, for example)?
2. what was the uncertainty in the statistical model used to estimate the likelihood of scours at different depths?

Further, deeper levels could be associated with the alternative mechanisms associated with generating scour (ice heave during freezing versus grounded ice during thaws), and so on.

7.7 PRIMARY RESPONSES

The next step involves searching for and classifying responses for each recognised source of risk, in the process *documenting, verifying, assessing* and *reporting* what is involved.

Very often the identification of a possible response to a particular source of risk is a simple task. Once a risk has been identified it is frequently obvious how one could respond. However, the most easily identified possible response may not be the most effective or the most risk-efficient response; other responses may be worth identifying and considering. Where sources of risk are particularly significant, a systematic examination of a range of possible responses, perhaps with a view to applying several responses in parallel, may be worthwhile.

There are nine types of response that can be considered, as shown in Table 7.3.

A key response option is to *modify objectives*, as noted in Section 7.4. For example, as a proactive response, the time allowed to complete a decommissioning task may be extended before a contract for the work is let because an assessment of the base plan shows that the initial target would be virtually impossible to meet. As a reactive response, certain performance targets may be relaxed during the execution and termination phases of the PLC, if difficulties in meeting original targets become insuperable or the value of achieving the original targets is reassessed. Setting different levels of cost, time or quality objectives can have varying effects on the achievement of other objectives. These effects depend on a variety of situational factors, not

Table 7.3 Generic response types.

Type of response	method of handling uncertainty
Modify objectives	reduce or raise performance targets, change trade-offs between multiple objectives
Avoid	plan to avoid specified sources of uncertainty
Prevent	change the probability of occurrence
Mitigate	modify the impact of a source of uncertainty
Develop contingency plans	set aside resources to provide a reactive ability to cope
Keep options open	delay choices and commitment, choose versatile options
Monitor	collect and update data about probabilities of occurrence, anticipated impacts, and additional risks
Accept	accept risk exposure, but do nothing about it
Remain unaware	ignore the possibility of risk exposure, take no action to identify or manage risk

least of which are the nature of the project and the behaviour of the contractors and professionals employed. For example, good quality building work is fostered by allowing contractors time to analyse and properly price what is required, and to conduct the work without excessive haste and paring of costs. In setting goals for attainment on each project objective, trade-offs must be made between levels of attainment on each objective. Unfortunately, deciding trade-offs is often complicated by uncertainty about the nature of the interdependencies between the different performance objectives. Thus, a decrease in the time available to complete a project can cause an increase in total project cost, but it may cause a decrease. Similarly, improvements in quality can mean an increase or a decrease in project time associated with an increase or a decrease in project cost.

In the face of these difficulties, a pragmatic approach is common. Trade-offs may be expressed simply in terms of one objective having clear priority over another. For example, under JCT 87 Management Contract conditions there is an implied instruction to the management contractor to put completion on time before cost control (Joint Contracts Tribunal, 1987, p. 5). Alternatively, project objectives are often expressed in terms of satisfying target levels of achievement which are assumed to be mutually compatible. This typically results in a series of *ad hoc* trade-offs being made through the life of the project. For example, in a construction project, the client's representative on the building site might accept work of lower performance than specified in the contract where specifications appear excessively tight, in exchange for work of higher performance in other areas, to secure an overall balance in the terms of exchange.

A second response, *avoidance*, is often a feasible and desirable response to identified risks. However, risk management strategies formulated as avoidance options in practice may operate only as prevention or mitigation options. This may still be useful, but the residual risk should be recognised.

In a multi-party context transferring risk to another party may be perceived by the transferring party to be an obvious and natural way of avoiding one or more sources of risk. However, risks may not be eliminated for the party transferring the risk unless the party receiving the risk adopts appropriate risk management strategies, and the consequences may include secondary risks which fall on the party who thought they had transferred the risk. This is a particularly significant issue in contractual relationships, often with profound implications for risk management and project performance. This issue is examined in more detail in Chapters 9 and 15.

A third response option is *prevention*. This is a very common type of response which typically has the intention of reducing the probability of adverse events occurring. Viewing risk management as opportunity management suggests a variation which involves increasing the probability of desirable events occurring. This perspective implies a concerted attempt to identify opportunities as well as risks.

A fourth response option is *mitigation*. This involves modifying the potential impact of a source of uncertainty on project performance. It certainly includes reducing adverse impacts, for example reducing delays likely to be caused should a particular event occur. However, mitigation may also involve modifying potential impacts by changing their nature, perhaps by transforming an impact on one performance criterion into an impact on another criterion. For example, if an event occurs which will delay the project, it may be possible to counter this, and plan to do so, by paying for overtime work or other additional resources.

A fifth type of response option is to *develop contingency plans*. This involves consciously accepting risk but setting aside resources to provide a reactive capability to cope with impacts if they eventuate. Thus the project manager may set aside a contingency reserve of physical resources, finance or time in case of need. Risk analysis may be useful to determine the appropriate level of contingency provision.

A sixth type of response, to *keep options open*, involves deliberate delaying of choices, limiting early commitment, and actively searching out versatile project strategies that will perform acceptably under a variety of possible future conditions.

Monitoring, a seventh type of response, implies a willingness to undertake more active risk management at some point, but the criteria for active management intervention may not be clearly articulated. Delaying risk management is always an option. Uncertainty may decrease (or increase!), risks may change, and the need for real-time problem solving may increase or decrease. Adopting this response ought to involve conscious assessment of the likely costs and benefits of delaying more active responses.

Acceptance, with recognition of the risk exposure, but with no further action to manage or monitor risk, is an eighth type of response.

In an important practical sense the final response option is to *remain unaware* that the risk exists. This is a sensible option in cases where such risks can be dealt with effectively and efficiently as and when they arise. It has obvious dangers in other cases. Remaining unaware is a default option if none of the other options in Table 7.3 are pursued.

The scope for complex risk/response management is clearly considerable. Example 7.6 provides an extension to Example 7.1 to clarify part of what is involved. Example 7.7 illustrates some further issues, complementing Example 7.6.

Example 7.6

Consider the potential occurrence of a pipe 'wet buckle'.

One kind of response is purely reactive, after-the-fact, using readily available resources: the buckled pipeline can be repaired. This involves sending down divers to cut off the damaged sections and put a cap on the pipe containing valves. A 'pig', a torpedo-like metal cylinder, is then sent through the pipe under air pressure from the other end, to 'dewater' the pipeline. The pipeline can then be picked up and pipelaying recommenced.

A second kind of response is proactive and preventive, up-front action which reduces the chance of risk being realised: a more capable lay barge could reduce the risk of a buckle occurring (capability for this purpose being maximum wave height conditions for safe working). This response is also a proactive mitigating response, because buckle repair can be completed more quickly in the face of bad weather with a more capable barge.

A third kind of response is also after-the-fact, but requires essential prior actions: the buckled pipeline can be abandoned, and a new pipeline started. If the buckle occurs before very much pipe has been laid, and sufficient additional spare pipe has been ordered in advance, this is a cost-effective solution because of the time saved. This kind of response is an example of a proactive/reactive combination.

Some responses have important implications for other responses, risks or the base plan, all of which need to be identified. For example, a more capable barge reduces the chances of a buckle, and it also allows faster repair of buckles as noted. It also allows faster pipelaying, especially in the face of bad weather, with an impact on base plan performance.

Simply accepting the risk of a buckle, in the sense of living with it with no direct risk management response, was not an option. However, oil majors operating in the North Sea in the 1980s often transferred some of the risk associated with buckles to their contractors, via fixed price contracts for a complete pipeline. This did not transfer all the risk, as contractors could not bear the consequential costs or lost revenues associated with delaying the start of oil or gas production. Insurance for such risks was taken into account, but generally considered inappropriate.

Designing out buckle risk, by using flexible pipe and reel barges, was not to our knowledge explicitly identified as a response to 'buckles' in the early days of North Sea pipelaying, but it might have been.

Example 7.7

Spending August sailing a small yacht from Southampton to Falmouth in Cornwall and back, along the south coast of England, is Chapman's idea of an ideal summer holiday project. Bad weather is the central risk. It can be designed out only by staying at home. Monitoring, keeping flexible, and changing objectives when appropriate, are the basic response strategies.

The trip each way is planned to take a week to ten days, with four or five stops on the way, sailing in daylight. The most desirable stops are anchorages in sheltered bays, which are usable only in certain wind conditions. A buoy in a quiet river is the next preference, a marina a poor third, unless water or fuel are required. Stopovers are for walks, pub meals, and visits to historic houses, gardens and other places of interest. Staying in port is also a response to a poor weather forecast. Avoiding planning long passages without alternative ports if the weather is bad, or potentially bad, is an important variant of this response to the monitoring process. If the forecast is bad for a week, going anyway becomes almost inevitable as priorities change. Further responses once underway include shortening sail (reefing or, in extremes, changing to a storm jib and/or tri-sail), putting on life-lines, and securing the main hatch. The basic objective is enjoyment while on passage, but extensive delays can make getting there more of a priority, and the ultimate priority is the safety of the boat and crew. Sometimes carrying on to the planned destination has to be replaced by heading for the nearest port in a storm, and in extremes that may have to be abandoned in favour of making sea room.

Many new strategic information systems projects for competitive advantage share most of these characteristics, as do a wide range of other projects, even if having fun is not the basic intent, and ending up dead in the water is not a potential outcome in a literal sense.

Most experienced sailors, and most experienced managers in other contexts where monitoring, keeping flexible, and changing objectives when appropriate is the basis of risk management, can recount tales of when it all went wrong, with disastrous or near-disastrous consequences. Yachting magazines carry regular features in this vein, which make educational as well as interesting reading for those with this inclination. Corporate disaster stories also receive such attention. Common features are a series of largely unpredicted events whose significance was not recognised, coming together at a time when options were reduced for predictable reasons, and a failure to take radical action based on a change of objectives early enough.

In a first pass at least one response should be identified for each specified primary risk, if only because the impact of a risk cannot be considered without some assumed response. This initial response may be simply 'accept the risk', but such a response may not be feasible, and a more active response would need to be identified. For example, in Example 7.6 there is a range of things that can be done, but just accepting the risk exposure is not one of them. On a first iteration one response per risk may be enough, especially for those risks which are clearly unlikely to prove significant. Later iterations can add additional responses for risks of importance. Very important risks may warrant careful consideration of possible options under each type of response in Table 7.3.

Sometimes it is particularly important to stress and extensively develop the primary response part of the Identify phase. One reason is to address low project team morale. Looking for problems can be very depressing when a project which is your sole source of income is already looking decidedly risky. Encouraging the project team to look for responses to each risk before going on to the next risk can be a vital aspect of success.

Another reason to stress primary response development arises where a project is based on a design which is so tentative that a major risk is best dealt with by redesign.

A third reason arises where a project's objectives are an essential aspect of success and the response 'if at first it doesn't look like you will succeed, redefine success' is a viable proposition.

Whether or not primary responses are stressed for the kinds of reasons just cited, it is very important to see responses in terms of all six Ws as part of a process concerned with maximising flexibility and enabling appropriate monitoring.

7.8 SECONDARY RISKS AND RESPONSES

The seventh step associated with the Identify phase involves identifying secondary risks and responses as appropriate, and documenting what is involved. The extent to which it is worth identifying and documenting secondary, tertiary and further consequential risks and responses is very much a matter of judgement, necessarily dependent on a variety of issues. Once again, the key lies in not overlooking any important issues. An extension of Example 7.6 illustrates this point.

Example 7.8

If 'repair' becomes the response to a pipe buckle, an important secondary risk involves the 'pig' running over a boulder or other debris, and becoming stuck.

A secondary response is to send down divers, cut off the pipe behind the pig, put a cap on the shortened pipeline, and try again. Another secondary response is to increase the air pressure, hoping to pop the pig through, with the tertiary risk that the pipeline may fail to withstand the additional pressure some considerable distance from the stuck pig, resulting in the loss of even more pipe and even more delay.

It was very important to identify these secondary and tertiary risk chains, for several reasons.

First, it clearly makes sense to assess, well in advance, how far the air pressure should be turned up in the event of a stuck pig. This is not a decision which should be left to a lay barge operator in the midst of a crisis. The decision requires the expertise of pipeline designers and pipeline manufacturers, who will understand the safety margins in their design and production, and are best placed to judge the probability of damage and the extent of that damage as the pressure increases. It also requires the expertise of those members of the project team who understand the cost implications of delay to the pipelaying, the likely effect on the project or activity, and the cost implications of delays to the project as whole, including opportunity costs.

Second, once it is clear that 'repair' involves considerable scope for loss of pipe, and that additional pipe will have to be ordered if a repair strategy is adopted, 'abandon and start again' begins to look a much more attractive option, and fast supply of extra pipe becomes a key issue.

Ultimately such considerations motivated fundamental changes in design, including the use of more flexible pipe laid from reel barges. This change in technology subsequently avoided buckles and greatly speeded up the whole process of pipelaying.

A key issue illustrated here is the insight provided by the process. Insight and understanding is what motivates and drives the process.

Many analysts prefer to look at risk-response-secondary risk chains within each activity, on a chain basis. However, there is some merit in taking the steps in order for the project as a whole.

In a risk management process centred around monitoring, keeping flexible, and changing objectives when appropriate, a further characteristic of actual or near disasters is a presumed primary response, or set of primary responses, which don't work. For example, on a sailing trip the radio needed for a 'mayday' may not work because the mast carrying the aerial has fallen down, and the emergency aerial, perhaps tested when new, has been stored for many years in a way which has led to its failure.

7.9 PROCESS ALTERNATIVES

In addition to the ponder approach to risk and response identification, there are a number of alternative approaches which serve to stimulate imaginative thinking and draw on the experiences of different individuals. Possible approaches include interviewing individuals, interviewing groups, various group processes such as brainstorming and decision conferencing, and approaches based on 'prompt lists' or 'checklists'.

Harnessing Creativity and Experience

The use of formal procedures to systematically capture personal experience can be very effective in identifying risks and possible responses. However, it is important that the experiences of a wide range of personnel are sought, particularly early on in the Identify phase, to ensure a comprehensive list of risk drivers is identified. Individual project managers may not have sufficient breadth of experience to provide this comprehensive view. Pooling of experience needs to include not only project managers, but specialists concerned with all aspects of projects, including, for example, designers, engineers, lawyers, financial personnel, and managers responsible for administration, sales, personnel, logistics, and so on. Even with input provided from a variety of sources, the quality of what is obtained depends heavily on the ability of individuals to recall events accurately, without selectivity. Some risks may not be identified because they were effectively managed in the past and are not so readily brought to mind.

An obvious limitation of identification based on experience is that such experience may not be entirely applicable to future projects. In particular, it may be of limited value in respect of changing project environments and novel aspects of future projects. 'The real risks are the one's you can't identify' is a common view, recognising that the 'unknown' can have a far greater effect on projects than all of the anticipated risks. For example, Hall (1975) cites examples of firms which were taken by surprise by substantial environmental changes: a mining company's assets seized by a foreign government, and the rapid rise in oil price in the early 1970s. These are perhaps examples of risks a project manager should be able to regard as 'external' project risks (as discussed in Chapter 6) and indicate a failure to identify and manage 'external' risks rather than a failure to identify and manage 'internal' project risks. Although we may wish to place responsibility for 'external' risks higher in the organisational hierarchy than the project manager, the Identify phase still needs to identify both 'external' and 'internal' risk drivers.

'Thinking the unthinkable' calls for some creativity and imagination. One of the best known techniques for fostering creativity is brainstorming, which is used to improve problem analysis by providing more possible solutions and unusual approaches to a problem. The process typically involves a group of six to twelve individuals with a variety of backgrounds in order to facilitate the analysis of a problem from different points of view. In a typical brainstorming session the emphasis is on generating a large number of ideas. In problem-solving situations it is hoped that this will increase the chances of obtaining an excellent idea. In the initial ideas-generation session, wild ideas are encouraged on the basis that ideas are easier to modify than to originate, and participants are encouraged to utilise the ideas of others to develop additional ideas. Throughout this process judgement of ideas is withheld. Ideas generated are criticised and evaluated in a later stage. Large problems may need to be made more manageable by breaking them into smaller parts, and samples should be available if products are being discussed (Whiting, 1958).

A less well-known but potentially significant technique is synectics, developed by Gordon (1956, 1968). A synectics team consists of a carefully selected group of individuals best equipped, intellectually and psychologically, to deal with problems unique to their organisation. After selection members are assigned to the synectics team on a full-time basis to solve problems for the entire organisation (Crosby, 1968). The synectics process involves two steps. The first step is 'making the strange familiar'. It requires that a problem and its implications be understood. The second step is 'making the familiar strange'. It involves distorting, inverting and transposing the problem in an attempt to view the problem from an unfamiliar perspective.

In the context of risk identification, creativity techniques such as brainstorming and synectics may be too creative. So many potential risk drivers may be identified that the project team becomes overwhelmed with the number of items to consider. Nevertheless, certain features of these approaches are attractive for risk identification purposes, including: the involvement of individuals with a variety of backgrounds, withholding judgement about identified risks, utilising the thoughts of others, and attempting to view situations from an unfamiliar perspective.

More recently a number of 'decision-conferencing' techniques have been developed (see, for example, Dennison and Morgan, 1994; Finlay and Marples, 1991; Marples and Riddle, 1992). Decision-conferencing techniques are designed to improve the efficiency and effectiveness of group processes involving the exploration of problems and decision-making situations. Typically decision-conferencing techniques involve a facilitator and real-time computer support operated by one or more analysts. The facilitator manages the group's deliberations, guiding discussion in appropriate directions as necessary. Computer support may be used to help the group develop an understanding of the different aspects of the problem being addressed and to document the proceedings. For example, Williams *et al.* (1995) describe the development of a cognitive map during a decision-conferencing process which was used to elicit an enhanced, shared understanding among the project management team of the reasons for project cost overruns.

What About Checklists or Prompt Lists?

It is important in the search for risks and possible responses not to unduly constrain the process if available experience and expertise is to be fully exploited. We explicitly advise against the use of highly structured techniques such as questionnaires which can straitjacket respondents, and strongly caution over-reliance on checklists to drive the identification of risks and responses. Given the popular appeal of checklists, this advice warrants some explanation.

A simple, 'checklist' approach to risk identification is often taken on the grounds that a 'quick and dirty' approach can yield substantial benefits despite its conceptual shortcomings. The checklist approach typically takes a view of project uncertainty which is very simple. The approach is illustrated in Table 7.4, which shows a typical list of broad headings under which individual risk drivers might be identified. Risk drivers are presumed to be independent, and are presented in a standard list. This list may be very extensive and cover a variety of categories. It may be extended as risk management experience accumulates over time.

Table 7.4 The checklist approach.

Risk driver	Impact	Likelihood	Exposure
Definition of project			
Concept and design			
Financing arrangements			
Logistics			
Local conditions			
Resource estimates			
Industrial relations			
Communications			
Project organisation			

Checklist approaches can be very effective in focusing attention on managing project risks, provided they are supported by appropriate administrative procedures. For example, a corporate risk manager or team may operate an internal audit function using the checklist as a basis for interrogating project managers at key stages in the life cycle of projects. More detailed documentation related to individual risk drivers and progress in managing them may accompany the checklist, as considered necessary.

Selection of the risk drivers to be included on a checklist is usually based on experience. An initial list may be drawn up by a small group of experienced project managers, with a view to augmenting the list in the light of new experiences. Even without the help of creativity techniques, some checklists, developed and added to over several years, can become very intimidating, particularly to new members of project teams. Worse still, the length of some checklists may actively discourage further, more detailed, selective analysis of a subset of risk drivers.

There is no doubt that the checklist approach is a convenient and relatively simple way of focusing attention on project risk management. However, the checklist approach has a number of potentially serious shortcomings, as follows:

1. Important interdependencies between risk drivers are not readily highlighted.
2. A list, particularly a long one, provides limited guidance on the relative importance of individual risk drivers.
3. Individual entries may encompass a number of important, separate risk drivers implicitly.
4. Risk drivers not on the list are likely to be ignored.
5. The list of risk drivers may be more appropriate for some projects than others.
6. Individual risk drivers may be described in insufficient detail to avoid ambiguity and varying interpretations.

7. A checklist presents an overly simplistic view of potential effects of individual risk drivers.
8. A checklist does not encourage the development of a more sophisticated attitude to assessing and quantifying risk.

The main problem is that a checklist does not offer a sufficiently structured examination of sources of risk from which to discover key risk drivers in a cost-effective manner. In our view, if any kind of 'checklist' is used it should be referred to as a 'prompt list', and used in that spirit as a catalyst and stimulant, not as a definitive statement of possibilities.

7.10 THE ONGOING NATURE OF THE IDENTIFY PHASE

A straightforward ponder approach to the Identify phase in a first pass can be useful, to guide a second pass back through the Focus phase, and to provide a basis for further passes through the Identify phase. Alternatively, more resource intensive techniques could be applied from the outset, or applied to selected areas where earlier passes suggest the additional resource commitment would be worthwhile.

Choosing between alternative identification techniques is a question of trading off different levels of analysis costs against effectiveness, a judgement which has to be made in relation to the importance of the uncertainty at all levels. It may require very different approaches in different areas, and successive passes of the process as a whole may be used to distinguish between those areas which warrant the most effective process available and those which do not.

If experience in the area being addressed is limited, more people can be used, but 'the clean sheet of paper and a pencil' is still the starting point. In terms of increasing effectiveness, and increasing cost, obvious choices are 'brainstorm'-driven group processes and individual interviews.

There is a very strong case for making the Identify phase as complete as possible before proceeding to the next phase. If risks, and responses, and associated secondary risk (response chains) are not properly understood, any subsequent risk management can be a complete waste of resources.

That said, time management pressures and the availability of key people may require getting on with some of the next phase while the Identify phase is still in progress. Delays associated with an incomplete Define phase can aggravate this difficulty. Regarding the risk management process as a project in its own right, this is 'fast tracking' in a fairly extreme form, rather like starting to put up a building before the foundations are fully in place. Any attempt to 'fast track' the risk management process needs to be managed with great care.

Chapter 8

Develop the Analysis Structure: The Structure Phase

... for want of a nail the shoe was lost; for want of a shoe the horse was lost; and for want of a horse the rider was lost.

Benjamin Franklin, 1758

8.1 INTRODUCTION

All the earlier phases in the risk management process (RMP) necessarily involve structuring. For example, the risk identification process in the Identify phase requires classification and characterisation of risks as illustrated by Example 7.1. The Structure phase is concerned with reviewing and extending this earlier structuring. The objective is to improve understanding of the relative importance of different sources of risk given identified responses, to explore more thoroughly the interactions between project activities, risks and responses, and to test the assumptions implicit or explicit in all earlier steps. This can lead to refinement of existing responses and prompt the development of new, more effective responses. It can also lead to new models or analyses.

In general, we want the structure used to be as simple as possible, but not misleadingly so. The Structure phase involves testing simplifying assumptions, and developing a more complex structure when necessary. Failure to do so can render project risk management dangerously misleading. For example, assuming a large number of risks are independent will allow their individual impacts to tend to cancel out with respect to the overall impact, on a 'swings-and-roundabouts' basis. If, in practice, they are positively correlated (things tend to go well or badly at the same time), this cancelling effect will be significantly reduced, and such circumstances need to be appreciated. Failure to structure can also lead to lost opportunities. For example, some responses to particular risks operate in practice as general responses in that they can deal with whole sets of risks, possibly all risks up to that point in a project, including risks which have not been identified. It is important to recognise the opportunities provided by such general responses.

Structuring involves three specific tasks:

1. *refine classifications*—this involves the review and development (where appropriate) of existing classifications, in the sense that a 'new' response may be defined because the understanding associated with an 'old' one may be refined, and in the sense that a new classification structure may be introduced, distinguishing between specific and general responses, for example;
2. *explore interactions*—this involves reviewing and exploring possible interdependencies or links between project activities, risks and responses, and seeking to understand the reasons for these interdependencies;
3. *develop orderings*—this involves possible revisions to the precedence relationships for project activities assumed in the Define phase. An ordering for risks is also needed for several purposes, including priorities for project and process planning, and for expository (presentation) purposes. In addition, this step involves developing a priority ordering of responses which takes impacts into account, including secondary risks.

In terms of documentation, the Structure phase involves completing the generation of a set of pictures or graphs, and defining associated mathematical models where appropriate, which capture all the key relationships in terms which are as simple as possible.

The key deliverable of the Structure phase is a clear understanding, on the part of the analysts and all users of the analysis, of the implications of any important simplifying assumptions about the relationships between risks, responses, base plan activities and all the other Ws.

Most RMPs concerned with project risk do not promote an explicit, separate, stand-alone Structure phase. Some traditional approaches, such as the basic PERT approach, do not need a separate Structure phase because the modelling approach used inherently assumes a particular simple standardised structure. However, a variety of techniques have been developed by a number of individuals and organisations in a project risk management context and in other contexts which are directly concerned with structuring.

This chapter attempts to integrate them in a six-step process as shown in Figure 8.1. Each of these steps may involve all three of the above specific tasks, as well as the four common repetitive tasks. Figure 8.1 portrays the process in a simplified form, consistent with Figures 5.1, 6.1 and 7.1.

This six-step process is more detailed than any other implicit or explicit structuring process we are aware of, and we hope it offers some useful new insights. The approach to the first five steps is comparable to the 'ponder' approach associated with a first pass through the Identify phase, prior to considering alternative processes. It is the sort of process a single analyst could take, and should use as a precursor to background process, or check on, any specific diagramming techniques adopted in the sixth step.

8.2 PONDER THE ACTIVITIES

Chapter 5 indicated the need for a summary level activity structure represented by an activity-on-node (precedence) diagram and a Gantt chart. Part of the purpose of the present step, 'ponder the activities', is to ensure that no important sources of precedence flexibility have been overlooked, and that the constraints on precedence flexibility are clearly defined where they are important. A simple, direct approach to this task is to question each and every precedence assumption, to make sure that no potentially significant assumptions of convenience are treated as inflexible imperatives. Example 5.7 illustrates the potential value in considering this explicitly: a precedence sequence was assumed so that the same resources could be used but the rationale for the precedence relationship was not documented.

Part of the rationale for the top-down risk appreciation of Chapter 6 is to clarify the difference between internal risks owned by the project and external risks owned by the corporate management team or some other party. This, together with subsequent risk and response analysis, has to be used to clarify which aspects of the project are relevant for risk management purposes. Important judgements about discarding or acquiring aspects of project responsibility may be necessary somewhere in the overall process. This step is concerned with ensuring that they are not overlooked. Important links may drive these decisions, as illustrated by the following.

Example 8.1

The engineering and construction of a major pipeline planned to take Arctic oil to markets in the USA was clearly the project manager's responsibility, but he preferred to assume that regulation risk was an 'external', corporate risk. However, preliminary risk analysis of the permissions process, using lawyers experienced in such processes, indicated that regulatory risk was a major source of project risk, and management of this risk could not be effective if it was treated separately from

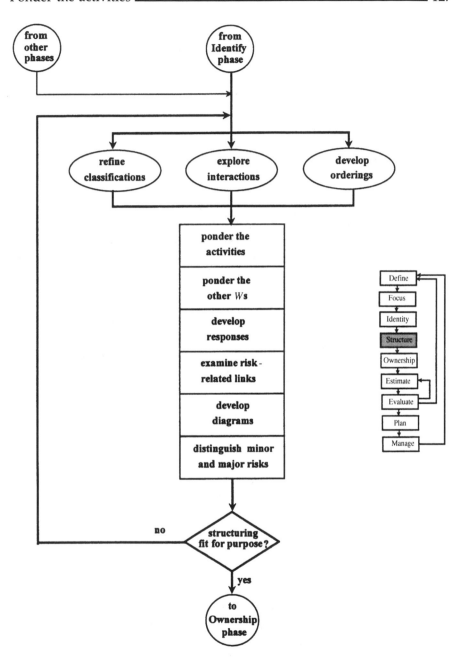

Figure 8.1   Structure phase specific tasks.

the management of technical and construction risks. Consequently, the project was redefined to recognise the need for this integrated treatment, and the regulatory risk lawyers became key players in the project team.

When clarifying project boundaries, it is often useful to recognise pervasive activities, sometimes associated with pervasive risks. For an environmentally sensitive project 'maintain public confidence' may be such an activity, linked to one or more specific permission process activities, but also linked to other specific corporate activities within and beyond the project. It may be very important to recognise such pervasive activities formally, in order to ensure basic things get done to avoid the obvious risks.

A further aspect of this step is making sure all activity definitions correspond to a common date for the 'snap-shot' that the risk management process will provide. This is a change control aspect of the risk management process (as distinct from the project). However, addressing change control for the risk management process may serve as a reminder to ensure all necessary project change control processes are in place, as part of the risk assessment of the project management process. This illustrates the cross-checking which the risk management process can stimulate. Having captured one new important idea or link, the instinctive question that should be asked is 'does this apply anywhere else?'

The goal of this step is a documented structure for the activities which reflect interactions with all other aspects of the analysis and portray the project *whichway* in terms which are both effective and efficient. Some of the interactions will be clarified later in the Structure phase, as part of the iterative nature of this phase, but drawing together all the interactions and their effects which were identified earlier in the risk management process is a sensible first step.

8.3 PONDER THE OTHER *W*s

Analogous issues may need to be dealt with for other project *W*s and some basic structural linkages between the *W*s usually require attention. Consider some illustrations.

A Gantt chart, defined by the precedence relationships between activities and base estimates for activity durations, provides a base estimate of the overall project *when*. It may be useful to ensure that formal links between Gantt charts and activity-on-node network diagrams are in place in terms of a joint computer-based model at this stage. This allows rapid assessment of the impact of a change in the *whichway* on the *when* and vice versa.

Project resource usage can be linked to Gantt charts via standard resource-planning models. If resource usage is a potential area of restriction, it may be worth using these models to explore just how much flexibility is available.

In the limit some projects are resource driven and should be managed in a manner which reflects this.

Project direct and indirect costs can be linked to Gantt charts via resource usage and cost, or directly via time-cost functions. These can be used to explore the flexibility associated with the project *when*, in overall project terms, and in relation to specific activities. The possible use of such models was alluded to in Chapter 7. At this stage ensuring such a model is not required if it is not already in place becomes an issue.

It may be useful to recognise formal links between project *whichway/when/ wherewithal* issues and the project *what*. For example, decision trees can be used to embed design change decisions into a base plan network, using what are called decision nodes as well as precedence nodes. For example, if a test on a high risk component is successful, the project proceeds using it, but if the test fails, an alternative approach is adopted.

8.4   DEVELOP RESPONSES

Responses require development at this stage for much the same reasons as the project's six Ws do. Three aspects of the process are worth highlighting:

1. distinguishing between specific and general responses;
2. ordering specific and general responses;
3. cross-checking for other links.

Distinguish Between Specific and General Responses

Some responses are specific to particular risks. For example, in relation to a pipeline 'buckle', discussed earlier in Example 7.6, 'repair' or 'abandon and start again' are feasible specific responses. Other responses may be identified in the context of a particular risk, but serve as general responses in the sense that they offer a solution to a wide range of risks. This step involves a careful and systematic search for all general responses. As a simple, practical matter, all project managers should try to make sure they have at least one general response available to deal with combinations of risks, including risks they may not have been able to identify. Consider a further extension of our 'buckle' example, from Example 7.1.

Example 8.2

It was recognised that the delay associated with a pipe buckle could be recovered by using a second lay barge working from the other end, with a submarine connection to join the two parts of the pipeline, provided that an option on a second barge was in place if needed. This response would also recover time lost due to bad weather, equipment failures, a delayed start to pipelaying, and a wide range of other difficulties, including some which may not have been identified in the first place.

Laying pipe from both ends using two barges was not a cost-effective base plan. However, it was a very powerful way to buy back lost time. This made the preservation of an option on the use of a second barge in case of need a particularly important issue. If this powerful general response was not available when needed because the importance of the option was not recognised earlier, a major failure of the proactive risk management process would have occurred.

Example 1.2 (concerned with the implications of a take-or-pay gas contract for a CCGT electric power project) provides a further illustration of the important role of this step in the process. The key here lies in being aware of any particularly useful general responses, and ensuring that they can be implemented if necessary, if it is cost effective to do so.

General responses can be viewed as a source of flexibility, building in flexibility being a key generic response to risk which deserves attention from several perspectives.

Ordering Specific and General Responses

Next it is useful to identify a preliminary ordering of responses in a preferred sequence in terms of which response is the most effective first choice, and if that fails what is the next best choice, and so on. Ordering of responses may be required for each set of specific responses associated with particular risks, and for each set of general responses associated with particular activities. While comparable to the ordering of activities in precedence terms to some extent, ordering of responses is a rather different process, with no prior formal analysis to provide its basis. In early iterations the judgements may be purely intuitive. Later on in the process analysis can be used to test these intuitions.

Examining Response-Generated Links

Often the response to one source of risk impacts other aspects of the project in important ways. If 'accept delay' is recognised as an important common response, associated impacts can be widespread and profound. One of the reasons many major projects get into serious difficulties is the failure to address knock-on impacts that delay in one activity may have for following activities.

At this stage in the analysis it can be useful to start a systematic search for all links associated with all identified responses which are reasonably likely to be implemented, using a cross-checking approach. For each of the relevant possibilities this involves asking the question 'if this response is implemented will it affect other activities, responses, or risks?'

One product of these searches will be the addition of a generic risk 'delay to preceding activities' for most activities. It is important to acknowledge this risk explicitly, especially for activities late in an overall project sequence, when the delays may be a matter of months or even years, with possible contractual implications of great importance.

Another product of these searches will be the identification of responses which are mutually exclusive or incompatible, or which affect other activities in an adverse manner. For example, if a decision is made to install the modules on an offshore oil production platform before they are complete, their completion offshore will have significant knock-on effects.

A further product of these searches will be the identification of statistical or causal dependencies which are response generated. For example, in a construction project based on the use of two cranes, if one crane should fail, and the response is to press on using only one crane, a significant increase in use may be required from the surviving crane, possibly increasing its failure probability. In the limit such dependencies can cause a cascade or domino effect. Reliability engineers are familiar with the need to understand and model such effects, but many project managers are not.

8.5   EXAMINE RISK-RELATED LINKS

This step involves reassessing all specific and pervasive risks, in the light of preferred responses and secondary risks. The basic approach is to address each risk in relation to each other risk, response or base activity and ask 'is there a link here?' In the context of responses to other risks and base activities, a useful complementary check is 'could this risk initiate problems in this response or base activity?'

Ensuring any pervasive risks have been identified as pervasive risks is an essential starting point, comparable to and linked to the search for pervasive activities, and similar to the search for general responses. Pervasive risks may be sources of risk which operate as underlying causal factors for several different 'level one' risks, or sources of risk which impact on a number of different activities or responses.

Example 8.3

When considering pipelaying in the North Sea, 'weather' was a major risk in terms of its direct impact on the ability to operate equipment. A '3 metre' barge is a barge deemed capable of working in wave conditions up to a nominal 3 metres maximum, so 'weather' in terms of wave height was a direct risk driver in relation to pipelaying performance.

   In addition to this direct effect, bad weather greatly increased the risk of a buckle, and the probability of a buckle increased significantly as the amount of work in the 'shoulder season' (early spring or late autumn) increased. It was important to recognise and model this effect.

Often dependence between different risks can be identified in causal terms. Sometimes the relationship is not clearly definable in these terms, and may be best described in terms of statistical dependence (see Chapter 11). For example, preliminary 'macro' level assessments of the relationship between capital cost items and direct cost rates associated with North Sea projects suggested an average of about 70% to 80% dependence. This level of dependence was driven by the prevailing level of construction activity and other specific market pressures as well as more general economic conditions. Attempts to describe this dependence in causal terms were not fruitful, in the sense that too many different factors were clearly driving a similar joint movement to make individual identification and modelling of the factors worthwhile. However, it became clear that it was essential to model this statistical dependence to avoid bias which otherwise made cost risk estimates meaningless and misleading to a dangerous degree.

It may be important to address dependence very carefully. Failure to do so, as in using a basic PERT model and assuming independence which does not exist, can be dangerously misleading, as well as a complete waste of time. For example, in the context of a basic PERT network, with activity A followed by activity B, the durations of activities A and B may be positively statistically dependent. If A takes longer than expected, B may also take longer than expected. This can arise because the risk drivers for A and B are common or related. Causal relationships underlying this statistical dependence might include:

1. the same contractor is employed for both activities, who if incompetent (or particularly good) on activity A will be the same for activity B;
2. the same equipment is used for both;
3. the same labour force is used for both;
4. the same optimistic (or pessimistic) estimator provided estimates for both activity duration distributions.

An important form of dependency is 'knock-on' or 'ripple' effects. In the simple example above, when things go wrong in activity A, the cost of A goes up and the delays impact on B. The cost of B then increases as a consequence of contingency responses to stay on target. As a consequence of contingency responses, which induce negative time dependence, the positive statistical dependence between the durations of A and B tends to disappear from view. However, the negative dependence introduced into the activity structure by contingency planning induces strong positive dependence between associated costs. If A costs more than expected, B tends to cost very much more than expected, because of the need to keep the project on target, quite apart from other market-driven sources of dependence. Put another way, cost and duration modelling of uncertainty which does not explicitly consider contingency planning tends to estimate time (duration) risk erroneously (usually optimistically and fails to structure or explain it, and it tends grossly to underestimate direct cost risk. Considering the impact of contingency planning will clarify apparent time (duration) risk, and increase apparent direct cost risk.

Common causes of 'knock-on' effects are design changes and delays, which not only have a direct impact but also cause 'ripple' effects which are termed 'delay and disruption'. Often direct impacts can be assessed fairly readily in terms such as the number of man-hours required to effect a change in design drawing and the man-hours needed to implement the immediate change in the project works. 'Ripple' effects are more difficult to assess and may involve 'snowballing' effects such as altered work sequences, conflicting facility and manpower requirements, skill dilution, undetected work errors, and so on.

Example 8.4

In 1991 apparently small changes in the design of fire doors on Channel Tunnel rolling stock was expected to lead to a delay of up to six months in providing a full service for car and coach passengers, substantially reducing expected revenue for Eurotunnel, operators of the tunnel. The problem was caused by the insistence of British and French authorities that the width of the fire doors separating the double-deck car shuttles should be widened from 28 inches to 32 inches (Taylor, 1991).

Example 8.5

Cooper (1980) has described how a computer simulation based on influence diagrams was used to resolve a $500 million shipbuilder claim against the US Navy. By using the simulation to diagnose the causes of cost and schedule overruns on two multi-billion dollar shipbuilding programmes, Ingalls Shipbuilding (a division of Litton Industries Inc.) quantified the costs of disruption stemming from US Navy responsible delays and design changes. In the settlement reached in June 1978, Ingalls received a net increase in income from the US Navy of $447 million. It was the first time the US Navy had given such a substantial consideration to a delay and disruption claim.

The need to appreciate fully the implications of 'knock-on' effects in a project is clear. As the last example illustrates, this process of appreciation can be greatly facilitated by appropriate diagramming of activity–risk–response structures and their interdependencies.

8.6   DEVELOP DIAGRAMS

The use of a range of diagrams is advantageous throughout the Structure phase to document and help develop insights in the structuring process. Precedence networks and Gantt charts are key documents because they capture key aspects of the base plan. However, other diagrams are important in terms of capturing a range of wider considerations. For example, if a formal model is used to link Gantt charts to resource usage and associated resource constraints, these issues will require appropriate diagrams. If direct/indirect cost models are used, other standard diagrams will be required. Of particular concern here is diagrams which summarise our understanding of risk/response structures, and links between activities, risks and responses.

Ensuring that the earlier steps in the Structure phase result in a set of diagrams which summarise the classification, ordering and linking issues is extremely important. Complexity is inherent in most projects, but it must be made manageable to deal with it effectively, and a summary diagram structure which all those who need to be involved can discuss as a basis for shared understanding is very important. Organisations which have used such diagrams often stop doing so because they are difficult to construct, but start again because they realise they are difficult to produce precisely because they force a proper disciplined understanding which is otherwise not achieved. One such diagram is the risk/response diagram of Figure 8.2, which was initially developed for offshore oil projects, and subsequently adopted by a range of organisations.

In principle an annotation process of the kind discussed earlier could be used to drive a computer-generated version of Figure 8.2, but manual approaches, with computer graphics when appropriate, have been employed to date.

Example 8.6

Figure 8.2 provides an illustration of risk/response diagrams in the context of the fabrication of an offshore project jacket (the structure which sits in the water to hold production and accommodation facilities), the first section of a diagram which went on in the same vein for several pages. The '7' in the large triangle (arrow head) indicates this is the start of the diagram for activity 7 (jacket fabrication). The '7b' label at the end of the diagram's horizontal centre line(s) indicates a continuation to a further page (diagram section) which will start with '7b' on the left-hand side.

Primary risks are represented by circles along the diagram's horizontal centre line(s). The first risk (labelled 1) in a time of realisation sense is 'yard not available', because another jacket is still under construction in the contracted yard (a dry dock construction area like a big shipyard), and our jacket has to await its completion. A close second in this time of realisation sense (labelled 2) is 'mobilisation problems': we can get access to the yard, but it has not been used for some time, so it will take time to get up to speed.

These two risks are mutually exclusive—we can have one or the other, but not both, the reason they appear in parallel. All the other risks are in series, indicating they can all occur, without implying additive or multiplicative effects at this stage. Their sequence is nominal. Dependence relationships could be indicated on the diagram and lead to ordering risks, but independence is assumed with respect to those risks shown.

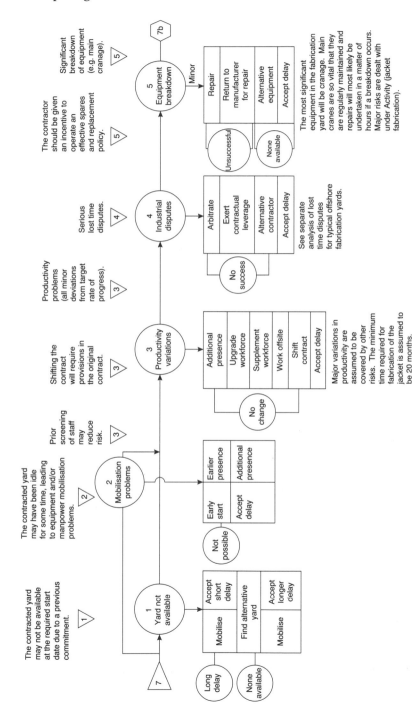

Figure 8.2 Risk/response diagram.

Links in this diagram are limited to links in from earlier activities discussed in notes along the top of the diagram. Links could appear as arrows between risks or responses, with links out to other diagrams if appropriate. Identification of all these links, dependence and ordering issues is part of the Structure phase steps identified earlier.

Responses are represented by boxes, ordered to reflect the preferred implementation sequence. Secondary risks are represented by circles by the side of primary responses. For example, if the yard is not available, the preferred response is to 'mobilise' (get ready to start work, making temporary use of another site) and 'accept a short delay'. The secondary risk here is a 'long delay', which would lead to the secondary response 'find an alternative yard'. The secondary risk here is 'none available', at which point 'mobilise' and 'accept a long delay' is the only remaining option.

These responses and secondary risks illustrate further the complexity of the generic types of response we may have to consider to capture the most effective response to risk. They also make it clear why a diagram to capture the structure provided earlier is a very good test of understanding, which may lead to redefinitions in earlier steps.

The final risk on the last page of the risk/response diagram for each activity is a collector/dummy risk which represents residual risk after specific responses. The ordered boxes which appear below this residual risk collector are the general responses. The importance of the structuring process as a whole is highlighted by the need for this feature. It also indicates that the residual risk of real interest is the combined effect of all individual risks (net of specific responses), *less the effect of general responses* (to emphasise further the importance of structure).

Implicit in the Identify phase is a very complex decision tree which will remain an implicit, ill-understood 'bushy mess' unless the structure phase is pursued until risk/response diagrams like that of Figure 8.2 can be drawn. Completion of such diagrams by risk analysts, and subsequent verification by all relevant players on the project team, is a watershed in the overall risk management process.

Fault Trees and Event Trees

Two common approaches used in a system-failure analysis context, which underlie the Figure 8.2 approach, are fault-tree analysis and event-tree analysis. It can be useful to adopt these approaches in their basic or standard forms as a preliminary or an alternative to the use of risk/response diagram formats like Figure 8.2. A good classic reference is NUREG (1975).

Event-tree analysis involves identifying a sequence of events that could follow from the occurrence of particular risk driver configurations, and representing the possible scenarios in a tree diagram where each branch represents an alternative possibility.

In fault-tree analysis the process is reversed, working backwards from a particular event (known as the top event) in an attempt to identify all possible sequences of events giving rise to the top event.

Ishikawa or fishbone diagrams (Ishikawa, 1986) adopt a similar approach, showing necessary inputs to a particular final position.

Influence Diagrams

In event-tree and fault-tree analysis there is still the problem of ensuring completeness in the set of possible failure modes. A more versatile representation of causes and effects can be achieved with influence diagrams, as used in 'systems dynamics' (Forrester, 1958, 1961; Richardson and Pugh, 1981; Senge, 1990) and 'cognitive mapping' (Eden, 1988). One advantage of influence diagrams over tree diagrams is that much more complex interactions can be shown, including feedback and feedforward loop effects.

Example 8.7

Williams *et al.* (1995a, 1995b) describe the study of a large design and manufacturing engineering project, undertaken as part of a 'delay and disruption' litigation. Design changes and delays in design approval would have caused delay to the project and in order to fulfil tight time constraints, management had to increase parallel development in the network logic, reducing delay but setting up feedback loops that markedly increased the total project spend. Cognitive mapping using specialist computer software called 'Graphics Cope' was used to elicit the relationships. The cognitive map contained some 760 concepts, 900 links and over 90 positive feedback loops were identified, illustrating the complex dynamics of the real situation. Figure 8.3 summarises some of the key feedback loops.

Figure 8.3 Key feedback loops in Example 8.7.

The situation in Example 8.7 is similar to that described in Example 8.5. It is unfortunate that the very considerable benefits of constructing cognitive maps to explore risk/response interdependencies were sought *after* these projects got into serious difficulties, rather than *before*.

Influence diagrams such as Figure 8.3 are essentially a qualitative tool, although they can provide a starting point for quantitative, systems dynamics models. They do not indicate the magnitudes or the timing of influence relationships which would be quantified in systems dynamics model simulations. Thus a link between two factors X and Y does not indicate the strength of the link, whether it is continuous or intermittent, and whether the impact on the influenced factors is immediate or delayed. Nevertheless, an influence diagram can be a useful aid to understanding a complex situation, particularly if effectively interpreted. It explores positive and negative feedback loops in a way Figure 8.2 does not accommodate, providing a very useful complementary or alternative technique. Diffenbach (1982) suggests a number of guidelines for interpreting influence diagrams:

1. *Isolated factors.* A factor not linked to any other factor suggests either that the isolated factor is not relevant to the depicted situation or that not all important links and factors have been identified.

2. *Influencing only factors.* A factor that influences other factors but is not itself subject to influence from other factors prompts questions about overlooked links and factors which might influence this factor.

3. *Influenced only factors.* A factor that does not influence any other factors prompts questions about overlooked links and factors by which this factor might influence.

4. *Secondary and higher order consequences.* Chains of influence suggest possible secondary and higher order consequences of a change in a given factor in the chain.

5. *Indirect influences of A on B.* Chains can reveal potentially significant indirect influences of one factor on another.

6. *Multiple influences of A on B.* One factor may influence another in more than one way. These multiple influences could be direct (by link) or indirect (by chain) and of the same or opposite sign.

7. *Self-regulated loops.* A chain with an odd number of negative links which cycles back to meet itself is a self-regulating, negative loop. Successive cycles of influences result in counteracting pressures.

8. *Vicious circles*. A chain with zero or an even number of negative links which cycles back to meet itself is a self-reinforcing, positive loop. Since it is unlikely that vicious circles will operate endlessly, unresisted by countervailing forces, one should look for one or more negative loops that are interrelated with the positive loop by means of a common factor.

The process of construction and interpretation of influence diagrams goes beyond mere identification of risk drivers and cause-effect relationships. This process also assists in identifying potentially important sources of uncertainty, such as the behaviour of risk drivers associated with vicious circles, or particular factors which influence many other factors either directly or indirectly. Increased understanding of cause–effect relationships can also prompt the formulation of additional risk responses.

More General Soft Systems Models

The use of influence diagrams can be viewed as a special (reasonably 'hard') version of a range of 'soft' approaches usually referred to as soft systems, soft Operational Research, or other labels which span the two, like problem (situation) structuring methods (Rosenhead, 1989; Checkland and Scholes, 1990). All these ideas are directly relevant to the Structure phase.

8.7   DISTINGUISH MINOR AND MAJOR RISKS

If the risk management process is not to become an overwhelming task in the face of a large number of identified risk drivers and complex cause–effect relationships, then it is necessary to assess the relative significance of different sources of uncertainty so as to guide subsequent risk management effort.

In particular it can be useful to formally identify some risks as 'minor' at this stage, to eliminate them further from consideration (if their impact is negligible), or to collect them together into a 'risks treated collectively' category or pool of the 'productivity variations' variety, leaving a relatively small residual of 'risks treated separately' which are all 'major' risks by definition.

The basic rules of thumb for collective/separate treatment are:

1. put all high-impact risks into the separate category if their responses are unique, and consider treating high-impact risks with a common response as a single risk;
2. put all low-impact risks with similar or common responses into the collective category;

3. consider all intermediate cases on their individual merits, in terms of the value of insights expected from separate treatment versus the cost/effort/time required.

Statistical dependence is one of the issues which can make judgements related to the third category complex.

There is a natural tendency simply to omit recording some risks altogether in the Identify phase because they are immediately considered to be of a minor nature. The merit in not doing so, leaving such judgements until now, is to ensure that:

1. there is a complete audit trail, to protect organisations and careers should these risks occur and questions are asked about their identification;
2. apparently minor problems which do not have an effective response are less likely to be overlooked;
3. prior to any estimation effort, risks are given an effective and efficient estimation structure, with separate treatment of risks which are worth separate treatment, and collective treatment of those which are not;
4. the nature of the risks treated collectively is clarified, with a rich range of examples which makes underestimation of the effect of such risks less likely.

A common alternative to both the minor/major risk distinction and later quantitative risk assessment is the use of probability impact matrix (or grid) diagrams, as illustrated by Figure 8.4

Such grids involve characterising risks as specific risk events with a probability of occurrence and a degree of impact. Typically probabilities and impacts are assessed qualitatively in terms of scenarios with labels like 'High' (H), 'Medium' (M) or 'Low' (L). Figure 8.4 illustrates such a grid where risks in the boxes labelled 1, 2 and 3 are the highest, intermediate and lowest priority respectively.

Some of the shortcomings of applying a grid approach to ranking risk drivers are fairly obvious, and result from the limitations of checklists indicated in Chapter 7. These shortcomings will be especially severe if a simple checklist is the only identification approach used and there is no detailed consideration of possible responses and interdependencies.

As part of a comprehensive Structure phase, the grid approach can be regarded as a refinement of a simple minor/major categorisation. Using it as such, and as a precursor to quantitative estimation, can be useful. However, it is usually more effective to concentrate on the major/minor distinction first, then go straight to the quantitative estimation of Chapter 10, for reasons discussed later.

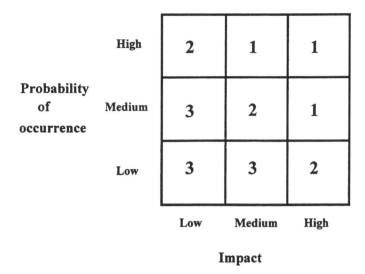

Impact

Figure 8.4 A probability impact grid.

8.8 CONCLUSION

The Structure phase as described here is a very important part of the risk management process. It is about transforming the information generated earlier into a qualitative model of project risk, ideally summarised in diagrams, with underlying computer-based models to handle changes where appropriate and feasible. The richer the information generated in the Identify phase, the greater the need for care in the Structure phase, to provide a sound basis for inferences to follow.

In the authors' experience some key points to bear in mind in the Structure phase are:

1. independence, or lack of it, is one of the most important assumptions made in any modelling of uncertainty;
2. the most effective way to understand uncertainty dependence is to model it in causal terms;
3. 'statistical' dependence is best thought of as a causal dependence of several kinds which cannot be sorted out, or which it is not cost effective to sort out at this stage;
4. in a cost dimension high levels of dependence are endemic, and in an activity dimension important instances of dependence are endemic;
5. if dependence cannot be estimated effectively it may be better not to attempt any quantitative analysis: assuming independence will allow most of the uncertainty to cancel out, promoting unfounded optimism,

while assuming perfect positive correlation will allow none of the uncertainty to cancel out, promoting unfounded pessimism.

As with other phases of the risk management process the Structure phase is typically an iterative process. In particular, we cannot assess the importance of some risks until we have identified responses and considered possible interactions between risks and responses. However, some assessment of the importance of identified risks is necessary to guide subsequent, more detailed evaluation and refinement of responses.

Changes to the Structure phase outputs may be triggered by changes to identified risks and responses later in the process. However, the Structure phase should always be as complete as possible given the progress made in the Identify phase before moving on to the Ownership phase.

Chapter 9

Clarify Ownership Issues: The Ownership Phase

It is an equal failing to trust everybody, and to trust nobody.

18th century English proverb

9.1 INTRODUCTION

In principle, making sure that every risk has an owner, and a manager, is recognised as basic, standard good practice for project risk management. In practice, this worthy ambition is not often achieved. One obvious reason for this is a failure to identify risks early in the project life cycle (PLC) which later prove to be a serious source of difficulties. Another is a failure to identify relationships between risks which prove to be a serious source of difficulty. These are failures of earlier phases in the risk management process (RMP). However, even if risks are duly identified and links between them appreciated, effective management of these risks requires appropriate and effective allocation of risks to those parties involved in a project.

Failures of risk management associated with the ownership and allocation of risks tend to arise because this activity is not recognised explicitly, or not given sufficient attention. This chapter attempts to provide a framework for efficient and effective risk allocation processes, to facilitate effective risk management. Explicit treatment of the Ownership phase can have such great importance that it may be worth treating this phase as a project in its own right, in the same way as the earlier Focus phase.

As indicated earlier, this chapter assumes a 'client' perspective, one organisation with one project, and RMP initiated at the Plan stage of the PLC.

The Ownership phase described here has three purposes:

1. to distinguish the risks and associated responses that the client is prepared to own and manage from those the client wants other organisations such as contractor(s) to own or manage;
2. to allocate responsibility for managing risks and responses owned by the client to named individuals;
3. to approve, if appropriate, ownership/management allocations controlled by contractor(s).

The first of these three purposes should be achieved before moving on to a first cut at the Estimate and Evaluate phases of the RMP. Some organisations will consider this first purpose as a part of project strategy, which the Define phase will identify. Deferring achievement of the other purposes until later is usually appropriate, as indicated by Figure 4.2. This suggests modest effort initially, increasing in subsequent cycles as the first purpose is replaced by the second and third.

The deliverables provided by the Ownership phase are clear allocations of ownership and management responsibility, efficiently and effectively defined, and legally enforceable as far as practicable. The tasks required to provide this deliverable may be very simple or extremely complex, depending upon contract strategy. For expository purposes we assume no fixed corporate contracting policy. In these circumstances the Ownership phase involves two specific tasks:

1. *scope the policy*—this task concentrates on issues such as what are the objectives of the ownership strategy (the *why*), which parties are being considered (the *who*), and what kinds of risk require allocation (the *what*). This task culminates in a policy for risk allocation issues;
2. *plan the contracts*—this task builds on the policy definition of the *what*, considers the details of the approach (the *whichway*), the instruments (the *wherewithal*), and the timing (the *when*). This task transforms risk ownership policy into operational contracts.

Figure 9.1 elaborates the structure of the Ownership phase. It portrays starting the Ownership phase in *scope the policy* mode. Each of the first three Ws is addressed in turn, in detail, with outline attention to the last three Ws. A specific *assess* task initiates possible loops back to the first three Ws, until the policy is 'fit for purpose'. The process then moves on in *plan the contracts* mode, working within the policy with respect to each of the last four Ws. This phase concludes with two specific *assess* tasks. If necessary

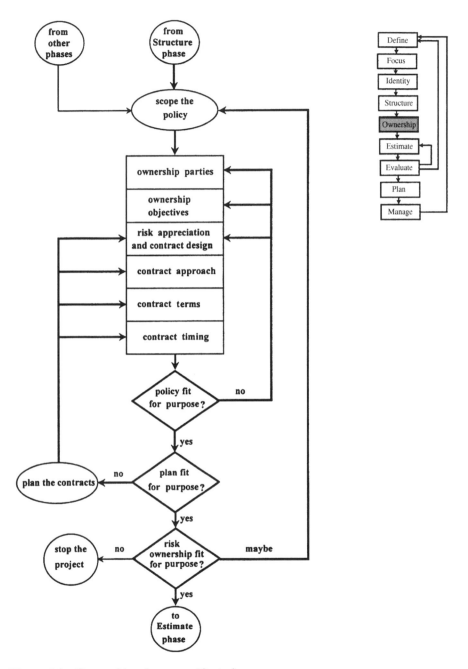

Figure 9.1 Ownership phase specific tasks.

the process loops back to the last four Ws as appropriate to fill in gaps until the contract plan is considered 'fit for purpose'. A final specific *assess* task considers more fundamental overall ownership issues, with stopping the project as an option.

Figure 9.1 is an idealisation to capture and illustrate the spirit of the process, recognising that in practice more complex processes may be effective. The difficulty separating risk appreciation and contract design issues at policy and plan levels is the basis of the three separate specific *assess* tasks put together in sequence. As in previous phases, recurring common *document*, *verify*, *assess* and *report* tasks are not shown, to keep the diagram simple.

9.2   IDENTIFY OWNERSHIP PARTIES, THE *WHO*

The first step in *scope the policy* involves identifying parties who could be expected to own some project-related risk. An obvious starting point is the list of key players identified in the Define phase of the RMP. As noted in Chapter 5, this list includes agents of the client such as contractors and subcontractors, and 'other stakeholders' such as parent organisations, regulatory bodies, competitors and customers. Clearly not all of these parties are relevant for ownership purposes, although potential owners of risk need not be confined to the client and agents of the client. For example, customers might be potential owners of some risks. Other potential risk owners might have been implicitly identified in the consideration of responses in a first cut of the Identify phase of the RMP. For example, additional third parties such as potential insurers need to be identified at this point. It is also important to identify likely groups and individuals within the client, contractors, subcontractors, and third parties, such as insurers.

Within the client's organisation, it is clearly important to distinguish between 'the project' and 'the board'. Further subdivisions within the project are often important, in terms of the control budget structure and the associated ownership of risk. For example, if the project is an information systems (IS) project undertaken by an external third party and managed by an internal IS group for an internal client, risk associated with the external third party, the internal client, the IS group and the board may need to be identified and managed separately.

Within 'the contractors', even if there is a 'prime contractor' (to whom all subcontractors report), similar issues can be involved.

9.3   CLARIFY OWNERSHIP OBJECTIVES, THE *WHY*

From a client's point of view, the fundamental reason for being concerned about who owns what risks is that this will influence how risks are managed and whether risks are managed in the client's best interest. This suggests that a client needs to consider explicitly who might own the various project risks and make conscious decisions about how risks should be allocated to various parties.

Risk allocation always occurs in any situation where more than one party is responsible for the execution of a project. Just as roles and responsibilities are allocated to the parties concerned, so too are the risks associated with the enterprise. However, allocation of risk can take place by default and need not be explicit, intentional or clearly articulated. The consequences of an allocation, particularly a default allocation, may not be fully appreciated, and the manner in which allocated risks are to be managed may be unclear, if they are managed at all.

Risk allocation is a very important aspect of ownership because it can strongly influence the motivation of parties and the extent to which risk is assessed and managed by each party. Insofar as individual parties perceive risks differently, and have different abilities and motivations to manage risk, then their approach to risk management will be different. In particular, any one party is likely to try to manage risk primarily for their own benefit, perhaps to the disadvantage of other parties.

Effective risk management requires that there is:

1. a clear specification of the required activities and associated risks;
2. a clear perception of the risks being borne by each party;
3. sufficient capability and experience to manage the risks;
4. adequate incentive to manage the risks.

The rationale for allocating risk between the client and other parties ought to be based on meeting these conditions as far as possible. Failure to meet any one of these conditions, for example by inappropriate allocation of risk or failure to allow adequate financial rewards for bearing a risk, is very likely to bring about added moral hazard risks for the client.

Example 9.1

Oil majors with North Sea projects in the 1970s typically took a very 'hands-on' approach to risk management. They paid their contractors on a piece or day rate basis for pipelaying, for example. Some risks, like bad weather, they left to their contractors to manage, monitoring performance, but they took the cost consequences of unexpected bad weather and all other external risks of this kind, like buckles. The rationale was based on the size and unpredictability of risks like buckles, the ability of the oil companies to bear such risks relative to the ability of the contractors to bear them, and the charges contractors would have insisted upon if they had to bear them.

By the late 1980s, many similar projects involved fixed price contracts for laying a pipeline. The rationale was based on contractor experience of the problems, and lower charges because of this experience and market pressures.

This example illustrates the way the rationale for a particular risk allocation policy can change within a given organisation, over the dimension 'hands-on' to 'hands-off eyes-on' (as the use of fixed price contracts is referred to in the UK Ministry of Defence).

In principle, decisions about the allocation of risk ought to be motivated by a search for risk efficiency and favourable trade-offs between risk and expected performance as described in Chapter 3. An obvious example is decisions about purchasing insurance cover. Insurance is best regarded as one way of developing contingency plans (one of the nine types of risk response listed in Table 7.3), where payment of insurance premia ensures the ability to make some level of restitution in the event that an insured risk eventuates. The insured party may take steps to reduce the possibility of loss or mitigate the impact of any insured risk, and reasonable efforts to do this may be required by the insurer. Insurers are third parties who take on specific risks with a view to making a profit. If the premium they can charge is not greater than the expected cost of the risk, giving them a positive expected profit, they will not take on the risk. In this sense they are subcontractors, competing for risks which might be better left with other contractors or the client.

The basic maxim for risk efficient insurance purchase is only insure risks which you cannot afford to take, because an uncovered event would cause serious financial distress which would distort other basic operations, or because dealing with an uncovered event would cause other forms of distress it is worth paying to avoid. For example, employment injury liability insurance may be worthwhile on both counts. A project may not be able to meet large claims without financial distress, but it may be just as important to avoid a position of conflict with employees over claims.

Given the opportunity, a client should favour risk efficient allocation of risk between parties to a project which simultaneously reduces risk and improves project performance for the client, be it in terms of lower expected cost or higher expected profits or some other measure of performance. However, in client–contractor relationships at least, a common aim of clients appears to be to avoid risk as far as possible by allocating as many risks as possible to contractors. Such behaviour is often encouraged by legal advisers concerned to put their client's legal interests first. In legal circles debate about risk allocation is usually about clarifying and ensuring the effectiveness of allocation mechanisms such as contract clauses, rather than concern with whether an intended allocation is appropriate.

If one party, typically the client, is in a position to allocate risks, then this party may regard allocating all risks to other parties as a perfectly acceptable allocation, even if the other parties are not very happy with this. The weakness in this simple but extreme strategy is that it may not produce risk management that is in the interests of the allocating party, either by design or neglect of the other parties. Moreover, in many situations, a careful consideration of risk allocation can produce a situation where risk is managed effectively for the benefit of all parties concerned. This issue is explored in more detail in Chapter 15.

As a second step in the Ownership phase of RMP, clarifying ownership objectives is not usually about project specific issues. The key principles are generic ones, and they are usually equally applicable to all projects undertaken by the organisation. Nevertheless it is useful to distinguish this step to ensure that these principles are duly acknowledged by the appropriate personnel.

9.4 RISK APPRECIATION AS A BASIS FOR CONTRACT DESIGN, THE *WHAT*

As noted in Section 6.4, an important reason for undertaking a top-down risk appreciation of the project context in the Focus phase of the RMP is to determine where the limits of the project manager's responsibilities for managing project-related risk lie. This involves deciding what risks are 'internal' to the project and therefore the project manager's responsibility to manage, and which risks are 'external' to the project and therefore risks which the project manager is not expected to manage.

Ownership of a risk implies responsibility for the management of that risk as well as responsibility for bearing its consequences. However, in certain circumstances it may be important to distinguish between responsibility for managing a risk and responsibility for bearing the consequences of the risk. In particular it may be desirable to allocate these responsibilities to different parties, recognising that the party best able to manage a risk may not be the party best able to bear the consequences of that risk. Thus, while one party, perhaps a contractor, may be best placed to manage a source of risk, it may not be appropriate or desirable for that party to bear all the associated financial risk. The following example illustrates the nature of this issue. It is explored in more detail in Chapter 15.

Example 9.2

An example of a risk which raised this responsibility issue occurred in the context of a late 1970s analysis of a North Sea oil pipeline which had to cross three other existing pipelines. Given the way lay barges were positioned, with lots of anchor in front under considerable tension, the risk of damaging one (or more) of the existing pipelines was seen as significant. The consequences, if one was fractured, were very significant. Apart from the environmental impact and clean up costs, and compensation required by the other pipeline owners, pipelaying equipment would have to be diverted from the task in hand to sort out the damaged pipeline, which would involve the loss of a weather window and cost a season.

This risk was a good example of large impact, low-to-medium probability risks that do not average out with other risks. They either happen or they do not, with a major impact either way relative to the expected outcome. For example, assume a £200 million impact in this case, a 0.10 probability, an expected cost of £200 million × 0.10 = £20 million. If this risk had been quantified and rolled into the analysis used by the corporate board to set the budget for the project, the implicit effect would have been to give the project manager ownership of this risk, with a budget of £20 million. If the risk was subsequently realised, this budget would not have sufficed and the project manager would have had to go back to the board for more money. If the risk was not subsequently realised, the project would have had £20 million to spend on other things which the board would not have appreciated. Whatever the outcome, it would not be appropriate to give the project this kind of risk.

There was a clear need to recognise the importance of this risk. It was clearly important to develop procedures and plans to avoid it being realised. It was also important to develop contingency plans should it happen. It might have been worth indicating to those responsible for avoiding the risk what sort of unpleasant futures might be forthcoming if the risk was realised. But there was no point in making the project responsible for it with an extra £20 million in the budget. Responsibility for this risk in financial terms had to be retained by the board, and managed along with a portfolio of other similar risks associated with other projects.

In addition to a simple distinction between project management and board level responsibilities, some organisations are moving towards distinguishing between risks held by the managing director, risks held by those at the sharp end of specific aspects of the project, and risks held by a number of intermediate management levels, in the context of control budgets which recognise the target, expected value and commitment distinctions discussed in Chapter 3. Control budgets and associated risk allocations in a hierarchical structure represent an interlocking set of organisational agreements, all of which can be viewed as 'contracts' for present purposes. External contracts and subcontracts with other organisations extend this structure. It is important to define, and in some instances to design, this structure. Example 9.2 illustrates what is involved in terms of one major risk across one boundary, its virtue as an example resting in part on its simplicity.

9.5   SELECT A CONTRACT APPROACH, THE *WHICHWAY*

The *plan the contracts* specific task involves considering how the ownership strategy is to be implemented, in terms of formal and informal contracts, first addressing the contract approach or *whichway* question, to expand on the closely related *what* or contract design question.

The contract approach is highly dependent on the parties involved in working on the project and the way in which project tasks have been divided and distributed between these parties. For example, the novelty and technical nature of a construction project may warrant the employment by the client of an architect, engineer, quantity surveyor, prime contractor and a variety of subcontractors. The presence of these parties may imply clear allocation of particular risks to particular parties. A very different and perhaps simpler risk allocation strategy is implied for a client who opts for a 'turnkey' contract to procure a building, where the client has only to deal with a single prime contractor.

In a given project, different divisions of labour and organisational arrangements may be possible, and the choice between these may be usefully driven by risk management considerations, as well as the physical nature of the project works. For example, a large construction project which Chapman was associated with recently involved a risk management process which included examining all the major components of the project in relation to their key risks and responses with a view to minimising the number of risks and responses which would require managing across contractor boundaries. The number of contractors and the division of work between them were designed to minimise the risk associated with the risk management process during construction. A very important consideration is that the need for separate parties to a project to work efficiently and effectively together creates associated sources of risk which also need to be allocated and managed.

Example 9.3
Management contracting systems involve the employment by the client of an external management organisation to coordinate the design and construction phases of the project and to control the construction work. The concept underlying management contracting systems is that the management contractor joins the client's team of professional advisers and devotes his efforts unequivocally to pursuing the client's objectives. He is able to do this by being employed on a fee basis so that there is no clash of interest on his part between looking after the client and protecting his own earnings. He normally accepts no liability for the site works other than any detriment to the client which is attributable to the management contractor's negligence.

The management contractor is normally brought in at an early stage in the preconstruction period in order that he can contribute his management and construction expertise to the design, and prepare a construction schedule linking works packages with design decisions. Competitive tenders are sought by the management contractor from construction contractors for specific packages of construction work. As the construction work is let in a succession of packages, each one can reflect the particular conditions and risks applicable to that part of the work. In this way the risks can be looked at separately and decisions made upon the extent to which a risk needs to be incorporated in a work package contract.

Four types of management contracting system can be distinguished in the construction industry:

1. construction management;
2. management contracting;
3. design and manage;
4. design, manage and construct.

The basic form of management contracting involves the management contractor directly employing works contractors to undertake all construction packages. The management contractor does no construction work himself. He exercises coordination, time, cost, and quality control over the work package contractors and provides facilities for their common use. The permanent works are constructed under a series of construction contracts placed by the management contractor after approval by the client.

A variation of this system which is more frequently used in North America is termed 'construction management'. It involves the management contractor performing the same coordination and control functions, but contracts for construction are formed between the client and the work package contractors. This arrangement gives the client more direct contractual involvement with the construction work, but can reduce the managerial impact of the management contractor.

Recognition of the importance of managing design has led to the emergence of a third variation, the 'design-and-manage' system. This system gives the management organisation a specific responsibility to oversee the design work on behalf of the client. This responsibility is normally exercised in a purely professional manner, and gives the management organisation a seniority among the designers that ostensibly enables it to impose a stronger discipline.

The fourth kind of management contracting system, 'design, manage and construct', places a degree of responsibility upon the management contractor for the performance of the construction operations. It moves the management contractor away from a purely professional role in which he can only be held liable for his negligence in performing his duties. The additional liability can occur in two ways. First, the management contractor is allowed to take on some elements of the construction work using his own workforce. Second, he is expected to accept some responsibility for achieving cost and time targets, and for meeting quality specifications.

The above example illustrates the potential complexity of risk ownership issues when considering the various forms of management contracting systems. Because the parties in each system and the contractual arrangements between them are different, each system gives rise to somewhat different sets of risks and allocations of risk, and each system varies in its ability to manage project risks. Choice between the different systems is not clear cut and depends on a variety of factors including the nature of the project and performance criteria, the skills of the management contractor, and the role the client is willing to take during project execution. A detailed discussion of these issues is given in Curtis, Ward and Chapman (1991).

9.6   SELECT CONTRACT TERMS, THE *WHEREWITHAL*

Wherewithal in an ownership phase context can be associated with contract details, including budgets, fees and penalties, the operational details which make internal or external contracts work. The contract may identify and allocate certain project risks explicitly, but very often particular risks are not identified and allocation of risks is implicit in the nature and size of contract payment terms. In these cases, the consequences of such allocation may not be fully appreciated, and, in particular, the manner in which risk is to be managed may be unclear.

This is one reason for the development of a wide range of 'standard' forms of contract which serve as familiar 'models' for the contracting process. For example, the New Engineering Contract has been designed so that its implementation should contribute to rather than detract from the effectiveness of management of the work. This is based on the proposition that foresighted, cooperative management of the interactions between the parties can shrink the risks inherent in construction work (Institute of Civil Engineers, 1995). The NEC main options offer six different basic allocations of risk between the 'employer' and contractor, and whatever variations in strategy between different contracts within a project are adopted, the majority of the procedures will be common to all contracts.

Internal contracting, models for establishing budget and target setting mechanisms, have not received the same attention, but the problems can be equally complex and equally important. Intelligent choices which reflect the circumstances can be crucial to effective and efficient allocation and subsequent management of risks.

9.7 DETERMINE CONTRACT TIMING ISSUES, THE *WHEN*

'When should transfer of responsibility take place?' is an important basic question with a number of associated issues which need early consideration. Where project risks are ongoing, answering this question can substantially alter the allocation of risk between parties. Obvious examples include the length of warranties, or the determination of 'vesting' or handover dates. Such issues cannot be addressed in detail until the earlier steps in this phase have been addressed comprehensively. However, failure to consider them early enough in the risk management process can lead to project delays and contract arrangements which are not risk efficient.

A further important (but often neglected) aspect of ownership assessment timing is the time allowed for tenders and contract negotiations. In particular, bidding contractors ought to be given sufficient time to price for the risks they will be expected to carry. This issue is discussed in more detail in Chapter 15.

9.8 ASSESS OWNERSHIP AS A WHOLE

Separate *assess* tasks for the policy and the contracts as shown in Figure 9.1 need no further comment, but the final *assess* task does. It provides a convenient place to pause and consider the risks associated with the contracting strategy as a whole as well as individual planned contracts developed to this point, and the associated risks to the client. The possibility of multiple contracts with many parties makes this overall integrative assessment crucial. It is worth explicitly addressing the possibility of stopping at this stage, or going back to rescope the policy, or passing on to the next phase.

9.9 THE ONGOING NATURE OF THE OWNERSHIP PHASE

This is a short chapter, because the issues are not usually treated as a part of the mainstream process of project risk management, and we do not want to unduly interrupt the flow of the other chapters. However, the issues involved are of fundamental importance. We believe providing the skeleton of an elaborated process is important as a part of basic RMP. These issues warrant further consideration. Some further consideration is provided later, in Chapters 12 and 15.

The Ownership phase should start early at the policy level, although contract planning at a detailed level may be fairly late in the overall process. Figure 4.2 indicated the way effort expended in the Ownership phase might be expanded. Initial concern in the next phase of the RMP, the Estimate phase, may be restricted to risks the client proposes to own, as identified in the Ownership phase. However, estimating contractor costs and verifying contractor cost estimates will require estimation of all associated risks, possibly using a somewhat different approach and different people. Part of the rationale for being clear about who owns risks and responses before estimation is to verify the feasibility of the assumed response and its impact for each risk. For example, client-initiated redesign is a response which may invalidate all allocations of risk to a contractor, with knock-on cost implications which are orders of magnitude greater than the cost of the redesign itself.

Chapter 10

Estimate in Terms of Scenarios and Numbers: The Estimate Phase

But to us, probability is the very guide of life.

Bishop Joseph Butler, 1756

10.1 INTRODUCTION

This chapter, and the next, may seem too technical to be of interest to senior managers. In our view this is not the case. Probability as it is addressed here is not new high science, it is old-fashioned common sense captured in a new manner, providing structure to guide decision making. The principles discussed, and their implications, need to be understood by everyone involved in risk management processes (RMPs).

As indicated in Chapter 4, the Estimate phase should have two purposes, which are related but important to distinguish:

1. to identify areas of the project which *may* involve significant uncertainty and *may* need more attention in terms of data acquisition and analysis;
2. to identify areas of the project which *clearly* involve significant uncertainty and *clearly* require careful decisions and judgements by the client team.

A single pass to achieve the second purpose is not usually a cost-effective approach to analysis. We want to minimise the time spent on relatively minor risks and risks with simple response options, so as to spend more time on major problems involving complex response options. To do this, a first pass with a focus on the first purpose can be used, looping back until the second purpose can be achieved with confidence. Further loops may be useful to provide more attention to detail and some revisions in relation to all the previous phase outputs in those areas where unresolved risk issues suggest it is worth applying more effort. Attempting to achieve all the required outputs via a single pass process is neither efficient nor effective, because it will involve attention to detail which proves unnecessary in some areas, as well as skimping in areas where more effort would be very productive. Loops back can involve just the Estimate and Evaluate phases, illustrated in Figure 4.2 by one such loop (sub-cycle) within each of the three complete loops back to the Define phase. This further increases the efficiency of the process.

The deliverables provided by the Estimate phase are estimates of likelihood and impact in terms of cost, duration, or other project criteria for risks identified earlier. Some specific project risk management methods suggest numeric probability distributions from the outset. Others suggest likelihood and criteria ranges associated with scenario labels such as 'High' (H), 'Medium' (M) and 'Low' (L) initially, as a form of qualitative assessment, and numeric measures later if appropriate. However, qualitative statements of beliefs about uncertainty are of limited use and open to different interpretations by different people. This book suggests using this approach only as a refinement of the minor/major risk distinction in the Structure phase, or as part of a 'Simple Scenario' approach developed in this chapter.

Example 10.1

As part of a seminar on decision analysis conducted for a private company, the seminar leader included a demonstration called the 'Verbal Uncertainty Exercise'. This exercise was designed to show that different individuals assign very different probabilities to the same qualitative expressions. In the exercise the seminar participants were individually asked to assign probabilities to common expressions such as 'very likely to occur', 'almost certain to occur', etc. The seminar leader had just completed the demonstration and was about to move on to another topic when the president of the company said, 'Don't remove that slide yet.' He turned to one of his vice presidents and, in essence, said the following: 'You mean to tell me that last week when you said the Baker account was almost certain, you only meant a 60 to 80% chance? I thought you meant 99%! If I'd known it was so low, I would have done things a lot differently' (from Merkhofer, 1987).

Some people argue that quantitative analysis is a waste of time if it has to be based on subjective estimates of probabilities. There are obvious concerns about the basis for such estimates and their validity. These concerns are reinforced by the recognition that no probability assessment (except 1 or 0) can be proven to be wrong. However, given that individuals are guided by their perceptions of uncertainty whether or not quantification is attempted, it makes sense to articulate these perceptions so that uncertainty can be dealt with as effectively as possible. Quite apart from the general benefits of quantifying uncertainty set out earlier in Chapter 3, quantifying subjective beliefs encourages more precise definition of risks, motivates clearer communication about uncertainty, and clarifies what is and what is not important.

Desirable as quantification is, concerns about the basis for subjective estimates of probability and their validity are reasonable concerns. Any method used to elicit probability estimates from individuals needs to address these concerns.

Sometimes good data are available to provide 'objective' probability estimates. One of the benefits of breaking out various sources of risk is the ability to use such data.

Example 10.2

Equipment laying pipe in the North Sea is designated by maximum wave height capability: 1.6 metre, 3 metre, and so on. Even in the early days of North Sea offshore projects, weather data spanning fifteen or so years was available which indicated the number of days in each month that waves were above various nominal heights, by sea area (see, for example, Mould, 1993). This provided a very good basis for estimating how many days a lay barge might operate or not due to weather. Direct use of these data in a semi-Markov process context allows very complex weather window effects to be modelled directly, enhancing understanding with good hard data (Cooper and Chapman, 1987).

It is worth recognising that even this example introduces a subjective element into the assessment process. In practice, a lay barge operator does not stop immediately when waves go above the equipment's nominal wave height, and start again as soon as the waves drop below the nominal wave height. For important practical reasons, judgements are made about carrying on for short spells of bad weather, stopping early for anticipated prolonged bad spells, and starting later after prolonged bad spells, because starting and stopping pipelaying may involve picking up or putting down a pipeline which are operations prone to 'buckles'.

There is always a gap between the assumed reality for data analysis purposes and actual practice. Deciding to ignore such gaps is always required, and its basis is inherently subjective. In this sense there is no such thing as a truly objective probability estimate for practical problems. Even the card or dice player has to make important assumptions about bias and cheating. All practical estimates are conditional on assumptions which are subjectively assumed to hold, and we need to recognise the fact that in practice such assumptions never hold exactly. The issue is the extent to which these assumptions fail to hold. In this sense, any 'objective' conditional estimate is necessarily 'subjective' in the unconditional form required for practical analysis.

Often there are aspects of a project where uncertainty is very important but appropriate data are not available. Even where past experience is relevant, the required data may not have been collected, may not exist in sufficient quantity or detail, or may not have been recorded accurately or consistently. In such situations, quantification may have to rely heavily on subjective estimates of probability distributions.

Assessment of some risks may be best handled by identifying them as conditions, with associated assumptions, deliberately avoiding estimation in the usual sense. Earlier chapters have emphasised the importance of this part of the process. On occasion, estimation in the usual numeric (or even H/M/L scenario) terms may be a waste of time and best eliminated: for example, if on a first pass the concern is identifying and then managing any 'show-stoppers', estimation reduces to looking for show-stoppers. Again, the importance of this aspect is emphasised.

The key deliverable of the Estimate phase is the provision of a basis for understanding which risks and responses are important. Three specific tasks are required to provide this deliverable, as follows:

1. *select an appropriate risk*—as the basis of a process of successive estimation of a set of risks, select an appropriate place to start, and each successive risk, in terms of initial estimates and refinement of those estimates;
2. *scope the uncertainty*—provide a simple numeric subjective probability estimate, based on the current perceptions of the individual or group with the most appropriate knowledge, to 'size' the risk;
3. *refine earlier estimates*—if the impact of the risk being estimated given chosen responses warrants, or the sensitivity of associated response decisions warrants, refine the initial scoping estimate. This may be undertaken in conjunction with refining the response-related decision analysis.

These last two specific tasks are so different that they divide the Estimate phase into two quite different sub-phases, Scope Estimates and Refine Estimates, each associated with its own version of the specific task *select an appropriate risk*, and its own specific *assess* tasks, as illustrated by Figure 10.1.

Figure 10.1a portrays starting the Estimate phase in the Scope Estimates sub-phase, in *select an appropriate risk* mode. Making sure that the first selected risk is the most appropriate place to start is worth specific attention, as part of the process of determining an effective sequence. Assessing each successive risk in terms of the question 'is it useful to quantify this risk?' follows.

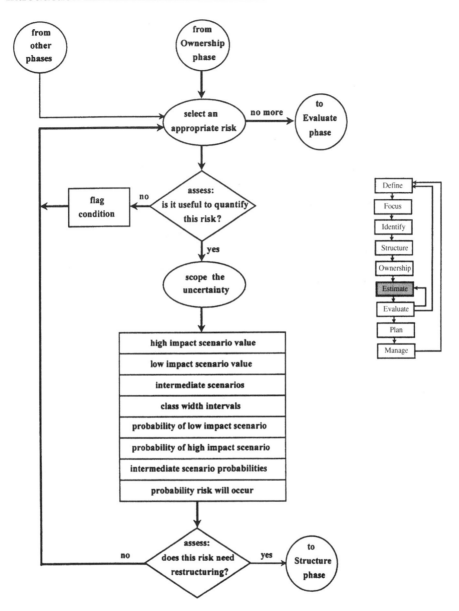

Figure 10.1a Estimate phase specific tasks: Scope Estimates sub-phase.

Estimating then moves into *scope the uncertainty* mode. The objective is an unbiased 'sizing' of the risk, in crude scenario terms with an explicit numeric interpretation, which are understood to be crude by all concerned, referred to here as the 'Simple Scenario' approach.

The final aspect of the Scope Estimates sub-phase involves another specific form of the *assess* task, asking the question 'does this risk need restructuring?' If the risk is too small to worry about separately, it may be convenient to add it to a pool of 'productivity variations' (or the equivalent). If the risk is surprisingly large, it may be appropriate to restructure immediately in order to understand the underlying structure better. If neither of these circumstances applies, a loop back to *select an appropriate risk* follows, moving on to the Evaluate phase if no further risks need scoping.

Figure 10.1b portrays the Refine Estimates sub-phase. This usually follows on from, and is motivated by, an earlier pass through the Evaluate phase. This sub-phase also starts in *select an appropriate risk* mode, asks 'is it useful to refine this risk's estimate?', and then moves into *refine earlier estimates* mode. The ultimate objective is estimation of all sources of risk involving a level of precision and estimation effort which reflects the value of that precision and the cost of the effort, recognising that different risks are likely to merit different levels of attention.

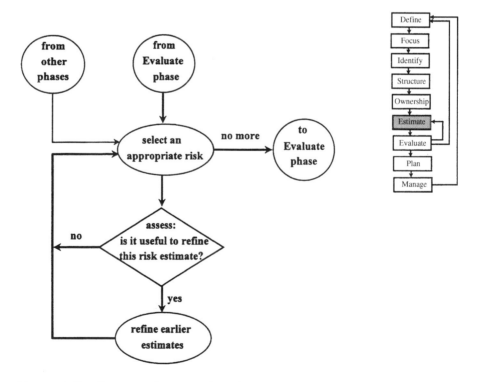

Figure 10.1b   Estimate phase specific tasks: Refine Estimates sub-phase.

For simplicity, a detailed step structure is not shown in Figure 10.1b, but a step structure is provided in Figure 10.1a for *scope the uncertainty* in terms of the Simple Scenario approach. As in earlier phase diagrams, the recurring common tasks of *document, verify, assess* and *report* are not shown, to keep the diagram simple. Further, in practice more complex processes may be effective—Figure 10.1 is an idealisation to capture and illustrate the spirit of the process.

This chapter adopts a section structure based on Figure 10.1. The following six sections outline the processes associated with each of the tasks associated with the operational stages of Figure 10.1 in turn. Subsequent sections consider more closely specific techniques for probability elicitation and detailed practical issues, to support and develop the Simple Scenario approach, and explain the nature of some alternatives.

For simplicity all of the following discussion assumes that the uncertainty of interest is related to time (duration) risk, and all risks have a chance of being realised (or not). Reasonably obvious transformations are necessary if risks always occur (like weather, which may be good, bad or indifferent, but it will be something), the issue being only one of degree.

10.2 SELECT AN APPROPRIATE RISK IN THE SCOPE ESTIMATES SUB-PHASE

Starting the Estimate phase by selecting the risk which earlier phases suggest is the most important is a simple and effective rule of thumb. This rule of thumb generalises to successive selections based upon an overall ordering of the risks for treatment in terms of a crudely perceived order of importance, perhaps within activities or other subdivisions of the project, which in turn may be selected because of the relative importance of risks as currently perceived. No matter how crude the basis of this judgement, it is preferable to using an alphabetic ordering, or some other totally arbitrary ordering.

Any estimation process involves 'getting up to speed', even if everyone involved is experienced in this kind of analysis. If inexperienced people are involved, going down a learning curve is part of the process. It makes sense to spend extra time as part of this process on the most important issues. It also makes sense to grip people's interest and involvement by starting with particularly important issues. When in doubt, err on the side of issues which have aspects which intrigue or touch on common experience, provided this is a cost-effective use of training time.

Having identified a suitable candidate in these terms, a key question follows: 'is this a useful risk to quantify?'

10.3 ASSESS THE USEFULNESS OF QUANTIFYING THE SELECTED RISK

There are two reasons why in some projects it may be useful to quantify no risks at all:

1. the client is not prepared to accept any significant risks, so all significant risks need to be transferred to other parties or avoided in some other manner, and quantitative risk analysis is not required;
2. one or more 'show-stoppers' have been identified earlier, and managing the show-stoppers is the most effective next move.

Example 10.3

A multi-national weapon platform project was approaching an early feasibility assessment. It was the first project those responsible had subjected to a formal risk analysis process. Most other risk analyses undertaken elsewhere in the organisation were quantitative. However, while quantitative risk analysis was an objective, it was not a commitment. When qualitative risk analysis clearly defined a small set of 'show-stoppers', risk management focused on managing away the 'show-stoppers'. There was no need at this stage for quantitative analysis, because it would not have served any useful purpose.

Assuming these general reasons do not apply, a range of other specific reasons for non-quantification might apply.

Example 10.4

The North Sea offshore pipelaying project examples cited earlier involved a number of risks which were usefully quantified in most cases: buckles, weather, equipment failures, and so on. Of the 40 or so pipelaying risks typically identified, about 30 were not quantified, but flagged as important 'conditions', assumptions which the analysis depended upon.

As an example of a risk not usefully quantified, one project involved an identified risk that 'the management may change its mind where the pipeline is to go' (because the company was drilling for oil on an adjacent site, and a strike would probably lead to replanning a 'collector network'). It was important to keep the plan as flexible as possible, to respond effectively to a possible change in route. However, the board owned this risk, not the project, and there was clearly no point going to the board with an estimate which says 'we think there is an x% chance you will change your mind about what you want, and if you do, it will cost y and take z days longer'.

It is important to stress that the identification of 'conditions' of the kind illustrated by the above example can be *much more* important than the identification of risks which are subsequently quantified. Such conditions may be the key to effective contract design, claims for 'extras', and risk avoidance or reduction management which is central to the overall risk management proces. As well as quantified risks, flagged conditions are an important output of the Estimate phase.

10.4 SCOPE THE UNCERTAINTY USING A SIMPLE SCENARIO APPROACH

The next task, *scope the uncertainty*, the first part of the Simple Scenario approach, involves making simple scenario-based estimates to roughly 'size' the risk. 'Sizing' the risk involves roughly assessing the range of possible impacts and associated probabilities. Example 10.5 illustrates what is involved, but first consider a description of each step, summarised in Figure 10.1a.

1. Nominal Maximum Impact, the 'High' Impact Scenario (H Value)

The first step in this task is to estimate the range of possible impacts commencing with the 'nominal' maximum impact value, defining a 'High' impact scenario H, if the risk in question is realised. This estimate should be 'nominal' in the sense that it has:

1. a rounded value, to make it easy to work with, and to indicate clearly its approximate nature;
2. an initially perceived chance of being exceeded of the order of 10% (given the risk is realised), without being specific at this stage.

This estimate should represent a plausible downside scenario, not too extreme, and representative of what can happen if things go wrong.

2. Nominal Minimum Impact, 'Low' Impact Scenario (L Value)

The next step in this task is to estimate a complementary nominal minimum impact value, defining a 'Low' impact scenario L, if the risk in question is realised. This estimate should also have a deliberately rounded value, on a scale common to the nominal maximum. In this case it should involve an initially perceived chance of a lower value of the order of 10%. This nominal minimum represents a credible upside scenario, representative of what can happen if things go well.

3. Intermediate Scenarios

The third step in this task is to designate one or two intermediate points defining intermediate scenarios between the nominal minimum and maximum scenario value. Usually it is convenient to choose these intermediate points such that the distances between each pair of adjacent points are equal. Call this distance d. With one intermediate point $d = (H - L)/2$, with two intermediate points $d = (H - L)/3$.

4. Class Width Intervals

The fourth step in this task is to define class width intervals centred on each of the designated points. Usually it is convenient to make these class width intervals equal to d.

Rationale for Steps 1 to 4

The rationale for this procedure in terms of beginning with the extremes, initially the maximum, is to mitigate against 'anchoring' effects which are discussed later. Other aspects support this concern and attempt to 'keep it simple'. With a bit of practice, H and L can be selected on a common scale with one or two intermediate points on the same common scale such that a common class width interval d can be used. The simplicity of the scenario set is more important than whether the probabilities associated with values exceeding H or being less than L are 0.1, 0.05 or 0.15. If 0.01 is approached, a rethink may be advisable. But 'keep it simple' is the priority.

The next part of the Simple Scenario process is concerned with assessing the probabilities associated with each of the designated intervals, *working to one significant figure*. For *scope the uncertainty* purposes it is convenient to assume that all values in a particular interval are equally likely.

5. Probability of L Scenario

Step 5 involves assessing the probability associated with the interval centred on the nominal minimum point L. Given the nominal 10% percentile interpretation of the point L, a probability of 0.2 is a reasonable estimate for this interval. An estimate of 0.3 may be preferred, and 0.1 is a possibility. However, usually these are the only viable choices, a simplicity driven by the choice process for L. Even modest experience makes selecting the most appropriate value in the context of this first pass process fairly quick and efficient.

6. Probability of H Scenario

Step 6 involves assessing the probability associated with the interval centred on the nominal maximum point H. Given an estimated 0.2 probability for the interval centred on the nominal minimum point L, and the complementary nominal 90 percentile interpretation of the maximum point H, 0.3 is a reasonable expectation for the interval centred on H, rounding up to reflect the usual asymmetry of delay duration distributions. An estimate of 0.2 may be preferred, and 0.4 is a possibility, but 0.1 would be a cause for query. As in the context of the nominal minimum, the process is efficient and quick for participants of even modest experience, with a simplicity driven by the choice process for H.

7. Intermediate Scenario Probabilities

Step 7 involves assessing the probabilities associated with the central intervals. If a single intermediate value is involved, it is simply residual. Two intermediate values require a split, rounding to the nearest 0.1. Again simplicity is the key, with a little practice giving an easy, fast and efficient process.

8. Probability Risk will Occur

Step 8 involves assessing the chance that the risk will occur at all, again to one significant figure (to the nearest 0.1, 0.01, 0.001, etc.).

Rationale for Steps 5 to 8

The rationale for the sequence of steps 5 and 6 is to encourage an assessment which spreads the distribution. The rationale for step 8 coming last is clarifying the overall nature of the risk realisation scenarios before estimating the probability that the risk will be realised.

An Illustration

The following simple example illustrates the procedure.

Example 10.5

Suppose the occurrence of a given risk could give rise to delay in a project with a nominal maximum duration of the delay given that the risk arises of 12 months, and a nominal minimum of 8 months. A single value of 10 months is the obvious single mid-point choice. If the minimum and maximum points were 11 and 14 months, respectively, it would be more convenient to use two intermediate points, 12 and 13.

If 8, 10 and 12 months are the points identified, the intervals centred on these points are each of 2 months width: 7 to 9, 9 to 11, and 11 to 13.

Assuming all values in a given interval are equally likely, suppose probabilities of 0.2 and 0.3 are assigned respectively to the intervals 7 to 9 and 11 to 13. The interval 9 to 11 is assigned the residual 0.5 probability.

Figure 10.2 shows the resulting probability density function and the associated piece-wise linear cumulative probability distribution. The 0.2 probability associated with the interval centred on the nominal minimum of 8 months is uniformly distributed over the range 7 to 9 in Figure 10.2a, causing the cumulative probability to rise from zero to 0.2 over the interval 7 to 9 in Figure 10.2b. The two other classes involve similar relationships.

Finally, assume the probability that the risk will occur is assessed at 0.2.

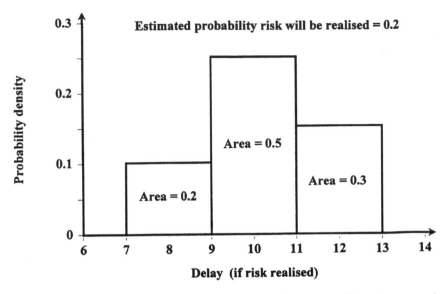

Figure 10.2a Distributions for interpreting Example 10.5: conditional rectangular density function.

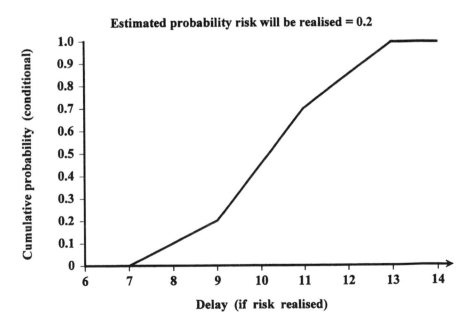

Figure 10.2b Distributions for interpreting Example 10.5: conditional piece-wise linear cumulative function.

In practice it may be convenient for elicitation purposes to treat the possible risk impact as a discrete variable, assigning probabilities to three scenarios corresponding to the two extreme points and the centre point as shown in Table 10.1. This data can then be converted to give a continuous variable interpretation if necessary in the manner described above.

Table 10.1 Nominal probability example, conditional tabular format.

Probability risk is realised	Impact if realised (months)	Conditional probability
0.2	8	0.2
	10	0.5
	12	0.3

More sophisticated conversion processes embedded in suitable computer software could dispense with the use of a common class interval, while keeping the basic simplicity of a Simple Scenario approach.

Comparison with Qualitative H, M, L Scenario Approaches

The Simple Scenario approach as described in this section is not fundamentally different to the use of H/M/L scenarios which are assessed in qualitative terms but clarified by defining percentile probability boundaries between H and M, M and L, *except* that it is explicit about a crude probabilistic basis which includes an upper boundary for H, a lower boundary for L, a distribution shape between these boundaries, and a sequence for the estimation process. The value of being explicit is important. It drives a need for more detail if and when this detail is seen as useful, it facilitates combining estimates in the Evaluation phase, and it forces consideration of dependence. The value of the sequence of steps is also important. The cost of being explicit is nominal and negligible relative to the benefits, which should be clear by the end of Chapter 11.

10.5   ASSESS THE NEED FOR RESTRUCTURING

The process of scoping the uncertainty associated with a given source of risk next leads to an assessment of whether the revealed risk warrants more detail or simplification. If the Simple Scenario approach as described so far indicates that the risk involves a very modest impact, restructuring in terms of putting this risk into a 'productivity variations' pot of risks not worth separate quantitative treatment may be an obvious useful short cut. This is a second cut at the 'minor risk' process of identifying such risk earlier, or it could be an alternative.

If the Simple Scenario approach indicates that the risk involves a major impact, it may be worth immediate restructuring in terms of decomposing the risk into components which clarify its nature and facilitate more accurate estimation.

In both these cases Figure 10.1 indicates a branch out to the Structure phase of the RMP, because restructuring is what is involved. Subject to any revisions being made to the structuring of the risk, the process can then recycle and address another appropriate risk. When no more risks remain, the process can pass on to the Evaluate phase.

10.6 SELECT AN APPROPRIATE RISK IN THE REFINE ESTIMATES SUB-PHASE

A first pass through the Evaluate phase will be primarily concerned with using the Scope Estimates sub-phase to identify which risks warrant further attention, to help allocate estimating time effectively and efficiently. How this is done will be addressed in the next chapter. This section assumes that it has been done, and some risks worthy of further attention have been identified in the Evaluation phase. In practice, some risks may be so obviously important that it is advisable to move on to the Refine Estimates sub-phase without an intervening pass through the Evaluate phase.

The purpose of the Refine Estimates sub-phase is to refine initial scoping estimates in a credible and useful manner. Concerns in this sub-phase include:

1. what level of detail to aspire to;
2. what approach to use to obtain more detailed estimates;
3. the reliability of estimates;
4. how best to manage the elicitation of probabilities;
5. the relationship between objective data and subjective probabilities.

These concerns are discussed in the remainder of this chapter.

For reasons similar to those discussed in Section 10.1, it makes sense to start this sub-phase with one of the most significant and interesting risks. For present purposes assume it is characterised by Table 10.1 and Figure 10.2.

Table 10.2 provides an unconditional form and expected values (conditional and unconditional) which may be useful outputs from the Evaluate phase. The perceptions Table 10.2 depicts are the same as Table 10.1, but Table 10.2 clarifies the discrete nature of the zero impact case if continuous distributions are used for the unconditional equivalents of Figures 10.2a and b. The simple rectangular histogram format of Figure 10.2a and the associated piece-wise linear format of Figure 10.2b mean that expectations for

Table 10.2 Nominal probability example, unconditional tabular format.

Impact (months)	Probability
0	0.8
8	0.04
10	0.10
1	0.06
expected impact (unconditional) 2.04	
expected impact (conditional) 10.20	

the continuous variable forms are the same as expectations for the discrete variable form of Table 10.1 or 10.2.

10.7 ASSESS THE USEFULNESS OF REFINING THE SELECTED RISK'S ESTIMATE

Even if a risk is of only moderate importance, presenting results to the project team may raise unnecessary questions if the portrayal is too crude, particularly if members of the project team are inexperienced in the use of the Simple Scenario approach. All risks modelled separately may require more probability distribution detail as a cosmetic issue. Further precision and accuracy may be required because a risk is recognised as important. Still more precision and accuracy may be required because demonstrating the validity of decisions dependent on the risk is important.

The task here is assessing how much precision and accuracy is appropriate with respect to this pass through the Estimate phase for each risk being addressed.

10.8 PROVIDE MORE PROBABILITY DISTRIBUTION DETAIL

A reasonable concern about estimates like Table 10.1/Figure 10.2 is its clearly nominal nature. People may be uncomfortable making significant decisions based on estimates which are so overtly crude.

Second and Third Cuts to Develop the Simple Scenario Approach

More detail can be associated with Table 10.1 as a development of the Simple Scenario approach without significantly altering the intended message, as illustrated in Table 10.3.

The 'second-cut' probabilities of Table 10.3 are typical of the effect of still working to one significant figure, but pushing an estimator to provide more detail in the distribution tails—the probability associated with the central value of 10-month drops, from 0.5 to 0.3, to provide the probability to fill

Table 10.3 Conditional probabilities: nominal, second- and third-cut examples, tabular format.

Impact (months)	Conditional probabilities		
	Nominal	Second cut	Third cut
4			0.05
6		0.1	0.10
8	0.2	0.2	0.15
10	0.5	0.3	0.25
12	0.3	0.2	0.20
14		0.1	0.15
16		0.1	0.10
expected impact	2.04	2.12	2.12
conditional expectation	10.20	10.60	10.60

out the tails. It might be argued that if the second cut is unbiased, the first cut (nominal estimate) should have had a 0.3 probability associated with 10 months. However, this implies probability values for 8, 10 and 12 months of 0.3, 0.3 and 0.4, which sends a different message. Further, we will argue later that most probability elicitation techniques are biased in terms of yielding too small a spread. The design of the process described here is explicitly concerned with pushing out the spread of distributions, to deliberately work against known bias.

The 'third-cut' probabilities of Table 10.3 are typical of the effect of pushing an estimator to provide still more detail in the tails, using a 20-division probability scale instead of 10, working to the nearest 0.05. A further slight decline in the central value probability is motivated by the need for more probability to fill out the tails.

It is worth noting that the expected values do not differ significantly. If expected value was the key issue, the second cut would provide all the precision needed, and the first would suffice for many purposes. The difference in expected values between cuts is a function of the skew or asymmetry of the distribution, modest in this case.

It is worth noting that the variance (spread) increases as more detail is provided. This is a deliberate aspect of the process design, as noted earlier. It is also worth noting that the third cut provides all the precision needed for most purposes in terms of variance.

A range of alternative approaches to providing more detailed estimates are available which may or may not help in a given situation. Some of these approaches are considered below.

Provide a Probability Distribution Function

Some people believe specific probability distribution functions provide more reliable estimates than the Simple Scenario estimating approach described in its basic form in Section 10.3 and above. However, while specific probability distribution functions can provide more precision, this is usually spurious, and specific probability distributions usually provide less accurate estimates. The exceptions to this rule arise when the assumptions inherent in some distribution functions clearly hold, and a limited data set can be used to estimate distribution parameters effectively. In such cases it may be appropriate to replace a specification like that of Table 10.1 with a distribution function specification. However, it is counterproductive, if not dangerous, to do so if the nature of these assumptions are not clearly understood and they are not clearly applicable. For example, Normal (Gaussian) distributions should not be used if the 'Central Limit Theorem' is not clearly understood and applicable (for a discussion of what is involved, see Gordon and Pressman (1978) for example). Table 10.4 indicates distributions often assumed, and associated assumptions.

Table 10.4 Applicability of theoretical probability distributions.

Distribution	Applicability
Poisson $P(n) = \lambda^n e^{-\lambda}/n!$ mean $= \lambda$, variance $= \lambda$	Distribution of the number of independent rare events, n, that occur infrequently in space, time, volume or other dimensions. Specify λ, the average number of rare events in one unit of the dimension (e.g. the average number of accidents in a given unit of time).
Exponential $f(x) = \begin{cases} e^{-x/k}/k, k > 0; \\ \quad 0 \le x \le \infty \\ 0 \quad \text{elsewhere} \end{cases}$ mean $= k$, variance $= k^2$	Useful for modelling time to failure of a component where the length of time a component has already operated does not affect its chance of operating for an additional period. Specify k, the average time to failure, or $1/k$ the probability of failure per unit time.
Uniform $f(x) = \begin{cases} 1/(U - L) \\ \quad L \le x \le U \\ 0 \quad \text{elsewhere} \end{cases}$ mean $= (U + L)/2$, variance $= (U - L)^2/12$	Where any value in the specified range $[U, L]$ is equally likely. Specify U and L.

Table 10.4 (*continued*)

Distribution	Applicability
Standard Normal $f(x) = \exp(-x^2/2)/\sqrt{2\pi}$ mean $= 0$, variance $= 1$	Appropriate for the distribution of the mean value of the sum of a large number of independent random variables (or a small number of Normally distributed variables). Let $Y_1, Y_2, \ldots Y_n$ be independent and identically distributed random variables with mean μ and variance $\sigma^2 < \infty$. Define $x_n = \sqrt{n}(\bar{Y} - \mu)\sigma$ where $\bar{Y} = \sum_{i=1}^{n} Y_i$. Then the distribution function of x_n converges to the standard normal distribution function as $n \to \infty$. Requires μ and σ^2 to be estimated.
Standard Normal $f(x) = \exp(-x^2/2)/\sqrt{2\pi}$ mean $= 0$, variance $= 1$	If y represents the number of 'successes' in n independent trials of an event for which p is the probability of 'success' in a single trial, then the variable $x = (y - np)/\sqrt{np(1-p)}$ has a distribution that approaches the standard normal distributions as the number of trials becomes increasingly large. The approximation is fairly good as long as $np > 5$ when $p \leq 0.5$ and $n(1-p) > 5$ when $p > 0.5$. Requires specification of p and n.

Instead of estimating parameters for an appropriate theoretical distribution, an alternative approach is to fit a theoretical distribution to a limited number of elicited probability estimates. This can serve to reduce the number of probabilities that have to be elicited to produce a complete probability distribution.

This approach is facilitated by the use of computer software packages such as 'MAINOPT' or '@Risk'. 'MAINOPT' is a tool which models 'bath-tub' curves for reliability analysis. The generic 'bath-tub'-shaped curve shows the probability of failure of a component at a particular time given survival to that point in time. The analyst specifies parameters which specify the timing of the 'burn-in', 'steady-state' and 'wear-out' periods, together with failures rates for each period. The software then produces appropriate 'bath-tub' and failure density curves. Woodhouse (1993) gives a large number of examples in the context of maintenance and reliability of industrial equipment.

A popular choice for many situations is the triangular distribution. This distribution is simple to specify, covers a finite range with values in the middle of the range more likely than values of the extremes, and can also show a degree of skewness if appropriate. As shown in Figure 10.3, this distribution can be specified completely by just three values: the most likely value, an upper bound or maximum value, and the lower bound or minimum value.

Alternatively, assessors can provide 'optimistic' and 'pessimistic' estimates in place of maximum and minimum possible values, where there is an $x\%$ chance of exceeding the optimistic value, and a $(100 - x)\%$ chance of exceeding the pessimistic value. A suitable value for x to reflect the given situation is usually 10%, 5%, or 1%.

In certain contexts, estimation of a triangular distribution may be further simplified by assuming a particular degree of skewness. For example, in

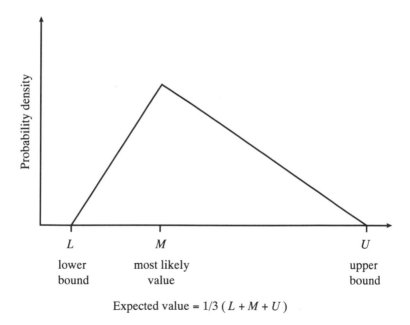

Expected value = $1/3 \, (L + M + U)$

Figure 10.3 The triangular distribution.

the case of activity durations in a project planning network Williams (1992) and Golenko-Ginzburg (1988) have suggested that durations tend to have a 1:2 skew, with the most likely value being a third along the range (that is, $2(M - L) = (U - M)$ in Figure 10.3).

The triangular distribution is often thought to be a convenient choice of distribution for cost and duration of many activities where the underlying processes are obscure or complex. Alternative 'theoretical' distributions such as the Beta, Gamma, and Berny (1989) distributions can be used to model more rounded, skewed distributions, but analytical forms lack the simplicity and transparency of the triangular distribution (Williams, 1992). In the absence of any theoretical reasons for preferring them, and given limited precision in estimates of distribution parameters, it is doubtful whether use of Beta, Gamma or Berny distributions have much to offer over the use of the simple triangle distribution.

In our view, for reasons indicated earlier, it is doubtful that triangular distributions offer any advantages over the use of the approach illustrated in Example 10.5, and they may cause significant underestimation of extreme values. The use of an absolute maximum value also raises difficulties discussed in the next subsection, whether or not the absolute value is solicited directly from the estimator.

Fractile Methods

A common approach to eliciting subjective probabilities of continuous variables is the 'fractile' method. This involves an expert's judgement being elicited to provide a complete, cumulative probability distribution for a selected variable.

The basic procedure as described by Raiffa (1968) is:

1. Identify the highest (x_{100}) and lowest (x_0) possible values the variable can take. There is no chance of values less than x_0. There is a 100% chance that the variable will be less than x_{100}.
2. Identify the median value (x_{50}). It is equally likely that the actual value will be above or below this figure (i.e. 50% chance of being below x_{50} and a 50% chance of being above x_{50}).
3. Subdivide the range x_{50} to x_{100} into two equally likely parts. Call the dividing point x_{75} to denote that there is a 75% chance that the true value will be below x_{75} and a 25% chance that it will be in the range x_{75} to x_{100}.
4. Repeat the procedure in step 3 for values below x_{50} to identify x_{25}.
5. Subdivide each of the four intervals obtained from step 3 and step 4, depending on the need to shape the cumulative probability distribution.

6. Plot the graph of cumulative percentage probability (0, 25, 50, 75, 100) against associated values (x_0, x_{25}, x_{50}, x_{75}, x_{100}). Draw a smooth curve or series of straight lines through the plot points to obtain the cumulative probability curve.

A variation of Raiffa's procedure is to trisect the range into three equally likely ranges, rather than bisect it as in step 2 above. The idea of this variation is to overcome any tendency for the assessing expert to bias estimates towards the middle of the identified range.

In our view this approach is fundamentally flawed in the context of most practical applications by the dependence upon identification of x_{100} in the first step. Most durations and associated risks are unbounded on the high side (there is a finite probability that the activity may never finish), because the project may be cancelled, for example. This means any finite maximum is a conditional estimate, and it is not clear what the conditions are. Further, it is very difficult in practice to visualise absolute maximums. For these reasons most serious users of PERT models redefined the original PERT minimum and maximum estimates as 10 and 90 percentile values thirty years ago, as discussed, for example, by Moder and Philips (1970). The alternative provided by Tables 10.1 and 10.3 avoids these difficulties. However, variants of Raiffa's approach which avoid the x_0 and x_{100} issue may be useful, including direct interactive plotting of cumulative probability curves.

Relative Likelihood Methods

A common approach to eliciting subjective probabilities of discrete possible values like Table 10.3 is the method of relative likelihoods (Moore and Thomas, 1976). The procedure to be followed by the assessing expert as Moore and Thomas describe it is as follows:

1. Identify the most likely value of the variable (x_m) and assign it a probability rating of 60 units.
2. Identify a value below x_m which is half as likely to occur as x_m. Assign this a probability rating of 30 units.
3. Identify a value above x_m which is half as likely to occur as x_m. Assign this a probability rating of 30 units.
4. Identify values above and below x_m which are a quarter as likely as x_m. Assign each of these values a probability rating of 15 units.
5. Identify minimum and maximum possible values for the variable.
6. On a graph, plot the probability ratings against associated variable values and draw a smooth curve through the various points.

7. Read off the probability ratings for each intermediate discrete value. Sum all the probability ratings for each value and call this R. Divide each individual probability rating by R to obtain the assessed probability of each discrete value.

The above procedure may be modified by identifying variable values which are, for example, one-third or one-fifth as likely to occur as the most likely value x_m.

In our view the Table 10.3 development of the Simple Scenario approach is simpler, but some of the ideas associated with this Moore and Thomas procedure can be incorporated if desired.

10.9   RELIABILITY OF SUBJECTIVE ESTIMATES OF UNCERTAINTY

Techniques used to encode subjective probabilities ought to ensure that estimates express the estimator's true beliefs, conform to the axioms of probability theory, and are valid. Testing the validity of estimates is extremely difficult, since it involves empirical observation over a large number of similar cases. However, it is possible to avoid a range of common problems, if these problems are understood.

An important consideration is ensuring honesty in estimates, and that explicit or implicit rewards do not motivate estimators to be dishonest or biased in their estimates. For example, a concern to avoid looking inept might cause estimates to be unrealistically optimistic.

Even if honest estimating is assumed, estimates may still be unreliable. In particular, overwhelming evidence from research using fractiles to assess uncertain quantities is that people's probability distributions tend to be too tight (Lichtenstein, Fischoff and Phillips, 1982, p. 330). For example, in a variety of experiments Alpert and Raiffa (1982) found that when individuals were asked to specify 98% confidence bounds on given uncertain variables, rather than 2% of true values falling outside the 98% confidence bounds, 20–50% did so. In other words, people tend to underestimate the range of possible values an uncertain variable can take. The Simple Scenario approach associated with Tables 10.1 and 10.3, deliberately pushing out the tails, helps to overcome this tendency.

Slovic, Fischoff and Lichtenstein (1982) suggest that 'although the psychological basis for unwarranted certainty is complex, a key element seems to be people's lack of awareness that their knowledge is based on assumptions that are often quite tenuous'. Significantly, even experts may be as prone to overconfidence as lay people when forced to rely on judgement.

The ability of both the layperson and experts to estimate uncertainty has been examined extensively in the psychology literature (e.g. Kahneman,

Slovic and Tversky, 1982). It is argued that, as a result of limited information processing abilities, people adopt simplifying rules or heuristics when estimating uncertainty. These heuristics can lead to large and systematic errors in estimates.

Adjustment and Anchoring

Failure to specify adequately the extent of uncertainty about a quantity may be due to a process of estimating uncertainty by making adjustments to an initial point estimate. The initial value may be suggested by the formation of a problem or by a partial computation. Unfortunately, subsequent estimates may be unduly influenced by the initial value, so that subsequent estimates are typically insufficiently different from the initial value. Moreover, for a single problem different starting points may lead to different final estimates which are biased towards the starting values. This effect is known as 'anchoring' (Tversky and Kahneman, 1974).

Consider an estimator who is asked to estimate the probability distribution for a particular cost element. To select a highest possible cost H it is natural to begin by thinking of one's best estimate of the cost and to adjust this value upward, and to select the lowest possible cost L by adjusting the best estimate of cost downwards. If these adjustments are insufficient, then the range of possible costs will be too narrow, and the assessed probability distribution too tight.

Anchoring bias can also lead to biases in the evaluation of compound events. The probability of conjunctive 'and' events tends to be overestimated while the probability of disjunctive 'or' events tends to be underestimated. Conjunctive events typically occur in a project where success depends on a chain of activities being successfully completed. The probability of individual activities being completed on time may be quite high but the overall probability of completion on time may be low, especially if the number of events is large. Estimates of the probability of completing the whole project on time are likely to be overoptimistic if based on adjustments to the probability of completing one activity on time. Of course, in this setting unbiased estimation of completion time for identified activities can be achieved with appropriate project planning software, but the anchoring may be an implicit cause of overestimation when a number of conjuncture events or activities are not explicitly treated separately.

The rationale for the process of Section 10.4 starting with the nominal extremes is minimisation of this anchoring effect.

The Availability Heuristic

The availability heuristic involves judging an event as likely or frequent if instances of it are easy to imagine or recall. This is often appropriate insofar as frequently occurring events are generally easier to imagine or recall than unusual events. However, events may be easily imagined or recalled simply because they have been recently brought to the attention of an individual. Thus a recent incident, recent discussion of a low probability hazard, or recent media coverage, may all increase memorability and imaginability of similar events, and hence perceptions of their perceived likelihood. Conversely, events which an individual has rarely experienced or heard about, or has difficulty imagining, will be perceived as having a low probability of occurrence irrespective of their actual likelihood of occurring. Obviously experience is a key determinant of perceived risk. If experience is biased, then perceptions are likely to be inaccurate.

In some situations, failure to appreciate the limits of presented data may lead to biased probability estimates. For example, Fischoff, Slovic and Lichtenstein (1978) studied whether people are sensitive to the completeness of fault trees. They used a fault tree indicating the ways in which a car might fail to start. Groups of subjects were asked to estimate the proportion of failures which might be due to each of seven categories of factors including an 'all other problems' category. When three sections of the diagram were omitted, effectively incorporating removed categories into the 'all other problems' category, subjects overestimated the probability of the remaining categories and substantially underestimated the 'all other problems' category. In effect, what was out of sight was out of mind. Professional mechanics did not do appreciably better on the test than laypeople.

Such findings suggest that fault trees and other representations of sources of risk can strongly influence judgements about probabilities of particular groups of risk occurring. Tables 10.1, 10.2 and 10.3 can be interpreted as a way of exploring the importance of these kinds of issues.

Presentational Effects

The forgoing discussion highlights that the way in which risks are expressed or presented can have a significant impact on perceptions of risk. This suggests that those responsible for presenting information about risk have considerable opportunity to manipulate perceptions. Moreover, to the extent that these effects are not appreciated, people may inadvertently be manipulating their own perceptions by casual decisions about how to organise information (Slovic, Fischoff and Lichtenstein, 1982). An extreme but common situation is where presentation of 'best estimates' may inspire undue confidence about the level of uncertainty. The approach recommended here is designed to manipulate perceptions in a way which helps to neutralise known bias.

10.10 MANAGING THE SUBJECTIVE PROBABILITY ELICITATION PROCESS

It should be evident from the forgoing section that any process for eliciting probability assessments from individuals needs to be carefully managed if it is to be seen as effective and as reliable as circumstances permit.

Spetzler and Stael von Holstein (1975) offer the following general principles to avoid later problems in the elicitation process:

1. Be prepared to justify to the expert (assessor) why the variable is important to the project.
2. Variables should be structured to show clearly any conditionalities. If the expert thinks of a variable as being conditional upon other variables, it is important to incorporate these conditions into the analysis to minimise mental acrobatics. For example, sales of a new product might be expected to vary according to whether a main competitor launches a similar product or not. Eliciting estimates of future possible sales might be facilitated by making two separate assessments, one where the competitor launches a product and one where they do not. A separate assessment of the likelihood of the competitor launching a rival product would then need to be made.
3. Variables to be assessed should be clearly defined to minimise ambiguity. A good test of this is to ask whether a clairvoyant could reveal the value of the variable by specifying a single number without requesting clarification.
4. The variable should be described on a scale that is meaningful to the expert providing the assessment. The expert should be used to thinking in terms of the scale used, so in general the expert assessor should be allowed to choose the scale. After encoding, the scale can be converted as necessary to fit the analysis required.

Developing point 2 in a slightly different manner, if a number of potential conditions are identified, but separate conditional assessments is too complex because of the number of variables or the partial dependency structure, the Simple Scenario approach can be developed along the lines of the more sophisticated approaches to scenario building used in 'futures analysis' or 'technological forecasting' (Chapman, Cooper and Page, 1987, Chapter 33). That is, estimation of the L and H scenarios can be associated with consistent scenarios linked to sets of high or low values of all the conditional variables identified. This approach will further help to overcome the tendency to make estimated distributions too tight.

For example, instead of asking someone how long it takes them to make a journey which involves a taxi in an unconditional manner, starting with the H value, suggest it could be rush hour (so taxis are hard to find and slow), raining (so taxis are even harder to find) and the trip is very urgent and important (so Sodd's law applies).

Example 10.6

An instructive case study which illustrates many of the issues involved in probability elicitation is described by Keeney and van Winterfeldt (1991). The purpose of this study, funded by the US Nuclear Regulatory Commission, was to estimate the uncertainties and consequences of severe core damage accidents in five selected nuclear power plants. A draft report published in 1987 for comment was criticised because it:

1. relied too heavily on scientists of the national laboratories;
2. did not systematically select or adequately document the selection of issues for assessing expert judgements;
3. did not train the experts in the assessments of probabilities;
4. did not allow the experts adequate time for assimilating necessary information prior to assessment;
5. did not use state-of-the-art assessment methods;
6. inadequately documented the process and results of the expert assessments.

Following criticisms, project management took major steps to improve substantially the process of eliciting and using expert judgements. Subsequently probabilistic judgements were elicited for about 50 events and quantities from some 40 experts. Approximately 1000 probability distributions were elicited and, counting decomposed judgements, several thousand probability judgements were elicited. Given the significance of this study it was particularly important to eliminate discrepancies in assessments due to incomplete information, use of inappropriate assumptions, or different meanings attached to words.

Nevertheless, uncertainties were very large, often covering several orders of magnitude in the case of frequencies and 50% to 80% of the physically feasible range in the case of some uncertain quantities.

Various protocols for elicitation of probabilities from experts have been described in the literature (Morgan and Herion, 1990, Chapter 7). The most influential has probably been that developed in the Department of Engineering–Economic Systems at Stanford University and at the Stanford Research Institute (SRI) during the 1960s and 1970s. A useful summary of the SRI protocol is provided by Spetzer and Stael von Holstein (1975), and Merkhofer (1987). A similar but more recent protocol is suggested by Keeney and van Winterfeldt (1991) drawing on their experience of the study in Example 10.6 and other projects. Their procedure involves several stages as follows:

1. Identification and selection of issues;
2. Identification and selection of assessing experts;
3. Discussion and refinement of issues;
4. Assessors trained for elicitation;
5. Elicitation interviews;
6. Analysis, aggregation and resolution of disagreements between assessors.

For completeness each stage is described briefly below, but it will be noted that stages 1–3 relate to the Define, Focus, Identify and Structure phases examined in previous chapters. Stage 3 raises the question of restructuring via disaggregation of variables, which is shown as an *assess* task in Figure 10.1.

1. Identification and Selection of Issues

This stage involves identifying questions about models, assumptions, criteria, events and quantities that could benefit from formal elicitation of expert judgements and selecting those for which a formal process is worthwhile.

Keeney and van Winterfeldt (1991) argue for the development of a comprehensive list of issues in this stage, with selection of those considered most important only after there is reasonable assurance that the list of issues is complete. Selection should be driven by potential impact on performance criteria, but is likely to be influenced by resource constraints which limit the amount of detailed estimation that is practicable. This stage encapsulates the spirit of the Focus, Identify and Structure phases discussed in earlier chapters.

2. Identification and Selection of Experts

A quality elicitation process should include specialists who are recognised experts with the knowledge and flexibility of thought to be able to translate their knowledge and models into judgements relevant to the issue.

Analysts are needed to facilitate the elicitation. Their task is to assist the specialist to formulate the issues, decompose them, to articulate the specialist judgements, check consistency of judgements and help document the specialist's reasoning. Generalists with a broad knowledge of many or all project issues may be needed in complex projects where specialists' knowledge is limited to parts of the project.

3. Discussion and Refinement of Issues

Following issue and expert selection, a first meeting of experts and analysts should be organised to clearly define and structure the variables to be encoded. At the start of this first meeting, the analyst is likely to have only a rough idea of what needs to be encoded. The purpose of the meeting is to enlist the expert's help in refining the definition and structure of variables to be encoded. The aim is to produce unambiguous definitions of the events and uncertain quantities that are to be elicited. For uncertain quantities the meaning, dimension and unit of measurement need to be clearly defined. All conditioning events also need to be clearly defined.

At this stage it is usually necessary and desirable to explore the usefulness of disaggregating variables into more elemental variables. Previous chapters have discussed the importance of breaking down or disaggregating sources of risk and risk drivers into appropriate levels of detail. A central concern is to ensure that sources of uncertainty are identified in sufficient detail to understand the nature of significant project risks and to facilitate the formulation of effective risk management strategies. From a probability elicitation perspective, disaggregation is driven by a need to assess the uncertainty of an event or quantity derived from a combination of underlying, contributory factors.

Disaggregation can be used to combat motivational bias by producing a level of detail that disguises the connection between the assessor's judgements and personal interests. Disaggregation can also help to reduce cognitive bias (Armstrong, Denniston and Gordon, 1975). For example, if each event in a sequence of statistically independent events has to occur for successful completion of the sequence, assessors are prone to overestimate the probability of successful completion if required to assess it directly. In such circumstances it can be more appropriate to disaggregate the sequence into its component variables, assess the probability of completing each individual event, and then computing the probability of successful completion of the whole sequence.

Often more informed assessments of an uncertain variable can be obtained by disaggregating the variable into component variables, making judgements about the probabilities of the component variables, and then combining the results mathematically. In discussions between analyst and assessor a key concern is to decide on an appropriate disaggregation of variables. This will be influenced by the knowledge base and assumptions adopted by the assessor.

Example 10.7

A project involved a contract to lay 24 km of gas pipe over land by a certain date. The project manager wanted to know the probability that the pipe would be laid on time. Estimating this probability directly might have been feasible if sufficient experience of laying similar pipelines could have been drawn on. However, this not being the case, the project was decomposed into individual weeks of pipelaying, so that focus was on the more detailed activities in each week. With this focus the site supervisor was able to specify the possible weekly lay rates and associated

Table 10.5 Calculation for Example 10.7.

End week	Length laid (km)	Computation				Probability	Probability (rounded)
0	0					1	1
1	5	0.3 × 1				0.3	0.3
	6		0.5 × 1			0.5	0.5
	7			0.2 × 1		0.2	0.2
2	10	0.3 × 0.3+				0.09	0.09
	11	0.3 × 0.5+	0.5 × 0.3+			0.30	0.30
	12	0.3 × 0.2+	0.5 × 0.5+	0.2 × 0.3		0.37	0.37
	13		0.5 × 0.2+	0.2 × 0.5		0.20	0.20
	14			0.2 × 0.2		0.04	0.04
3	15	0.3 × 0.09+				0.027	0.03
	16	0.3 × 0.30+	0.5 × 0.09			0.135	0.13
	17	0.3 × 0.37+	0.5 × 0.30+	0.2 × 0.09		0.279	0.28
	18	0.3 × 0.20+	0.5 × 0.37+	0.2 × 0.30		0.305	0.30
	19	0.3 × 0.04+	0.5 × 0.20+	0.2 × 0.37		0.186	0.19
	20		0.5 × 0.04+	0.2 × 0.20		0.060	0.060
	21			0.2 × 0.04		0.008	0.01
4	20	0.3 × 0.027+				0.0081	0.01
	21	0.3 × 0.135+	0.5 × 0.027+			0.054	0.05
	22	0.3 × 0.279+	0.5 × 0.135+	0.2 × 0.027		0.1566	0.16
	23	0.3 × 0.305+	0.5 × 0.279+	0.2 × 0.135		0.258	0.26
	24	0.3 × 0.186+	0.5 × 0.305+	0.2 × 0.279		0.2641	0.26
	25	0.3 × 0.060+	0.5 × 0.186+	0.2 × 0.305		0.172	0.17
	26	0.3 × 0.008+	0.5 × 0.060+	0.2 × 0.186		0.0696	0.07
	27		0.5 × 0.008+	0.2 × 0.060		0.016	0.02
	28			0.2 × 0.008		0.0016	0.00

probabilities as follows:

Kilometres per week	Probability
5	0.3
6	0.5
7	0.2

This assessment can be used to calculate a distribution for the time required to lay 24 km by a single aggregation calculation shown in Table 10.5.

The expected length of pipe laid after four weeks is 4 × 5.9 = 23.6 kilometres. Table 10.5 indicates a probability of about 0.5 of completing the 24 kilometres of pipelaying by the end of the fourth week. The distribution of possible progress after four weeks is clearly more detailed and significantly different from an assessment which only assesses three possible values and associated probabilities for a four-week period directly.

Cooper and Chapman (1987; Chapter 11) give an example of disaggregation in which more detailed representation of a problem can be much easier to use for estimating purposes than an aggregated representation. Disaggregation also facilitates explicit modelling of complex decision rules or conditional probabilities and can lead to a much better understanding of the likely behaviour of a system.

4. Training for Elicitation

In this stage the analyst leads the training of specialist and generalist assessors to familiarise them with concepts and techniques used in elicitation, to given them practice with assessments, to inform them about potential biases in judgement, and to motivate them for the elicitation process.

Motivating assessors for the elicitation process involves establishing a rapport between assessor and analyst, and a diplomatic search for possible incentives in which the assessor may have to prove an assessment which does not reflect the assessor's true beliefs.

Training involves explaining the nature of heuristics and cognitive biases in the assessment of uncertainty and giving assessors an opportunity to discuss the subject in greater depth if they wish. Training may also involve some warm-up trial exercises based around commonplace variables such as the journey time to work. This familiarisation process can help assessors to become more involved in the encoding process and help them understand why the encoding process is structured as it is. It can also encourage assessors to take the encoding process more seriously if the analysts are seen to be approaching the process in a careful and professional manner (Morgan and Herion, 1990).

In the study outlined in Example 10.6, Keeney and van Winterfeldt (1991) found that the elicitation process worked largely due to the commitment of project staff to the expert elicitation process and to the fact that the experts were persuaded that elicitation of their judgements was potentially useful and worthy of serious effort. Also they considered that training of experts in probability elicitation was crucial because it reassured the experts that the elicitation process was rigorous, and showed them how biases could unknowingly enter into judgements.

5. Elicitation

In this stage structured interviews take place between the analyst and the specialist/generalist assessors. This involves the analyst reviewing definitions of events or uncertain quantities to be elicited, discussing the specialist's approach to the issue including approaches to a decomposition into component issues, eliciting probabilities, and checking judgements for consistency.

Conscious bias may be present for a variety of reasons, such as the following:

1. An assessor may want to influence a decision by playing down the possibility of cost escalation, or by presenting an optimistic view of possible future revenues.
2. A person who thinks they are likely to be assessed on a given performance measure is unlikely to provide an unbiased assessment of

uncertainty about the performance measure. Estimates of the time or the budget needed to complete a task are likely to be overestimated to provide a degree of slack.

3. A person may understate uncertainty about a variable lest they appear incompetent.
4. For political reasons a person may be unwilling to specify uncertainty that undermines the views or position of other parties.

Where such biases are suspected, it may be possible to influence the incentive structure faced by the assessor, and additionally to modify the variable structure to obscure or weaken the incentive for bias. It can also be important to stress that the encoding exercise is not a method for testing performance or measuring expertise.

Spetzler and Stael von Holstein (1975) distinguish three aspects of the elicitation process: conditioning, encoding and verification. Conditioning involves trying to head off biases during the encoding process by conditioning assessors to think fundamentally about their judgements. The analyst should ask the assessor to explain the bases for any judgements and what information is being taken into account. This can help to identify possible anchoring or availability biases. Spetzler and Stael von Holstein (1975) suggest that the analyst can use availability to correct any central bias in estimates by asking the assessor to compose scenarios that would produce extreme outcomes. Careful questioning may be desirable to draw out significant assumptions upon which an assessment is based. This may lead to changes in the structure and decomposition of variables to be assessed.

Encoding involves the use of techniques such as those described earlier, beginning with easy questions followed by harder judgements. Spetzler and Stael von Holstein (1975) provide some useful advice for the encoding analyst:

1. Begin by asking the assessor to identify extreme values for an uncertain variable. Then ask the assessor to identify scenarios that might lead to outcomes outside of these extremes and to estimate the probability of outcomes outside the designated extremes. This uses the availability heuristic to encourage assignment of higher probability extreme outcomes to counteract central bias that may otherwise occur.
2. When asking for probabilities associated with particular values in the identified range, avoid choosing the first value in a way that may seem significant to the assessor, lest subsequent assessments are anchored on their value. In particular, do not begin by asking the assessor to identify the most likely value and the associated probability.

3. Plot each response as a point on a cumulative probability distribution and number them sequentially. During the plotting process the assessor should not be shown the developing distribution in case the assessor tries to make subsequent responses consistent with previously plotted points.

The final part of the elicitation stage involves checking the consistency of the assessor's judgements and checking that the assessor is comfortable with the final distribution. Keeney and van Winterfeldt (1991) suggest that one of the most important consistency checks is to derive the density function from the cumulative probability distribution. This is most conveniently carried out with on-line computer support. With irregular distributions, the cumulative distribution can hide multi-modal phenomena or skewness of the density function. Another important consistency check is to show the assessor the effect of assessments from decomposed variables on aggregation. If the assessor is surprised by the result the reasons for this should be investigated, rechecking decomposed assessments as necessary.

6. Analysis, Aggregation and Resolution of Disagreements

Following an elicitation session the analyst needs to provide feedback to the assessor about the combined judgements if this was not possible during the elicitation session. This may lead to the assessor making changes to judgements made in the elicitation session.

Where elicitation of a variable involves more than one assessor it is necessary to aggregate these judgements. This may involve group meetings to explore the basis for consensus judgements or resolve disagreements. Keeney and van Winterfeldt (1991) found that whether or not substantial disagreements existed among expert assessors, there was almost always agreement among them that averaging of probability distributions (which preserved the range of uncertainties) was an appropriate procedure to provide information for a base case analysis.

It should be clear from the forgoing discussion that probability encoding is a non-trivial process, which needs to be taken seriously for credible results. To be effective the encoding process needs to be carefully planned and structured and adequate time devoted to it. The complete process should be documented as well as the elicitation results and associated reasoning. For subsequent use, documentation should be presented in a hierarchical level of detail to facilitate reports and justification of results in appropriate levels of detail for different potential users. In all of these respects the encoding process is no different to other aspects of the risk analysis and management process.

10.11 MERGING SUBJECTIVE ESTIMATES AND OBJECTIVE DATA

Subjective probability estimates often have a basis in terms of objective data. The use of such data was touched on earlier, in the introduction, and in relation to fitting specific probability distribution curves to data, for example.

On occasion there is a need to make important subjective adjustments to data-based estimates, to reflect issues known to be important, even if they are not immediately quantifiable in objective terms.

Example 10.8

When Chapman was involved for the first time in assessing the probability of a buckle when laying offshore pipelines in the North Sea in the mid 1970s, data were gathered. The number of buckles to date was divided by the number of kilometres of pipe laid to date to estimate the probability of a buckle. When the result was discussed with experienced engineers, they suggested dividing it by two, because operators had become more experienced, and equipment had improved. In the absence of time for revised time series analysis (to quantify the trend), this was done, on the grounds that dividing by 2 was a better estimate than not dividing by anything.

When Chapman worked for IBM in the 1960s, advice provided by a 'wise old timer' on the estimation of software costs was 'work out the best estimate you can, then multiply it by 3'. A more recently suggested version of this approach is multiply by π, on the grounds that it has a more scientific ring about it, and it is closer to reality on average. Such advice may seem silly, but it is not. Formal risk management processes are driven at least in part by a wish to do away with informal, subjective, hidden uplifts. However, the operative words are informal and hidden. Visible, subjective uplifts are dispensed with only by the very brave, who can be made to look very foolish as a consequence.

10.12 DEALING WITH CONTRADICTORY DATA OR A COMPLETE ABSENCE OF DATA

As argued earlier subjective estimates for the Scope Estimates sub-phase are useful even if no data exist, to identify which aspects of a situation are worth further study.

Where no data exist, or the data are contradictory, it can be useful to employ sensitivity analysis directly. For example, a reliability study

(Chapman, Cooper and Cammaert, 1984) involving liquefied natural gas (LNG) plant failures used increases and decreases in failure probabilities by an order of magnitude to test probability assumptions for sensitivity. Where it didn't matter, no further work was undertaken with respect to probabilities. Where it did, extensive literature searches and personal interviews were used. It transpired that LNG plant failure probabilities were too sensitive to allow operators to provide data or estimates directly, but they were prepared to look at the Chapman *et al.* estimates and either nod or shake their heads.

In some situations, where experience and data are extremely limited, individual assessors may feel unable or unwilling to provide estimates of probabilities. In such situations providing the assessor with anonymity, persuasion, or simple persistence may be sufficient to obtain the desired cooperation (Morgan and Herion, 1990, Chapter 7). However, even where assessors cannot be persuaded to provided probability distributions, they may still provide useful information about the behaviour of the variables in question.

Nevertheless, there can be occasions where the level of understanding is sufficiently low that efforts to generate subjective probability distributions are not justified by the level of insight that the results are likely to provide. In deciding whether a probability encoding exercise is warranted, the analyst needs to make a judgement about how much additional insight is likely to be provided by the exercise. Sometimes a parametric analysis or simple order-of-magnitude analysis may provide as much or more insight as a more complex analysis based on probability distributions elicited from experts, and with considerably less effort. In the following example, probability estimates were unavailable, but it was still possible to reach an informed decision with suitable analysis.

Example 10.9

During a study of the reliability of a water supply pipeline Chapman was asked by a client to advise on the risk of sabotage. The pipeline had suffered one unsuccessful sabotage attack, so the risk was a real one, but with experience limited to just one unsuccessful attack there was clearly no objective basis for assessing the subsequent chance of a successful attack. Any decision by the client to spend money to protect the pipeline or not to bother needed justification, particularly if no money was spent and there was later a successful attack. In this latter scenario, the senior executives of the client organisation could find themselves in court, defending themselves against a charge of 'professional negligence'.

The approach taken was to turn the issue around, avoiding the question 'What is the chance of a successful sabotage attack?', and asking instead 'What does the chance of a successful sabotage attack have to be in order to make it worthwhile spending money on protection?' To address this latter question, the most likely point of attack was identified, the most effective response to this attack was identified, and the response and consequences of a successful attack were costed. The resulting analysis suggested that one successful attack every two years would be necessary to justify the expenditure. Although knowledge was limited it was considered that successful attacks could not be this frequent. Therefore, the case for not spending the money was clear and could be defended.

Had a successful attack every two million years justified the expenditure, a clear decision to spend it might have been the result.

A middle ground result is not a waste of time. It indicates there is no clear case one way or another based on the assumptions used. If loss of life is an issue, a neutral analysis result allows such considerations to be taken into account without ignoring more easily quantified costs.

The key issue this example highlights is *the purpose of analysis is insight, not numbers*. At the end of the day we usually do not need defendable probabilities. We need defendable decisions. The difference can be very important.

Example 10.9 illustrates a number of issues in relation to two earlier examples in this chapter:

1. Data availability is highly variable, ranging from large sets of directly relevant data to no relevant data.
2. Analysis of *any* available and relevant data is a good starting point.
3. To capture the difference between the observed past and the anticipated future, subjective adjustment of estimates based on data is usually essential.
4. Even when good data are available, the assumptions used to formulate probability distributions which describe the future are necessarily subjective. Thus it is useful to think of all probability distributions as subjective, some based on realistic data and assumptions, others more dependent upon judgements made in a direct manner.
5. The role of probabilities is to help us make decisions which are consistent with the beliefs of those with relevant expertise and knowledge, integrating the collective wisdom of all those who can usefully contribute. The validity of the probabilities themselves is not really relevant unless misconceptions lead to ill-advised decisions. Understanding why some decision choices are better than others is what the process is about.
6. The validity of probability distributions in terms of our ability to verify or prove them may be an issue of importance in terms of legal or political processes. In such cases it may be easier to demonstrate the validity of recommended strategies instead.

10.13 CONCLUSION

This chapter suggests a particular process, based on the Simple Scenario approach, which can be developed in various ways. In its simplest *scope the uncertainty* form it provides a simple alternative to H/M/L scenarios defined in purely qualitative terms, explicitly linking a Simple Scenario approach to full quantitative analysis via a simple quantitative interpretation of the scenarios. The sequence of the steps suggested was selected to respond to known bias.

There is a very large literature on probability elicitation, for good reason. Much of it complements the approach suggested here, but some of it is contradicted by the discussion here. We hope sufficient detail has been provided to indicate which is which, for those who wish to develop deep expertise in this area. We also hope those not concerned with the finer points of these arguments will feel comfortable applying the suggested approach.

Chapter 11

Evaluate the Estimates and their Implications: the Evaluate Phase

'Five to one against and falling ...' she said, 'four to one against and falling ... three to one ... two to one ... probability factor of one to one ... we have normality ... Anything you still can't cope with is therefore your own problem.'

D. Adams, *The Hitchhiker's Guide to the Galaxy*

11.1 INTRODUCTION

The Evaluate phase is central to the iterative nature of the overall risk management process (RMP), which is in turn central to effective development of insight about the nature of project risk, which is in its turn central to the understanding of effective responses to manage that risk. In this sense the Evaluate phase is at the core of understanding risk in order to respond to it. The Evaluate phase does not need to be understood at a deep technical level in order to manage risk. However, some very important concepts, like statistical dependence, need to be understood properly at an intuitive level in order to manage risk effectively. An understanding of what is involved when distributions are combined is part of this. This chapter endeavours to provide that understanding, without technical detail which goes beyond this basic need.

All project RMPs have an Evaluate phase, as indicated in Chapter 4. Its purpose is evaluation of the results of the Estimate phase, with a view to client assessment of decisions and judgements. The Evaluate phase usually includes the synthesis of individual risk estimates, as is the case here.

As indicated in Chapter 4, the deliverables will depend upon the depth of the preceding phases achieved to this point. Looping back to earlier phases before proceeding further is likely to be a key and frequent decision at this stage. For example, an important early deliverable might be a prioritised list of risks, while a later deliverable might be a diagnosed potential problem associated with a specific aspect of the base plan or contingency plans, and suggested revisions to these plans to resolve the problem. The key deliverable is diagnosis of any and all-important opportunities or threats, and comparative analysis of the implications of responses to these opportunities or threats. The Evaluate phase should be used to drive and develop the distinction between the two main tasks of the Estimate phase indicated earlier. A first pass can be used to portray overall uncertainty and the relative size of all contributing factors. A second pass can be used to explore and confirm the importance of the key risks, obtaining additional data and undertaking further analysis of risks where appropriate. Further passes through the Estimate and Evaluate phases can further refine our understanding.

Some of these decisions and judgements are generally viewed as part of the Plan and Manage phases. However, it is convenient to treat the diagnosis of the need for such decisions and the development of the basis for appropriate judgements as part of the Evaluate phase, because they are closely coupled to the Estimate–Evaluate phase loops.

It is convenient to consider the specific tasks under four headings:

1. *select an appropriate subset of risks*—as the basis of a process of combining successive subsets of risks, choose an appropriate place to start, and each successive risk, using a structure which reflects dependence and/or the most effective story line to support cases for changes;
2. *integrate the subset of risks*—combine the risks, using addition, multiplication, division, greatest operations or other operations as appropriate, and restructure to simplify dependence as appropriate, computing summary parameters as appropriate;
3. *portray the effect*—design a presentation for overall and intermediate results to provide insights for the analysts in the first instance, to tell useful stories for risk analysis users as the plot of these stories emerges;
4. *diagnose the implications*—use the presentation of results to acquire the insight to write the appropriate stories.

Figure 11.1 portrays the way these specific tasks relate to key *assess* tasks, without complicating the diagram with other common tasks (*document, verify, assess,* and *report*).

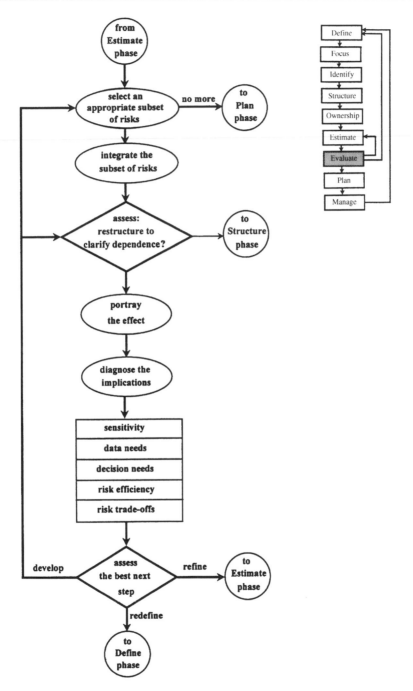

Figure 11.1 Evaluate phase specific tasks.

Figure 11.1 also portrays starting the Evaluate phase in *select an appropriate subset of risks* mode. A step breakdown is not provided. The objectives initially are making sure that the selected risk subset is the most appropriate place to start, for reasons comparable to those discussed in Chapter 10. The rationale becomes more complex later, when dependence becomes a key issue, and developing and telling stories becomes the concern. Evaluation then moves into *integrate the subset of risks* mode. This task is not represented in terms of steps, but a complex range of considerations is involved. The objective is effective and efficient synthesis of all the earlier analysis, with a view to understanding what matters and what does not. Assessing dependence may lead to an identified need to restructure, the role of the *assess: restructure to clarify dependence?* task.

Portray the effect follows, without showing steps. In the subsequent *diagnose the implications* task a number of steps are distinguished, representing an attempt to provide a checklist of the different aspects of diagnosis which need to be addressed in an orderly manner at this stage. Early passes through the process should focus on the early steps, with the focus moving to later steps as the iterative process matures.

The final aspect of the Evaluate phase is another form of the common *assess* task: *assess the best next step*, with a view to going back to the Estimate phase to refine the available information, going back to the Define phase for a more fundamental rethink, going back within this phase to assess the possible need to restructure, or moving on to selecting a wider or different subset of risks, until no more require evaluation and proceeding to the Plan phase is appropriate.

The structure of this chapter follows the structure of Figure 11.1 in Sections 11.2–11.7, with alternative integration procedures addressed in Section 11.8.

11.2 SELECT AN APPROPRIATE SUBSET OF RISKS

As indicated in Chapter 10, it may be important to start with one or more subsets of risks which are interesting enough, and sufficiently familiar to all those involved, to provide a useful basis for an educational process which may be central and essential to the early use of risk management processes. At this point in the RMP it may also be important to throw light on a pressing decision. Alternatively, it may be important to provide those contributing to the risk management process with results of immediate use to them, to show them an early return for the effort they have invested in the analysis process.

If a semi-Markov process is used to model risks, as discussed in Example 10.7, the initial subset may be a single risk.

Example 11.1

Early offshore North Sea project risk analyses which Chapman was involved with often started with the core risk in the pipelaying activity, weather risk. The effect of weather risk on the pipelaying schedule was modelled as a semi-Markov process. The calculation started with the state of the system when pipelaying begins (no pipe laid). A progress probability distribution for the first time period was applied to this initial state to define the possible states of the system at the start of the second time period. A progress probability distribution was then applied to this state distribution to define the possible states of the system at the start of the third time period, and so on. (Example 10.7 used this modelling approach, and Cooper and Chapman (1987) provide a further example.)

Only after this central core risk had been modelled and understood, and tentative decisions made about the best time of year to start pipelaying for a particular project, did the analysis move on to further risks. Further risks were added one at a time, to test their importance and understand their effect separately. Each successive risk was added in a pair-wise structure to the accumulated total effect of earlier risks. Because some of these risks (like buckles) were themselves weather dependent, it was essential to build up the analysis gradually, in order to understand the complex dependencies involved.

If semi-Markov processes are not involved, and dependence is not an issue, it may be appropriate to treat the subset of time or schedule risks associated with each activity as a base-level risk subset.

11.3   INTEGRATE THE SELECTED SUBSET OF RISKS

Integrating or combining risks together so that their net effect can be portrayed is a central task of the Evaluate phase. Typically this integration task is carried out with the aid of computer software based on Monte Carlo simulation (Hertz, 1964). This makes it relatively straightforward to add large numbers of risks together in a single operation to assess their overall impact. Unfortunately, this convenience can seduce analysts into a naive approach to risk combination which tends to overlook the importance of dependency between individual sources of risk. It also encourages analysts to set up the combination calculations to present the end result and ignore intermediate stages for specification and computational convenience. Also, the mechanics of how individual distributions are combined is not transparent to the user. Together these factors can lead to a failure to appreciate insights from considering intermediate stages of the combination process and dependencies between individual sources of risk.

Below we use a simple form of the Simple Scenario probability specification introduced in Chapter 10 and an approach based on basic discrete probability arithmetic to demonstrate the nature of dependency and illustrate its potential significance. Section 10.8 briefly relates this approach to alternatives.

Independent Addition

The simplest starting point is the addition of two independent distributions, each defined on the same common interval scale, a common interval (CI) variant of standard discrete probability calculus (Chapman and Cooper, 1983a).

To keep the example as simple as possible, assume we are combining the costs of two items, A and B, each with the same distribution of costs represented by three values shown in Table 11.1, defining C_a and C_b.

Table 11.2 shows the calculation of the distribution of $C_i = C_a + C_b$ assuming the costs of A and B are independent.

The calculation associated with the joint cost of 16 is the product of the probabilities of individual costs of 8, the 0.04 probability reflecting the low chance of both items having a minimum cost. Similarly, the joint cost of 24 reflects the low chance of both items having a maximum cost. In contrast, a joint cost of 20 has a relatively high probability of 0.37 because it is associated with three possible ways of obtaining a cost of 20: 8+12, 10+10, or 12+8. The probabilities associated with joint costs of 18 (via combinations 8+10 and 10+8), or 22 (via combinations 10+12 and 12+10), are closer to the 20 central case than they are to the extremes because of the relatively high probability (0.5) associated with $C_a = 10$ and $C_b = 10$.

Successive additions will make the probability of extreme values smaller and smaller. For example, ten items with this same distribution will have a minimum value of 80, with a probability of 0.2^{10}, zero for all practical purposes in the present context.

Table 11.1 Cost distributions for items A and B.

Cost (£k), C_a or C_b	Probability
8	0.2
10	0.5
12	0.3

Table 11.2 Distribution for $C_i = C_a + C_b$ assuming independence.

Cost (£k), C_i	Probability computation	Probability
16	0.2×0.2	0.04
18	$0.2 \times 0.5 + 0.5 \times 0.2$	0.20
20	$0.2 \times 0.3 + 0.5 \times 0.5 + 0.3 \times 0.2$	0.37
22	$0.5 \times 0.3 + 0.3 \times 0.5$	0.30
24	0.3×0.3	0.09

Positive Dependence in Addition

Positive dependence is the most common kind of statistical dependence, especially in the context of cost items. If item A costs more than expected because of market pressures, and B is associated with the same market, the cost of B will be positively correlated with that of A. Similarly, if the same estimator was involved, and he or she was optimistic (or pessimistic) about A, the chances are they were also optimistic (or pessimistic) about B.

Table 11.3 portrays the distribution of $C_p = C_a + C_b$ assuming perfect positive correlation. The probabilities shown are the same as for values of C_a and C_b in Table 11.1 because the addition process assumes the low, intermediate and high values for C_a and C_b occur together. That is, the only combinations of C_a and C_b possible are 8 + 8, 10 + 10, and 12 + 12. Table 11.3 shows clearly how the overall variability is preserved compared with C_i, the addition of $C_a + C_b$ assuming independence. In this simple, special case where A and B have identical cost distributions, C_p has the same distribution with the cost scaled up by a factor of two. Successive additions assuming perfect positive correlation will have no effect on the probability of extreme values. For example, ten items with the same distribution will have a minimum scenario value of 80 with a probability of 0.2. Compare this with the independence case cited earlier, where the probability of the minimum scenario value is 0.2^{10}.

Figure 11.2 portrays the addition of A and B assuming perfect positive correlation using the continuous variable cumulative forms introduced in Chapter 10 and procedures discussed at length elsewhere (Cooper and Chapman, 1987). The two component distributions are added horizontally. That is, the addition assumes costs of 7 and 7 for A and B occur together, costs of 8 and 8 occur together, and so on. More generally, all percentile values occur together. Plotting Figure 11.2 directly from Table 11.3 provides the same result.

Figure 11.3 replots the C_p curve of Figure 11.2 in conjunction with a cumulative curve for C_i derived directly from Table 11.2. For C_i the minimum cost of 15 in contrast to the minimum cost of 14 for C_p reflects a small error in the discrete probability calculation of Table 11.2 if it is recognised that the underlying variable is continuous. This error is of no

Table 11.3 Distribution for $C_p = C_a + C_b$ assuming perfect positive correlation.

Cost (£k), C_p	Probability
16	0.2
20	0.5
24	0.3

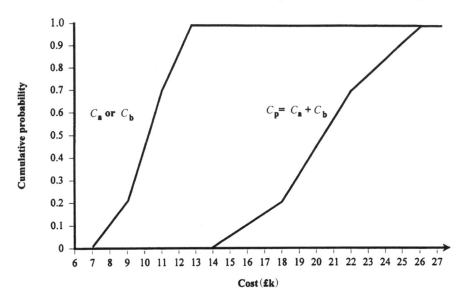

Figure 11.2 $C_p = C_a + C_b$ assuming perfect positive correlation.

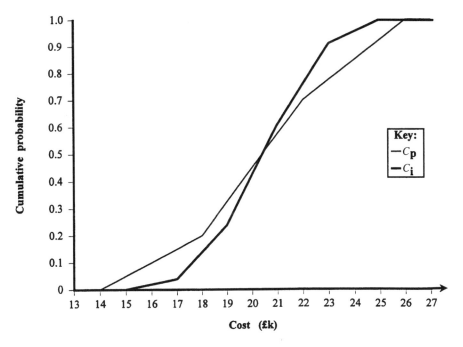

Figure 11.3 Comparison of C_p and C_i cumulative probability curves.

consequence in the present discussion (see Cooper and Chapman, 1987, Chapter 3, for a detailed discussion).

In practice assuming perfect positive correlation for cost items is usually closer to the truth than assuming independence. As indicated in Chapter 8, extensive correlation calibration studies associated with steel fabrication costs for North Sea oil and gas offshore projects in the early 1980s suggested 70–80% dependence on average, defining 'percent dependence' in terms of a linear interpolation between independence (0% dependence) and perfect positive correlation (100% dependence). For most practical purposes, percentage dependence is the same as 'coefficient of correlation' (defined over the range 0–1, with 0.5 corresponding to 50%) (see Yong, 1985, for a more detailed discussion).

In the absence of good reasons to believe otherwise, the authors assume about 80% dependence for cost items, a coefficient of correlation of 0.8, representing a slightly conservative stance relative to the 70–80% observed for North Sea projects. For related reasons, 50% is a reasonable working assumption for related project activity duration distributions, unless there is reason to believe otherwise. This avoids the potential pessimism of 100% dependence and the undue optimism of complete independence. Example 11.2 indicates the misleading effect unfounded optimism about dependence can have.

Example 11.2

A complex military hardware project had a planned duration of about 12 years. A PERT model involving several hundred activities was estimated, yielding individual activity probability distributions those involved felt were reasonable. It was evaluated assuming independence, yielding an overall duration suggesting 12 years ± about 5 weeks. It was believed ±5 years would have been a better reflection of reality. It was understood that assuming independence in conjunction with a large number of activities effectively assumed away the real variability, making the model detail a dangerous waste of time. However, the response was to use fewer activities in the model. This did not directly address the question of dependence and obscured rather than resolved the basic problem.

In practice, assuming independence is always a dangerous assumption if that assumption is unfounded. It becomes obviously foolish if a large number of items or activities is involved. However, it is an apparently plausible understatement of project risk that is the real evaluation risk.

Negative Dependence in Addition

Negative dependence is less common than positive dependence, but it can have very important impacts, especially in the context of successive project activity durations, and 'insurance' or 'hedging' arrangements. For example, if A and B are successive activities, and B can be speeded up (at a cost) to compensate for delays to A, the duration of B will be negatively correlated with that of A (although their costs will be positively correlated, as discussed in Chapter 8).

In terms of the simple discrete probability example of Table 11.1, perfect negative correlation (-100% dependence) implies that when C_a takes a value of 8, C_b is 12, and vice versa (overlooking for the moment the different probabilities associated with these outcomes). Call the distribution of $C_a + C_b$ under these conditions C_n. In terms of the continuous variable portrayals of Figure 11.2, C_n is a vertical line at a cost of 20 (overlooking the asymmetric distributions for A and B). Negative correlation substantially reduces variability, and perfect negative correlation can eliminate variability completely.

From a risk management point of view, positive correlation should be avoided where possible, negative correlation should be embraced where possible. Negative correlation is the basis of insurance, of 'hedging' bets, of effectively spreading risk. Its value in this context is of central importance to risk management. The point here is that while independence may be a central case between perfect positive and perfect negative correlation, it is important to recognise the significant role that both positive and negative dependence have in specific cases, and the fact that positive and negative dependence cannot be assumed to cancel out on average.

Other Combining Operations

Evaluation of risks in a cost estimate may involve multiplication ('product') and division ('quotient') operations. Evaluation of profit may involve subtraction ('difference') operations. Evaluation of precedence networks can involve 'greatest' operations at a merge event. The mathematics can become more complex. In particular, simple common interval calculations become much more complex than the calculation of Table 11.2. However, the principles remain the same, and the effects of positive and negative correlation can become even more important. For example, if costs are perfectly positively correlated with revenues, profit is assured, while perfect negative correlation implies a high gearing up of the risk.

11.4 ASSESS THE NEED TO RESTRUCTURE TO CLARIFY DEPENDENCE

One of the obvious difficulties associated with non-expert use of percentage dependence or coefficient of correlation assessments of dependence is the need for mental calibration of what these measures mean. If this is an issue, or if dependence is too complex to be captured adequately by simple

Table 11.4 Conditional cost distribution for
C_b given C_a.

C_a (£k)	Probability	C_b (£k)	Probability
8	0.2	8	0.7
		10	0.3
10	0.5	8	0.2
		10	0.5
		12	0.3
12	0.3	10	0.3
		12	0.7

Table 11.5 Distribution for $C_c = C_a + C_b$ assuming the specification of Table 11.4.

C_c (£k)	Probability computation	Probability
16	0.2×0.7	0.14
18	$0.2 \times 0.3 + 0.5 \times 0.2$	0.16
20	0.5×0.5	0.25
22	$0.5 \times 0.3 + 0.3 \times 0.3$	0.24
24	0.3×0.7	0.21

measures like percentage dependence, conditional specification of dependence is an effective solution. Table 11.4 provides a simple example, based on the cost of item A with the same C_a distribution as in Table 11.1, but with the distribution of the cost of item B, C_b, dependent or conditional on the level of C_a.

Table 11.5 shows the calculation of the distribution of the cost $C_c = C_a + C_b$ assuming the conditional specification of Table 11.4.

The computational effort is not increased by the conditional specification. In this particular example it is actually reduced. However, specification effort is increased, and it would increase exponentially if we wanted to consider three or more jointly dependent items in this way. It is this specification effort which constrains our use of conditional specifications to occasions when it adds value relative to simple percentage dependence or coefficient of correlation specifications.

Comparison of C_c with C_i and C_p is provided in Table 11.6 and Figure 11.4.

Figure 11.4 (and the C_p values in Table 11.6) uses the continuous variable approach developed in Cooper and Chapman (1987) and the C_p bounds of 14 to 26 to correct partially for the errors noted in Section 11.3 because this makes interpretation of the curves easier. Table 11.6 and Figure 11.4 should make it clear that even the simple dependence structure of Table 11.4 does not yield a simple interpolation between C_i and C_p. However, for most

Table 11.6 Comparison of the distribution for C_c with C_i and C_p.

Cost (£k)	Probability		
	C_i	C_c	C_p
16	0.04	0.14	0.15
18	0.20	0.16	0.17
20	0.37	0.25	0.25
22	0.30	0.24	0.19
24	0.09	0.21	0.24

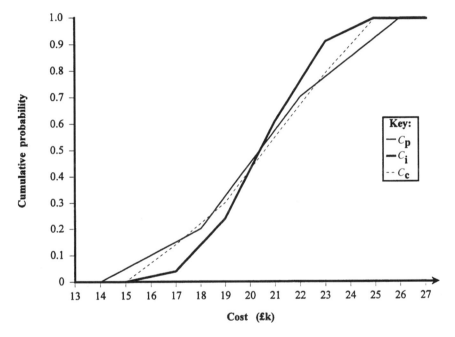

Figure 11.4 Comparison of C_p, C_i and C_c cumulative probability curves.

practical purposes 80–90% dependence is a reasonable interpretation of the level of dependence portrayed by Table 11.4, and other levels of dependence could be mentally calibrated in a similar manner. This example should also make it clear that very high levels of dependence are both plausible and common.

In addition to the use of conditional specifications like Table 11.4 to calibrate simpler dependence measures, this form of specification is very useful for more complex forms of dependence (Cooper and Chapman, 1987). In this context the use of conditional specifications can become a form of restructuring, asking questions about why B ought to vary with A in a particular pattern. Once these questions are raised, it is often more practical to explicitly address the possible need for restructuring.

If, for example, the reason the costs of items A and B are correlated is that they will be the responsibility of either contractor X or contractor Y, X being very efficient and Y being very inefficient, but political pressures determining the outcome, it may be useful to model this choice directly, as indicated in Table 11.7. Table 11.8 computes the associated cost distribution, defined as C_m, the 'm' subscript denoting causally *modelled*.

Those who do not follow the probability tree calculations imbedded in Table 11.8 do not need to worry about the computational detail. What matters is the simplicity and clarity of a format like Table 11.7 relative to a format like Table 11.4, and the quite different results they yield. The result provided in Table 11.8 involves much stronger dependence than even C_p, with very little chance of a value of 20, and 16 or 24 much more likely. That is, the example provided by Tables 11.7 and 11.8 has been chosen to illustrate a 'bimodal' result which can be so extreme as to virtually eliminate any chance of a central value, one or other of the extremes becoming the likely outcome. This is an even more extreme form of positive dependence than the perfect positive correlation illustrated by C_p, which some people see as a very pessimistic extreme or bound on the impact of positive correlation. More generally, perfect positive correlation and perfect negative correlation are the most extreme forms of *well-behaved, simple dependence*,

Table 11.7 Causal model of dependence example specification.

Probability X will be responsible for both A and B = 0.6	
Probability Y will be responsible for both A and B = 0.4	
Cost (£k) for A or B if X responsible	Probability
8	0.8
10	0.2
Cost (£k) for A or B if Y responsible	Probability
10	0.1
12	0.9

Table 11.8 Distribution for $C_m = C_a + C_b$ assuming the causal model of Table 11.7.

Cost (£k)	Computation	Probability
16	$0.6 \times 0.8 \times 0.8$	0.384
18	$0.6 \times 0.8 \times 0.2 + 0.6 \times 0.2 \times 0.8$	0.192
20	$0.6 \times 0.2 \times 0.2 + 0.4 \times 0.1 \times 0.1$	0.028
22	$0.4 \times 0.1 \times 0.9 + 0.4 \times 0.9 \times 0.1$	0.072
24	$0.4 \times 0.9 \times 0.9$	0.324

but more complex forms of dependence can produce extremes which go significantly beyond the bounds of simple perfect correlation. Cooper and Chapman (1987) develop these ideas in more detail.

More generally still, if a causal structure which can be articulated underlies any complex form of dependence, it is usually efficient and effective to explore that structure using some form of probability or decision tree. An important part of the overall process is defining the structure in a manner which simplifies our understanding of complex issues (Cooper and Chapman, 1987, also develop these ideas in more detail).

11.5 PORTRAY THE EFFECT

Graphs like Figures 11.3 and 11.4 are clearly useful when assessing the nature and importance of dependence, and the possible need to reconsider the way dependence might be modelled. Such figures help to develop the story a completed analysis will tell. Even if dependence is not involved, this story needs to be developed a bit at a time, as each successive distribution is combined with the subset considered to date, or at intervals as subsets are compiled. Figures 11.5 and 11.6 illustrate other formats which are often useful.

Figure 11.5 portrays the build-up of six risks within a given activity. The curve labelled '6' represents all six risks. The curve labelled '1' represents just the first, the curve labelled '2' is the sum of the first two, and so on. The gaps between the curves indicate the relative importance of each contribution, risk 5 ('industrial disputes') being the most important in this example. This example is based on the 'jacket fabrication' case used to illustrate risk–response diagrams earlier.

Each activity in a network can be portrayed using the format of Figure 11.5. Less important risks can be combined, to keep the story simple, six separate risks or risk subsets being close to the upper limit of effective portrayal in this format.

Relationships between activities can then be portrayed using the format of Figure 11.6. Like Figure 11.5, Figure 11.6 is based on a North Sea oil project case used earlier in several publications (Chapman, 1990).

The format of Figure 11.5 is also extremely useful for building up a cost structure in a nested fashion.

Example 11.3

A deep mining project for which Chapman advised on risk management processes was addressed via top-down risk analysis as an early part of an integrated set of risk management processes.

The starting point was a 'base cost' estimate already in place, and a set of conditions or assumptions, mostly explicit, which had been made when producing this 'base cost' estimate. Senior members of the project team provided a subjective

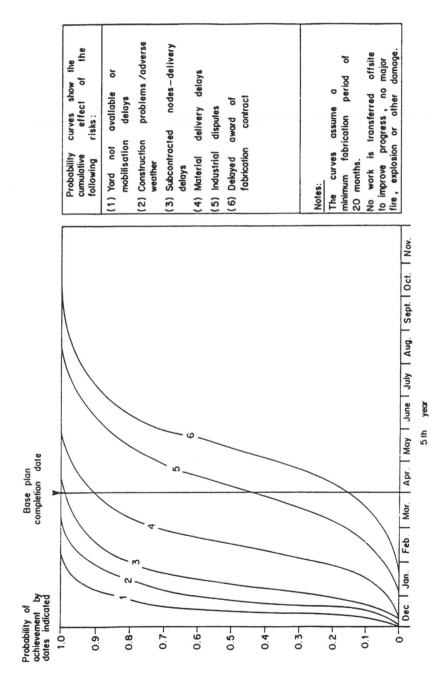

Figure 11.5   Initial level output for offshore project.

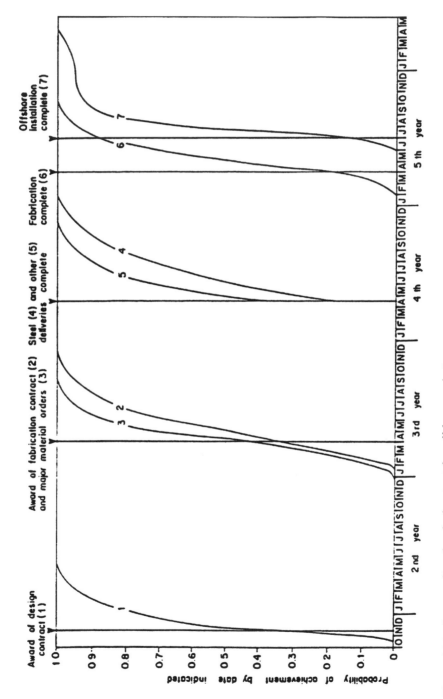

Figure 11.6 Intermediate level of output for offshore project.

estimate of the variability associated with the base estimate given all the conditions held, defining a distribution called B.

Conditions were then grouped into four sets of 'specific risks', the first three of which were assumed to share a high level of common dependence within each group:

1. 'geology risks', all related to geological uncertainty with direct cost implications;

2. 'geology/design risks', all related to design changes driven by geology uncertainty;

3. 'geology/planning risks', all related to planning approval risks driven by geology uncertainty;

4. 'independent risks', which could be assumed to be largely independent of each other and other specific risks.

Various experts contributed to subjective estimates of 'direct cost' (ignoring the knock-on effects of delay) probability distributions within each of these four sets, designated: G1, G2, etc.; GD1, GD2, etc.; GP1, GP2, etc.; IR1, IR2, etc.

Based on discussions with the experts during the elicitation of these distributions, Chapman provided initial estimates of a percentage dependence level within and between each set. These were used with the estimates to provide five figures in the Figure 11.5 format. Four defined:

$$G = G1 + G2 \text{ etc.}$$

$$GD = GD1 + GD2 \text{ etc.}$$

$$GP = GP1 + GP2 \text{ etc.}$$

$$IR = IR1 + IR2 \text{ etc.}$$

The fifth defined:

$$SR = G + GD + GP + IR$$

In the light of earlier discussions about specific risks, senior members of the project team then provided estimates of the probability of delay to the project (D), and the probability distribution for the indirect cost of delay per unit time (CT). Further graphs in the format of Figure 11.5 showed:

$$CD = CT \times D$$

$$C = B + SR + CD$$

As indicated, the final curve for C was built bottom-up, but the complete set of curves was presented top-down in three levels:

1. $C = B + SR + CD$

2. $CD = CT \times D$
   $SR = G + GD + GP + IR$

3. $G = G1 + G2 \text{ etc.}$
   $GD = GD1 + GD2 \text{ etc.}$
   $GP = GP1 + GP2 \text{ etc.}$
   $IR = IR1 + IR2 \text{ etc.}$

The project team as a whole then discussed these results in relation to the underlying assumptions to assess:

1. whether it told an overall story which was consistent with their beliefs;
2. where the uncertainty was a cause for concern which needed attention in terms of a clear need for more data and analysis of those data;
3. where the uncertainty was a cause for concern which needed attention in terms of a clear need for exploration of alternative ways of addressing the six *W*s.

This kind of analysis can be undertaken in days or weeks, hours if really pressed, and used to drive the start of a more detailed bottom-up analysis.

11.6 DIAGNOSE THE IMPLICATIONS

Diagnosis is central to the risk evaluation process. It is discussed here in a layered structure, starting with the most obvious issues needing early treatment, then moving on to the more subtle issues best left until later in the risk management process.

Sensitivity

All effective quantitative modelling requires sensitivity analysis, so the analysts and the users of analysis can understand the relative importance of the components the analysis uses. Figures such as 11.5 provide a direct built-in sensitivity analysis. If partial results are not accumulated and displayed in this way, this sensitivity analysis information is lost.

There are ways of partially recovering such information. For example, a common approach is to hold each parameter at its expected value, and let one parameter vary. Another is to use a set of values representing the range for each parameter, letting the others vary. However, a nested structure using the approach illustrated by Figure 11.5 is simpler to compute and use. It requires planning the sequence of the evaluate operations in advance, but in practice this a very small price to pay for the convenience and insight which follows such evaluation operations.

Data Needs

A very important aspect of the iterative approach to the overall risk management process is its use to allocate data acquisition and analysis time efficiently.

Example 11.4

Figure 11.5 reflects the story told by a first cut analysis based on subjective probability estimates provided by the group responsible for this activity. When the relative importance of 'industrial disputes' was observed, industrial dispute data for all the yards likely to be used for the fabrication of the jacket were gathered and analysed. The analysis confirmed the relative importance of industrial disputes, and the sizing of the risk in Figure 11.5. It was worth spending extra time on this risk, but not on comparatively unimportant risks.

Decision Needs

Another important aspect of the iterative approach to the overall risk management process is its use to allocate decision analysis time efficiently.

Example 11.5

Figure 11.5 suggests a probability of achieving the 'base plan' completion date of about 0.15, an unsatisfactory outcome. Once it was confirmed that the picture portrayed by Figure 11.5 was valid, improving the prognosis was in order, by changing the base plan or contingency plans, with particular reference to key risk areas. In the process of 'industrial dispute' data acquisition and analysis, the hypothesis that a carefully drafted contract with the yard would be an effective response was explored. Analysis suggested such contracts actually had little effect on these industrial disputes. Such industrial disputes mainly occurred during the last 10% of a contract if no more work was anticipated in that yard on completion. Recognition of this cause led to effective action—smoothing the flow of work to yards to the extent possible by all the oil companies involved. It was recognised that this resolved the particular problem diagnosed by Figure 11.5, and the more general 'industrial disputes' problem. It was also recognised that this smoother work flow reduced jacket fabrication costs by avoiding bidding up the price when demand peaked.

Further Risk Efficiency-Motivated Changes

Example 3.1 illustrated the risk efficiency concept in the content of a decision to use a 3 metre wave height capability barge to perform a hook-up instead of the 1.6 metre barge initially chosen. The need to consider an alternative decision was flagged by the analysis results, akin to the Figure 11.5 situation just discussed. However, often improvements in risk efficiency which are possible are not flagged in this way. In such cases we must search for them. Typical examples include: using more capable equipment than the minimum requirements suggest; using more resources initially, then releasing them if rapid progress is made; starting earlier; purchasing insurance; designing out the key sources of risk recognised by this stage in the analysis; writing contracts to allow more flexible responses to possible threats and opportunities.

Comparison of alternative ways of achieving an activity or a project as a whole can be portrayed in terms of diagrams like Figure 11.7. Figure 11.7 uses simple uniform distributions to clarify the messages discussed here.

Figure 11.7 portrays a comparison between approaches A, B and C in terms of cost probability distributions. It shows that in terms of cost as

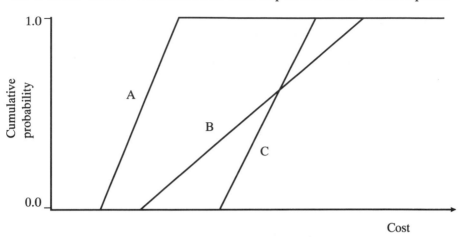

Figure 11.7 Comparison of approaches A, B and C.

measured, approach A is the risk efficient choice. The expected cost of A is less than that of B and C. In addition, the risk is less, in the sense that the probability of the cost exceeding any given level is higher for B and C than for A. This case involves clear 'stochastic dominance', indicated by the distributions for B and C being clearly and entirely to the right of the distribution for A.

If A were not available B would generally be preferable to C. It does not 'dominate' completely, indicated by the crossing of the curves. But the increase in potential extreme values associated with B relative to C is offset by the reduced expected value, and the reduced expected value will make up for the additional variability of B relative to C in most contexts.

The use of diagrams like Figure 11.7 to portray the comparative implications of alternative approaches is one way to pursue changes in base plans and contingency plans which involve an increase in risk efficiency. In practice 'S' curves like those of Figure 11.5 are more usual than the simple linear cumulative distributions of Figure 11.7, but multi-modal distributions can be involved, resulting in curves like '7' in Figure 11.6, the flat portion around 0.9 probability indicating a 10% chance of missing a 'weather window'.

Further Risk/Expect Cost Balance-Motivated Changes

Example 3.2 illustrated trade-offs between risk and expected cost which may require attention. Often these are not flagged—they must be searched for. Further, often they reflect opportunities people are not prepared to take if they are not protected from the 'bad luck/bad management confusion'. These are key opportunities to address, particularly in the early stages of introducing formal risk management processes into an organisation.

Typical examples are the flip side of the examples cited in the last subsection context of risk efficiency improvements if the numbers (probabilities) are different. They include: using less capable equipment than maximum requirements suggest; using fewer resources initially, with fall-back plans in place when appropriate; starting later; not purchasing insurance (self-insuring); designing in the possible ability to capture possible opportunities recognised at this stage of the analysis.

Figure 11.7 portrays a comparison between approach C and approach B in terms of cost probability distributions. It shows that in terms of cost as measured, neither is more risk efficient. A trade-off is involved. Approach B has a lower expected cost, but the tail of the distribution crosses that of approach C, implying more risk. In this case most would find this risk worth taking, but the more profound the overlap and the closer the expectations, the more difficult the choice.

Using diagrams like Figure 11.7 to portray the comparative implications of alternative approaches is one way to pursue changes in 'base plans' and 'contingency plans' which involve trade-offs between expected values of the key performance measure and associated risk. They provide a way of portraying what the trade-off involves so that those responsible can make informed choices.

Further Changes Motivated by Other Trade-offs

Further trade-offs may also require consideration at this stage. For example: if an activity was given a less generous time provision, would the direct cost increase be less than the revenue increase; if the performance or quality specification for a component was decreased, would the related decrease in time or cost be worthwhile; and so on.

In concluding this section, it is important to reiterate that all the above forms of diagnosis require attention as the subset of risks grows. Effective and efficient choices cannot be left until all the risks have been jointly evaluated. Careful attention to partial results as the evaluation process proceeds will suggest changes to those looking for such changes.

11.7   ASSESS THE BEST NEXT STEP

Sensitivity analysis and subsequent data or decision needs analysis may suggest a need to re-estimate, as indicated in Examples 11.4 and 11.5. Further forms of diagnosis may also indicate a need for a loop back to the Estimate phase. More profound loops back to restructuring may also be suggested, as portrayed in Figure 11.1. Otherwise a loop back to enlarge the subset of risks may be appropriate, unless all the risks have now been considered, and moving on to the Plan phase is appropriate. Selecting the next risk to be considered may need to follow a complex nesting structure, like that implicit in Example 11.2. In this case base level subsets of risks are combined, then second level risks, and so on.

11.8 ALTERNATIVE INTEGRATION PROCEDURES

Those not interested in computational issues, computer software selection or hands-on analysis may skip this section. It is arguably the least relevant section in this book for senior managers. However, at least a skim read is still advisable.

The simple controlled interval approach of Table 11.2 involves a systematic error associated with the discrete value approximation of a continuous variable distribution, as explained elsewhere (Cooper and Chapman, 1987, Chapter 3). To indicate the size (importance) of the error, note that the Figure 11.2 C_i curve assumes 15 is the absolute minimum, while exact integration indicates that 14 is the absolute minimum, with a probability of 0.05 of a value less than 15. The more intervals used to represent a distribution, the smaller this systematic error becomes. Even with only three intervals, this error is not significant for present purposes. To overcome this error a Controlled Interval and Memory (CIM) approach has been developed, as explained elsewhere (Cooper and Chapman, 1987). This approach also overcomes the complications associated with operations other than addition. Software developed to use this approach by BP International (Clark and Chapman, 1987; Yong, 1985) and K&H (PERK) has been used on a wide range of projects, but it is not currently readily available. In its original forms it requires pair-wise specification of a sequence for combining all distributions. This can raise difficulties, when irreducible networks are involved, for example (Soukhakian, 1988). It requires expert use to make effective use of the pair-wise structuring, and it can be tedious to use if pair-wise structures are not helpful.

As noted earlier, Monte Carlo simulation is the usual method employed to combine risks in standard risk analysis software packages like '@Risk' (see APM, 1995, for a summary of available software). Monte Carlo simulation is based on 'sampling'. For example, to add the probability distributions for items A and B of Table 11.1 assuming independence to define C_i, we start by taking a 'sample' from the distribution for A. The mechanics of this 'sample' reduce to using a 'pseudo random number generator' to obtain a random number in the range 0–1, using this sampled value to reference the probability scale of a cumulative distribution for item A like that of Figure 11.2, and reading off the corresponding cost. For example, a generated random number value of 0.1 would yield a sample cost of 8. Assuming the random numbers are uniformly distributed over the range 0–1, this can be shown to result in costs sampled from the assumed distribution for C_a.

A similar sample for item B can be added to define a sample for $C_a + C_b = C_i$. Repeating this procedure a hundred times results in a frequency distribution for C_i which approximates the true integration with sufficient accuracy for most purposes. However, the 0.05 probability error noted in relation to Figure 11.3 could require a thousand samples or more to estimate with reasonable precision, a similar number being required for a resulting curve which is smooth, without visible sampling error. Using ten thousand samples gives the same level of precision as a CIM procedure with about 30 classes, the latter being about a thousand times faster (Yong, 1985).

Non-random sampling procedures ('Latin Hypercubes', for example) can be used to speed up the production of smooth curves. In principle, such procedures are a partial move towards the completely systematic sampling procedure which CI or CIM procedures use, partially reducing sampling error while inducing some systematic error. In practice, the systematic error is unlikely to be important, though it can be.

Simple discrete probability methods suitable for manual computations in a decision tree or probability tree context, and Controlled Interval and Memory (CIM) developments of these methods, provide alternatives to Monte Carlo simulation. The key points about the CIM process in the present context are:

1. it requires combining successive pairs of risks, for computational reasons;
2. this requirement encourages thinking about a structure for these successive pairs which reflects dependence and the story to be told;
3. a byproduct of this computational structure is built-in sensitivity analysis, as discussed in Section 11.5;
4. for reasons discussed in Section 11.5 the use of CIM procedures or exposure to the results of their use should persuade any expert analyst or user of analysis without access to CIM software to use Monte Carlo-driven packages as if they were CIM driven to some extent, if not to the point of always using a pairing structure.

The approach described in this chapter assumes Monte Carlo simulation-driven software will be used, but the lessons from CIM-driven analysis learned by the authors are worth incorporating in the process. In the long term, software which uses expert system technology to select CIM or

Monte Carlo processes as appropriate should be practical and forthcoming. In the short term any sampling software which allows for dependence used with reasonable care is effective, if not efficient.

Monte Carlo-driven software can usually accommodate dependence in coefficient correlation or percentage dependence equivalent forms. In practice, 'industry standard' packages can cause difficulties when modelling dependence, and care needs to be exercised. Analysts need to understand dependence well enough to realise when results do not make sense.

Earlier 'industry standard' methods based on statistical moments, typically 'mean-variance', as used in the original PERT calculations (Moder and Philips, 1970), are worth understanding, at least in outline. The 'mean' or 'expected value' of a variable is the sum of all the possible values for the variable weighted by the associated probabilities of each value. This represents a single estimate of what will happen on average. Expected values have the useful property that they are additive. That is, the expected cost of a sum of costs is equal to the sum of the expected values for each individual cost.

It is important to distinguish between the expected value and other 'measures of central tendency' associated with a distribution, such as the 'median' (that value which has a 50% chance of being exceeded), and 'the most likely value' (most probable, often referred to as the 'best estimate'), which do not have this additive property in general.

For example, the cost of items A and B of Table 11.1 each have an expected value of $(8 \times 0.2) + (10 \times 0.5) + (12 \times 0.3) = 10.2$. This means that the expected cost of a thousand such items is 10 200 (£k). The most likely costs of 10 for each item cannot be added to obtain a most likely value for more than one item. The median cost will lie between the expected cost and the most likely value of total cost. The 2% difference between the expected value of 10.2 and the most likely value of 10.0 is negligible, but it is small only because of the nearly symmetric shape of these distributions. For completely symmetric distributions, this difference would be zero. If 8 were the most likely value, with a probability of 0.5, while 10 and 12 had probabilities of 0.3 and 0.2, respectively, the expected value would be $(8 \times 0.5) + (10 \times 0.3) + (12 \times 0.2) = 9.4$.

With this skewed distribution the difference between the most likely value and the expected value is substantial, some 18% of the most likely value. Such a difference in magnitudes is common, arising from much less extreme asymmetry but much longer distribution 'tails'. In general, the more low probability/high impact risks a probability distribution embodies, the longer the right-hand tail of the distribution, and the greater the gap between the expected value and the most likely or median values. Chapman and Ward (1996) provide a plausible nuclear power cost per kWh example where the expected cost is more than double the most likely cost.

The 'variance' of a distribution is a useful single measure of the average amount of dispersion or spread in a distribution. Variances for *independent* random variables are additive. That is, the variance of a sum of costs is equal to the sum of the variances for each individual cost. For example, the cost of items A and B of Table 11.1 have a variance (in $£^2k^2$) of $[(8 - 10.2)^2 \times 0.2] + [(10 - 10.2)^2 \times 0.5] + [(12 - 10.2)^2 \times 0.3] = 1.96$. This means that the variance of a thousand such items is 1960 and the standard deviation (square root of 1960) is about 44 (£k). The Central Limit Theorem implies that the sum of n independently distributed random variables of any distribution has a distribution which approximates to the Normal distribution for sufficiently large n. (In practice, quite small n will do. A simple practical illustration is provided by the distribution of outcomes when rolling dice (n die): $n = 1$ (uniform), 2 (triangular), 3 (already looking roughly Normal), and so on.) Using standard Normal tables, this implies that the expected value of the sum of our one thousand cost items should fall in the range $10\ 200 \pm 44$, that is within one standard deviation of the mean, about 68% of the time, and almost certainly falls within the range $10\ 200 \pm 132$, defined by three standard deviations either side of the mean (a 99% confidence band). This result suggests an extraordinary degree of certainty about the sum of our one thousand cost items! The absurdity of this result should reinforce Example 11.2 and the importance of dependence. More generally, it illustrates the way independence induces a square root rule reduction in variability as n increases. The standard deviation of the cost of one of our cost items, 1.4 (square root of 1.960), is about 14% of 10.2, but 44 is about 0.43% of 10 200, a reduction by a factor of about 32 (equal to the square root of 1000). More generally, compared with a single item ($n = 1$), $n = 4$ increases total variability by a factor of 2, $n = 16$ increases total variability by a factor of 4, $n = 64$ increases total variability by a factor of 8, and so on.

'Mean-variance' approaches need not assume independence, and an expert system-driven probability evaluation package could usefully embrace moment-based approaches as well as CIM and Monte Carlo. Moment-based approaches offer speed and precision when appropriate assumptions hold, but catastrophic systematic errors (bias) when appropriate assumptions do not hold.

To summarise this section, three types of procedure can be considered, each with their advantages and disadvantages. Current 'industry standard' software based on Monte Carlo simulation is effective if used by experts with adequate understanding of dependence in a manner reflecting the usage of CIM approaches, but it is not a simple, efficient solution to all Evaluate phase issues. It needs to be used with care, and better software is feasible, even for the simple treatment of dependence discussed in this section.

11.9 CONCLUSION

In a fully developed risk management process, the Evaluate phase is the pivotal point which directs where and how successive iterations develop the analysis. Figure 4.1 indicates two main or key loops back, but in practice loops back to other phases (like the Structure phase) will also be important.

The effectiveness and the efficiency of the risk management process as a whole depends upon how well this iterative process works, in terms of the ability of the analysts to detect what is important and what is not, before spending too much time on the unimportant, without overlooking important threats or opportunities which do not stand out initially. Extensive probabilistic analysis based on carefully researched data can be very useful, but often such analysis is not appropriate. What is usually essential is a rough sizing of uncertainty from all the key sources which require management. With notable exceptions, this should be the goal of the first pass through the RMP. It provides the initial understanding of which areas need the most attention, and which can receive less. This assessment is itself prone to risk which must be managed. But doing nothing is not an option, and treating all aspects as equally important is foolish.

In the early 1990s it became fashionable to use High, Medium and Low (H/M/L) scenarios to assess risk probabilities and impacts in qualitative terms as a first pass technique. For those unfamiliar with the use of subjective probabilities, nervous about the validity of their probability estimates, such an approach can be very attractive. It is seductive because it is deliberately crude, making estimators more comfortable with their uncertainty about uncertainty. However, properly presented, the deliberately crude numerical probability Simple Scenario approach of the Estimate phase in Chapter 10 should give nervous estimators the same confidence. The benefits of a numerically based process in the Evaluate phase relative to one dependent upon H/M/L scenarios with a purely qualitative interpretation should be self-evident. Efficient and effective evaluation depends on our ability to combine risks. Numbers lend themselves to the process of combining risks. Categories, and associated combination processes based on weighting schemes, tend to obscure more than they clarify. Given a little practice, the Simple Scenario approach is no more difficult than an H/M/L qualitative scenario approach, and it makes all the difference to effective evaluation.

First pass probabilities used to initiate the Evaluate phase should be seen as simple statements of belief by those reasonably able to judge, brought together to provide a basis for discussing what matters and what does not. The numbers should be simple order-of-magnitude assessments, with a clear overall health warning to the effect that no one will be held accountable for their accuracy. Only when and if it becomes clear where data analysis and objectively estimated probabilities might be useful should the accuracy of such estimates become a concern.

The approach recommended here is based upon a need for efficient and effective decision taking, understanding that the probabilities used are a means to an end, not an end in themselves. What matters at the end of the day is the quality of the decisions taken, not the validity of the probability estimates. Efficiently derived quality decisions require estimation effort allocated in proportion to the benefits associated with that effort, a 'catch 22' situation unless a numeric probability-based iterative process is used.

The results we get when we combine probability distributions are critically dependent upon the dependence assumptions used. Assuming independence when this is not an appropriate assumption renders probabilistic risk analysis misleading and potentially dangerous, not just useless. Those who are not prepared to understand and reflect important dependencies should avoid probabilistic risk analysis. Those using risk analysis results provided by others should pay particular attention to the understanding of dependence displayed by their analysts, and totally reject any probabilistic analysis which suggests a failure to deal with dependence in an appropriate manner. One clear and valid defence for an H/M/L scenario approach to qualitative assessment is an inability or unwillingness to confront dependence, but this can cripple the pursuit of benefits like a distinction between 'target', 'expected' and 'commitment' values.

If the range of values associated with an important variable is clearly misjudged by a factor of 10, the associated risk analysis is clearly suspect. If independence is assumed between half a dozen key variables when 50% dependence (or a coefficient of correlation of 0.5 or some equivalent level of dependence) is appropriate, the associated risk analysis is much more misleading. A factor of 10 error on a single variable may be a trivial error in comparison. Understanding dependence and understanding structure are related issues. The most effective way to deal with dependence in a statistical sense is to give it a causal structure which explains it. Statistical dependence is causal dependence we have failed to identify and structure.

Sometimes a causal structure for dependence is not feasible, and other times it is not cost effective. In such cases experienced analysts can effectively employ measures like percentage dependence or coefficients of correlation. However, to develop that experience, working with causal structures and conditional specifications is an important part of the learning process.

Chapter 12

Plan the Project and the Management of its Risk: The Plan Phase

Plans are nothing, planning is everything.

Napoleon Bonaparte

12.1   INTRODUCTION

The plans produced in the Plan phase of the risk management process (RMP) may be 'nothing' in the sense that the one thing we can be sure of is that things will not happen as planned. However, the process of developing these plans, including all previous phases, is essential. This development warrants reference to three very different types of plans: 'reference plans', 'base plans', and 'contingency plans'.

'Reference plans' serve as a reference point which we use to compare with 'today's recommendations'. They are the project plans prior to (the current) risk analysis defined in terms of all six Ws.

'Base plans' are the recommended planning basis, our proposed starting position for project implementation. Base plans also embrace all six Ws. However, they differ from the reference plans in several important respects:

1. they reflect 'targets', what we are aiming for, as distinct from what we believe may happen on average;
2. embedded in base plans are all the proactive risk management measures our risk analysis has led us to recommend;

3. to the extent necessary, base plans contain detail for implementation purposes which reference plans do not normally address, including milestones initiating payments and an associated expenditure profile.

'Contingency plans' are the recommended supplementary plans building on the base plans, including trigger points (decision rules) initiating reactive contingency responses. They reflect anticipated potential departure from our targets which we believe deserve planning attention now, whether or not resource commitments are involved now.

Planning horizons are important for any kind of plans. Planning horizons may not receive explicit attention with respect to reference plans, but prior to implementation both base plans and contingency plans require explicit attention to planning horizons, in particular what we will call 'action horizons', the initial periods of the planning horizon which involve commitments, different resources sometimes being associated with different action horizons. 'Action plans' are the associated front-end base plans and contingency plans which involve a commitment to implementation.

Distinguishing action plans, other base plans and contingency plans is grounded on the different purposes they serve. Action plans are a direct guide to action. Following base plans and contingency plans are required to shape action plans and provide a basis for subsequent action plans, but they do not require a commitment to action yet.

Consider a very simple analogy based on the game of chess. An experienced chess player usually begins a game with a strategy. As the game progresses, the strategy develops, and tactics evolve. Action plans always involve a single move, linked to subsequent moves defined by a base plan and contingency plans. Most project plans may be less subject to uncertainty than the plans of a chess player, but the analogy has value in terms of clarifying the distinction between current action plans and the rest of the base and contingency plans in successive action horizons.

Some of the key specific deliverables any RMP Plan phase should provide are:

1. base plans in activity terms, at the detailed level required for implementation, with timing, precedence, ownership and associated resource usage/contractual terms where appropriate clearly specified, including milestones initiating payments, other events or processes defining expenditure, and an associated base plan expenditure profile;
2. risk assessment in terms of threats and opportunities, prioritised, assessed in terms of impact given no response if feasible and potentially desirable, along with an assessment of alternative potential proactive and reactive responses;
3. recommended proactive and reactive contingency plans in activity terms, with timing, precedence, ownership and associated resource

usage/contractual terms where appropriate clearly specified, including trigger points (decision rules) initiating reactive contingency responses, and impact assessment.

Proactive responses will be built into the base plans, and reactive responses will be built into the associated contingency plans, when they become part of the overall project plans. All phases of the RMP should be closely coupled with project planning in general, but the need for this coupling is perhaps particularly obvious in this phase. As indicated earlier, organisational constraints may suggest an undesirable formal separation between issues owned by the project management function and issues owned by the project risk management function. It is important to recognise the need to live with this separation if it cannot be dissolved, working across it with processes designed to minimise its impact. However, even if this potential divide is completely dissolved, with risk management a fully integrated aspect of project management, for quite different reasons it can be very important to distinguish between reference plans, base plans, and contingency plans in RMP.

It is convenient to treat the specific tasks of the Plan phase under three headings:

1. *Consolidate and explain*—document, verify, assess and report (all the common tasks) the reference plans and the risk analysis, completing a current update of the process which will have been ongoing since the project risk management process began, providing a 'snapshot' of the current state of play.
2. *Select and elaborate*—use the reference plans and the risk analysis to select the management strategies and tactics, and develop these into base plans and contingency plans, including action plans, using all the common tasks.
3. *Support and convince*—explain why the base plans and contingency plans are effective and efficient, providing a case which is as convincing as the analysis to date will allow.

Figure 12.1 portrays the way these three specific tasks and associated steps relate to a final key specific *assess* task. The structure of this chapter follows that of Figure 12.1. Figure 12.1 shows no iterations within this phase. In practice, some will be involved, but they are inconveniences to be managed, not opportunities to be seized. In contrast, it is important to try to complete a first pass through the foundations of the Plan phase as part of the Evaluate phase as early as possible on the overall risk management process, looping back from the Evaluate phase to earlier phases, as portrayed in Figure 4.1. Early passes through the complete RMP to the end of the Evaluate phase will concentrate on the foundations for the earlier aspects of the

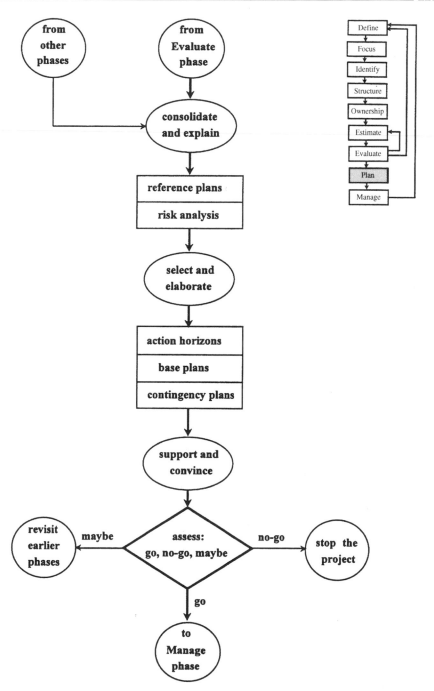

Figure 12.1   Plan phase specific tasks.

Figure 12.1 process, with completion of the later parts left for later passes. Some branches back to earlier phases are associated with the final *assess* task, and stopping the project is a possibility.

12.2 REFERENCE PLANS

Reference plans are the current version of the output of the Define phase as noted at the end of Chapter 5. As indicated earlier, senior executives and directors often comment on the immense value to them of a carefully crafted simple explanation of the nature of the project which reference plans should provide. Project staff working 'at the sharp end' are usually incapable of writing such a document. By nature they tend to want to slay dragons, not tell stories. Risk analysis can fill a gap of importance by ensuring an appropriate reference plan is available. Ensuring it is available in an appropriately polished form can be seen as the essence of this step in the Plan phase, drawing to an effective conclusion a process which started at the outset of the project risk management process.

Users of risk management processes at the senior executive and director level should see the presence of a sound reference plan as a key test of an appropriate formal risk analysis process. If a 'go' decision is anticipated, at this stage in the RMP no significant project management errors of omission or commission should remain. Sometimes it is not feasible to produce such a plan, because of unresolved issues. This is usually a clear sign of impending problems which are unnecessary if addressed at this point.

A reference plan is a dialogue between those deeply involved in the project and those who must make judgements about it, structured by risk analysis in a way which ensures 'a simple honest tale' all can subscribe to. 'An honest tale' is essential from a pragmatic perspective, apart from any moral or ethical considerations which may be appropriate. If the corporate culture requires deliberate falsification, in the sense 'if I tell the truth I will be shot, or my project will be shot and I will go with it', the organisation faces a serious corporate risk which needs urgent attention. Any approach to project management, with or without RMP, will be a castle built on sand, and the wrong castles will be built in the wrong places. No one can reasonably blame the builders of these castles if they have no obvious alternative forms of employment. Everyone should blame the senior management if they fail to respond to a clear indication of the implications for their organisation, or if they fail to ask the relevant questions in the first place.

It is important to recognise that reference plans will be dynamic, with relationships to initial plans which may not be worth elaboration. Reference plans can usefully capture some earlier misconceptions, to provide convenient 'straw men', to be knocked down by the risk analysis. Unlike base plans, reference plans need not be credible given today's understanding. But if reference plans seriously embarrass any major players, they put the whole formal risk management process at risk. Helping all major players to bury their embarrassing misconceptions in revised reference plans is a key part of successful risk management processes. Selective memory is often expedient. That said, a key purpose of risk analysis processes is uncovering aspects of project reference plans or associated project planning processes which need changes. Sometimes, provided those changes are made, they are best kept confidential to the risk analyst and those responsible, to avoid any unnecessary embarrassment. Assuring all involved that this will be the case is an important starting point at the beginning of the analysis. It is comparable to the confidentiality agreement any consultant signs before he or she starts work, except that it is informal and it is a separate arrangement with each individual player. Operative words here are *avoiding unnecessary embarrassment, provided necessary changes are made*. The practical reason why it is important to adopt this position, and make it very public at the outset in the Define phase, should be obvious. If this is not done, people will be inhibited and defensive in a way which is both natural and entirely reasonable given their perspective, to the detriment of the project as a whole from the client's perspective. Our ultimate purpose is to help the project's owners succeed. 'Impartial science' operating like a loose cannon will be recognised as a danger by all concerned, and properly treated as such.

Our concern here is the project as a whole from the client's perspective. Extending these notions of tact and honesty to painting optimistic pictures for potential bankers or third party investors or insurers raises some different issues. Putting aside moral issues, there are some serious practical issues here, beyond the scope of this book. For example, it is self-evident that if people believe all project risk assessments are optimistic, an honest appraisal may kill a project that should proceed. Squaring this circle is a non-trivial proposition. But it is not effectively dealt with by avoiding all risk assessments. It requires making all the users of the results part of the overall process, making them understand the nature of the process and its outputs as part owners of that process.

Early in the process of introducing risk management into an organisation, if formal risk management processes are used to test project plans produced by others, the term base plan may be used for reference plans. It can be worth avoiding this potential confusion, limiting the use of base plan to a recommended plan related to targets determined after risk analysis. While pre-risk analysis reference plan durations may be tested by risk analysis, base plan durations should be set in the light of risk analysis. As risk analysis becomes more embedded in the project management process, reference plans will become more flexible and less rigid in nature, more concerned with the link between proposed actions and the goals or benefits these actions are designed to achieve, and less concerned with the specifics of proposed actions.

12.3   RISK ANALYSIS

Risk analysis needs to be documented to back up associated recommendations in the base plans and contingency plans. A bottom-up risk analysis process involves a bottom-up documentation process, but it needs to be presented top-down, for reasons indicated in Example 11.3.

The process of interpreting the risk analysis in top-down terms can be regarded as the essence of this step in the Plan phase. This top-down perspective can produce new insights, and it is important to give it the time and space in the overall process which it deserves. Like writing the executive summary for a report, attempting to explain what we understand can be an important process in clarifying and developing that understanding.

A risk analysis report at a very early stage in the process should include as a minimum a comprehensive list of threats and opportunities, prioritised, assessed in terms of impact given a response, if this is feasible and potentially desirable, along with an assessment of alternative potential proactive and reactive responses.

A more comprehensive risk analysis report later in the process may include well-developed contingency plans, including trigger points and decision rules—in short, a complete basis for both project base plans and contingency plans.

12.4   ACTION HORIZONS AND ACTION PLANS

Risk management for some projects requires early consideration of appropriate planning horizons with respect to project reference plans. Often these are captured in the definition of distinct project phases. For example, a project planned to take 15 years may involve a 'phase one' which is effectively the first three or four years, followed by several subsequent phases in the form of Figure 2.3a. Usually these project phases are defined in terms of deliverables, such as feasibility, development, permission to proceed from a regulator, an operational prototype, production of the 'first of class', and so on.

Sometimes these distinctions are driven by very different types of decisions requiring very different decision processes, an issue which can be very important (for example, see Chapman and Ward, 1996). However, the general basis is less need for detail as we look further into the future, but more need for flexibility with respect to strategic choices, over a continuum. The nature of possible fundamental discontinuities is not considered here.

Whether or not a project has a duration long enough to warrant a planning horizon phase structure with respect to the project's reference plan, project planning which embeds and reflects formal risk management processes requires explicit formal recognition of an 'action horizon' concept during the Plan phase. This is done to distinguish between action plans, which have been developed as far as formal planning processes can usefully take them, ready for implementation, and plans which follow on from action plans which can be *formally* revisited. Formality is an important qualification because in practice even action plans will need some revision during implementation. The distinction between action plans and other base plans or contingency plans is grounded in the lack (or otherwise) of an opportunity to formally reassess them before implementation is attempted.

Project management processes which are not integrated with formal risk management tend to use common levels of detail for the whole of each phase, often at two or more levels connected by a 'hammocking' structure, which tends to be fairly detailed at the most detailed level. The basic notion is different levels of detail for different purposes.

Experience with formal risk management processes suggest that much detailed planning beyond the action horizon is wasted effort. It involves planning effort better spent on risk management at a higher level of planning, with detailed planning for implementation purposes restricted to the action horizon. Detailed planning beyond the action horizon is typically undertaken on the implicit assumption that a reference plan is what will happen, the one thing we can be fairly sure will not happen.

It would be convenient if an action horizon could be given a simple, single time period, say three months, associated with a regular review and revision of plans as necessary. It is useful to use a single period as a basis for planning. However, some aspects of most plans will have to involve longer horizons—ordering critical materials or contracting for critical plant, for example. Hence, it is usually useful to choose a lowest common denominator review period like a week or a month, but recognise an action horizon which adds to this duration for specific types of resource.

Effective use of action horizons, in terms of a significant saving in detailed planning effort, involves a culture change. In the absence of formal risk management processes it is detailed planning which gives people confidence in higher level plans. However, this is detailed planning based on the implicit assumption that reference plans will go as planned. Once people become used to the detail being associated with base plans and contingency plans, and a review pattern is clear, if they are encouraged to provide detail for implementation purposes only within the action horizon, they will be grateful for the avoidance of what will then be clearly perceived as unnecessary effort.

The distinction between action plans and other base and contingency plans will be developed further with examples in Section 13.4.

The focus of all the discussion so far has been effective and efficient implementation of a project, with no special attention being paid to associated forecasting or programme integration issues. If such issues are important, perhaps dominant, it will be important to have considered this in the Focus phase, reflect it in the whole of the analysis which follows, and distinguish where appropriate between different concerns at this point in the Plan phase.

12.5   BASE PLANS

Base plans differ from reference plans because they serve a different purpose. This difference in purpose is driven in part by the imminent implementation associated with base plans. However, it is essential to remember that the whole of a base plan is not going to be implemented at once. Various action horizons will be involved. Where long lead times are involved, early commitments may be vital, and interfacing with these commitments may require detailed planning. However, detailed planning beyond a period of immediate concern may be a complete waste of time and resources.

Put the other way around, it is important to preserve flexibility, and avoid making commitments before we have to. Base plans which develop detail before it is needed tend to inhibit flexibility. *In extremis*, people acquire an emotional attachment to plans which should never have been made, and distort organisational decision taking to preserve 'their children'.

Hence, a key step in this part of the Plan phase is deciding what has to be decided now, what has to be decided by the next review point, and what decisions can be left beyond that point. Once this is clear, we can start making provisional decisions where such decisions are necessary, including decisions about trigger points related to decisions which must be made before the next review point.

Base plans must incorporate all proactive risk management measures, including prior risk reduction and mitigation measures, and actions which facilitate or enable contingency plans. Put at its simplest, preparing a base plan involves building on the reference plan using the risk analysis to formulate a plan which is operational provided a range of specified risks are not realised. These risks are associated with separate after-the-fact contingency plans, although the base plans will contain related prior actions.

Such a plan will involve target cost and performance measures as well as target durations. It is vital to understand the difference between such targets and expected values, and the difference between expected values and commitments.

The large numbers of low to moderate impact risks with a moderate to high probability of being realised which face most projects ought to be embedded in the base plan, with suitable responses implicit if not explicit in the activity definitions. Target performance measures ought to reflect the expected impact of those risks in this category which the target owner is responsible for. Higher levels of responsibility may imply wider risk ownership, which in turn implies target costs which do not sum directly unless provision is made for additional risks.

12.6 CONTINGENCY PLANS

Some low probability, high impact risks are best identified as conditions or assumptions which all planning requires, and left at that. The world may end tomorrow. The client our risk management process serves may go bankrupt. However, between these conditions or assumptions, and the risks best embedded in the base plan, lies a range of events which may be worthy of separate explicit contingency plans. Such plans are best presented in a manner that integrates them with the base plan. However, contingency plans are usefully seen as somewhat separate, and worthy of special attention because:

1. they change the nature of the project and its plans;
2. they raise ownership issues;
3. they require revisions to control budgets or other performance measures.

As in the context of base plans, it is important to restrict the development of detailed contingency plans to an 'as needed' basis, to avoid unnecessary planning costs, and to avoid loss of flexibility, using the action horizon concept to restrict the action plan aspects of the contingency plan.

Hence, a key step in this part of the Plan phase is deciding what has to be decided now, what has to be decided by the next review point, and what decisions can be left beyond that point. Once this is clear we can start making provisional decisions where such decisions are necessary, drawing on all the earlier work to date.

12.7 SUPPORT AND CONVINCE

Providing support to convince those responsible for a project *go/no-go/maybe* decision to agree to a '*go*' may be part of a single document emanating from the whole of the Plan phase. However, it is worth recognising this as a separate specific task, which builds on everything which precedes it, but adds some important new ingredients and involves a change in the mode of operation.

Those experienced with the use of formal analysis to assist with decision taking clearly understand that formal analysis does not make decisions for people, it simply guides decision taking. Routine public reminders that this is the case are important. No matter how detailed and comprehensive the analysis, only those issues amenable to formal analysis will be addressed. A wide range of other issues will not be addressed. Formal analysis necessarily abstracts from the real world, to clarify certain issues. It is essential to interface such analysis with the real world to use it effectively. This task is concerned with providing that interface.

For example, an information systems project may be seen as a central competitive weapon in an organisation's strategy. The implications of a one-year delay to its completion, or a failure to achieve performance specifications, may be virtually impossible to assess in formal terms. The support and convince task may have to tackle these issues directly without any direct measures, perhaps by explaining what can be measured in relation to alternative scenarios, so that each key decision taker can make subjective assessments of trade-off without attempting explicit discussion, never mind consensus.

At the end of the day communicating insights is the ultimate goal. Analysis has serious limitations, and a failure to address these limitations when attempting to offer advice is a very serious mistake, possibly the most serious mistake an analyst can make. Consider a reasonably simple example to illustrate what is involved.

Example 12.1

A major international computer company wanted a formal system to address bidding for 'systems integration' projects, involving the supply of hardware, new software, revisions to existing software, revamped physical facilities, and retrained staff. The approach developed, often used by the authors as the basis for a case study for teaching purposes, employs a simplified version of the process explained in earlier chapters of this book to making some technical choices and choices between alternative subcontractors in order to derive an estimated expected cost for the project. Suppose the expected cost is estimated at £15 million.

The process then involves assessing a 'probability of winning' curve like that of Figure 12.2, and using it together with the expected cost to define a table like Table 12.1.

Figure 12.2 implies that attempting to 'buy the work' with a bid below about £13 million is counterproductive, and winning the bid with certainty is not possible. Once the bid is above the expected cost of £15 million the probability of winning drops rapidly although the rate of decline of the probability of winning as the bid continues to increase has to drop off as the probability approaches zero.

Table 12.1 implies that bidding at the expected cost involves zero expected profit; each £1 million added to the bid increases the conditional expected profit (the expected profit given we win) by £1 million; each £1 million added to the bid increases the unconditional expected profit (profit times probability of winning) by an amount which peaks at a £17 million bid, thereafter declining because of the rate of decline of the probability of winning.

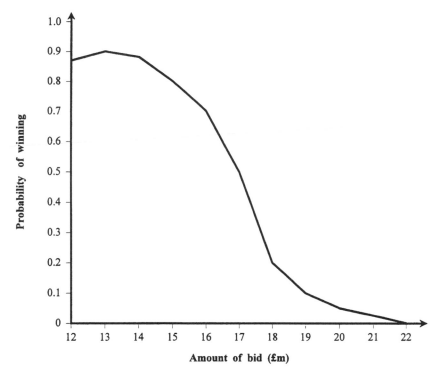

Figure 12.2 Probability of winning against amount bid.

Table 12.1 Profitability of different bids in Example 12.1.

Bid (£m)	Probability of winning	Profit if win (£m)	Expected profit (£m)
13	0.90	−2.0	−1.80
14	0.88	−1.0	−0.88
15	0.80	0.0	0.00
16	0.70	1.0	0.70
17	0.50	2.0	1.00
18	0.20	3.0	0.60
19	0.10	4.0	0.40
20	0.05	5.0	0.25

The 'textbook' solution which maximises expected profit is to bid at £17 million. In practice, what is vitally important is not providing the decision takers with a recommendation 'bid £17 million', but instead giving them Table 12.1, and explaining:

1. if the expected cost is of the order of £15 million and if Figure 12.2 is roughly consistent with their beliefs, then bidding at £17 million will maximise short-term expected profit, but:

(a) a bid of £16 million increases the chance of winning from 0.50 to 0.70, with an expected profit reduction of £0.3 million;
(b) a bid of £15 million increases the chance of winning from 0.50 to 0.80, with an expected profit reduction of £1.0 million;

2. these trade-offs will not be significantly affected by minor changes to the expected cost or Figure 12.2, any decision takers' 'what ifs' being amenable to modelling;
3. if such analysis is used regularly, recording the probability of winning as forecast by curves like Figure 12.2 will allow feedback to correct any bias in the estimation of such curves;
4. such curves are implicit in any bidding process, as are the trade-offs which lead to departures from the short-run profit maximising bid;
5. the use of a table like Table 12.1 allows quantification and data accumulation to test subjective estimates where this is feasible and useful, facilitating the use of this information in conjunction with management judgements about softer issues such as long-term market advantages associated with winning a bid, and the advantages of work to keep otherwise idle or redundant staff busy.

Finding the most effective manner to explain the implications of analysis is a craft, not a science, and it is an important aspect of the craft skills required to achieve successful risk management processes.

12.8 ASSESS: *GO/NO-GO/MAYBE*

It can be argued that assessing a *go/no-go/maybe* decision ought to precede the *select and elaborate* task, because detailed planning for implementation in the action plan sense is a waste of time if *no-go* is decided. The questions this raises are more profound than just resequencing Figure 12.1. More efficient forms of risk analysis from start to finish can be applied to decision processes where *go* or *no-go* is the sole concern, without reference to how implementation will take place if it proceeds. This is the kind of analysis which ought to lie behind a situation like that illustrated by Example 12.1.

The most convenient way to address this within the simplifications of an idealised process description like that provided here is as follows.

Start the risk analysis process with a first pass analysis which is primarily concerned with *go/no-go*. So long as *no-go* is a serious possibility, concentrate on that aspect of the assessment, ignoring implementation issues. However, when implementation is anticipated, start to develop a plan for implementation. Even on the final pass, immediately before implementation begins, ensure that no important *no-go* issues are ignored. As with the preceding phases, it is a question of shifting the emphasis from earlier steps to later steps as the process reiterates and matures.

12.9 CLARIFICATION OF TARGET, EXPECTED VALUE AND COMMITMENT ESTIMATES

Setting control budgets, and controls related to base plan activity durations and performance measures, is an important aspect of the Plan phase. It is considered last in this chapter for expository convenience. In practice, the whole RMP needs to recognise the difference between target, expected value and commitment estimates, using appropriate values for each part of the process, all three being relevant in some contexts.

The use of estimates for control purposes requires an understanding of which risks are the responsibility of which partners. Disputes are the result of misunderstanding, unintentional or wilful. The basis of all control estimates should be expected values given the risks the owner of the estimate is responsible for, including 'provisions' for those risks. These estimates should be 'targets' in the sense that they should exclude all risks better held at a higher level in the control structure. At the highest level in a control estimate process we need 'contingency' to provide an appropriate chance of meeting commitments, on average the 'contingency' uplift not being required. At all levels we need 'provisions', on average needed, related to the risks held at that level in the control process.

If no risks outside a control estimate occur, the owner of that estimate should be expected to achieve the target implied by the control estimate. If risks outside the control of the owner of the estimate occur, relaxation of the time, cost or performance requirements should be allowed, automatically. Because those at the 'sharp end' will not own many of the risks, they will be unlikely to achieve their targets.

Consider development of Example 12.1.

Example 12.2

Assuming for the moment that the distinction between expected value estimates and commitment estimates is not an issue, target values should be defined as expected values given the risks owned by the target holder. Control estimates should be set up in terms of (conditional) expected values associated with these targets and risk provisions, with additional contingency funds at higher levels in the structure.

Suppose the expected cost of £15 million in Example 12.1 is made up of:

	Expected cost £millions
1. hardware	5
2. new software	3
3. revisions to existing software	4
4. facilities	2
5. training	1
total	15

Suppose the expected hardware cost is based on the hardware division's estimates as follows:

specified equipment cost	£4.4 million
extra memory installed later if needed	
cost if needed £1.0 million	
chance needed 0.6	
expected cost (provision) 0.6 × 1	£0.6 million
Total expected cost	£5.0 million

The expected cost for control purposes (target) for the hardware division will be £4.4 million, not £5 million, an expected cost which is conditional on extra memory not being needed. The project manager would probably hold the £0.6 million provision for extra memory. Assume this is the case. If extra memory is required, an extra £1 million would have to be released to the hardware division, leaving the project manager £0.4 million short on this item.

If the project manager would have difficulty recouping the £0.4 million shortfall on hardware just discussed, and if his or her reputation or income depended upon staying within budget, a 0.6 chance that he or she would be £0.4 million short might not be acceptable. More generally, the project manager might request a budget such that an 80% chance of delivery within budget was feasible, on the grounds that there is an asymmetry in the penalty function: being under budget is not as costly (for the project manager) as being over budget.

The above example should make it obvious that a single unconditional budget estimate may provide no effective basis for either planning or control. In situations like this example, the gap between the model which implicitly underlies a single estimate and the reality which needs to be managed is a significant one.

Project managers who have to go back to a client or board for more time or money if they fail to meet their target will need contingency if the rewards or penalties associated with over- or underachievement are not symmetric. Ideally these asymmetries are designed out of the process except at the highest levels, to simplify the management process.

Consider a simple example. If the expected duration of a trip to a railway station is 30 minutes, and there are trains every 30 minutes to the required destination, most people will allow an extra 5 minutes or so—a modest contingency being justified by a modest increase in inconvenience if a train is just missed, relative to the inconvenience of arriving early. However, if the train in question is the last one that day, and missing it means very serious difficulties, most people will allow more than a 5 minute contingency. The asymmetry of the penalty function involves a high cost of being late relative to the cost of being early in such a case. This example involves an individual setting their own 'control budget' of time to get to the station, based on their assessment of the consequences of making it too high or too low, as well as the expected outcome given appropriate underlying planning decisions.

By making life difficult for project managers to obtain additional funds, easy for them to give back (or spend) residuals, organisations will induce a strong and well-founded wish for contingency on the part of project managers. Convention suggests a 70% or 80% level of confidence to define a suitable contingency sum. Convention may have it about right, but the rationale is not clearly visible, is questionable, and is well worth exploration.

If the cost to the organisation of being over or under budget is also asymmetric, in line (in relative terms) with the impact on the project manager, there is a good case for adding a contingency sum to the budget. There is also a good case for ensuring consistent penalty functions. In particular, if the cost to the organisation of the project being over or under commitment is symmetric, and this symmetry is passed on to the project manager, there is no case for a contingency sum. That is, a symmetric penalty function implies expected costs should be used for control purposes. Chapman and Ward (1996) outline a simple model used to assess early or late duration target planning in a form of analysis which could be used to assess this issue.

These issues can be associated with a concept of 'enlightened controls', which is complementary to but different from 'enlightened gambles' and 'enlightened caution' described in Chapter 3.

'Enlightened control setting' is concerned with avoiding setting up control estimates which are too high or too low given appropriate underlying decisions. If people are given contingency they do not need, they will usually find a way to use it, sometimes via unenlightened caution, with direct cost or profit implications. If they are not given contingency they need, they will be frustrated, they may be punished inappropriately, and they may be encouraged to take unplanned, unenlightened gambles, on the grounds that 'one might as well be hung for a sheep as a lamb'. 'Enlightened control adjustment' is concerned with revising control estimates appropriately in the light of out-turns which depart from expectations.

'Enlightened controls' require enlightened control setting and adjustment, as well as underlying planning which encourages enlightened gambles and enlightened caution. The issue is aligning the controls people will work to with the best interests of the organisation in a manner which goes beyond specific identifiable planning decision choices, although it needs to embrace such decisions in a consistent manner.

12.10 CONCLUSION

Much of the Plan phase as it might be conceived is embedded in earlier phases as described in this book. However the earlier phases are described, the purpose of the Plan phase is to use all previous analysis to develop a plan which passes a *no-go/maybe* test and then a *maybe/go* test, producing a plan ready for implementation, or an early and appropriate *no-go* decision.

The key messages of this chapter are tied to the three specific tasks.

Consolidating and explaining the reference plans and the risk analysis is the first mode of analysis peculiar to the Plan phase as described here. The material this is based on must be produced in the required form from the outset, in a very real sense 'writing the final report' beginning on day one of the risk management process. However, the editing, the explaining, the focus on telling stories which need to be told, requires a different style of analysis in this phase. Like the Focus phase, it involves a lot of craft and a very clear understanding of why analysis is being undertaken, using that understanding to shape the evolution of the whole analysis process as successive iterations are completed. There is nothing magic about craft. It is based on experience in a learning environment, as understood by crafts-people as far back as one cares to go. The science in terms of a systematic structure provided by modern risk management processes does not replace craft skills. It makes them more demanding and more useful.

Selecting and elaborating action horizons, other purposes for plans, base plans and contingency plans also draws together everything which came before with a purpose and focus peculiar to the Plan phase. Again, craft skills, and a clear grasp of purposes and possibilities, are important.

Support and convince is not decomposed into steps, and this task is illustrated by one quite specific example, Example 12.1. However, the bridge it provides between what can and cannot be formally analysed is of vital importance. It interfaces the abstraction of analysis with the messy details of reality, the need for different people with different perspectives and concerns to use the same analysis to reach joint decisions. It is the ultimate test of a risk analyst's craft skills. Example 12.2 further develops this bridge in terms of target, expected value and commitment estimate issues.

Chapter 13

Manage the Project and its Risk: The Manage Phase

I have never known a battle plan to survive a first contact with the enemy.

19th Century General

13.1   INTRODUCTION

If project 'management' is decomposed into 'planning' and 'control', a classic binary division, we are now leaving the realm of 'planning', and moving into 'control', maintaining an ongoing interest in 'planning'. Even the very best of plans need adjusting in the heat of battle, but this chapter is also about the role of initiative and training to bridge the gap between what needs to be done and plans that work.

'Planning' in this general sense has been decomposed extensively in the earlier chapters of this book. It could be argued that the simple treatment of planning and control offered in this chapter seriously understates the importance of the doing as opposed to the thinking about the doing. For example, leadership, motivating people to 'reach for the sky', and motivating people to work as a team, can be more important to project success than anything discussed in this book. However, these issues are also central to the whole of the earlier process. This chapter concentrates on building on the results of the earlier risk management process (RMP) phases to assist the project risk management process. There is no intention to play down the importance of other issues.

The basic message of this chapter is that once a project starts, there are four quite different new specific tasks associated with the RMP Manage phase: *manage planned actions, monitor, manage crises,* and *roll action plans forward.* These four tasks have to be managed in parallel in conjunction with one basic *assess* common task, as indicated in Figure 13.1. The format of this chapter follows Figure 13.1.

A unique characteristic of Figure 13.1 relative to earlier equivalents is the parallel nature of the specific tasks. Effort on all four fronts may not be continuous, but this phase does not involve an iterative process in terms of sequential treatment of these four specific tasks. This has important practical

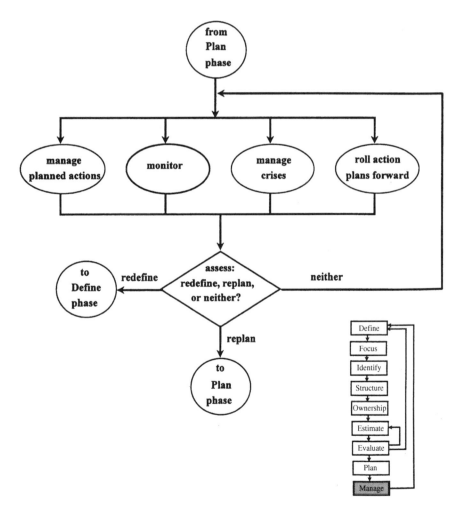

Figure 13.1 Manage phase specific tasks.

implications. For example, for a large project, if one person is formally responsible for all four specific tasks, problems are almost inevitable if they do not delegate each to a suitable champion, and they do not regularly remind themselves of the need to manage all four simultaneously. Just as earlier phases of the RMP make extensive use of iterations, so iterations are central to the Manage phase. However, the four specific tasks require parallel treatment.

13.2 MANAGE PLANNED ACTIONS

Operational plans for the immediate 'action horizon' require implementation in the Manage phase. This is the basis of progressing the achievement of the project's objectives. Managing this aspect of the project is the basis of project management in the Manage phase.

Translating plans into actions is seldom entirely straightforward. Some see the key as planning detail. We see the key as insight about what might happen, as distinct from what we hope will happen, with particular reference to the motivation of the parties involved, and a clear vision of what really matters and what does not.

Excessive planning detail in a deterministic framework can be a serious handicap. A simply defined deterministic base plan embedded in even a simple understanding of the uncertainties involved can be much more effective. It can also be much more 'fun' for those involved, 'empowering' them to make decisions which encourages 'seizing opportunities', providing 'ownership', and generating improved performance through a proper understanding of the project team as a collection of people with all that implies.

Consider an analogy, based on North American (Canadian or US) football. A distinguishing feature of North American football relative to European football is 'downs'. Leaving aside opening and post 'touch-down' (scoring) 'kick-offs', play starts when the ball is lifted from the ground by the offensive team. Play stops when a forward pass is dropped, the ball carrier is tackled, the ball leaves the field, an offence is committed, or scoring takes place. Each of these 'plays' is separated by a period of reorganisation for the next down. This allows detailed planning for the next play in the 'huddle'. When the quarter back says 'number 93' (play number 93), each player knows what he is supposed to do. The plan for a play specifies base plan actions for all players. On most plays, a score is the planned result if everyone does what they are supposed to. The self-evident failure to score with every play does not detract from the value of the planning. Nor does the planning inhibit a skilled running back (ball carrier), or a skilled blocker.

Most project plans are not prespecified plays, and most projects follow their base plans more closely than North American football players. However, the analogy has value in terms of clarifying the distinction between successive action plans and what has to be done to actually move the ball forward. Formal planning in terms of what the play specifies for each play requires additional informal planning by each player. More generally, the higher the skill levels of the players, the less players need to be instructed in detail, and the more they are able to interpret plans flexibly and effectively in response to what is happening on the ground in 'real time'. Effective use of contingency plans is part of the training, not part of the plan *per se*, but base plans without such contingency plans are of limited use.

Routine project planning meetings concerned with implementing planned actions should have some of the characteristics of a North American football 'huddle', including each member of the team being reminded what everyone else is planning to do, how and why they may fail, and reaffirming team 'bonding'. Project activity between meetings should have some of the characteristics of a successful offensive North American football play, including each member of the team doing their best at their own prescribed task, capitalising on opportunities, and minimising the impact of team-mate failures.

European football involves less formal play planning, without the 'downs' structure. This chapter's failure to develop the analogy to include European football should not be seen as a matter of bias. Some time was spent speculating on analogies, but their development is left to the reader.

13.3   MONITOR

The North American football example of the last section is a useful analogy to carry forward. In the context of the *monitor* specific task it facilities a clear distinction between formal and informal monitoring, at different levels of authority.

For example, a running back with the ball under his arm has to monitor play and respond instinctively in fractions of a second. At the end of each play, the quarterback has to monitor progress to choose the next play. The coach will also monitor at this level, and may intervene, directly specifying the next play. The manager may get involved at this level, and will do so in terms of half-time and end-of-game reviews. End-of-game and end-of-season reviews may involve still higher levels of monitoring.

Projects involve very important informal monitoring as well as formal monitoring and change control processes at various levels. As in most other aspects of project risk management, simple devices are usually the best unless there is clear reason for more complex devices. An example which has proven useful for a century is the Gantt chart, as discussed earlier, indicating planned progress in relation to progress achieved to date.

A useful update on the classical statistical control chart (plotting actual outcomes within preplotted confidence bands) are charts plotting actual outcomes (in cost, duration or other performance terms) in relation to preplotted target, expected and commitment values.

Each time the project plan is reviewed, eliminating the risks which have now been realised or avoided, confidence band assessments should contract, unless new risks are envisaged. Plotting how this process is progressing can be useful, especially if some serious set-backs have been experienced but the chance of achieving commitments is stable or improving. However, this is an example of a relatively complex portrayal of the monitoring process, best used infrequently at high levels. The lower the level and the more frequent the monitoring activity, the simpler the devices have to be.

It is worth remembering that people directly involved in a project are usually all too well aware when things are going wrong. Usually the issue is not a need for devices to detect when things are going wrong; it is having ways of explaining what is going wrong in order to persuade appropriate people to take appropriate action. More generally, the issue is to ensure that processes are in place which encourage this level of communication to take place in an effective manner.

The distinction between target, expected value and commitment estimates is of substantial importance in relation to the *monitor* specific task. Managing the process of reconciling what actually happens to these three types of estimates is essential if the monitoring process is to facilitate an understanding of the implications of departures from base plans. Example 12.2 should make it clear that this kind of monitoring involves key risks or conditions, like the extent to which documentation is 'adequate', 'inadequate' or 'disastrous'.

Given a *monitor* specific task which is defined to reflect these links and generate responses using the whole of the RMP outlined earlier, monitoring is not a mechanical reactive task. It is a flexible and creative proactive task, concerned with understanding what is happening in 'real time' in relation to what was planned, anticipating future departures from plans, and initiating all necessary revisions to earlier plans.

13.4 MANAGE CRISES

Managing planned actions as discussed in Section 13.2 can embrace the variations from base plans which do not warrant contingency plans, and the management of variations via contingency plans. A major concern of formal risk management is to avoid nasty surprises which give rise to crises, requiring crisis management. However, it is very unwise to be unprepared for crisis.

'Crisis' might be defined as 'a time of acute danger or difficulty', or 'a major turning point'. The best responses in general terms are based on insight, effective and efficient information systems, being prepared, being able to respond rapidly, and being decisive. Viewing crisis management as contingency management for significant unspecified and unanticipated events, a more effective crisis management strategy will make it effective and efficient to devote less time to contingency planning for specified and anticipated events. This view connects with the concern to develop 'general responses' discussed earlier in Chapter 8 in relation to Example 8.2.

13.5   ROLL ACTION PLANS FORWARD

The 'action horizon' concept developed in Chapter 12 is very important, to avoid wasteful and inhibiting detailed planning. It is part of knowing what is not important, and is just as vital as knowing what is important. If the importance of this distinction is grasped, rolling action plans forward becomes a vital ongoing aspect of the Manage phase.

In terms of the earlier North American football analogy, we need to call the next play. The formality of calling the next play is perhaps the most appropriate analogy for project risk management purposes, but the chess analogy also has value. In a chess player's terms, we need to plan moves as far ahead as our capabilities allow, with a view to the next move, but even chess 'masters' do not plan games to 'checkmate' from the outset. A risk management planning horizon needs to be limited for similar reasons. Until we see what happens, some aspects of detailed planning are an inhibiting waste of time. But anticipation in broad strategic terms needs to go beyond the next move or play. A key difference between chess masters and other chess players is the effectiveness of the way they anticipate what will happen without detailed analysis of all possible moves. Devices which can be useful in this context include:

1. updated detailed plans for all activities to be undertaken during the action horizon, with ownership of and responsibility for risks clearly indicated, as well as anticipated progress;
2. a short prioritised list of risk/response issues requiring ongoing management attention, with changes in priority emphasised and trends assessed, and both ownership and responsibility clearly defined.

13.6   ASSESS: REDEFINE PLANS, REPLACE PLANS, OR NEITHER?

Any unplanned significant events, significant planned events, and the completion of review time cycles should initiate assessment. That assessment may simply confirm that the project can proceed as planned. However, it may indicate a need to loop back one phase to the Plan phase, it may indicate a need to go right back to the Define (the project) phase, or it may indicate a need for an intermediate loop back. Figure 4.1 shows only the basic inter-phase loop back to the Define phase, but judicious use of a loop back to the Plan phase can be efficient if the RMP is effective.

Exception or change reporting issues need to be addressed in this context, 'change control' being a thorny issue requiring special care. An adequate grasp of the importance of this issue at the outset can have a profound effect on the whole of the project. For example, the nature of all contracts, the nature of the design, and the basic technologies employed can reflect a need to minimise changes, or to respond effectively to changes which are inevitable.

13.7   CONCLUSION

This is the shortest chapter of the nine addressing each phase of RMP. The Manage phase draws on all the earlier phases of the process. This chapter only addresses new issues. Even so, there is clearly scope for considerable development of the material addressed in this chapter, and for further issues to be addressed in the context of an effective Manage phase.

Part Three

Modifying the Generic Process

Chapter 14

The Impact of Different Project Life Cycle Positions

Experience is not what happens to you, it is what you do with what happens to you.

Aldous Huxley

14.1 INTRODUCTION

Part Two (Chapters 5–13) made three key assumptions to facilitate discussion of the generic risk management process (RMP). These assumptions were:

1. the RMP is concerned with 'the client perspective', and 'the client' is one organisation with one project;
2. the RMP is initiated in the Plan stage of the project life cycle (PLC);
3. a comprehensive RMP is required.

Part Three considers the implications of relaxing each of these three assumptions, in Chapters 14–16. Part Three also considers introducing RMPs into an organisation as a project in its own right, in Chapter 17.

This chapter is about when in the PLC to get some RMP experience, and what to do with it. A central concern is how this experience may differ for RMP in different stages of the PLC. This chapter considers the rationale for choosing to initiate RMP at the Plan stage in a project to control and enhance the learning process. It also considers the implications of using

RMP at some stage in the PLC other than at the Plan stage. Introducing RMP at a stage other than the Plan stage should lead to some modifications and changes of emphasis in the generic RMP described in Part Two. As Table 2.2 shows, the reason for undertaking risk analysis can change significantly over the PLC, because the project itself changes, and because what is known about the project changes. Both can change in quite profound ways. In general, the earlier risk analysis begins in a PLC, the greater the scope for effective risk management. However, experience suggests that the earlier risk analysis begins, the more difficult it is, because the greater scope is a challenge as well as an opportunity. For example, risk management in the Conceive stage needs to be very wide in scope, and very foreseeing, concerned with issues like product or design fault liability, but it would be unreasonable to expect all the risks of relevance in all eight PLC stages to be fully assessed in 'concept evaluation'. Getting the balance right is a major issue.

A key issue in planning for risk analysis and designing an appropriate RMP is the stage of interest in the PLC. An important related issue is how much risk analysis of earlier stages in the PLC is available as a starting point. The *stage* structure of the PLC and the *phase* structure of the RMP yield a matrix of possible combinations of phase and stage location in the PLC, shown in Table 14.1. This matrix provides a useful framework for the discussion that follows.

An obvious starting point is to distinguish between RMP which takes place *before* the Plan stage in the PLC and RMP that takes place *after* the Plan stage. Implementing RMP for the first time earlier than the Plan stage in the PLC is in general more difficult, because the project is more fluid, and less well defined. A more fluid project means more degrees of freedom, more alternatives to consider, including alternatives which may be eliminated as the project matures, for reasons unrelated to the RMP. A less

Table 14.1 Matrix defined by stages of the PLC and phases of the RMP.

Stages of the PLC	Phases of the RMP								
	Define	Focus	Identify	Structure	Ownership	Estimate	Evaluate	Plan	Manage
Conceive									
Design									
Plan*									
Allocate									
Execute									
Deliver									
Review									
Support									

*The plan stage is the assumed position in the PLC in Part Two

well-defined project means appropriate documentation is hard to come by, and alternative interpretations of what is involved may not be resolvable. RMP earlier in the project life cycle tends to be:

1. less quantitative;
2. less formal;
3. less tactical/more strategic;
4. more creative;
5. more concerned with the identification and capture of opportunities.

That said, implementing RMP earlier in the PLC is in general much more useful if it is done effectively. There is scope for much more fundamental improvements in the project plans, perhaps including a risk-driven redesign, or initial design of the product of the project. Undertaking formal risk management in an objectives–benefits–design–activities framework clearly demands explicit attention to the risk management process as early as possible, preferably in the Conceive stage. Further, it suggests planning in more formal terms the progression from the Conceive stage to later stages in the PLC. The opportunity management aspects of the process can be a particularly important reason for early RMP. For example, an early RMP facilitates lateral thinking about pre-emptive responses to risks which may address entirely new ways of achieving objectives.

As indicated in Chapter 5, the activities concerned with designing, planning and costing in large engineering and construction projects are often undertaken by three different groups of people with significantly different cultures and perspectives, with good reason. The skills required are quite different. However, integration of these functions is critical. Undertaking formal risk management generally makes it clear to everyone involved that early integration of this trio is desirable. Once this message is understood, implementation of risk management earlier in the PLC for subsequent projects is usually perceived as a useful vehicle for earlier integration of these functions. This is not a new perception, but it is still not widely appreciated.

Implementing RMP for the first time later in a PLC gives rise to several difficulties, without any significant worthwhile compensating benefits. The basic problem is like the one that evokes the response to a request for directions, 'if I were going there, I wouldn't start from here'. After the Plan stage, contracts are in place, equipment has been purchased, commitments are in place, reputations are on the line, and managing change is comparatively difficult and unrewarding. That said, even a later RMP can and should encompass routine reappraisal of a project's viability. In this context early warnings are preferable to late recognition that targets are incompatible or unachievable. In general, better late than never.

Using the structure of Table 14.1 to expand on these general observations, each following section of this chapter addresses a PLC stage. Section 14.2 starts with the Plan stage, in terms of a rationale for choosing this stage for a learning process. Section 14.3 considers the implications of moving the initiation of RMP back to the Design stage. Moving further back, to the Conceive stage, follows in Section 14.4. Later sections move on from the Plan stage, first to the Allocate stage, then to the Execute stage, and so on. In each section the starting point for the discussion is moving the initiation of the generic RMP from the Plan stage to another PLC stage, followed where appropriate by comments about building on earlier stage RMPs.

14.2   INTRODUCING RMP IN THE PLAN STAGE

Part of the rationale for assuming that RMP is initiated at the Plan stage of the PLC in Part Two is based on the view that this is the easiest stage to describe, because it is the most straightforward. Another closely coupled part of the rationale is based on the view that this is the easiest place to start for first-time users, with the best chance of success in what is a fairly high risk venture in its own right. By the Plan stage a fair amount of information about a project is available, but scope for significant contributions to project performance by pursuit of formal risk management is likely to remain. If the introduction of RMP into an organisation is *voluntary*, try to choose a project at this stage.

If formal RMP is introduced on a *voluntary* basis in a multi-project organisation, it also makes sense to choose a project to learn on which has three characteristics:

1. it has been very well managed to date;
2. despite its successful management to date, it raises risk-driven concerns which need to be addressed to the satisfaction of those granting sanction;
3. there is sufficient time to undertake a comprehensive RMP.

The essence of the argument is 'learn to walk on a carpeted floor before you try to run on difficult terrain', and 'learn about the terrain as a whole before you attempt short cuts under pressure'. If these three characteristics apply, first-time formal risk management at the Plan stage of a project can be comparatively rewarding and trouble free.

If RMP is applied for the first time on a *non-voluntary* basis, the Plan stage is the most likely point at which it will be required. The requirements of banks and boards motivate many first-time users to employ RMP with a stick, and the Plan stage is usually when the threat can no longer be avoided. Moreover, *prudent* boards and banks will *require* a *comprehensive*

RMP if first-time users of RMPs are involved. Hence, we hope the reader interested in direct application of the ideas developed earlier in this book will be able to try them out before confronting directly the issues yet to be discussed. However, a broad appreciation of what follows should precede any RMP application.

14.3 USING RMP IN THE DESIGN STAGE

RMP initiated in the PLC Plan stage starts with a Define phase based upon a reasonably complete design. Shifting the initiation of RMP from the Plan stage back to the Design stage of the PLC necessarily involves more attention to the project *what*, less attention to the project *whichway*, but it still needs to consider the implications of all later stages. Initiating RMP in the Design stage involves a significant change in emphasis, but not a totally new process.

Define Phase

When addressing the six Ws in the RMP Define phase, the emphasis will switch from the *whichway* and *when* to the *what* (design), but all six Ws will still require coordinated treatment.

The process will be more demanding because the design itself will be more fluid, perhaps with a range of quite different concepts requiring comparison and choices. It will also be more demanding because the six W issues associated with later stages in the PLC will usually require more effort. For example, life cycle cost and revenue issues, up to and including final disposal of the product of the project in some cases, are likely to be subject to much greater uncertainty due to more limited clarification to date.

Because there is much more scope to change design to reflect these issues, it is much more important to understand them properly in order to seize the opportunities provided by the earlier initiation of RMP.

Additional effort invested in developing an understanding of whole project life cycle issues as a consequence of introducing RMP at the Design stage will have ongoing benefits in the later stages of the RMP, as well as the direct immediate benefits to the project as a whole.

Focus Phase

When addressing how best to plan the risk analysis effort, the shift in emphasis to design choice issues is critical. A very similar process to the generic RMP may be appropriate, but at the very least significant cosmetic changes may be essential, and more fundamental structural changes may be necessary. The underlining issue is an appropriate design for the RMP, and the extent to which this design needs to be different because the RMP is concerned initially if not primarily with the Design stage of the project.

Example 14.1

A client wanted a risk analysis undertaken to confirm (or otherwise) a design decision. The decision was the sizing of storage for LNG (liquefied natural gas) as a buffer between LNG production and shipping. The production and storage facilities being considered were proposed for Meville Island, in the Canadian High Arctic. The proposed shipping involved ice-breaking tankers, taking the LNG to East Coast USA.

One team of consultants addressed variable shipping patterns. Another addressed LNG plant reliability issues. As discussed elsewhere (Chapman, Cooper and Cammaert, 1984), analysis indicated a need for a second compression chain in the LNG production facility, as well as confirming the storage sizing:

Cosmetic changes to the generic RMP were important. For example, 'activities' were replaced by 'components' and 'sub-systems', sources of 'risk' became reasons for 'outages', the probability of a risk occurring was couched in terms of 'mean time between failures', and so on. That is, the activity–risk–response–impact structure became a component–outage–response–impact structure. But the change in labels did not affect the models or the computer software used.

The cited paper discussing this example specifically addresses what cosmetic changes were necessary in this case, and what was portable. For a more general discussion of these issues and other references see Chapman (1992b).

Identify Phase

In terms of the Identify phase of the generic RMP, a shift in emphasis from activity-based plans to underlying project design involves a shift in the scope of risks of interest which can be very important.

Example 14.2

A client wanted a risk analysis undertaken to make a design decision in a manner which could be justified with respect to a number of interested parties. The decision was how to get a proposed very large gas pipeline (48 inch) across the Yukon river in Alaska. The gas pipeline was following the route of a very large oil pipeline. The obvious choice was putting the gas pipeline in an empty spare pipe rack on a road bridge built to carry the oil pipeline. Concerned parties included the owners of the oil line, the State of Alaska Transport Department as owners of the bridge (which had generated considerable road traffic), the local indigenous people (who were particularly concerned about the possible pollution impacts of any oil spills caused by bridge failure), and the US Federal Government Department of Energy (who were concerned about a significant portion of the US energy supply being exposed to potential sabotage on a single bridge).

An early issue of concern was which parts of the pipeline's life cycle should be the focus for the risk analysis. Construction, operation and maintenance were addressed, but the emphasis was on the operation of the pipeline.

'Risks' in the project construction plan sense were replaced by 'failure' risks. In this case catastrophic failures were the concern, not minor operating difficulties. The

RMP design aspects of the Focus phase had to reflect more significant changes in this case than in the Example 14.1 case, including the need to explicitly demonstrate the relative merits of alternative structures to different groups of people with quite different concerns, as discussed elsewhere (Chapman *et al.*, 1985), but the fundamentals of Part Two still applied.

For example, the project manager (Debelius) was a very experienced and pragmatic former senior officer in the US Army Corps of Engineers. He made it clear at the outset that the insights gained during the course of the study must be summarised by a clear defence of a recommended choice on one side of a single sheet of A4 paper. The study was a large and complex one, involving about 30 people working full time for about 3 months at its peak. The challenge of summarising its results on one page in this way was formidable, but its value has been remembered for all subsequent studies, a lesson worth learning well. The purpose of the analysis was gaining the insight required to write very simple stories. The main story in this case was a surprising story for many. The recommended approach, a separate aerial crossing, was the least likely option as perceived by all parties involved at the outset. Moreover, it was not difficult to explain the rationale for the preferred approach, in terms of effective rapid recovery from loss of the separate aerial crossing by temporary use of the bridge pipe rack if the bridge survived, and a reasonable degree of independence between threats to the aerial crossing and threats to the bridge. Complex risk/response dependencies which were not anticipated could be reduced to a simple story once their impact was understood.

It is perhaps worth observing that if some of the time typically spent on risk identification in the PLC Plan stage is devoted to RMP in the PLC Design stage, considerable benefit might be gained. The operating state of a building or piece of plant may be much more important than its construction, and deserving of much more attention. For example, even for comparatively straightforward and routine projects like a speculative office block, making sure there are no design features which will threaten future net rental income (and hence capital value) because of concerns driven by tenants, owners, local authorities and others may be much more important than construction cost issues which often receive much more attention.

Structure Phase

The design of RMP Structure phases requires an understanding, developed in the Focus phase, of those aspects of structure which need explicit attention, and those that do not. All the concerns addressed in Chapter 8 are relevant for a Design stage RMP Structure phase, but the extent to which structural issues are clear in the Focus phase of the process may be significantly reduced. This makes the Structure phase more important, and more demanding. Chapman *et al.* (1985) develop this issue.

Ownership Phase

Ownership issues of special interest as a consequence of the shift in emphasis from plan to design include the impact of design–build–operate concepts. Risk and response ownership discussions develop a distinctive new flavour when project whole life issues involve designers directly. More generally, ownership issues can become much more complex in the PLC Design stage, because all the other PLC stages require clear recognition and attention.

Estimate, Evaluate, Plan and Manage Phases

Subsequent phases of the RMP (Estimate, Evaluate, Plan and Manage) follow on in a way largely determined by the earlier phases and the general principles discussed in Chapters 10 to 13. However, it is worth emphasising that if RMP embraces the Design stage from the outset, project change control issues right back to design become part of an integrated and ongoing evaluate, plan and manage process. For example, the distinction between 'target', 'expected' and 'commitment' values becomes an essential part of the language of design, with the management of expectations about design achievement linked to the management of expectations about time, cost and performance achievement.

14.4   USING RMP IN THE CONCEIVE STAGE

Taking the initiation of RMP back into the Conceive stage of the PLC intensifies and further develops all the issues discussed in the previous section.

Define Phase

The distinctions between PLC Design stage and Conceive stage approaches to the Define phase of the RMP can be relatively unimportant, because of the overlapping nature of these stages. For instance, Example 14.1 relates to a project which was quite explicitly a concept-proving exercise, part of the PLC Conceive stage of a broader project. This context did not significantly affect the approach taken to the Define phase. Example 14.2 could also be viewed as an example of a Conceive stage approach.

However, if the emphasis switches to the *who* (parties) and the *why* (objectives), the resulting distinction between approaches to the Define phase of the RMP in the Design and Conceive stages of the PLC can be very important, and the impact of this difference can be extreme. For example, most textbooks on decision analysis emphasise examples which involve Conceive stage decisions, basic decision tree models being useful for simple representations of such choices. At their simplest and most fundamental level, the Define phase in the PLC Conceive stage may describe alternative approaches to a business proposition in terms which leave implicit all the issues to be addressed other than the profit or cost of each alternative. A one sentence description of each option may suffice in the limit.

Example 14.3

In 1979, Maritime Engines and Motors (MEM), a medium-sized British firm manufacturing outboard engines and motors for pleasure craft, was considering the introduction of a new product based on modifications to one of its best-selling models.

Recently, this model had been banned in the United States because it did not meet federal emission standards. Fortunately this was not an important market for MEM, but the managing director was concerned that similar emission controls might be introduced in Britain. Consequently, MEM was considering introducing a new motor with a redesigned carburation system using conventional but up-to-date technology. However, the existing model was so well established that any change to its design might cause a loss of market share, and in any event the new product might soon be overtaken by motors using microchip technology produced by a German competitor.

A decision tree showing different possible scenarios was developed and supported by a financial model which calculated the Net Present Value (NPV) of each scenario over a ten-year planning horizon. The first part of the decision tree developed is shown in Figure 14.1.

The tree starts with a decision node representing the choice between going for the new redesigned product or staying with the old one. If the new product option were chosen it was estimated that there was a 0.4 probability of various signifi- cant possible sources of trouble in introducing the new product. Nodes A–E were followed by further branches showing possible scenarios relating to sales levels and the penetration into the market of products using microchip technology. The

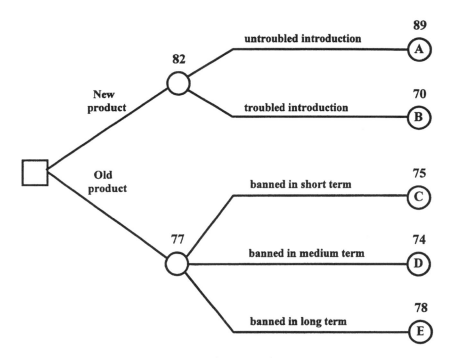

Figure 14.1 First part of decision tree in Example 14.3.

numbers above each node correspond to the expected NPV in millions of pounds of all scenarios to the right of the node in the tree. It will be noticed that the expected values (in £millions) at nodes C, D and E, 75, 74 and 78, respectively, are not very different. Whatever the probability assignments, the expected value for the old product cannot be less than 74 or more than 78, and it is always less than the expected value with the new product. Sensitivity analysis tended to support this conclusion. Thus the uncertainty that had motivated the analysis initially turned out to be unimportant because the decision was insensitive to the entire range of possible probability assignments for the 'banned' event. This insensitivity arose because developing the decision tree had forced the managing director to think strategically about the consequences of a ban in the light of the microchip threat and expected NPVs at nodes C, D, E reflected responses that had been developed to cope effectively with a ban.

While the difference between the expected NPV for the new product and the old product (82 − 77 = 5) is small, the expected NPV following an 'untroubled introduction' is £12 million more than the expected NPV for the old product. This highlighted the value of developing responses to increase the probability of an 'untroubled introduction'. Eventually, the managing director called in an outside design consultant to redesign the new product so it would look as good as the old product, and several thousand pounds were spent to ensure that the marketing of the new product was done as well as possible.

(summarised from Phillips, 1982)

The distinctions between PLC Design and Conceive stage approaches to the Define phase of the RMP can also be important but less extreme in its impact, giving rise to a range of approaches between the relatively complex formal models of Examples 14.1 and 14.2 and the relatively simple model of Example 14.3.

Example 14.4

The State of Alaska electric power authority had to choose between a major hydro-electric power project or incremental development of coal-fired power units. RMP developed to assist with this decision (Chapman and Cooper, 1983b) avoided direct probabilistic modelling of any of the parameters of the standard Net Present Value (NPV) decision framework, because the key parameter uncertainties involved issues such as the rate of inflation of fuel prices relative to general inflation and the terminal value (at a 50-year planning horizon) of a hydroelectric power unit, which are by nature only amenable to subjective probability distribution estimates and highly correlated. This approach is 'parametric' in that it systematically identified how far parameters had to move from their expected values to change ('flip') the decision, comparing that movement to plausible ranges of values to identify the relative importance of risks. It facilitates a simple story in a framework most suited to the key parameter risk. For example, instead of NPV as a framework for discussing the hydro/coal choice, it suggests a Terminal Value (TV) approach. TV = 0 is a standard assumption many would insist upon, but a terminal value for the hydroelectric project in money of today before discounting greater than the cost of construction was a plausible possibility in this case (90% of the capital cost was roads, dams and other civil works which might be more valuable in 50 years than their cost today, if properly maintained, given inflation in construction costs and further relative escalation in fuel costs). It was useful to indicate what minimum TV would indicate hydro was the preferred choice under various expected value assumptions for other parameters.

Example 14.5

A more recent study which used the parametric discounting framework of Example 14.4 as a starting point addressed the question 'should the UK defer the disposal of intermediate level nuclear waste for 50 years, or not?' In the process of the analysis a number of the parameters received probabilistic treatment within the parametric framework (Chapman and Howden, 1995). For example, costs associated with temporary surface storage of nuclear waste were assessed probabilistically because the engineers responsible for the estimated costs felt much more comfortable with estimates structured around a formal representation of what reprocessing and other safety measures might and might not be required. Also, the risk of losing the proposed site as a consequence of delay was accepted as high (above 80%), and this was considered to be a key issue which could greatly increase costs.

Of particular importance in this decision is the discount rate. The UK Treasury see the discount rate as a policy variable. The cited paper suggests this is a very high risk strategy. If the appropriate discount rate as economists would measure it with hindsight is slightly less than the Treasury policy rate, the decision 'flips', from 'deferral' to 'non-deferral'. The scope for actual appropriate discount outcomes below the policy rate is vast, relative to the scope for actual appropriate discount rates above the policy rate. This gives rise to an asymmetric risk, with very serious implications associated with deferral being selected and proving non-optimal relative to the implications if non-deferral is selected and proves non-optimal. That is, if the UK does not defer disposal and in 50 years' time history suggests deferral would have been the best choice, the opportunity loss will probably be small relative to the opportunity loss if the UK does defer disposal and in 50 years' time history suggests non-deferral would have been the best choice.

Examples 14.3, 14.4, 14.5, 14.1 and 14.2 (in that order) can be seen as an ordered set illustrating the range of complexity of appropriate approaches to the Define phase when RMP is initiated in the Conceive stage of a PLC. This may be useful. However, it is important to note that some projects may require quite different styles of analysis. For example, a focus on issue identification may make a 'soft' approach preferable. The absence of both detail and structure can make 'soft' or situation-structuring methods particularly useful.

Focus Phase

The Focus phase may change dramatically as a consequence of initiating RMP during the PLC Conceive stage rather than the Design stage. Changes in approach may not be significant, but when they are, the shift is away from an elaborate predesigned RMP like those of Examples 14.1 and 14.2, towards the use of simple decision tree models as in Example 14.3, parametric approaches as in Examples 14.4 and 14.5, and 'soft' situation structuring methods (Rosenhead, 1989).

Following Phases

The nature of following phases of the RMP (Identify, Structure, Ownership, Estimate, Evaluate, Plan and Manage) will be coloured by the earlier phases and the general principles discussed in Part Two. The details are not worth development here. However, it is worth emphasising that if RMP embraces the Conceive stage from the outset, change control issues right back to setting objectives become part of the ongoing RMP process. For example, the uncertainty associated with opportunity cost or value associated with delayed availability of a finished capital investment item becomes an essential aspect of the whole decision process, including design and concept development. For instance, the basic design of a speculative office block may be heavily influenced by assessed uncertainty about construction cost escalation and rent increases, and the basic design of an electric power station may become heavily influenced by assessed uncertainty about construction cost escalation and growth in the demand for electric power. In both cases the approach to basic design concept development may be driven by the wish to minimise the period between committing to construction and completing construction, in order to facilitate management of cost escalation risk, demand and revenue risk.

It can be extremely important to define expectations about the achievement of project objectives in RMP terms at the outset, with a clear understanding of the difference between targets, expectations and commitments. One obvious and important benefit of doing so in a management of expectations context is ensuring a reasonable chance of regular delivery of good news. If a messenger always brings bad news, some will argue he or she deserves to be shot.

14.5   USING RMP IN THE ALLOCATE STAGE

Delaying the initiation of the RMP from the PLC Plan stage as assumed in Part Two until the Allocate stage should have a profound impact. We move from project planning with a strategic planning tone towards project planning with a tactical planning tone. Our project may or may not resemble the 'charge of the light brigade', but the tone of appropriate thinking moves sharply from 'reason why' towards 'do or die', and RMP must accommodate this shift.

That said, the Allocate stage is the last of three stages (Design, Plan and Allocate) often referred to as the 'planning phase' (see Table 2.1), so without our refined PLC stage structure this delay is not detectable. Further, the Allocate stage still precedes the Execute stage when the project is well and truly underway (see Table 2.1). It is still not too late to go back to 'square one' if major potential difficulties are identified, although it is a very good idea not to be responsible for having overlooked those potential difficulties earlier.

As Table 2.1 and associated discussion in Chapter 2 indicate, we are now concerned with the allocation of resources to implement our plans. Within the relevant 'action horizons', we have to put contracts in place to a completed presigning stage, get ready to make commitments, and define appropriate 'action plans'.

When implementing RMP for the first time at this PLC stage, a lack of RMP-based strategic plans can be a major problem. It can mean that RMP tactical plans are largely a waste of time at a general overall level, because they will be based on a wide range of assumptions which in general will not hold, with no clear understanding of the implications of the failure of these assumptions. Generally speaking, to add value effectively, effort needs to be focused on specific tactical areas and decisions, or fairly massive effort needs to readdress Plan, Design and even Conceive stage issues which should have been addressed earlier in RMP terms.

By way of contrast, if Conceive, Design and Plan stage RMP has been employed, Allocate stage RMP can use the framework these earlier RMPs provide to assist with the tactical planning for the action horizon within a strategy which is already well developed. Indeed, where strategic choices required an understanding of tactical issues, as modelled in conventional decision tree analysis, tactical choices may simply require refining at an operational level.

Define Phase

When addressing the six Ws in RMP terms for the first time in the Allocate stage, the emphasis will be *wherewithal* (resources), but all six Ws will still require coordinated treatment.

Project manager expectations of RMP introduced at this stage may be assistance with pressing tactical issues, or it may be confirmation that the planning has been properly done and imminent 'release of funds', a project '*go*', is appropriate, or some combination of these. Most project team members will have similar expectations, although a board or banks about to give approvals will have quite different concerns. Questioning earlier strategic planning assumptions at this stage is rarely a popular activity, but it is an inevitable part of a proper RMP introduced for the first time at this stage. An audit of the quality and effectiveness of project management to date is a key part of RMP at this stage, and considerable tact and strength of character are key prerequisites for the risk analysts. External (to the project) guidance for the RMP which is resistant to project team coercion is vital. When banks or other external funders are involved, authority and independence in relation to the client organisation can also be important.

The 'quality audit' tone of the process becomes much more of a concern than for earlier RMP introduction. However, it remains very important to provide useful feedback to the whole project team as soon as possible. If those responsible for implementing the RMP are not accepted by the project team as part of the team, serious problems will follow. The RMP on the whole project may be aborted as a consequence.

Empowerment from the top, and experienced analysts, are essential if a purely cosmetic analysis is to be avoided. Purely cosmetic analysis at this stage is not just a waste of time; it is dangerously misleading, and the basis of some well-founded mistrust of RMPs. Most people who are seriously suspicious of RMPs have been 'burned' by ineffective RMPs at this stage, and have not understood that it was the particular RMP practitioners who were at fault, or those who hired and directed them, not the basic idea of such a process. There are RMPs and there are RMPs. Each needs to be used in an appropriate way at an appropriate time. Further, there are RMP practitioners and RMP practitioners. Some are very good with specific familiar problems, but are not flexible enough in terms of conceptual education or experience to deal effectively with situations they have not encountered before. It is important to see RMP design skills as part of a craft which requires serious attention. It is not something which provides something to do for engineers who are past their 'sell by date' and given a two-day intensive course. We do not want to put people off who wish to have a go. But we are particularly anxious that mistakes and the ongoing consequences of those mistakes are avoided if the uninitiated tackle the infeasible or inappropriate.

In effect, the Define phase properly done requires the initiation of RMP which covers all the important issues which should have been done earlier, if this is feasible. If this is not feasible, detailed bottom-up analysis of the whole project is a dangerous waste of time. Time is much better spent on two alternative forms of analysis, with an emphasis dependent upon relative priorities:

1. bottom-up risk analysis of specific tactical issues;
2. top-down risk analysis of the project and its context as a whole.

If RMP was introduced earlier in the PLC, and our concern is revisiting an ongoing RMP in the Allocate stage, some revisiting of strategic decisions in the light of new information will be essential, but the Define phase can concentrate on filling in detail in relation to action plans, in preparation for tactical risk management. Getting ready for 'the off' is the focus. Looking in more detail at the implication of plans over the 'action horizon' may reveal new insights which include unwelcome surprises. We have to look for such surprises, remaining sensitive to the possible need for a rethink. But such surprises should be the exception, not the rule, if earlier RMP has been effective.

Focus Phase

The nature of the Focus phase of RMP introduced for the first time in the Allocate stage is shaped by the concerns discussed in the last subsection. In practice, the feasibility of RMP shapes the Focus phase which in turn shapes the Define phase, breaking down both the separability and the assumed sequence of the Define and Focus phases. More generally, this is a good illustration of the complexity of the relationships between RMP phases which makes the whole of the PLC and RMP structure of Table 14.1 a useful conceptual model, which simplifies a complex underlying reality in a practical manner, without relieving us of the need to address considerations which go beyond this 'model' of the process of concern. For example, a decision to spend the time and resources available for a last minute RMP on strategic top-down risk analysis with a view to a possible decision to delay release of funds and the start of the Execute stage must be made very early in the RMP, because it involves a profoundly different approach to the Define phase than RMP with a focus on selected tactical decisions.

The nature of the Focus phase when RMP has been introduced earlier, and our concern is revisiting an ongoing RMP in the Allocate stage, is quite different. In this case, a choice between fundamentally different approaches may not be the issue. However, desirable changes in approach can be much more than refinement in detail. For example, earlier RMP may have more of the flavour of Examples 14.1 to 14.5 than the RMP described in Part Two, with a focus on the Design stage which was not fully transformed during the Plan stage. Ensuring a full transformation in relation to all strategic issues as well as due attention to 'action plans' may be necessary. A major change in analysis style is not necessarily an indication of earlier process failures. It is to be expected, given the change in focus and concerns. In principle, a smooth transition in the style of analysis used at successive stages in the PLC might seem desirable. In practice, more radical steps are easier to manage, and the exact timing of the changes need not follow the PLC stage structure exactly.

Following Phases

The nature of the following RMP phases (Identify, Structure, Ownership, Estimate, Evaluate, Plan and Manage) will be shaped by the earlier phases and the general principles discussed in Part Two. The details are not worth developing here. However, it is worth emphasising that if the Define phase and the Focus phase do not resolve the problems posed by late introduction of RMP, RMP will remain crippled for the rest of the PLC. Further, successful adaptation of earlier RMP to the needs of the Allocate stage will provide the necessary foundation for ongoing RMP which is successful in terms of both effectiveness and efficiency.

14.6   USING RMP IN THE EXECUTE STAGE

Delaying the initiation of RMP from the PLC Plan stage until the Execute stage will have a profound impact on the role of RMP. It is too late to stop the project without a loss of face which will necessitate some changes in the faces present. The project manager who asks for RMP to be introduced at this stage because his or her project is out of control should be looking for another employer at the same time.

That said, all the issues raised in the previous section remain relevant. The changes are a matter of degree. For example, in the Define phase, all six Ws will still require integrated treatment, but the emphasis may swing towards *whichway* (how), to the extent that *whichway* is a matter of detail without fundamental implications requiring much earlier focus. We have gone beyond planning over an 'action horizon', although such planning must be rolled forward as part of the project management process. We are into the details of doing it, executing the action plans. At this level planning may not be a centralised function any more, other than on an exception basis. Planning may be undertaken very locally, perhaps even to the level of each person planning their next step with no consultation required unless there is a major glitch or difficulty.

In the limit, it does not make economic sense to plan how every nut and bolt is put into a piece of machinery, how every weld goes into a bridge, how every element of software code will be written. Where the line is drawn is very important in terms of the efficiency of the management process, and inefficiency can degrade effectiveness.

In the authors' experience, a lack of detailed consideration of uncertainty impacts via appropriate RMP tends to go hand-in-hand with excessive detail in a deterministic planning process. One of the very important impacts of effective RMP is what might be viewed as 'empowerment' of those at the coal face or sharp end, by a reduced amount of centralised and formalised detailed planning, and by an increased degree to which goals and objectives and 'rules of engagement' are specified, with the details left to those in charge of implementing particular tasks.

Hence, if RMP is an ongoing process, revisiting the nature of that process in the Execute stage of the PLC can involve substantial savings in effort in the overall formal project management process, as well as much more effective use of both formal and informal processes. Battle commanders have understood this for hundreds of years. Professional sports coaches have also understood it for as long as they have been around—Roman gladiator coaches included. At this level people need to react the appropriate way by instinct. It is too late for any kind of planning. Part of the purpose of training is building in the appropriate instincts.

14.7   USING RMP IN THE DELIVER STAGE

The Deliver stage is the first of three PLC stages sometimes associated with the project 'Termination phase' (indicated in Table 2.1). As in the context of earlier PLC stages, the PLC decomposition provided by Chapter 2 is useful in terms of discussing how the RMP should adapt to a late appearance in the PLC.

The Deliver stage involves commissioning and handover. The 'basic deliverable verification' step of Table 2.2 involves verifying what the product of the project will do in practice, its actual performance as a whole system, as distinct from its design performance or its performance on a component-by-component basis during the Execute stage. It is too late for 'coordinate and control' in the Execute stage sense.

If the product of the project does not meet a contract performance specification, it is usually too late to introduce meaningful RMP for the first time, unless most of the project's senior staff are first relieved of their posts. Corporate sacred cows and individual reputations can get in the way of the radical thinking which will be required if RMP is introduced at this stage for the first time because serious problems are becoming self-evident.

There are exceptions which prove the rule. For example, if most of the problems were caused by the client or third parties, a contractor who has not previously used RMP may find it very useful to introduce a 'forensic RMP' at this stage to demonstrate why they should be paid very much more than the obvious direct cost increases which have been generated by feedback loops within the project environment (see Examples 8.4, 8.5 and 8.7). For example, a late design change for Channel Tunnel rolling stock due to the goal posts being moved by government safety inspectors together with no delay in the required delivery date by the client induced an increase in parallel working which in turn made the cost of subsequent redesign even more expensive, and an increase in staffing which in turn meant that the staff on average was less experienced and more likely to make mistakes, and so on. The methodology for this kind of 'forensic RMP' is quite different to the RMP discussed in Part Two in terms of its emphasis. In terms of the Focus phase, the risk analysis has to be designed to serve quite different purposes. It is not concerned with making effective decisions. It is concerned with explaining why effective decisions on the part of the contractor were not enough, given the behaviour of the client and third parties.

If project abort or not is the issue, a quite different approach to the Focus phase is appropriate, akin to those discussed earlier in the Design and Conceive stage contexts. However, prevention is better than cure. In particular, if RMP was introduced back in the Define or Design stage, performance will be defined in terms of 'targets', 'expected values' and 'commitments'. Modification of product performance achievement may be possible and effective, but modification of performance criteria can also be addressed within a framework which facilitates trade-offs because it was used to establish commitments in the first place. In particular, client/contractor negotiations may involve 'user-groups' within the client organisation in useful dialogues which go well beyond which 'commitments' to relax, considering where ambitious 'targets' might be approached or exceeded to capture opportunities.

For example, it may not be possible to achieve a maximum weight specification for a weapon system, but given the extra weight it may be possible to make it so much more effective that a smaller number of weapons on the same platform offers much better overall performance than the service in question expected. In such a case the defence procurement executive involved should want to encourage the capture of such opportunities, even if the contract involves a fixed price high performance penalty approach.

14.8   USING RMP IN THE REVIEW STAGE

The Review stage involves a documental audit after delivery of the product, including a full audit of the RMP.

If RMP was not in place early in the PLC, effective review is impossible. It is not just difficult. It is impossible. The authors know of no organisation with an effective review stage process which does not also have an effective RMP. Obvious reasons are:

1. the inability to distinguish between targets, expectations and commitments;
2. the inevitable difference of opinion about risks which were predictable and those which were not;
3. arguments about who owned which risks;
4. confusion about what the project was supposed to achieve in terms of basic objectives;
5. the natural wish to avoid witch-hunts and get on with the next project.

Perhaps not quite so obvious is the lack of a framework to allow effective and efficient capturing of corporate experience. For example, in the bidding context of Example 12.1, once RMP is in place, explicit estimates of the probability of winning each bid allow feedback on bids actually won to refine future estimates. Without the explicit prior estimates, this feedback is inefficient and ineffective. In a similar way, a decomposition of risks and responses as discussed in Part Two allows efficient development of databases for common risk sources and responses which could not be developed without the risk structure to build on which an effective RMP provides. More generally, effective database construction has to follow effective risk analysis which in the first instance may have to work without adequate data. In theory, it would be nice to have all the data for the first RMP, but in practice RMP has to be developed and used before we know what data we really want, and how we want them stored for effective retrieval. Trying to build databases in advance of the associated RMP is inefficient and ineffective, although a degree of simultaneous development is possible.

In a broad sense we must have some informal data gathering to postulate an approach to RMP design, and available data will directly affect our RMP process design, but detailed formal data gathering and capturing of related corporate experience in terms of how best to handle risks and responses depends upon the structuring of those issues adopted by the RMP.

To some extent this is counter-intuitive for most people who have not been directly involved in RMP. This makes it all the more important for everyone to understand that effective review must be built on the back of effective RMP, and effective data and corporate experience capture must be built on the back of an effective Review stage. No RMP means no Review which means no effective experience or data capture. This is an expensive and debilitating shortcoming for any organisation.

14.9   USING RMP IN THE SUPPORT STAGE

The Support stage involves living with the ongoing legacy of apparent project completion, possibly in a passive 'endure' mode. Product liability issues may go right back to the Conceive or Design stage. Reliability, maintainability and availability issues may go back to the Design stage, but they may relate to Plan, Allocate, Execute or Deliver stages. All these issues were risks earlier in the PLC which may not 'come home to roost' until the Support stage. They can be crisis managed in the Support stage, and earlier risk management planning can be developed, but it is too late for RMP to be initiated without a fairly catastrophic rethink.

Product withdrawal is an obvious classic example, as in the case of pharmaceutical products which are found to have dangerous side effects only after significant numbers of people have suffered these side effects. However, pharmaceutical companies are so obviously in the risk management game, that most of them should be managing this kind of potential liability issue from the outset. Product withdrawal associated with 'dangerous' car designs in the USA some time ago is perhaps a more useful example. What makes this example particularly instructive is the more recent practice of European car manufacturers to design cars for recycling at the end of their life, a movement towards a true whole life cycle view of basic design issues. In this sense the international automobile industry is a 'model' others might usefully learn from.

Those responsible for decommissioning nuclear facilities, particularly in the former Soviet block, no doubt wish their current concerns had received more attention in the Conceive and Design stages. However, it would be a serious mistake to be too heavily critical of the nuclear industry, in the sense that their approach was in general understandable, even if in some particular instances it may not be forgivable. At the time nuclear reactors currently being decommissioned were designed and built, very few organisations or industries had an effective RMP which embodied Support stage issues, and the change in political attitudes to such issues was not readily predictable. Some very reputable standard approaches left considerable room for further development (Anderson, Charlwood and Chapman, 1975).

Twenty years from now this defence will not be available, even to the builders of routine office blocks or highways. Designers of today's products who fail to give adequate consideration to Support stage issues and who plead ignorance of the law or good practice will be held accountable for their errors of omission or commission, in moral if not in legal terms. To avoid a potential guilty verdict, and associated damaging commercial consequences, they need to address these issues now.

Further, the industries responsible for projects in specific areas need to lead the development of appropriate definitions of good practice for their industries, drawing on the experience of all other industries which can teach them something useful. Collective sharing of good practice across industries is an important aspect of the process of evolution of RMP good practice.

14.10 CONCLUSION

This chapter provides a structure based around Table 14.1 for considering the impact of introducing RMP for the first time at stages in the PLC other than the Plan stage as assumed in Chapter 4 and Part Two. It also considers the impact of revising an ongoing RMP at different stages in the PLC. The analysis offered is necessarily incomplete, but the authors hope it indicates the nature of the issues, some useful ways to deal with them, and some insights into RMP design issues which would not be apparent if we did not take the discussion beyond the basic RMP of Part Two.

Some of the important conclusions to draw from this chapter are:

1. there is some merit in initially developing effective RMPs introduced at the end of the Plan stage of the PLC on the 'learn to walk before you can run' principle;

2. effective integration of the design–plan–cost trio is an important motivation for bringing the risk management process forward in the PLC;

3. explicit management of the parties–objectives–design–activities quartet is an even more important motive for bringing the risk management process forward in the PLC, but it will require a much more sophisticated RMP than that discussed here;

4. at present, soft systems and soft operational research methods are perhaps the most useful tools for formalisation of these early RMPs (Rosenhead, 1989), but experience should yield more specific methods and processes in time;

5. data and broader experience gathering systems are most effectively designed following successful design and implementation of RMP, rather than the other way around;

6. shifting RMP effort forward in the PLC, into the Design stage from the Plan stage, for example, tends to allow more focus on the latter stages or states (operating state for the product of the project, for example), which can lead to significant benefits;

7. among the benefits of earlier RMP, 'target', 'expected' and 'commitment' value distinctions become part of the language of design, which is of value throughout the PLC, particularly during the Deliver stage;

8. change control processes based on RMP which embrace changing objectives can be a major benefit of earlier RMP implementation, making 'the management of expectations' part of the basic process;

9. simple stories are essential as a summary of the insights provided by an analysis, no matter how complex the analysis;

10. empowerment from the top, and experienced risk analysts, are particularly important prerequisites for successful RMP if the process is introduced for the first time during the Allocate stage, making the Plan/Allocate stage distinction of Table 2.1 developed in Chapter 2 of considerable importance;

11. ineffectual RMPs introduced for the first time during the Allocate stage are responsible for RMPs having a bad reputation with many people who have been 'burned' without recognising that the problem was the specific process or what was asked of it, not the basic idea;

12. understanding RMP design issues which arise in the context of considering initiation of RMP at different stages in the PLC helps to understand the role of the separability assumed in earlier chapters, and how that separability can collapse in practice;

13. an effective RMP can encourage 'empowerment' of those directly implementing plans, with more attention to communicating objectives and 'rules of engagement', less attention to the details of *whichway*, and more attention to developing effective instincts;

14. an effective Review stage process demands an effective RMP introduced early in the PLC;
15. effective data and corporate experience capture depends upon an effective Review stage process;
16. no effective experience or data capture is an expensive and debilitating shortcoming for any organisation;
17. good practice should involve appropriate attention to Support stage issues in an RMP framework at the outset of the PLC even for routine projects;
18. sharing good practice across industries is an important aspect of the process of evolution of RMP good practice.

Chapter 15

Alternative Points of View: A Contractor Perspective

We must indeed all hang together, or most assuredly we shall all hang separately.

Benjamin Franklin, a remark to John Hancock at signing of
the Declaration of Independence, 4 July 1776

15.1 INTRODUCTION

Previous discussion in this book has largely assumed a client or project owner's perspective of project risk. To the extent that a client needs to consider the concerns of other parties, this perspective is a broad one, and a contractor can apply it directly to 'the contractor's project' defined as a subset of the parent project. However, we have not so far addressed the emphasis or special concerns of other parties, in terms of assisting those parties, or in terms of helping clients to understand these special concerns. This chapter addresses these concerns, using the context of a simple two-party situation involving a client and contractor to illustrate the basic issues.

A fundamental point is that different parties involved in a project frequently have different perceptions of project risk. As a consequence they may wish to adopt different strategies for managing project risks as they see them. One reason is that different parties typically have different knowledge and perceptions about the nature of sources of project risk. Another reason is that project parties are likely to have different objectives, or at least different priorities and perceptions of performance objectives, as noted in Section 7.3.

Example 15.1

Consider the nature of risk analysis carried out in three closely related but quite different contexts:

1. risk analysis by the client prior to putting a contract out to competitive tender;
2. risk analysis by a bidding contractor prior to submitting a tender;
3. post tender risk analysis by the winning contractor.

In each case the scope of the risk analysis undertaken will be influenced by the predominant concerns of the party undertaking the risk analysis, and the information about risks available.

Analysis by the client— Risks are evaluated and the project design is developed to manage risks in the client's best interests. Tender documentation and the contract may be drafted to allocate risk to the contractor. However, even with the help of advisers, the client may not be in a position to assess many of the risks associated with the project. Such risks may be better assessed by potential contractors. Some of the key risks will be associated with contractor selection and contract terms.

Analysis by a bidding contractor— Risk analysis by each bidding contractor could be based on the client's risk analysis if it is provided in the tender documentation. The greater the detail provided by the client in relation to risks which are to be borne in whole or in part by the contractor, the less the contractor has to price for risk related to the contractor's uncertainty about what the project involves. Risk analysis here needs to evaluate uncertainty about the tasks required to perform the work specified in the tender documents, but also assesses bids that give an appropriate balance between the risk of not getting the contract and the risk associated with profits and losses if the contract is obtained. Some of the key risks will be associated with client selection (is the client's business secure?, does the client behave in a reasonable manner?, etc.) and contract terms.

Analysis by the winning contractor— Risk analysis by the winning contractor should be undertaken to reduce uncertainty and risk associated with the contractor's profits, to pursue efficiency and check the risk/expected profit balance. If the client has already undertaken such an analysis, and provided it to all bidding contractors, the winning contractor can use it as a starting point. If the contractor has to start from scratch, several drawbacks are involved:

1. The scope for modifications to the project specification and base plan will be less than would be the case during the client's risk analysis. This implies a less efficient project specification and base plan.
2. The level of detail adopted by the contractor will be determined by the benefit to the contractor of more or less detail. Risks which involve costs which can be recovered from the client, and contingency plans associated with the contractor's possible bankruptcy, will not be relevant. This implies less efficient project specification, base and contingency plans.

It may be that these two effects discourage contractors from undertaking risk analysis. They certainly strengthen the case for a client's risk analysis prior to the development of tender documentation. If the client chose the wrong contractor, the contractor chose the wrong client, or both agreed to inappropriate contract terms, both may have serious problems on their hands which require crisis management more than risk management.

From the client or project owner's point of view, project success depends on the production of a deliverable which can be beneficially exploited, perhaps for purposes not originally envisaged, perhaps in the context of an original purpose which has gone away. Project completion by a certain time may not be an essential requirement. From the project manager's point of view, the focus of attention is on coordinating and controlling the project execution. With these concerns, it is not surprising that success at a project management level is often seen as delivery on time and within budget. How useful the final deliverable is to the project owners and subsequent users is a secondary concern. The gap between project owners or users and project managers that this suggests is clearly important.

Differences in perception of project success arise most obviously in client–contractor relationships. The question of 'success from whose point of view?' matters to even the most egocentric party. For example, in a simple single client and single contractor context, if the client or the contractor push their luck, the other party may walk away or go broke and cease to exist. It is often held that 'good project contracts stay in the drawer—as soon as either party loses the confidence of the other, both parties are in trouble' (Curtis, Ward and Chapman, 1991). Different people within the same client or contractor organisation can give rise to essentially the same problems, as can multiple clients or multiple contractors. A central difficulty is that such parties can have different objectives which are not congruent. Unless a shared perception of project success criteria is possible, these different, conflicting criteria for project success may imply very different perceptions of project-related risk, and different priorities in project risk management.

If RMP is carried out by the client prior to the Allocate stage of the PLC, then as discussed in Chapter 9, an important consideration is the appropriate allocation of risk between client and contractor. Rational allocation of risk depends on evaluation of risks under different project scenarios characterised by different contractual arrangements. A difficulty here is that perceptions of risk are dependent on assessment of subsequent risk avoidance and risk reduction actions likely to be taken by the contractor and other parties. Such actions depend in turn on the form of contract agreed and the consequent motivations and behaviour of the contract parties.

As noted in Chapter 7, in a client–contractor situation, the client exerts influence over the contractor primarily via conditions laid down in a contract between the two parties. The contract sets out what is to be produced, what the client will pay, how the client can assess and monitor what the contractor has done, and how things should proceed in the case of various contingent events. The contract may identify and allocate project risks explicitly, but very often particular risks are not identified explicitly and allocation of risks is implicit in the nature and size of contract payment terms. In these cases, the consequences of such allocation may not be fully appreciated. In particular, the manner in which risk is to be managed, if it gets managed at all, may be unclear.

15.2 CONSEQUENCES OF TWO SIMPLE CONTRACT PAYMENT TERMS

Two basic forms of risk allocation via contract payment terms are the fixed price contract and the cost plus fixed fee (CPFF) or 'reimbursement' contract. In the fixed price contract the contractor theoretically carries all the risk. In the CPFF contract the client theoretically carries all the risk. Neither is entirely satisfactory under all circumstances from a risk management perspective. Fixed price contracts are by far the most common, and frequently used inappropriately.

Cost Plus Fixed Fee (CPFF) Contracts

With a cost plus fixed fee (CPFF) contract the client pays the contractor a fixed fee and additionally reimburses the contractor for all costs associated with the project: labour, plant and materials actually consumed charged at rates that are checked and approved by open-book accounting. The cost of overcoming errors, omissions, and other charges is borne by the client.

Advantages for the client include the following: costs are limited to what is actually needed; the contractor cannot earn excessive profits; and the possibility that a potential loss for a contractor will lead to adverse effects is avoided.

However, CPFF contracts have a serious disadvantage as far as most clients are concerned in that there is an uncertain cost commitment coupled with an absence of any incentive on contractors to control costs. Under a CPFF contract, the contractor's motivation to carry out work efficiently and cost effectively is considerably weakened. Moreover, contractors may be tempted to pad costs in ways which bring benefits to other work they are undertaking. Examples include expanded purchases of equipment, excessive testing and experimentation, generous arrangements with suppliers, and overmanning to avoid non-reimburseable layoff costs, a problem which is more pronounced when the fee is based on a percentage of actual project costs.

A further difficulty is that of agreeing and documenting in the contract what are allowable costs on a given project. However, it is important that all project-related costs are correctly identified and included at appropriate charging rates in the contract. Particular areas of difficulty are overhead costs and managerial time. To the extent that costs are not specifically reimbursed, they will paid for out of the fixed fee, and contractors will be motivated to minimise such costs.

The use of a CPFF contract also presents problems in selecting a contractor who can perform the work for the lowest cost. Selecting a contractor on the basis of the lowest fixed fee tendered in a competitive bidding situation does not guarantee a least-cost outcome. It could be argued that it encourages a maximum-cost outcome.

Fixed Price Contracts

Common practice is for clients to aim to transfer all risk to contractors via fixed price contracts. Typically, a contract is awarded to the lowest fixed price bid in a competitive tender, on the assumption that *all* other things are equal, including the expertise of the tendering organisations. Competitive tendering is perceived as an efficient way of obtaining value for money, whether or not the client is relatively ignorant of the underlying project costs compared with potential contractors.

With a fixed price contract the client pays a fixed price to the contractor regardless of what the contract actually costs the contractor to perform. The contractor carries all the risk of loss associated with higher than expected costs, but benefits if costs turn out to be less than expected.

Under a fixed price contract, the contractor is motivated to manage project costs downwards. For example, by increasing efficiency or using the most cost-effective approaches the contractor can increase profit. Hopefully this is without prejudice to the quality of the completed work, but the client is directly exposed to quality degradation risk to the extent that quality is not completely specified or verifiable. The difficulty of completely specifying requirements or performance in a contract is well known. This difficulty is perhaps greatest in the procurement of services as compared with construction or product procurement. For example, it is very difficult to define unambiguously terms like 'cooperate', 'advise', 'coordinate', 'supervise', 'best endeavours', or 'ensure economic and expeditious execution', and it is silly to assume that contractors have priced work under the most costly conditions in a competitive bidding situation.

In the case of a high risk project, where uncertainty demands explicit attention and policy or behaviour modification, a fixed price contract may appear initially attractive to the client. However, contractors may prefer a cost reimbursement contract and require what the client regards as an excessive price to take on cost risk within a fixed price contract. More seriously, even a carefully specified fixed price contract may not remove all uncertainty about the final price the client has to pay. For some sources of uncertainty, such as variation in quantity, or unforeseen ground conditions, the contractor will be entitled to additional payments via a claims procedure. If the fixed price is too low, additional risks are introduced: for example, the contractor may be unable to fulfil contractual conditions and go into liquidation, or use every means to generate claims. The nature of uncertainty and claims, coupled with the confidentiality of the contractor's costs, introduce an element of chance into the adequacy of the payment, from whichever side of the contract it is viewed (Perry, 1986). This undermines the concept of a 'fixed price' contract and at the same time may cause the client to pay a higher than necessary risk premium because risks effectively being carried by the client are not explicitly so indicated. In effect, a cost reimbursement contract is agreed by default for risks that are not controllable by the contractor or the client. This allocation of uncontrollable risk may not be efficient. Client insistence on placing 'fixed price' contracts with the lowest bidder may only serve to aggravate this problem.

Such observations suggest that fixed price contracts should be avoided in the early stages of a project when specifications may be incomplete and realistic performance objectives difficult to set. A more appropriate strategy might be to break the project into a number of stages, and to move from cost-based contracts for early stages (negotiated with contractors that the client trusts), through to fixed price competitively tendered contracts in later stages as project objectives and specifications become better defined.

Normally, the client will have to pay a premium to the contractor for bearing the cost uncertainty as part of the contract price. From the client's perspective, this premium may be excessive unless moderated by competitive forces. However, the client will not know how much of a given bid is for estimated project costs and how much is for the bidder's risk premium unless these elements are clearly distinguished. In the face of competition, tendering contractors (in any industry) will be under continuous temptation to pare prices and profits in an attempt to win work. Faced with the difficulty of earning an adequate return, such contractors may seek to recover costs and increase earnings by cutting back on the quality of materials and services supplied in ways which are not visible to the client, or by a determined and systematic pursuit of claims, a practice common in the construction industry. This situation is most likely to occur where the supply of goods or services exceeds demand, clients are price conscious, and clients find suppliers difficult to differentiate. Even with prior or post bidding screening out of any contractors not deemed capable, reliable and sound, the lowest bidder will have to be that member of the viable set of contractors who scores highest overall in the following categories:

1. Most optimistic in relation to cost uncertainties. This may reflect expertise, but it may reflect a willingness to depart from implicit and explicit specification of the project, or ignorance of what is required.
2. Most optimistic in relation to claims for additional revenue.

3. Least concerned with considerations such as the impact on reputation or the chance of bankruptcy.
4. Most desperate for work.

Selecting the lowest fixed price bid is an approach which should be used with caution, particularly when:

1. uncertainty is significant;
2. performance specifications are not comprehensive, clear, and legally enforceable;
3. the expertise, reputation and financial security of the contractor are not beyond question.

The situation is summed up by Barnes (1984):

> The problem is that when conditions of contract placing large total risk upon the contractor are used and work is awarded by competitive tender, the contractor who accidentally or deliberately underestimated the risks is most likely to get the work. When the risks materialise with full force he must then either struggle to extract compensation from the client or suffer the loss. This stimulates the growth of the claims problem.
>
> The remedy seems to be to take factors other than lowest price into account when appointing contractors. In particular, a reputation gained for finishing fast and on time without aggressive pursuit of extra payment for the unexpected should be given very great weight and should be seen to do so.

An underlying issue is the extent to which clients and contractors wish to cooperate with an attitude of mutual gain from trade, seeing each other as partners. Unfortunately, the all too common approach is inherently confrontational, based on trying to gain most at the other party's expense, or at least seeking to demonstrate that one has not been 'beaten' by the other party. This confrontational attitude can breed an atmosphere of wariness and mistrust. It appears to matter greatly whether the client is entering a one-off non-repeating contractual relationship, or a relationship that may be repeated in the future. To the extent that the client is not a regular customer, the client can be concerned only with the present project and may have limited expertise in distinguishing the quality of potential contractors and bids. Competition is then used to 'get the best deal'. This is often manifested as seeking the lowest fixed price on the naive and rash assumption that all other things are equal. As indicated above, this practice brings its own risks, often in large quantities.

15.3 WELL-FOUNDED WILLINGNESS TO BEAR RISK

Many of the problems with claims and arbitration arise because of contractual parties' preoccupation with transferring risk to other parties, generally under fixed price contracts. To the extent that either clients or contractors believe that risks can be transferred or off-loaded onto the other, or some third party, such as a subcontractor, then any assessment or management of project risks on their part is likely to be half-hearted. Consequently, many contracting parties do not assess risks or share information about risks in any systematic way. As we have seen in the previous section, this behaviour may not be in the best interests of either party.

Abrahamson (1973) has commented on the problem in the following way:

> The strangest thing is that the pricing of risk item ... is resisted by both sides. Some contractors prefer a contentious right to their extra costs to a chance to price a risk, and indeed rely on the increase in their final account from claims to make up for low tenders. On the other hand, some clients and engineers prefer to refer to risks generally or as obliquely as possible, presumably in the hope of finding a contractor who will not allow for them fully in his price.
>
> These two attitudes are equally reprehensible and short sighted. What a sorry start to a project when they encounter each other!

Such behaviour is often encouraged by legal advisers concerned to put their client's legal interests first. In legal circles debate about risk allocation is usually about clarifying and ensuring the effectiveness of allocation arrangements in the contract. Lawyers are not concerned with the principles that should guide appropriate allocation of risk between contracting parties. It could be argued that they are pursuing their own best interests by maximising conflict, implicitly if not explicitly.

At first sight, appropriate allocation might be based on the willingness of parties to take on a risk (Ward, Chapman and Curtis, 1991). However, willingness to bear risk will only result in conscientious management of project risks to the extent that it is based on:

1. an adequate perception of project risks;
2. a reasoned assessment of risk/reward trade-offs;
3. a real ability to bear the consequences of a risk eventuating;
4. a real ability to manage the associated uncertainty and thereby mitigate risks.

Willingness to bear risk should not be a criterion for risk allocation to the extent that it is based on:

1. an inadequate perception of project risks;
2. a false perception of ability to bear the consequences of a risk eventuating;
3. a need to obtain work;

4. perceptions of the risk/return trade-offs of transferring risks to another party.

As noted earlier, these latter conditions can be an underlying reason for low tender prices on fixed price contracts.

To ensure that willingness to bear risk is well founded, explicit consideration of risks allocated between the contracting parties is desirable, preferably at an early stage in negotiations or the tendering process. In particular, contractors ought to be given an adequate opportunity to price for risks they will be expected to carry.

Unfortunately, the following scenario for a construction project is often typical.

Example 15.2

A project that has taken several years to justify and prepare is parcelled up and handed to tendering contractors who are given just a few weeks to evaluate it from scratch and commit themselves to a price for building it. The tenderers have been through an extensive and costly prequalification exercise that is designed to determine their capacity to undertake the work. Having the gratification of being considered acceptable, they would like to be allowed the time to study the tender documents in detail and to consider carefully their approach to the work. Instead they are faced with a tender submission deadline that only permits a scanty appraisal of the complex construction problems and risks that are often involved. Consequently, each tenderer proceeds along the following lines.

A site assessment team, which may include a project manager, estimator, planner, geologist and representatives of specialist subcontractors, is assembled and despatched to the site with instructions to gather in all method- and cost-related information needed for preparing the bid. This information, together with quotations from materials suppliers, subcontractors and plant companies, and advice on the legal, insurance, financial and taxation implications, is assessed by the estimating team working under great pressure to meet the deadline. Various construction techniques have to be investigated and compared, and temporary works proposals considered and designed. Lack of information on ground conditions, plant availability, materials supply, subcontractor capacity and many other important factors have to be overcome by further investigation and inspired guess-work. The contractual terms have to be explored to elicit the imposed risk strategy of the client. An assessment has to be made of the client's reaction to any qualifications in the bid. Possible claims opportunities are evaluated.

In the absence of adequate time and information, any evaluation and pricing of potential risk exposure is on an *ad hoc* basis. Evaluation of risks begins by questioning experienced managers in the contractor's organisation and arriving at a consensus of the 'gut feelings' expressed. The overall level of risk is assessed by looking at the overall programme, checking if it is very 'tight', considering the effects of delays by suppliers, and checking the basic conditions for any extension of time. Few, if any, calculations or references to specific results on previous contracts are made, the rationale being that any such references are unlikely to be applicable to the circumstances of the contract in question, even if any relevant data existed. The chairman ends up by pulling a figure out of the air based upon his feelings about the advice obtained.

Even if the contractor is prepared to undertake appropriate analysis of project risks, lack of information about project uncertainties coupled with lack of time to prepare a tender may preclude proper evaluation of project risks.

Joint identification of risks by client and tendering contractors is desirable, on efficiency grounds in terms of cost-effective identification of a comprehensive list, and to ensure that both parties are fully aware of the risks involved. If tendering contractors were simply given more time to tender without client involvement, they might undertake adequate analysis of project risks. While many project risks may be best assessed by knowledgeable contractors, it may be more efficient for the client to undertake analysis of certain project risks to expedite the tendering process and to ensure that all tenderers have similar information. For example, contractors should not be expected to bear risks which cannot be cost effectively quantified with sufficient certainty, such as variable ground on a tunnelling project. In such cases the price ought to be related to what is actually encountered (Barber, 1989). If clients are unduly concerned about bearing such risks, then it will be appropriate for them to undertake the necessary in-depth risk analysis themselves and require tendering contracts to price for the risk on the basis of the client's risk analysis. Sharing such risks is always an option. Obviously, the greater the detail provided by the client in relation to risks which are to be borne in whole or in part by the contractor, the less the contractor has to price for risk related to the contractor's uncertainty about what the project involves.

In determining a final bid figure, contractors need to consider several other factors besides estimates of the prime cost of performing the contract (Ward and Chapman, 1988). The intensity of the competition from other contractors, the costs of financing, insurance and bonding, the financial status of the client, terms of payment and project cash flow, and the level of the contingency allowance to cover risks, all affect the mark-up that is added to the prime cost of construction. Tendering contractors' risk analysis will have additional dimensions to the client's risk analysis. Each contractor requires a bid that gives an appropriate balance between the risk of not getting the contract and the risk associated with possible profits or losses if the contract is obtained.

Aside from allowing contractors sufficient time to properly consider the pricing of risk, clients need to be able to assess the extent to which contractors' tender prices are based on well-founded willingness to take on project risk. A useful 'transparent pricing' strategy is for the client to require fixed price bids to be broken down into a price for expected project costs and risk premia for various risks. Supporting documentation could also show the contractors' perceptions of risk upon which the risk premia were based. As in insurance contracts, pricing based on broad categories of risk rather than related to small details is a realistic approach. An important consideration in performing risk analysis is the identification of factors which can have a major impact on project performance. However, detailed risk analysis may be necessary to determine the relative significance of project risks. Pricing need not consider all project risks in detail, but it does need to be related to major sources of risk.

An important benefit of a 'transparent pricing' strategy to both client and contractor is clarification of categories of risk remaining with the client despite a fixed price contract. For example, there may be project risks associated with exogenous factors, such as changes in regulatory requirements during the project, which are not identified or allocated by the contract. Such factors are unlikely to be allowed for in bids, because tenderers will consider such factors outside of their control and the responsibility of the client.

A further benefit of 'transparent pricing' is that it helps to address an important potential 'adverse selection' problem. Contractors who can provide honestly stated, good-quality risk pricing may price themselves out of the market in relation to those who provide dishonestly stated, poor-quality risk pricing at low prices, if sufficient clients are unable to distinguish between good and poor quality, honesty and dishonesty. As Akerlof (1970) argues in a paper entitled 'The market for "lemons": quality uncertainty and the market mechanism', poor quality and dishonesty can drive good quality and honesty out of the market. Clients can address this problem by requiring transparent pricing of risk in tenders and by requiring tender submissions to include plans for managing risk. In this way comparisons between tenderers in terms of the extent of well-founded willingness to bear risk can be made on a more informed basis.

In practice, tenderers experienced in risk management may be able to demonstrate well-founded willingness to bear risk *and* submit lower tender prices than competitors. In such cases 'transparent pricing' should help to consolidate their advantage over less experienced contractors.

15.4   EFFICIENT ALLOCATION OF RISK

The acquisition of information about project risks plays a key role in the ability of contractual parties to allocate and manage risk. Given the potential conflict of contractual party objectives, a central issue is the extent to which contractual parties can obtain mutual benefit by sharing risk information. A related issue is how this information can be used to allocate risks on a rational basis and the extent to which risks can be allocated in a mutually beneficial way.

It is often suggested that cost risk should be allocated to the party best able to anticipate and control that risk. On this basis, a tentative conclusion is that fixed price contracts are appropriate when risks are controllable by the contractor, CPFF contracts are appropriate when risks are controllable by the client. However, this conclusion ignores the relative willingness of client and contractor to bear risk, and it ignores the ability of each party to bear risk. In particular, it ignores the pricing of risks, the client's attitude to trade-offs between expected cost and carrying risk, and the contractor's attitude to trade-offs between expected profit and carrying risk. Further, it fails to address questions about how risk which is not controllable by either party should be allocated.

Elsewhere (Chapman and Ward, 1994), we show in detail how the allocation of risk might be guided by consideration of the risk efficiency of alternative forms contract payment terms. In choosing between a fixed price or CPFF contract, the criterion of risk efficiency implies choosing the contract with the preferred combination of expected cost and risk. As explained in Chapter 3, if one option offers both lower cost and lower risk, then this is a risk efficient choice.

The approach in Chapman and Ward (1994) distinguishes three basic types of project cost uncertainty or risk: contractor controllable uncertainty, client controllable uncertainty, and uncontrolled uncertainty. The analysis suggests that different contractual arrangements may be appropriate for each type of uncertainty, in each case dependent on the relative willingness of the client and contractor to accept project-related risk. If a project involves all three types of uncertainty, the contract should involve different payment terms for each set of risks. To the extent that individual sources of cost uncertainty independently contribute to each of the three categories, it may be appropriate to subdivide categories and negotiate different payment terms for each major independent risk source. One simple, practical example of this approach is where a client undertakes to pay a lower fixed price if the client agrees to carry a designated risk via cost reimbursement in respect of that risk.

The analysis highlights the need for clients to consider project cost uncertainty explicitly in the form of a 'PC curve' (Probability distribution of Costs), and to identify the clien$T$'s 'equivalent' certain cost, T, corresponding to the maximum fixed price the client is prepared to pay. In the envisaged procedure, the client first identifies appropriate constituent groupings of project risks, constructing associated PC curves and identifying T values for each. The PC curve for the project as a whole is then obtained by combining the component PC curves. The total project PC curve together with the associated T value is used later for checking consistency and completeness of submitted bids rather than to determine a single payment method for the whole project. Tenderers are asked to submit for each group of project risks designated by the client:

1. fixed price bids R (the contracto$R$'s 'equivalent' certain cost);
2. the contribution to profit, or fee, K (a constant), required if a CPFF contract is agreed.

In addition, tenderers might be required or choose to submit their perceptions of constituent risk PC curves (which need not match the client's perceptions), to demonstrate the depth of their understanding of the project risks and to justify the level of bids, should these be regarded by the client as unusually low or high. Equally, a client might provide tenderers with the client's perceptions of constituent risk PC curves to encourage and facilitate appropriate attention to project cost uncertainties. If a spirit of cooperation and willingness to negotiate mutually beneficial risk sharing arrangements prevailed, the client and individual tenderers could exchange perceptions about constituent risk PC curves with a view to developing a consensus view of project risks. Such views expressed as PC curves would facilitate the negotiation of mutually beneficial risk-sharing agreements without the necessity for the PC curves themselves to have any legal status in the contract.

In assessing bids, the client would be concerned about the relative sizes of R and T values for each constituent risk PC curve. The contractor bidding with the lowest total sum of R values would not necessarily be the contractor with the most preferred pattern of R values.

Our analysis (Chapman and Ward, 1994) concludes the following about the risk efficiency of fixed price and CPFF contracts:

1. a fixed price contract is usually risk efficient in allocating contractor controllable risk;
2. a CPFF contract is usually risk efficient in allocating client controllable risk;
3. in respect of uncontrollable risk, a fixed price contract is risk efficient if the contractor is more willing to accept risk ($R < T$), but a CPFF contract is risk efficient if the client is more willing to accept risk ($T < R$).

An important conclusion is that even where client and contractor share similar perceptions of project cost uncertainty, a fixed price contract may be inefficient for the client, if the contractor is more risk averse than the client. In this situation the contractor will require a higher premium to bear the risk than the client would be prepared to pay for avoiding the risk. This situation can arise where the client is a relatively large organisation, for whom the project is one of many, but the contractor is a relatively small organisation, for whom the project is a major proportion of the contractor's business, a fairly common scenario.

We believe the results this analysis suggests are robust. These are not abstract arguments which will not withstand the impact of practical considerations. However, some clients have appeared to be willing to enter into CPFF contracts only as a last resort. For example, Thorn (1986) notes experience in the UK Ministry of Defence in which the desire to avoid non-risk contracts has frequently led to non-competitive contracts being placed on a fixed price basis, even when the specification has been insufficiently defined for a firm estimate to be agreed:

> In such cases, the contractor is unwilling to commit to a fixed price without a substantial contingency to cover any unknown risks, and the Authority is unable to accept the high level of contingency required by the contractor. The result is that prices have been agreed at such a late stage in the contract that the amount of risk eventually accepted by the contractor is substantially reduced and, in some cases, removed altogether. The Review Board has frequently expressed concern at delays in price fixing, and has advocated the use of incentive contracts. These are intended to be used when the risks are too great to enable fixed prices to be negotiated, but not so great as to justify the use of cost plus contracts.

15.5 RISK SHARING AND INCENTIVE CONTRACTS

Incentive contracts offer the possibility of sharing risk between the client and contractor and an intermediary position between fixed price and CPFF contracts. This is potentially a more risk efficient alternative for both client and contractor.

In the simplest form of incentive contract, where

C = the actual project cost (which is uncertain at the start of the project),
E = target cost,
b = the sharing rate, $0 < b < 1$,
F = the target profit level,

and E, b, and F are fixed at the commencement of the contract, payment by the client to the contractor is

$$C_T = F + bE + C(1 - b), \tag{15.1}$$

and the profit to the contractor is

$$P = F + b(E - C). \tag{15.2}$$

When $b = 1$, the contract corresponds to a fixed price contract. When $b = 0$, the contract corresponds to a CPFF contract.

Note that in Equation (15.2), if the cost C exceeds E by more than F/b, then the profit to the contractor becomes negative and the contractor makes a loss.

In the situation described by Equation (15.2), which is sometimes referred to as a budget-based scheme, tendering firms select a budget (target cost), and incentive profit is proportional to budget variance (Reichelstein, 1992). Three parameters are required to specify the contract: the sharing rate b, the target cost level E, and the target profit level F. In theory, the target cost level should correspond to the expected value of project costs. In practice, it is very important that this is understood, lest misunderstandings about the status of this figure arise. Instead of specifying F, a target profit rate r may be specified, where $F = rE$. With this specification the client must decide which (if any) values to preset for E, b and F or r prior to inviting tenders.

An alternative form of Equation (15.2) is

$$P = d - bC, \tag{15.3}$$

where d is a fixed profit fee, with

$$d = F + bE. \tag{15.4}$$

In Equation (15.3) only two parameters are required to specify the contract: the sharing rate b, and the fixed profit fee d. Tenders may be invited in the form of d if b is prespecified by the client, or for both b and d. Typically, if a 'uniform' value for b is prespecified by the client, the contract is awarded to the contractor submitting the lowest fixed profit fee d.

Selection of an Appropriate Risk-sharing Rate

Risk sharing arrangements may be risk efficient from the client's point of view when contractors are risk averse, have superior precontractual information, or limited liability under the proposed contract. The desirability of risk sharing will also depend on whether the cost risks are controllable by the contractor, controllable by the client, or controllable by neither. In the latter case, the party bearing the risk acts as a quasi-insurer (Ward, Chapman and Curtis, 1991), and the desirability of risk sharing is related to the relative levels of risk aversion of the contractor and client. In the case of cost risks that are controllable to some extent by either party, risk sharing influences incentives to manage those risks.

An inherent problem with risk sharing is the reduction in a contractor's sensitivity to adverse outcomes as the proportion of cost risk borne by the client increases. In the case of contractor controllable risk, the contractor's motivation to limit cost overruns and seek cost savings will be reduced as the client takes on more risk. It follows that different levels of risk sharing may be appropriate for categories of risk which are (a) controllable by the contractor, (b) controllable by the client, and (c) not controllable by either.

Samuelson (1986) shows that under 'general conditions', *some* level of risk sharing, with $0 < b < 1$, should be preferred by the client to either CPFF or fixed price contracts. The general nature of Samuelson's analysis does not lead to any specific optimal values for b, but the optimum value of b increases the more risk averse the client, and the more costs are controllable by the contractor. A further complication is that contractor risk aversion affects the actual level of contractor effort on controlling costs once the risk-sharing rate b has been negotiated. The greater the perceived risk of loss in a contracting situation, the more vigorously contractors strive to reduce costs for the sake of avoiding loss as well as for the sake of gaining increments of profit (Scherer, 1964). A similar difficulty exists in considering the efficiency of sharing client controllable risk. However, in specific situations, the client may be able to identify and cost various options available and evaluate these under different risk-sharing arrangements.

In the case of risk which is not controllable by either client or contractor, a plausible variation to the risk-sharing arrangement in (15.1) and (15.2) is to set $F = K + b^2(V - E)$, where K is the fee required by the contractor if a cost reimbursement CPFF contract were to be agreed, and V is set to the value R or T referred to in the previous section. Assuming variance (Var) is an appropriate measure of risk, this risk-sharing arrangement reduces the contractor's risk from Var $(E - C)$ to Var $b(E - C) = b^2$ Var $(E - C)$. Therefore the contractor's risk premium should be reduced from $(V - E)$ to $b^2(V - E)$ under this risk-sharing arrangement. With agreement between client and contractor on the value of the expected cost E, this arrangement is risk efficient for both client and contractor for a wide range of circumstances (Chapman and Ward, 1994b).

Of course, difficulties in specifying an optimum, risk efficient level for the risk-sharing rate need not preclude the use of incentive contracts and pragmatic definition of risk-sharing rates by the client. An alternative arrangement is for clients to require contractors to specify a value for the risk-sharing rate b as part of their bid. Contractors are then selected on the basis of bids for b and d in the situation described by Equation (15.3), or for b, E, and F or r in the situation described by Equation (15.2).

Selection of Efficient Contractors

If the client presets b and F (or r where $F = rE$), the selection of the contractor who bids the lowest value for E (or d) is not guaranteed to minimise procurement costs for the client. There may still be difficulties in selecting the most efficient contractor. For example, McCall (1970) has argued that incentive contracts awarded on the basis of the lowest bid leads to 'inefficient' firms being selected. McCall's analysis implies that relatively inefficient firms, whose actual costs are high, tend to submit estimated costs (bids E) that are lower than actual costs, because they can share some of their losses with the client. Conversely, relatively efficient firms, whose actual costs of production are low, tend to submit estimated costs (bids) that are higher than actual costs. With the client sharing in any cost underrun, the less an efficient firm's expected cost, the more it must bid to secure a profit equal to that obtainable elsewhere. Hence, if the client chooses among firms on the basis of the lowest bid, then it is possible that it will select relatively inefficient firms (high actual costs) instead of relatively efficient ones (low actual costs). The probability of selecting a high-cost instead of a low-cost firm increases as the declared sharing proportion decreases.

In addition, where F and b are fixed by the client, Baron (1972) shows that if two firms are bidding for a contract, other things being equal, the more risk-averse firm will submit the lower bid (in effect the lower estimate of E from Equation (15.4)), and the probability of a cost overrun will be greater if that firm is selected. Thus a low bid for d may reflect a contractor's wish to reduce the risk of not winning the contract rather than ability to perform the contract at low cost. This possibility is generally recognised in both fixed price and CPFF contract situations.

However, the above arguments by Baron and McCall are of limited relevance where clients do not preset the sharing rate b. More usually, it might be expected that the fixed profit fee d and sharing rates would be determined together, so that clients would bargain simultaneously for both low cost targets *and* high contractor share rates. Thus, in general, the tighter the negotiated cost target, the higher the sharing proportion desired by the client. In these circumstances, Canes (1975) showed that there is a systematic tendency toward cost overruns, because contractors tend to submit bids below their actual estimate of expected costs. According to Canes only a subset of efficient firms will be willing to compete by simultaneously increasing the share rate they will accept and reducing their target cost bid. Inefficient firms and the remainder of efficient firms will prefer to charge for higher share rates by raising target cost bids, and in Canes' analysis these firms correspond to the set of firms which submit bids below their expected costs. To the extent that tendering contractors are observed to charge for higher share rates in this way, cost overruns can be expected from such contractors. As a contract letting strategy, Canes suggests setting the target profit rate r (and hence the target profit level F) at zero while allowing firms to choose share rates subject to some minimum rate greater than zero. Canes argues that this policy should minimise clients' costs of procurement while inducing firms to reveal their true opportunity costs of production.

However, an important assumption in the analysis of Canes (1975) and McCall (1970) is that the contracting firms are assumed to be risk neutral (maximisers of expected profit). In situations where contractors are significantly risk averse, their conclusions need to be treated with caution.

Determining an Appropriate Target Cost

A further problem in ensuring a risk-efficient incentive contract is determining an appropriate value for the target cost E. Ideally, the client would like the target cost to correspond to the contractor's true estimate of expected cost. Obviously, the benefit to the client of an incentive element in the contractor's remuneration will be undermined if the target cost is higher than the contractor's true estimate of expected cost.

Suppose firms are invited to tender values for b and E. A disadvantage of this invitation is that it can encourage a generally high level of tender values for E. But the client would like to encourage truthful, unbiased estimates of the expected costs from tenderers. In principle, the client could achieve this by offering higher values of b for lower estimates of E. Then submitting an overestimate of expected cost will be less appealing to the contractor because the associated lower sharing rate limits the contractor's ability to earn large profits when costs turn out to be low. Conversely, if a contractor truly believes costs will be high, the threat of low profits if costs turn out to be high will dissuade the contractor from submitting an underestimate of expected cost.

Thus, the client could offer a menu of contracts, in terms of values of F and b for different values of E. By submitting a cost estimate, a tendering firm chooses one particular incentive contract given by the corresponding F and b values. Provided F and b are suitably defined, such a menu of contracts can induce firms to provide unbiased estimates of project cost.

A practical application of this menu approach for rewarding sales personnel in IBM Brazil is described by Gonik (1978). Gonik describes an incentive system which gears rewards to how close staff forecasts of territory sales and actual results are to the company's objectives. A sales forecast S is made by each sales person for a given period and sales region, and this is used to determine each person's level of bonus P. If the company quota is Q, actual sales achieved are A, and a base level of bonus payment preset by the company is B, then each person's level of bonus payment P is given by

$$P = BS/Q \quad \text{where } S = A, \tag{15.5}$$

$$P = B(A + S)/2Q \quad \text{where } S < A, \text{ and} \tag{15.6}$$

$$P = B(3A - S)/2Q \quad \text{where } S > A. \tag{15.7}$$

In general, for a given sales forecast S, bonuses increase as A increases, but for a given A, payments are maximised if $A = S$. Thus, sales personnel receive more for higher sales but are also better off if they succeed in fore-casting actual sales as closely as possible. In principle, a similar system could be adopted in contracting to encourage contractors to provide un-biased estimates of project costs and control these costs to the best of their ability (see, for example, Reichelstein, 1992).

Other Forms of Incentive Contract

The economic literature focuses on linear incentive contracts in the form of Equation (15.1), but in practice incentive contracts often involve more than one risk-sharing rate over the range of possible project costs, and they may incorporate minimum and maximum levels of allowable profit. Two main types of incentive contract are usually distinguished: the fixed price incentive (FPI) contract and the cost plus incentive fee (CPIF) contract. These differ mainly in the treatment of cost overruns beyond some ceiling. In both forms of contract the contractor's profit from cost underruns is subject to a ceiling value, but risk sharing takes place for costs in some range around the target or expected cost. With an FPI contract the contractor assumes a higher share of risk for cost overruns outside this range, and may carry all risk above some set cost level. With a CPIF contract the client takes all cost risk above some cost level and the contractor receives a minimum level of profit. Such variations on the simple linear incentive contract of the form of Equation (15.1), while of practical significance, make a general analysis of incentive contracts even more difficult. For example, Reichelstein (1992) notes that the introduction of cost ceilings may distort the incentives created by simple incentive contracts of form Equation (15.1). With a cost ceiling the contractor typically bears 100% of all costs in excess of the ceiling, and the contractor will be better off submitting a bid below the contractor's expected cost. Without a cost ceiling the contractor could be induced to submit a bid which was a true reflection of the contractor's expected cost, as noted in the previous section. However, in the presence of a cost ceiling, costs in excess of the ceiling will be penalised at the same rate irrespective of the bid. Therefore, the contractor has an incentive to bias his submitted cost estimate downwards.

15.6 CONCLUSION

Despite the risks inherent in the fixed price contract this is still a very common form of contract. CCFF contracts have weaknesses for the client which severely limit its use by risk-averse client organisations. Incentive contracts offer a variety of middle ground positions, but do not appear to be as widely used as they might be. This may be because of a lack of awareness of the shortcomings of typical fixed price contracts or because of a lack of appreciation of the value of incentive contracts in motivating contractors. However, the additional complexity of incentive contracts may make them difficult and time consuming to negotiate. In particular, there are problems in selecting the lowest cost contractor, and appropriate values for the sharing rate b and the target cost E. Unless firms can be motivated to provide unbiased estimates of costs (perhaps by arrangements such as those described above), client organisations may be wary of incentive contracts when they are unable to formulate realistic project cost targets for themselves. Incentive contracts may be confined to procurement projects where the client has a sound basis to estimate contract costs, there are uncertainties that make a fixed price contract impractical, but the uncertainties are not so great as to justify the use of cost plus contracts (Thorn, 1986). A further problem with incentive contracts is that the evaluation of the consequences of a particular incentive contract is not straightforward when project costs are uncertain. This can make it difficult to carry out negotiations on a fully informed basis, but such difficulties are not insurmountable (Ward and Chapman, 1995a). Perhaps the most significant obstacle to greater use of incentive contracts and risk sharing is the still widespread unwillingness of parties entering into procurement contracts to explore the effects of project risk and the possibilities for effective risk management.

Negotiating a fixed price contract with a trusted or previously employed contractor may be a preferred alternative for knowledgeable clients, and perhaps also worth pursuing by less knowledgeable clients. Also, a move away from 'adversarial' contracting towards 'obligational' contracting (Morris and Imrie, 1993) may be mutually beneficial for both clients and contractors and give rise to an atmosphere of increased trust and sharing of information. In these circumstances there will be opportunities for increased mutual understanding and management of contract risks.

From a risk management perspective, it is very important to identify categories of risk which are:

1. controllable by the contractor;
2. controllable by the client;
3. not controllable by either party.

Different payment arrangements should be adopted for each of these categories of risk, implying different levels of risk sharing for each category of risk, so that appropriate allocation and positive management of those risks is encouraged where possible. The flexibility of incentive contract forms of payment is attractive here, but more widespread use of such contracts may depend on the development of more 'obligational' contracting rather than 'adversarial' contracting.

Addressing alternative points of view in this chapter has been focused on a contractor perspective, in terms of a contractor pursuing the contractor's best interest and the implications for clients. The issues are not simple, and even with this limited focus, only an overview has been provided. Those seriously touched by these issues need to follow up the references provided.

A number of other alternative points of view are important and could be subjected to analysis with similar rigour. In some cases the situation may be even more complex. For example, a project may involve important interfaces with several regulators, concerned with issues such as: the implications of the project in terms of the efficiency and effectiveness of particular market places in the context of fair or unfair competition; the impact of the project approach on the health and well-being of future generations; the impact of the project on local industry or labour markets; or the impact of the project on the health and safety of its work force. Such regulators may shape the nature of a proposed project in ways which are both profound and complex, often worthy of at least as much attention as client–contractor relationships. Further organisations, like insurers (a form of subcontractor but with some special characteristics), may deserve special attention. As indicated in Chapter 7, issues such as employment injury liability may not be straightforward.

Chapter 16

Selecting Short Cuts

The art of being wise is the art of knowing what to overlook.

William James

16.1   INTRODUCTION

Partially for expository reasons, Part Two assumed that circumstances warranted a comprehensive risk management process (RMP). To understand the nature of *effective* risk management, it is essential to understand the nature of a comprehensive RMP. In practice, the comprehensive approach may need to be simplified to meet the practical needs of a particular context, to provide *cost effective* and *efficient* risk management. Knowing what to overlook, and how to take effective short cuts, is not a simple matter.

There are obvious opportunities for simplification or short cuts if the present risk analysis is an update of an earlier risk analysis, or a standardised model or prototype risk analysis process for comparable projects is available. This can improve the efficiency and perhaps the effectiveness of the risk management process. However, the key reason for seeking simplification or short cuts is to ensure *cost-effective* and *efficient* RMP in general, in the long term, if not the short term. Carrying out an RMP is not without costs, and a key concern is ensuring an appropriate trade-off between these costs and the effectiveness of the RMP.

Costs of RMP

Cost associated with RMP may arise in direct cash or time terms, but 'opportunity' costs can be even more important, and opportunity costs raise important issues in terms of long-term versus short-term decisions.

In the short term we may have to work within inflexible resource constraints. Key people's time may become extremely precious. In the terms economists would use, the marginal cost of an extra hour (or the last hour) spent on RMPs by *all* the staff involved (not just specialist RMP staff) ought to be assessed in terms of the value of the best alternative use these hours might be put to. At a critical point in the development of a project, the time of the staff involved will be very valuable, perhaps 2, 3 or even 10 times their gross salary cost, and effective use of their time is a key concern. The effects of this are easily observable in terms of the project team which is 'too busy fighting alligators to think about how to drain the swamp they are in'. Part of the effect of effective RMP will be avoidance of this kind of panic, but crisis management is not going to be eliminated if the project plan is risk efficient, and high short-term opportunity costs for the time required for RMPs is going to remain an issue. In the longer term we need to anticipate the opportunity costs associated with all staff involved in RMP, and resource RMP accordingly. This is a key consideration in the Focus phase. As indicated earlier, RMP can be a high risk project in its own right. Attempting to add RMP resources in a crisis (including more support for all those who need to be involved, not just specialist RMP staff) is not a good idea. It can have an effect comparable to 'attempting to put out a fire by pouring on petrol', like adding staff to a computer software project which is out of control, as indicated earlier.

The Trade-off Between RMP Effectiveness and Cost

Although assessing the direct costs of RMP is complex, assessing the effectiveness of RMP is even more complex. In any particular case there is a need to address the effectiveness of RMP in terms of the full set of motives (or benefits) of RMP discussed in Chapter 3 in relation to the full set of relevant project performance criteria and concerns addressed in Chapter 5. This assessment is clearly demanding in terms of skill and experience. It is too complex to deal with directly here.

However, choosing appropriate short cuts in the Focus phase (initially and as an ongoing aspect of RMP development) is driven by trade-offs between RMP effectiveness and RMP cost. There is no one best way to approach all RMPs, and given the complexity of both RMP effectiveness and cost, what we should mean by 'best' is an inherently complex issue.

To a significant extent this means we are in the realm of 'craft' rather than science. The authors know of no simple way to describe clearly what is involved. 'We know what we like when we see it, but we cannot describe what we like in abstract terms.'

That said, we cannot leave this issue unaddressed. It is perhaps the most important single issue a professional RMP specialist has to address, once the basics are understood. It would constitute a dereliction of duty on our part to ignore it. To make the discussion of this chapter as simple as possible, six dimensions have been chosen, as follows:

1. immediate versus long-term motives;
2. comprehensiveness of motives;
3. degree of anticipation;
4. degree of formality;
5. model complexity;
6. model quantification.

Each of these dimensions is discussed separately in subsequent sections, ordered to make a complicated story as easy to follow as possible. More dimensions might be used, or fewer. The authors are not suggesting six is a magic number. Six is simply a useful number for present purposes, in terms of a trade-off between the useful simplicity provided by a nominally separable structure for discussion purposes and an oversimplification of a complex reality which might obscure important connections or links.

16.2   IMMEDIATE VERSUS LONG-TERM MOTIVES

If the introduction of RMPs into an organisation is part of a long-term change in project management processes and organisational culture, it is very important to see early applications as part of a corporate learning process. Viewed in this light, the effectiveness of RMP relates to benefits derived from all subsequent impacts of the process on later projects as well as the project which is an immediate concern. Taking this to its logical conclusion, the first project subjected to RMP should be carefully selected to realise these long-term benefits. The understanding provided will allow informal choices about short cuts subsequently, with an understanding of both the costs and benefits of alternative approaches.

As an example of taking this to its limit, the very first application of the SCERT approach (Chapman, 1979) with BP International was a 'passive' (retrospective) analysis of a project just completed, to polish the process before its first test on a 'live' project. Most organisations do not need a 'passive' test, but it is very useful to see the first application as a test and as a learning experience.

As most people who have acquired some of their wisdom via the 'school of hard knocks' know, making mistakes is the only way to learn some of life's more important lessons, but it is important not to make mistakes which kill or cripple future opportunities. If mistakes are inevitable, we need to make mistakes we can live with.

As a simple illustration, when laying a course to sail a yacht across the English Channel from Southampton to Cherbourg, it is advisable to aim to hit the French coast several miles up-tide and/or up-wind of the destination, because it is comparatively easy to alter course at the last minute in a down-wind and down-tide direction, comparatively difficult to do so up-wind against the tide. We know we will get it wrong to some extent, and the error is not symmetric in its effect, so we aim for low cost errors. The magnitude of error assumed should reflect our proven navigation skill. Further, it is advisable to cross the Channel a reasonable number of times before attempting the Atlantic Ocean.

These ideas apply to choosing an appropriate level of RMP for the first attempt, as well as choosing an appropriate project.

An excessively sophisticated RMP will be a handicap, as will an excessively difficult project. But learning requires a challenge, and only by using a bit more sophistication than we need can we recognise when and where it is safe to take short cuts. As experience is gained, the emphasis can move from RMPs as a general risk management learning experience to RMPs as an effective way to deal with immediate concerns. Short cuts can be taken in the light of an understanding of how much effort will be saved by the short cuts and what the likely impact is in terms of the effectiveness of the project management process as a whole.

An important shortcoming of the Southampton to Cherbourg sailing analogy as just developed is worth emphasis. If an approach which is too simple is used, the benefit of a more sophisticated process may not be observed. For example, improvements in risk efficiency which a more sophisticated RMP might have provided may not be observable, unless a catastrophic mistake results.

Stretching the Southampton to Cherbourg sailing analogy a bit further, choosing a level of sophistication for a first RMP and observing the results is like hitting the French coast in the dark with no position-finding instruments and no knowledge of the coast. If you can safely assume you are up-tide and up-wind you can drift down-wind and tide until what looks like a major harbour comes into view. If you don't know which side of Cherbourg you are, you have a potential major problem on your hands.

Several pieces of practical advice follow from this line of argument, some of which were noted in earlier chapters:

1. The first time an organisation uses RMP, they should acquire expert advice involving the craft skills necessary to guide the selection of an appropriate initial approach.
2. The first project should be selected with care, looking for real challenges, but avoiding anything resembling a suicide mission.
3. In terms of RMP sophistication, initially some deliberate overkill is important, recognising it as such, as a way of better assessing future short cuts and ensuring we 'know which side of Cherbourg' we are.

4. Viewing RMP as a learning exercise initially is important, ensuring that the lessons learned are properly captured by the organisation as a whole.
5. An ongoing source of expert advice as new issues arise is very important. This can be provided by an ongoing relationship with particular consultants, ideally the ones who helped to start the process. As an organisation's RMPs mature, in-house experts may feel they do not need external consultants, but they should at least use available opportunities for sharing experience with others in their position.

It is perhaps worth noting that in our experience over the last 20 years most organisations have first used RMPs because of an organisational imperative, sometimes imposed by 'nature', sometimes imposed by regulators, bankers or other interested parties. However, once RMP is in place, most organisations have expanded their motives as an appreciation of the benefits has been acquired. In the past organisations have tended to 'learn the hard way', as have the authors. There is now no need for organisations to 'learn the hard way' to such an extent. The pioneers took a decade to learn what first-time users can now learn in a year. This doesn't mean there will be no learning curve. But to use the Southampton to Cherbourg sailing analogy yet again, other people have now made the crossing lots of times and written about their experiences, in some cases with guidance about specific passages. The *International Journal of Project Management*, particularly since 1990, is one good source of experience which may provide cases relevant to the reader's circumstances.

16.3 COMPREHENSIVENESS OF MOTIVES

The sophistication of the motives which drive the trade-off between the effectiveness of RMP and its cost is a key dimension of RMP choices requiring consideration in the Focus phase. At its simplest, RMP may address only relevant sources of catastrophic risk. For a contractor, this may be limited to reasons a project may cost more which cannot be passed on to the client. Delays, failure to meet performance requirements, and all other client problems may be ignored. Risks which put the contractor out of business may also be ignored if going out of business as a consequence of not getting a job is the only alternative. Risks which hurt the client to a catastrophic extent, but give the contractor significant extra profit, may be the opportunities which are the contractor's prime concern. Informal risk management processes tend to breed this kind of very limited scope. Part of the role of formality is clarifying the need for a richer set of motives, as well as helping the pursuit of that richer set of motives.

To use a simple analogy, one of the arguments supporting the early use of PERT (Moder and Philips, 1970) is that replacing a single point estimate with three (optimistic, pessimistic and most likely) helps to eliminate conscious and unconscious bias, by exposing the uncertainty dimension, and forcing an agreed representation of a duration probability distribution. This is a benefit which does not rely on the 'correctness' of the estimates. It is a benefit which arises because the question is asked, independent of the answer.

Using RMP to expose motives and associated trade-offs which may be different for different parties has the same effect. Both conscious and unconscious bias will be reduced, simply because important questions are asked in an explicit, formal manner.

16.4   DEGREE OF ANTICIPATION

One characteristic of RMP which influences the cost-effectiveness balance is the degree of anticipation sought. At one extreme a purely reactive approach could be adopted. At the other, an exhaustive proactive approach to managing uncertainty could be adopted.

Key issues here are the extent to which decisions are irreversible and the seriousness of the consequences of inappropriate decisions as judged after the fact. In the limit, a very flexible approach to a project involving no costs associated with feedback adjustments requires no RMP. However, there are usually practical limits on the level of flexibility possible, and efficiency gains associated with giving up some feasible flexibility. Hence, choosing an appropriate level of flexibility for the project should be related to choosing an appropriate level of sophistication for RMP.

Gilbert (1983) argues for an approach to project risk management which is based upon feedback as the key. Some might argue (with some justification) that a SCERT approach as initially described (Chapman, 1979) is excessively focused on proactive analysis. However, Cooper and Chapman (1987) consider the balance, and it is now very clear to both authors of this book that the key is choosing an intermediate position which best reflects the nature and approach of the project in question, and making conscious choices about the appropriate choice of approach to both the project and the associated RMP with these trade-offs in mind. The choices about the approach to the project itself are the primary choices, RMP choices secondary. For essentially the same reasons argued in Section 16.2, it is worth erring on the safe side with respect to those primary and secondary choices: a deliberately excessively flexible approach to the project, and a deliberately excessively proactive approach to planning, particularly while going down a learning curve.

To labour the original Southampton to Cherbourg sailing analogy a bit more in a different direction, consider making this passage for the first time. Reading a few sailing magazines will soon make it clear it is a good idea to make the first passage in daylight, in spring (when days are longest), starting at dawn, with a good stable weather forecast for several days ahead. Given this approach to the project, RMP based on a simplistic approach to navigation would suffice: assuming you take the Isle of Wight on your left, head due south from the Needles until you hit the French coast, then turn right. However, refining navigation skills when time is available, making course corrections which are designed to enhance knowledge rather than minimise passage time, making frequent checks with positioning instruments, and using visual checks where feasible, is a part of the fun which could be an invaluable investment for the future. Learning processes should be fun. Most people who go into project management as a career need a measure of fun to keep them on the job, as well as the stimulation of challenges to meet. A bit more fun and a bit less challenge than the norm can be a useful bias for early experience. The saying 'there are old pilots and bold pilots, but no bold old pilots' does not apply directly to project staff, but some of the bolder young project staff need to be explicitly taken on a few 'Channel crossings' with a pleasurable learning experience approach to the passage before letting them take on the 'Atlantic' on their own.

16.5   DEGREE OF FORMALITY

Another characteristic of RMP which influences the cost-effectiveness balance is the degree of formality sought in RMP. At one extreme a purely informal, intuitive approach could be adopted. At the other, a very high level of formality could be adopted, involving more cost but more benefits.

Formality is not about lots of long lists, although documentation is part of the issue. The key aspect of formality is structure, so we put our time to effective use. Everyone's time is relevant, with weightings reflecting the relevant value of different people's time. The formalisation of RMP developed in Part Two is not intended as a step-by-step guide to be followed literally, except possibly by inexperienced RMP users on a carefully selected learning process study. It is an illustrative formal process model, to be simplified as appropriate, based on the user's experience. However, we believe the most effective way to refine judgements about how to simplify effectively involves starting with some practice using RMP as close to that of Part Two as possible, with the time available to spend on some aspects of the process which may look unproductive at the outset.

Revisiting the first crossing from Southampton to Cherbourg example used earlier, developing navigating skills requires practice using formalised methods with ample time to compare and contrast alternative ways of determining the position (location) of the yacht. The experienced navigator can afford to take short cuts on a 'day sail' in good conditions, but an effective and efficient intuitive process is usually built around formalised methods which need practice. Navigating through a high risk project can be much more difficult than crossing the Channel in a yacht, and in general warrants more attention to formality, not less.

'Experts' are distinguishable from 'skilled amateurs' by virtue of skills that are intuitive or subconscious and not easily modified. A key lesson learned the hard way by Chapman in the context of 'knowledge engineering' aspects of building expert systems (Edwards and Connell, 1989) was that formalising intuitive 'expert' decision rules is very difficult. An example provided by an expert auditor in the context of assessing business risk associated with an organisation was that 'too many 7 series BMWs in the car park' is a signal something might be wrong that he had not been conscious of using until his knowledge was extensively probed as part of a very detailed 'knowledge engineering' exercise. A closely coupled lesson was that the formality of a knowledge engineering process was invaluable as a way of understanding what was involved as a basis of training auditors, even if an expert system to do the job was not a practical proposition. The authors do not believe in the formalisation of RMPs to the extent that expert systems are an efficient proposition except in very special cases. The issues are too complex for anything other than a very narrow or very naive expert system.

However, just as a three-estimate PERT approach reduces conscious and unconscious bias by asking questions, and a comprehensive treatment of motives raises useful questions, so does formalisation of RMP raise useful questions. Learning to ask the right questions is a skill worth acquiring. Formality of RMPs is partly about making sure the right questions get asked and answered, and partly about making sure everyone who needs to know understands the answers. Helping people to develop the right answers is a third aspect, which lies between these two aspects, but while it can be a focus of attention for risk analysts, it may be of no concern to everyone else. Giving people the comfort that all the key questions have been asked and addressed is the basic rationale of a formal RMP. *How* they are addressed is orders of magnitude less important.

In our view the *effectiveness* of RMP is largely driven by its ability to ask the right questions, and it is this need to ensure that the right questions are asked which is a key reason for formality at a comprehensive level. However, the *efficiency* of the RMP is also driven by formality. Only when it is clear what an exhaustive approach to formality buys can sensible decisions about informal short cuts be made with confidence.

Example 16.1

Example 12.1 considered a simple but formal bidding process. What this process reveals might be characterised as follows.

If only ten minutes are available to prepare a bid:

1. spend two minutes deciding how to do the project;
2. spend two minutes assessing its expected cost given step 1;
3. spend two minutes assessing the chance of winning given a bid equal to expected cost and two or three higher or lower bids;
4. spend one minute constructing a table like Table 12.1;
5. spend three minutes considering the most appropriate bid price in relation to criteria other than expected profit, in trade-off terms;
6. record your bid, your estimate of the associated probability of winning, and feedback analysis of this information into step 3 next time you bid.

As the authors' use of this bidding situation a large number of times as a case study clearly reveals, only spending much more time on each of these tasks reveals the true relative importance of steps 3, 4, 5 and 6. Most people instinctively spend most of their time on steps 1 and 2.

16.6   MODEL COMPLEXITY

As noted in Section 6.6, the degree of model complexity is a key aspect of designing effective RMPs, and indeed other management science intervention processes. An interesting survey of failures and successes of quantitative methods in management by Tilanus (1985) supports the widely held view that successful modelling requires approaches that are 'simple', flexible, easily understood, appropriate to the situation, and able to cope with low-quality data. A detailed discussion of the effectiveness of 'simple' is provided by Ward (1989), employing the objective concept of 'constructive simplicity' which describes the form and level of detail in a model. Constructive simplicity is distinguished from the subjective concept of transparency, which relates to user comprehension of a model. Usual arguments for constructive simplicity focus on model-building considerations such as model clarity, flexibility, and convenience, but constructively simple models can also provide an efficient way of learning about decision situations. Client managers may prefer constructive simplicity not only as a convenient way of ensuring transparent models, but also for reasons related to motivation, time constraints, implementation, and involvement of third parties (Ward, 1989). Such motives may need to be actively managed by model builders. A natural, further conclusion is that model builders ought consciously to consider the level of constructive complexity to incorporate in a given model. Ideally, decision makers seek *complete* models which capture all the *important* features of decision situations, but unfortunately completeness is potentially in conflict with both constructive and transparent simplicity. However, modelling involves a learning process and the potential conflict between completeness and simplicity (constructive or transparent) can be mitigated. Models can be elaborated as understanding develops. The learning process involves scrutiny of initial model output and querying results that do not correspond with intuitive understanding of the modelled situation. This leads to correction of errors, changes in model formulation, or the decision maker learning something new about the situation and 'updating intuition' (Little, 1970). Flexible, easily amended models may be more useful than technically accurate models.

A key theme here is that additional complexity should be introduced only if it is useful (Chapman, 1990). Usually additional complexity proves useful because:

1. it makes estimation easier;
2. it allows the integration of estimation expertise held by different people or different databases;
3. it clarifies what estimates measure and what they do not measure;
4. it provides richer insights about decision alternatives;
5. it provides more confidence that issues are properly understood.

As indicated in Chapter 6, the simplest formal quantitative model of uncertainty for project duration analysis is the basic PERT model; the most complex the authors are aware of in a risk–response–impact dimension is the basic SCERT model (Chapman, 1979). An earlier publication (Chapman et al., 1985) addresses making choices along the PERT–SCERT axis, and subsequent publications have discussed these choices in more detail (for example, Chapman, 1990). Other modelling complexity dimensions include systems dynamics models to capture feedback and feedforward loops (Forrester, 1961; Richardson and Pugh, 1981; Senge, 1990), cognitive mapping to capture other interdependencies in a qualitative manner (Eden, 1988), and more general 'soft' methods (Rosenhead, 1989; Checkland and Scholes, 1990), as mentioned in Chapter 8. Such modelling complexity dimensions are no doubt worth exploring with a view to more effective modelling of uncertainty.

However, the more modelling choices become available, the more difficult making the most appropriate choice becomes, unless we clearly understand what each model feature costs, and what it tends to yield. Only some very general guidelines can be offered here:

1. if activities involve repetitive processes, like laying a pipe, consider the use of Markov process models, especially if weather windows are involved;
2. if feedback or feedforward loops are important, consider the use of system dynamics models;

3. hang on to the idea of making sure all key risks are identified and associated with appropriate responses, whether or not formal quantitative modelling is feasible, if necessary at a 'single activity' or 'total project overview' top-down level of risk analysis;
4. hang on to the idea that responses are important, as part of opportunity management, as well as a prerequisite for dealing with downside risk;
5. don't attempt implementation or interpretation of quantitative analysis unless you understand prior underlying qualitative analysis.

16.7 MODEL QUANTIFICATION

Quantified models are usually a useful goal when designing the RMP in the Focus phase, with notable exceptions mentioned in Chapter 10, such as decision taker not prepared to take any risk, and the identification of major 'show-stoppers'. Quantification of all relevant risks is essential if the motives for RMP include distinguishing between target, expected value and commitment estimates, as indicated in Chapter 3. The general rule is quantify when and where it is useful to do so. Example 14.2 is an illustration where exhaustive quantification was essential, for reasons developed in Chapman *et al.* (1985).

Many experienced RMP users see the use of qualitative H/M/L (High, Medium and Low) risk probability and impact assessments for time, cost and performance criteria as a useful half-way position between purely qualitative analysis and numerical quantification in probability terms of those risks, but as indicated earlier, we prefer viewing H/M/L qualitative assessments as a refinement of the minor/major risk aspect of the Structure phase, with a numeric Simple Scenario approach to quantification in the Estimate and Evaluate phases.

Within this Simple Scenario probability framework a key issue is the degree of refinement of the numeric probabilities in the Estimate and Evaluate phase. In the limit the highly iterative approach to Estimate and Evaluate phases developed in this book suggests a first pass through the Estimate and Evaluate phases which puts first-cut probabilities on all risks, to 'size' them, then further Estimate–Evaluate (and Structure) phase iterations to develop a more refined understanding of what is important, and finally, further refinement to make defensible probability estimates critical to key decisions. The issue in this framework is not what is quantified but how well it is quantified. This kind of iterative process involves two separate sets of loops:

1. refinement or not for each risk's estimates, to drive the RMP's iterative nature with a view to developing understanding;

2. refinement or not for each risk's estimates, to defend a case, ensuring that quantification of risks critical to that case can withstand scrutiny.

The first set of loops may be all that is necessary to clarify all key decisions, two or three passes allowing an efficient allocation of largely subjective probability estimation effort. At the other extreme, this level of effort in the first set of loops may simply reveal the need for much more effort within the first loop set, and the second loop set may also require sustained effort for estimates which prove key for important decisions.

Particularly, if significant effort is required in the second set of loops, it may become useful to treat different kinds of uncertainty more formally. As in Example 7.5 (pipe burial in the Beaufort Sea), it may be important to distinguish carefully between

1. uncertainty inherent in nature;
2. uncertainty inherent in our data set;
3. uncertainty inherent in our basic science explaining the physical mechanisms or processes involved.

16.8 CONCLUSION

Planning a project can be viewed as a first-order process, with planning the planning (including the RMP) as an associated second-order process. In this framework Part Three of this book addresses planning the planning of the planning, a third-order process, and this chapter addresses this third-order process most directly.

This book offers reasonably well-structured advice about the first-order process, such advice being the primary thrust of this book. This book has also made a point of offering considerable advice and insight about the second-order process. The Focus phase, as discussed in Chapter 6 and referred to throughout, is concerned with planning the planning process. We believe direct formal development of this planning the planning process is worthwhile, and hope others will join us in attempting to do so. This chapter has made a point of attempting to explain the basis of the third-order process (in Section 16.1), and to offer some insights into choices available in six dimensions, which we also believe to be a useful endeavour. There is, of course, a fourth and further higher orders of planning within this framework. However, the authors believe practical usefulness stops at level three, and even at this level, formality and structure which is directly useful is difficult to come by. The absence of tables or figures in this chapter is not accidental. Chapters 14 and 15 attempted to provide some structure for the third-order planning process discussion, but the residual issues addressed in Chapter 16 are difficult to disentangle, and avoiding structuring the very complex to preserve a holistic perspective has merit.

It is an inability to formalise extensively beyond second-order planning which limits the future of expert systems in the RMP area, and ensures reasonable prospects of gainful employment for RMP specialists who have well-developed craft skills. This chapter is about how to go about developing these craft skills, with advice aimed at organisations which individuals may also find directly relevant.

In summary, some of the key messages of this chapter include:

1. The central issue when considering RMP short cuts is the trade-off between the effectiveness of the RMP and the cost of the RMP.
2. RMP effectiveness is a complex concept to assess, and it requires an understanding of risk efficiency in terms of all relevant criteria and a rich set of motives which include creating a 'learning organisation' which people want to be a part of.
3. RMP cost is also a complex concept to assess, requiring an understanding of opportunity costs which can vary sharply over the PLC and from day to day within particular stages of the project life cycle. In a crisis, time is particularly valuable.
4. The high opportunity cost of time in a crisis is part of the argument for much more proactive planning than might seem obvious. Time spent making conditional decisions in advance can mean time is available for other issues when a crisis occurs.
5. The high opportunity cost of time in a crisis is also part of the argument for much more proactive learning based on formal processes than might seem obvious. Time spent 'training', developing skills, developing judgement, so everyone is effective, efficient and cool in a crisis has advantages well understood by military commanders for tens of centuries. Lack of attention to such training and development is a plausible strategy for 'management' of any kind which has no formal content, no body of knowledge or guidelines or standards which are accepted by those responsible for deciding how to manage. Project risk management is now developing a formal content which deserves attention in terms of 'training'. The concepts developed in this book are part of that content.

Chapter 17

Organising for Risk Management

Unhappiness is best described as the difference between our talents and our expectations.

Edward de Bono

17.1 INTRODUCTION

This book has been largely about the application of effective risk management in the context of a single project. This chapter is concerned with institutionalising RMP so that it can be employed on an ongoing basis in a variety of projects over time. The issue here is ensuring that our corporate talents allow us to meet our expectations.

In the process of discussing effective risk management of individual projects we have generally assumed that a formal, institutionalised risk management process (RMP) is a goal, since this is an obvious way to fully exploit the benefits of project risk management. As a result we have given advice on institutionalising risk management at various points in this book. In this chapter we draw some of these ideas together with additional discussion to present a more coherent picture of an effective institutionalising process.

As noted in Chapter 6, the application of RMP to a given project can be a high risk project in its own right, warranting particular attention to the process *who* question in the Focus phase of the RMP. The process of instituting RMP procedures as a standard corporate policy is also not without risk. The essential risk is that the policy fails to bring sufficient benefits, perhaps because procedures are inappropriate, not properly implemented or only partially adopted. Once difficulties are encountered the credibility of the initiative may suffer, making it very difficult to revive an RMP initiative at a later date. Such risks and their underlying causes need to be recognised and managed in much the same way as any significant organisational change.

Walsham (1992) has suggested a management framework which views organisational change as a jointly analytical, educational and political process where important interacting dimensions are the context, content, and process of the change. Significant aspects of context include: stakeholders' perspectives and relationships between those affected by a particular project, the history of existing procedures and systems, informal networks and procedures, and infrastructure needs (for example, skills and resources required). The process of change involves the dynamics of interaction between participants in a project and others who are affected by it or who can affect it. Significant aspects of process include power-politics and organisational culture. Implementing a significant change like the introduction of RMP needs to take these dimensions into account.

Other writers on the management of change have related the implementation process to Lewin's (1947) model of planned change which involves three phases: unfreezing–changing–refreezing. Each phase is concerned with changes in the balance of (psychological) forces in the organisation and the degree to which they restrain or drive change. Unfreezing involves disturbing the equilibrium of the status quo by increasing the balance of driving forces over restraining forces, decreasing restraining forces, or a combination of these. Effective unfreezing generally involves increasing driving forces while managing a reduction in restraining forces, that is, reducing resistance to change. Refreezing involves the systematic replacement of the temporary change-inducing forces with more permanent forces which can maintain the new status quo.

Forces for change to institutionalising RMP are likely to be derived from a senior. management recognition of the potential benefits considered in the next section. Resistance to change may be due to some or all of the following:

1. parochial self-interest in maintaining the status quo;
2. inability to perceive a need for change;
3. pressure of other work;
4. concern about the costs of introducing new procedures;
5. individuals concerned that they will be unable to carry out the new procedures;
6. uncertainty and suspicion about the nature of the change.

Suggested strategies for reducing resistance to change often include education, communication, participation and involvement, facilitation and support, and offering incentives. Discussing the introduction of strategic planning as a significant organisational change, Ansoff (1984) has argued that maximum resistance is produced by a change process which seeks to impose administrative systems before addressing sources of behavioural resistance to change. In contrast, minimum resistance is created when a change process builds acceptance of change before introducing administrative systems.

In the context of introducing RMP, the minimum resistance route implies a process which first clarifies the need for and relevance of RMP, seeks to improve stakeholders' understanding of what is involved, and provides motivation for individuals to use RMP. Additionally, there is a need to ensure that risk management skills are developed, and that individuals have sufficient time and resources to operate RMP. Subsequently, administrative systems for coordinating and controlling RMP can be introduced.

These issues can be explored in more specific detail if we consider the setting up and operation of RMP as a project in its own right, and examine this 'RMP project' (set-up and operation) in terms of the eight-stage PLC framework of Chapter 2. Within this framework we can clarify what activities and institutional arrangements are appropriate for effective performance at each stage.

17.2   RMP CONCEPTION

As noted in Table 2.1, the Concept stage involves identifying a deliverable to be produced and the benefits expected from the deliverable. Chapter 4 provides an outline description of the deliverable in terms of a process that will be applied to future projects, with Part Two providing an elaboration of this description. The benefits of RMP, as described in Chapter 3 and elsewhere, have tended to focus on the manner in which improvements in performance of individual projects can be obtained. In the present context a more long-term corporate view of potential benefits is appropriate. Put simply the benefits of effective risk management processes are in terms of improved project performance in a stream of projects across the range of project performance objectives. But as noted in Section 16.3, part of the role of a formal RMP is clarifying the need for a richer set of motives, as well as helping pursuit of that richer set.

Figure 17.1 offers a view of corporate benefits that institutionalised formal RMP for all projects might bring in a contracting organisation. The diagram incorporates the benefits of documentation (Section 3.7) and

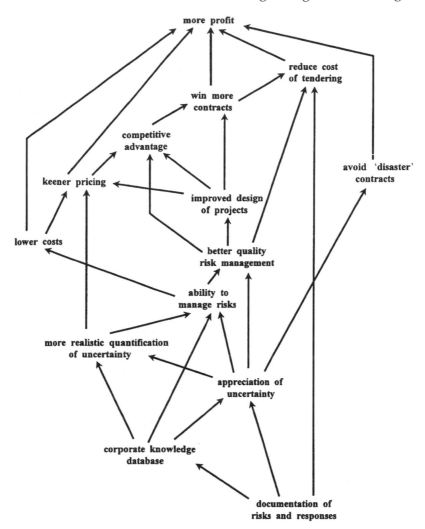

Figure 17.1 Corporate benefits of effective risk management.

corporate learning (Section 16.2) in a direct manner, with all other aspects of Chapter 3 working through 'ability to manage risks'. Assuming a contracting organisation undertakes risk management prior to and after tendering, then a number of interrelated benefits can accrue, all driving up profitability, through lower level benefits such as:

1. keener pricing, better design and stronger risk management abilities provide competitive advantage and improve chances of winning contracts;

2. better appreciation of uncertainty means more realistic pricing and the avoidance of potential loss-making 'disaster' contracts where uncertainty is too great;
3. ability to manage risks means lower project costs with direct profit implications;
4. reduced tendering costs mean higher profits.

Figure 17.1 does not explicitly address the very valuable culture changes which can be an important part of the process of introducing RMP. Making 'enlightened caution', 'enlightened gambles' and 'enlightened controls' part of an organisation's culture (as discussed in Chapter 3) can be central to killing a risk-averse culture based on 'uncertainty and risk are negative issues, and what you don't know won't hurt you', generating a new 'risk management' culture based on 'uncertainty is the source of our opportunities, and we need to understand our opportunities to seize them effectively'. Effective use of action horizons and other visible reductions in wasted effort and frustration can also be important. This kind of culture change can make an organisation more exciting to work for and make going to work more enjoyable. This in turn can lead to higher quality staff wanting to join (and stay with) the organisation, with obvious general benefits. Figure 17.2 portrays the spirit of this aspect of the impact of RMP. Figures 17.1 and 17.2 may be useful alongside a rereading of Chapter 3.

As with any corporate initiative, senior management support is crucial to empower the process, and to ensure the RMP reflects the needs and concerns of senior management. All relevant managers, but especially project managers, need to become involved at this early stage, to ensure that the proposed RMP is taken into the project management process.

Ideally, a manager for the RMP project should be appointed in this stage so that he or she can actively participate in elaborating the RMP concept and clarifying its purpose before the more detailed Design and Plan stages. It can be useful to involve a wider group of parties, including individuals in functional departments in the organisation, key customers, key contractors or subcontractors, potential partners, and external consultants to facilitate the RMP design and introduction.

There is increasing recognition in an ever growing number of organisations that failure to introduce formal RMPs as a routine aspect of project management is tantamount to 'commercial suicide'. Increasing competition, more demanding customers, the increasing pace of technological development and other changes, increasing complexity and novelty of business opportunities are all increasing the need for more systematic and effective approaches to managing uncertainty and project risks. It is unfortunate if acceptance of this message has to await the occurrence of a 'trigger event', like commercial failure in a major project, or failure to win a major contract.

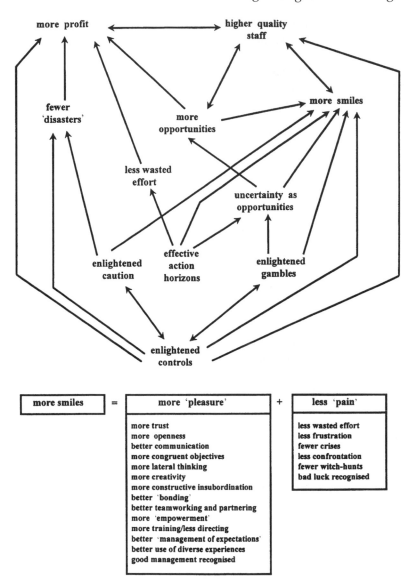

Figure 17.2 Corporate benefits of a risk management culture.

17.3   RMP DESIGN

The basic design of RMP has been set out in some detail in Part Two, and it is assumed that this forms the basis of the institutionalised process ultimately needed. However, strategies for aiming for this institutionalised process may vary.

A common approach is to begin with a simplified process, perhaps limited to probability impact diagrams and checklists, introduced fairly rapidly with a minimum of piloting. Following rapid introduction, the intention is to continue operating the simplified process in a well-defined administrative framework, without major changes in format.

In Chapter 16 we have argued against this approach, arguing that to understand the nature of effective risk management it is essential to understand the nature of a comprehensive RMP. Ideally this understanding needs to be developed on a widespread basis, not confined to one or two individuals charged with the (rapid) introduction of a new corporate risk management policy.

The approach advocated in this book is the pilot study approach, applying a comprehensive RMP to a project to learn on which has three characteristics:

1. it has been very well managed to date;
2. despite its successful management to date, it raises risk-driven concerns which need to be addressed to the satisfaction to those granting sanction;
3. there is sufficient time to undertake a comprehensive risk management process.

The aim is to build effective risk management capability which can pursue flexible tactics within the scope of a comprehensive process. If administrative processes for a simplified RMP which is limited in scope are introduced, this may delay and even discourage development of risk analysis and risk management expertise.

A pilot study approach may ultimately lead to more effective risk management procedures but may be relatively slow as a learning process. In contracting organisations retrospective analysis of recently completed projects may provide more time for the necessary analysis and learning, divorced from tight time schedules associated with tender formulation.

Another design consideration is the range of projects which will be subject to an RMP. A simple answer, adopted by the UK Ministry of Defence, is 'all projects'. We support this approach. However, it implies that different levels of RMP will be cost effective for different sizes and types of projects, which transforms the question into 'what kind of RMP should be used over the range of projects of interest?' In general, comprehensive risk management will tend to be most useful when projects involve one or more of the following:

1. substantial resources;
2. significant novelty (technological, geographical, environmental, or organisational);
3. long planning horizons;
4. large size;

5. complexity;
6. several organisations;
7. significant political issues.

In time, organisations institutionalising project risk management may apply different guidelines for RMP to projects dependent on the degree of presence of the factors listed above. However, such sophistication needs to wait on the development of experience with comprehensive RMP on selected projects.

A further design consideration is at what stage of a project's PLC an RMP will be applied. Chapter 14 discussed this issue in detail, making the observation that in general RMP was best applied as early as possible in a project's PLC. This is a significant point for contracting organisations. As indicated in Example 15.1, contractors may usefully undertake risk analysis in respect of a given contract first as part of tender development, to help determine whether to bid or not and at what price, and second as ongoing risk management of a contract that is actually won. Contracting organisations ought to institute RMPs which incorporate risk analysis and management at each of these stages. As indicated in Figure 17.1, this may lead to strategic decisions about the amount of effort to be applied to submission of tenders, the level of profits expected on individual contracts and an appropriate target success rate for submitted tenders.

17.4   RMP PLAN

The Plan stage of institutionalising RMP involves determining how the design will be executed, what steps to take in what order, what resources are required in broad terms, and how long it will take. This involves determining specific targets for establishing operative RMP, particularly in terms of the scope of the projects to be covered and the time scale in which this is to be achieved. To a large degree these targets will depend on the impetus behind the initiative, related to the parties involved and perceived need.

Plan development needs to include arrangements for capturing existing risk management expertise and disseminating it as part of developing risk management thinking and expertise in individual personnel. This may include in-house training courses and special interest group seminars (as a form of 'quality circle').

17.5   RMP ALLOCATION

As noted in Chapter 2, the Allocate stage of the PLC involves decisions about project organisation, identification of appropriate participants, and allocation of tasks between them.

Most organisations introduce project risk management processes using a 'risk analyst' ('riskateer' is a term some prefer) who may be an external consultant, an internal consultant, or a member of the project team who has undertaken some form of training or self-study programme on risk management. A sizeable team of analysts may be involved, or the part-time efforts of a single individual. Most organisations with mature risk management processes maintain a risk analysis team. In large organisations this team may be dedicated to project risk management. In small organisations this 'team' may be a single individual with other responsibilities. Even a very small organisation needs somebody to act as the repository of risk management skills and facilitate formal risk management.

As noted in Section 6.2 this team or individual may undertake risk analysis for individual project managers. However, they should not be regarded as risk *managers*, since proper integration of project risk management and project management more generally requires that the project manager take personal responsibility for all risk not explicitly delegated to managers of components of the project.

The provision of analytical support, while useful, is only part of institutionalising RMP. There is an additional need to ensure widespread, effective application of RMP, to monitor the quality of RMPs, and to ensure that risk management experience is captured and used to improve risk management in subsequent projects. The experience, seniority and role of the RMP project manager is obviously of critical importance here. That such a manager is appointed with these responsibilities is a basic tenet of effective project management.

17.6   RMP EXECUTION

The steps in the Execute stage of the PLC shown in Table 2.1 are:

1. coordinate and control;
2. monitor progress;
3. modification of targets and milestones;
4. allocation modification;
5. control evaluation.

These steps carried out in a continuous iterative process are part of the ongoing management of operating RMPs on a continuing basis. From this perspective the RMP project never terminates and the Deliver, Review and Support stages become part of the Execute stage. However, a first pass through the Execute stage might usefully involve a pilot exercise applying the proposed RMP to a suitable project, as indicated earlier. Lessons from this experience may influence the design of the RMP in a subsequent pass back through the Design, Plan and Allocate stages before application of the RMP on another project. This experience might also provide data in respect of sources of risk and efficacy of responses of direct relevance to other concurrent and subsequent projects. Such feedback clearly need not wait for termination of the subject project. As a general principle the institutionalising of RMP should include arrangements to disseminate the latest experience in managing risk as rapidly as possible. In this context it may be useful to see the RMP project as a programme of projects, in the sense of Figure 2.3.

17.7   RMP DELIVERY

As indicated in Chapter 2 the Deliver stage of a project involves commissioning and handover, with the steps shown in Table 2.1:

1. basic deliverable verification;
2. deliverable modification;
3. modification of performance criteria;
4. deliver evaluation.

In the context of completion of a pilot RMP such steps look very much like tasks which form a necessary part of a loop back through the Design, Plan and Allocate stages prior to further applications of the RMP on a wider scale. Subsequently, these steps are worth addressing periodically to check and appraise the effectiveness of RMP procedures. Over time this can lead to significant changes in the way RMPs are coordinated and controlled.

Example 17.1

In the late 1970s and early 1980s, an oil major began with a single risk analyst undertaking analysis late in the Plan stage of the PLC. Very soon a group of analysts were working in the same way, to cover all projects, often earlier in the PLC. This group of analysts reported direct to the project managers for the most part, as a service function for project managers independent of the design, planning and costing functions. After a few years, a more senior person was made head of the risk analysis function and the planning function, effectively integrating planning and risk management formally. Then a still more senior person was made responsible for risk management, planning and costing, extending the integration. As time went on analysis was undertaken earlier and earlier in the PLC, although to our knowledge it did not get back to the Design stage, which had separate risk analysis support, with a somewhat different (safety-, reliability- and availability-based) focus.

17.8   RMP REVIEW

Following each application of RMP to a project, a systematic appraisal of the RMP application is appropriate to evaluate the likely relevance and usefulness of both project specific results and process specific results, to inform both future projects and future risk management practice.

Periodically, a broadly based review of RMP procedures is appropriate to draw out lessons from the operation of RMP procedures across the organisation.

17.9 RMP SUPPORT

As indicated in Table 2.1 the Support stage of a project involves the following steps:

1. basic maintenance and liability perception;
2. development of support criteria;
3. support perception development;
4. support coordination.

There is a need to provide continuing support for risk management in future projects in both a facilitating and supervisory sense. Aside from analytical expertise which may be called upon by project management teams, there may well be a need for corporate management involvement in scrutinising individual RMPs to ensure an appropriately rigorous approach, to facilitate improvements in risk management practice, and to monitor the effectiveness of RMP procedures. The level of such support will need to be reassessed periodically to ensure it remains cost effective. As noted in Example 17.1, the level of analytical support may need to be increased over time, and it may need to change qualitatively, depending on the expertise and resources available within the project teams. Policy decisions may need to be made about the composition of project teams if the need for risk analysis increases. Apart from analytical support, senior management scrutiny of risk analyses and risk management plans may be well worth maintaining indefinitely as part of standard project appraisal procedures. This will help to maintain and improve standards of risk management, particularly through changes in personnel at all levels.

17.10 CONCLUSION

Many organisations have addressed the process of organising for risk management, and the development of appropriate documentation. Examples of references in the public domain which others may wish to draw on in this context include MoD(PE)-DPP(PM) (1991), PERAG (1991), Jordan, Lee and Cawsey (1988), Roberts (1994), HM Treasury (1993), NSWG (1993), and DAS (1992).

A number of other authors suggest approaches which we have incorporated at least in part in our approach. Readers may wish to consult these authors to flavour their own approaches. Some examples include: APM (forthcoming); Charette (1989); Thompson and Perry (1992); Gaisford (1986); Grey (1995); approaches cited in Chapters 5–13 (for example, Keeney and Winterfeldt, 1991); and a large number of papers in the *International Journal of Project Management*, particularly since 1990.

The approaches described in this book were developed with a range of organisations with a wide range of situations to assess as part of their RMP project. This chapter might have attempted a more complex structure using the full variety of these applications, based on the matrix of Table 14.1, for example. However, we strongly advise organisations introducing RMP for the first time to acquire guidance from those experienced in RMP implementation even if a straightforward route is adopted, and such advice becomes imperative if complex or non-standard application is involved.

Our concluding comment is:

1. keep it simple, in general;
2. make it more complex when it is useful to do so;
3. keep smiling, if you can.

References

Abrahamson, M. (1973). Contractual risks in tunnelling: how they should be shared. *Tunnels and Tunnelling*, November, pp. 587–598.

Adams, J. R. and Barndt, S. E. (1988). Behavioral implications of the project life cycle, Chapter 10 in Cleland, D. I. and King, W. R. (eds), *Project Management Handbook*. Second edition. New York: Von Nostrand Reinhold.

Akerlof, G. A. (1970). The market for 'lemons': quality uncertainty and the market mechanism. *Quarterly Journal of Economics*, **84**, pp. 488–500.

Alpert, M. and Raiffa, H. (1982). A progress report on the training of probability assessors, Chapter 21 in Kahneman, D., Slovic, P. and Tversky, A. (eds), *Judgment Under Uncertainty: Heuristics and Biases*. New York: Cambridge University Press.

Anderson, D. L., Charlwood, R. G. and Chapman, C. B. (1975). On seismic risk analysis of nuclear plants safety systems. *Canadian Journal of Civil Engineering*, December.

Ansoff, H. I. (1984). *Implanting Strategic Management*. Englewood Cliffs, NJ: Prentice-Hall International.

APM (forthcoming). *Association of Project Managers Project Risk Analysis and Management (PRAM) Guide*.

APM (1995). *Association of Project Managers—Project Risk Analysis Software Directory*.

Armstrong, J. S., Denniston, W. B. and Gordon, M. M. (1975). 'The use of the decomposition principle in making judgments. *Organisation Behaviour and Human Performance*, **14**, pp. 257–263.

Barber, J. N. (1989). Risks in the method of construction, in Uff J. and Capper P. (eds), *Construction Contract Policy: Improved Procedures and Practice*. King's College, London: Centre of Construction Law and Management.

Barnes, M. (1984). Effective project organisation. *Building Technology and Management*, December, pp. 21–23.

Barnes, N. M. L. (1988). Construction project management. *International Journal of Project Management*, **6**(2), pp. 60–79.

Baron, D. P. (1972). Incentive contracts and competitive bidding. *American Economic Review*, **62**, pp. 384–394.

Berny, J. (1989). A new distribution function for risk analysis. *Journal of the Operational Research Society*, **40**(12), pp. 1121–1127.

Brooks, F. P. (1975). *The Mythical Man-month: Essays on Software Engineering*. Reading, MA: Addison Wesley.

Canes, M. E. (1975). The simple economics of incentive contracting: note. *American Economic Review*, **65**, pp. 478–483.

CCTA (1995). *Management of Project Risk*. The Government Centre for Information Systems, ISBN 0-11-330636-9, London: HMSO.

Chapman, C. B. (1979). Large engineering project risk analysis. *IEEE Transactions on Engineering Management*, EM-26, pp. 78–86.

Chapman, C. B. (1988). Science, engineering and economics: OR at the interface. *Journal of the Operational Research Society*, **39**(1), pp. 1-6.

Chapman, C. B. (1990). A risk engineering approach to project management. *International Journal of Project Management*, **8**(1), pp. 5-16.

Chapman, C. B. (1992a). *Risk Management: Predicting and Dealing with an Uncertain Future*. Exhibit #748, Province of Ontario Environmental Assessment Board Hearings on Ontario Hydro's Demand/Supply Plan, submitted by the Independent Power Producers Society of Ontario, 30 September.

Chapman, C. B. (1992b). My two cents worth on how OR should develop. *Journal of the Operational Research Society*, **43**(7), pp. 647-664.

Chapman, C. B. and Cooper, Dale F. (1983a). Risk engineering: basic controlled interval and memory models. *Journal of the Operational Research Society*, **34**(1), pp. 51-60.

Chapman, C. B. and Cooper, Dale F. (1983b). Parametric discounting. *Omega—International Journal of Management Science*, **11**(3), pp. 303-310.

Chapman, C. B., Cooper, Dale F. and Cammaert, A. B. (1984). Model and situation specific OR methods: risk engineering reliability analysis of an L.N.G. facility. *Journal of the Operational Research Society*, **35**, pp. 27-35.

Chapman, C. B., Cooper, Dale F., Debelius, C. A. and Pecora, A. G. (1985). Problem solving methodology design on the run. *Journal of the Operational Research Society*, **36**(9), pp. 769-778.

Chapman, C. B., Cooper, Dale F. and Page, M. J. (1987). *Management for Engineers*. Chichester: John Wiley and Sons.

Chapman, C. B. and Howden, M. (1995). A case for parametric probabilistic NPV calculations with possible deferral of disposal of UK nuclear waste as an example. London Business School/IFORS First Joint Symposium, Energy Models for Policy Planning, London Business School, London, July.

Chapman, C. B., Phillips, E. D., Cooper, Dale F. and Lightfoot, L. (1985). Selecting an approach to project time and cost planning. *International Journal of Project Management*, **3**(1), pp. 19-26.

Chapman, C. B. and Ward, S. C. (1994). The efficient allocation of risk in contracts. *Omega—The International Journal of Management Science*, **22**(6), pp. 537-552.

Chapman, C. B. and Ward, S. C. (1996). Valuing the flexibility of alternative sources of power generation. *Energy Policy*, **24**(2), pp. 129-136.

Charette, R. N. (1993). Essential risk management: note from the front. Second SEI Conference on Risk Management, Pittsburg, Pennsylvania, ITABHI Corporation.

Charette, R. N. (1989). *Software Engineering Risk Analysis and Management*. New York: McGraw-Hill.

Checkland, P. B. and Scholes, J. (1990). *Soft Systems Methodology in Action*. Chichester: John Wiley and Sons.

Clark, P. and Chapman, C. B. (1987). The development of computer software for risk analysis: a decision support system development case study. *European Journal of Operational Research*, **29**(3), pp. 252-261.

Cooper, Dale F. and Chapman, C. B. (1987). Risk analysis for large projects—models, methods and cases. Chichester: John Wiley and Sons.

Cooper, K. G. (1980). Naval ship production: a claim settled and a framework built. *Interfaces*, **10**(6), pp. 20-36.

Crosby, A. (1968). *Creativity and Performance in Industrial Organisation*. London: Tavistock Publications.

Curtis, B., Ward, S. C. and Chapman, C. B. (1991). Roles, responsibilities and risks in management contracting. Construction Industry Research and Information Association, Special Publication 81, London.

DAS (1992). *Managing Risk in Procurement*. Commonwealth Procurement Guideline, Department of Administrative Services, Office for Better Buying, Australia.

Dennison, M. and Morgan, T. (1994). Decision conferencing as a management process—a development programme at Dudley MBC. *OR Insight*, 7(2), pp. 16-22.

Diffenbach, J. (1982). Influence diagrams for complex strategic issues. *Strategic Management Journal*, 3, pp. 133-146.

Eden, C. (1988). Cognitive mapping: a review. *European Journal of Operational Research*, 36, pp. 1-13.

Edwards, A. and Connell, N. A. D. (1989). *Expert Systems in Accounting*. London: Prentice-Hall in association with the Institute of Chartered Accountants in England and Wales.

Eisenhardt, K. M. (1989). Agency theory: an assessment and review. *Academy of Management Review*, 8(1), pp. 57-74.

The Engineering Council (1993). *Guidelines on Risk Issues*. London.

Finlay, P. and Marples, C. (1991). A review of group decision support systems. *OR Insight*, 4(4), pp. 3-7.

Fischoff, B. (1982). For those condemned to study the past: heuristics and biases in hindsight, Chapter 23 in Kahneman, D., Slovic, P. and Tversky, A. (eds), *Judgment Under Uncertainty: Heuristics and Biases*. New York: Cambridge University Press.

Fischoff, B., Slovic, P. and Lichtenstein, S. (1978). Fault trees: sensitivity of estimated failure probabilistics to problem representation. *Journal of Experimental Psychology: Human Perception and Performance*, 4, pp. 330-334.

Forrester, J. (1958). Industrial dynamics: a major breakthrough for decision making. *Harvard Business Review*, 36(4), pp. 37-66.

Forrester, J. (1961). *Industrial Dynamics*. Cambridge, MA: MIT Press.

Gaisford. R. W. (1986). Project management in the North Sea. *International Journal of Project Management*, 4(1), pp. 5-12.

Gilbert, G. P. (1983). The project environment. *International Journal of Project Management*, 1(2), pp. 83-87.

Golenko-Ginzburg, D. (1988). On the distribution of activity time in PERT. *Journal of the Operational Research Society*, 39(8), pp. 767-771.

Gonik, J. (1978). Tie salemen's bonuses to their forecasts. *Harvard Business Review*, May-June, pp. 116-123.

Gordon, G. and Pressman, I. (1978). *Quantitative Decision Making for Business*, Englewood Cliffs, NJ: Prentice-Hall International.

Gordon, W. J. J. (1956). Operational approach to creativity. *Harvard Business Review*, 34(6), pp. 41-51.

Gordon, W. J. J. (1968). *Creativity and Performance in Industrial Organisation*. London: Tavistock Publications.

Green, S. D. (1994). Beyond value engineering: SMART value management for building projects. *International Journal of Project Management*, 12(1), pp. 49-56.

Grey, S. (1995). *Practical Risk Assessment for Project Management*. Chichester: John Wiley and Sons.

Hall, W. K. (1975). Why risk analysis isn't working. *Long Range Planning*, December, pp. 25-29.

Hertz, D. B. (1964). Risk analysis in capital investment. *Harvard Business Review*, 42(1), pp. 95-106.

HM Treasury (1993). *Managing Risk and Contingency for Works Projects*. Central Unit on Procurement (CUP), CUP Guidance No. 41, London.

Institution of Civil Engineers (1995). *The New Engineering Contract*, 2nd edition. London: Thomas Telford.

Ishikawa, K. (1986). *Guide to Quality Control,* 2nd edition. White Plains, NY: Asia Productivity Organization/Quality Resources.

Joint Contracts Tribunal (1987). *Standard form of Management Contract.* London: Building Employers Federation.

Jordan, G., Lee, I. and Cawsey, G. (1988). *Learning from Experience: A Report on the Arrangements for Managing Major Projects in the Procurement Executive.* Report to the Minister of State for Defence Procurement, ISBN 0-11-772615-X, London: HMSO.

Kahneman, D., Slovic, P. and Tversky, A. (eds) (1982). *Judgment Under Uncertainty: Heuristics and Biases.* New York: Cambridge University Press.

Kahneman, D. and Tversky, A. (1973). On the psychology of prediction. *Psychological Review,* **80,** pp. 237–251.

Keeney, R. L. and Van Winterfeldt, D. (1991). Eliciting probabilities from experts in complex technical problems. *IEEE Transactions on Engineering Management,* **38**(3), August, pp. 191–201.

Klein, J. H. (1993). Modelling risk trade-off. *Journal of the Operational Research Society,* **44,** pp. 445–460.

Kletz, T. A. (1985). *An Engineer's View of Human Error.* Rugby: The Institution of Chemical Engineers.

Lemaitre, N. and Stenier, B. (1988). Stimulating innovation in large companies: observations and recommendations from Belgium. *R & D Management,* **18**(2), pp. 141–158.

Lewin, K. (1947). Frontiers in group dynamics. *Human Relations,* **1**(1), pp. 5–41.

Lichtenstein, S., Fischoff, B. and Phillips, L. D. (1982). Calibration of probabilities: the state of the art to 1980, Chapter 22 in Kahneman, D., Slovic, P. and Tversky, A. (eds), *Judgment Under Uncertainty: Heuristics and Biases.* New York: Cambridge University Press.

Little, J. D. C. (1970). Models and managers: the concept of a decision calculus. *Management Science,* **16,** pp. B466–B485.

Lyles, M. A. (1981). Formulating strategic problems: empirical analysis and model development. *Strategic Management Journal,* **2,** pp. 61–75.

Marples, C. and Riddle, D. (1992). Formulating strategy in the POD—an application of Decision Conferencing with Welwyn Hatfield District Council. *OR Insight,* **5**(2) pp. 12–15.

McCall, J. J. (1970). The simple economics of incentive contracting. *American Economic Review,* **60,** pp. 837–846.

Merkhofer, M. W. (1987). Quantifying judgmental uncertainty: methodology, experiences and insights. *IEEE Transactions on Systems, Man and Cybernetics,* SMC-17, 5, pp. 741–752.

Mintzberg, H. (1978). Patterns in strategy formation. *Management Science,* **24**(9), pp. 934–948.

MoD(PE)-DPP(PM) (1991) *Risk Management in Defence Procurement,* reference D/DPP(PM)/2/1/12, available from Ministry of Defence, Procurement Executive, Directorate of Procurement Policy (Project Management), Room 6302, Main Building, Whitehall, London SW1A 2HB.

Moder, J. J. and Philips, C. R. (1970). *Project Management with CPM and PERT.* New York: Van Nostrand.

Moore, P. G. and Thomas, H. (1976). *Anatomy of Decisions.* London: Penguin Books.

Morgan, M. G. and Herion M. (1990). *Uncertainty—A Guide to Dealing with Uncertainty in Quantitative Risk and Policy Analysis.* New York: Cambridge University Press.

Morris, P. W. G. and Hough, G. H. (1987). *The Anatomy of Major Projects.* Chichester: John Wiley and Sons.

Morris, J. and Imrie, R. (1993). Japanese style subcontracting—its impact on European industries. *Long Range Planning*, **26**(4), pp. 53–58.

Mould, G. (1993). Depending on the weather—assessing weather risk in North Sea oil production. *OR Insight*, **6**(4), pp. 13–17.

Newland, K. (1995) A methodology for project risk analysis and management. *Project*, September, pp. 7–9.

NSWG (1993). *Capital Work Investment Risk Management Guidelines*. ISBN 0-7310-2704-3, New South Wales Government, Sydney, NSW, Australia.

NUREG (1975). *An Assessment of Accident Risks in US Commercial Nuclear Power Plants*. US Nuclear Regulatory Commission Reactor Safety Study, WASH-1400 (NUREG—75/014).

PERAG (1991). Risk Management Information Pack (incorporating MoD(PE)-DPP(PM) 1991). MoD Procurement Management Group and Department of Management Development, Portsmouth University Business School.

Perry, J. G. (1986). Dealing with risk in contracts. *Building Technology and Management*, April, pp. 23–26.

Phillips, L. D. (1982). Requisite decision modelling: a case study. *Journal of the Operational Research Society*, **33**, pp. 303–311.

PMI (1992), Wildeman, M. (ed.). *Project and Program Risk Management: A Guide to Managing Project Risk and Opportunities*. The PMBOK Handbook Series—Volume 6, preliminary edition for trial use and comment, Project Management Institute, PO Box 43, Drexell Hill PA 19026-0043, USA.

Raiffa, H. (1968). *Decision Analysis: Introductory Lectures on Choices Under Uncertainty*. Reading, MA: Addison Wesley.

Reichelstein, S. (1992). Constructing incentive schemes for government contracts: an application of agency theory. *The Accounting Review*, **67**(4), pp. 712–731.

Richardson, G. P. and Pugh, A. L. (1981). *Introduction to Systems Dynamics Modeling with DYNAMO*. Portland, OR: Productivity Press.

Roberts, J. T. (1994). *The Management of Risk in ODA Activities*. Technical note No. 12, Aid Economics and Small Enterprises Department, London.

Rosenhead, J. (1989). *Rational Analysis for a Problematic World: Problem Structuring Methods for Complexity, Uncertainty and Conflict*. Chichester: John Wiley and Sons.

Samuelson, W. (1986). Bidding for contracts. *Management Science*, **32**(12), pp. 1533–1550.

Scherer, F. M. (1964). The theory of contractual incentives for cost reduction. *Quarterly Journal of Economics*, **78**, pp. 257–280.

Senge, P. M. (1990). *The Fifth Discipline: The Art and Practice of the Learning Organization*. New York: Doubleday.

Slovic, P., Fischoff, B. and Lichtenstein, S. (1982). Facts versus fears: understanding perceived risk, Chapter 33 in Kahneman, D., Slovic, P. and Tversky, A. (eds), *Judgment Under Uncertainty: Heuristics and Biases*. New York: Cambridge University Press.

Soukhakian, M. A. (1988). *Project Completion Times and Criticality Indices*. PhD dissertation, Department of Management, University of Southampton.

Spetzler, C. S. and Stael van Holstein, C. S. (1975). Probability encoding in decision analysis. *Management Science*, **22**(3), pp. 340–358.

Taylor, A. (1991). Four inch set back for 30 miles of Channel tunnel. *Financial Times*, Tuesday, 9 April.

Taylor, D. W., Beryl, P. L. and Block, C. H. (1958). Does group participation when using brainstorming facilitate or inhibit creative thinking? *Administrative Science Quarterly*, **3**(1), pp. 23–47.

Thamhain, H. J. and Wileman, D. L. (1975). Conflict management in project life cycles. *Sloan Management Review*, **26**(3), summer.

Thompson, P. A. and Perry, J. G. (1992). *Engineering Construction Risks: A Guide to Project Risk Analysis and Risk Management*. London: Thomas Telford.

Thorn, D. G. (1986). *Pricing and Negotiating Defence Contracts*. London: Longman, p. 229.

Tilanus, C. B. (1985). Failures and successes of quantitative methods in management. *European Journal of Operational Research*, **19**, pp. 170–175.

Turner, J. R. (1992). *The Handbook of Project Based Management: Improving Processes for Achieving Your Strategic Objectives*. New York: McGraw-Hill.

Turner, J. R. and Cochrane, R. A. (1993). Goals-and-methods matrix: coping with projects with ill-defined goals and/or methods of achieving them. *International Journal of Project Management*, **11**, pp. 93–102.

Tversky, A. and Kahneman, D. (1974). Judgment under uncertainty: heuristics and biases. *Science*, **185**, pp. 1124–1131; reprinted in Kahneman, D., Slovic, P. and Tversky, A. (eds) (1982). *Judgment Under Uncertainty: Heuristics and Biases*. New York: Cambridge University Press.

Uff, J. and Capper, P. (eds) (1989). *Construction Contract Policy: Improved Procedures and Practice*. Centre of Construction Law and Management, King's College, London.

Walsham, G. (1992). Management science and organisational change: a framework for analysis. *Omega—The International Journal of Management Science*, **20**(1), pp. 1–9.

Ward, S. C. (1989). Arguments for constructively simple models. *Journal of the Operational Research Society*, **40**(2), pp. 141–153.

Ward, S. C. and Chapman, C. B. (1988). Developing competitive bids: a framework for information processing. *Journal of the Operational Research Society*, **39**(2), pp. 123–134.

Ward, S. C. and Chapman, C. B. (1994). Choosing contractor payment terms. *International Journal of Project Management*, **12**(4), pp. 216–221.

Ward, S. C. and Chapman, C. B. (1995a). Evaluating fixed price incentive contracts. *Omega—The International Journal of Management Science*, **23**(1), pp. 49–62.

Ward, S. C. and Chapman, C. B. (1995b). Risk management and the project life cycle. *International Journal of Project Management*, **13**(3), pp. 145–149.

Ward, S. C., Chapman, C. B. and Curtis, B. (1991). On the allocation of risk in construction projects. *International Journal of Project Management*, **9**(3), pp. 140–147.

Whiting, C. S. (1958). *Creative thinking*. New York: Reinhold.

Williams, T. M. (1992). Practical use of distributions in network analysis. *Journal of the Operational Research Society*, **43**(3) pp. 265–270.

Williams, T., Eden, C., Ackermann, F. and Tait, A. (1995a). The effects of design changes and delays on project costs. *Journal of the Operational Research Society*, **46**, pp. 809–818.

Williams, T., Eden, C., Ackermann, F. and Tait, A. (1995b). Vicious circles of parallelism. *International Journal of Project Management*, **13**, pp. 151–155.

Woodhouse, J. (1993). *Managing Industrial Risk—Getting Value for Money in Your Business*. London: Chapman and Hall.

Yong, D. H. H. (1985). *Risk Analysis Software Computation Error Balancing for British Petroleum International Limited*. MSc dissertation, Department of Management, University of Southampton.

Index